W9-BOA-874

POCKET SIZE 1

AKIKO ON THE PLANET SMOO

The Complete Graphic Novel

THE MENACE OF ALIA RELLAPOR, PART ONE

The Akiko Series, Issues 1~7

SIRIUS ENTERTAINMENT
UNADILLA, NEW YORK

This book is dedicated
to my wife, Miki

AKIKO POCKET SIZE 1 JUNE, 2004.
FIRST PRINTING. PUBLISHED BY SIRIUS ENTERTAINMENT, INC.
LAWRENCE SALAMONE, PRESIDENT. ROBB HORAN, PUBLISHER.
KEITH DAVIDSEN, EDITOR. CORRESPONDENCE: P.O. BOX X, UNADILLA, NY 13849.
AKIKO AND ALL RELATED CHARACTERS ARE TM & © 2004 MARK CRILLEY. SIRIUS AND
THE DOGSTAR LOGO ARE ® SIRIUS ENTERTAINMENT, INC. ALL RIGHTS RESERVED. ANY
SIMILARITY TO PERSONS LIVING OR DEAD IS PURELY COINCIDENTAL.
PRINTED IN THE USA.

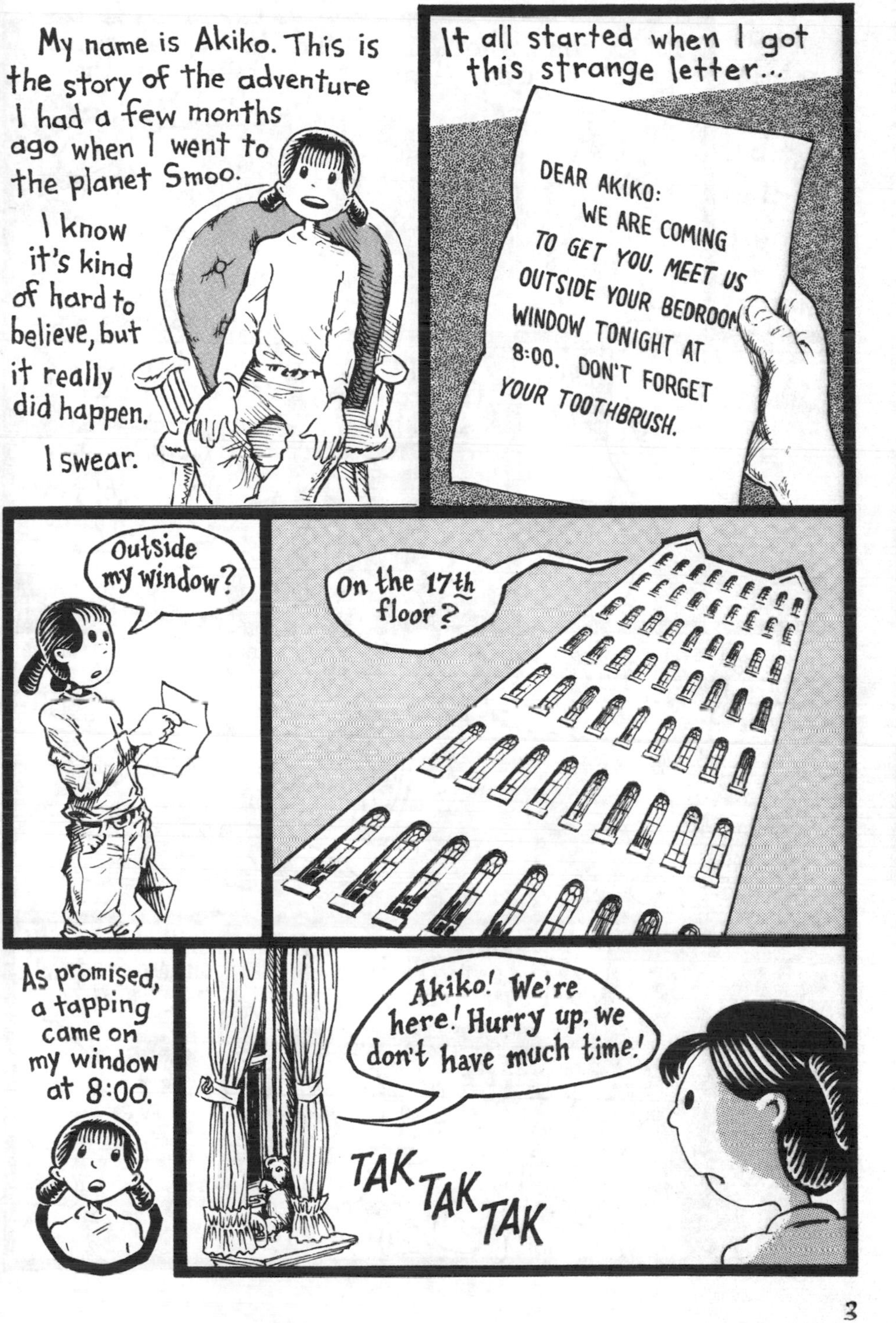
My name is Akiko. This is the story of the adventure I had a few months ago when I went to the planet Smoo.
I know it's kind of hard to believe, but it really did happen.
I swear.
It all started when I got this strange letter...
DEAR AKIKO:
WE ARE COMING TO GET YOU. MEET US OUTSIDE YOUR BEDROOM WINDOW TONIGHT AT 8:00. DON'T FORGET YOUR TOOTHBRUSH.
Outside my window?
On the 17th floor?
As promised, a tapping came on my window at 8:00.
Akiko! We're here! Hurry up, we don't have much time!
TAK TAK TAK

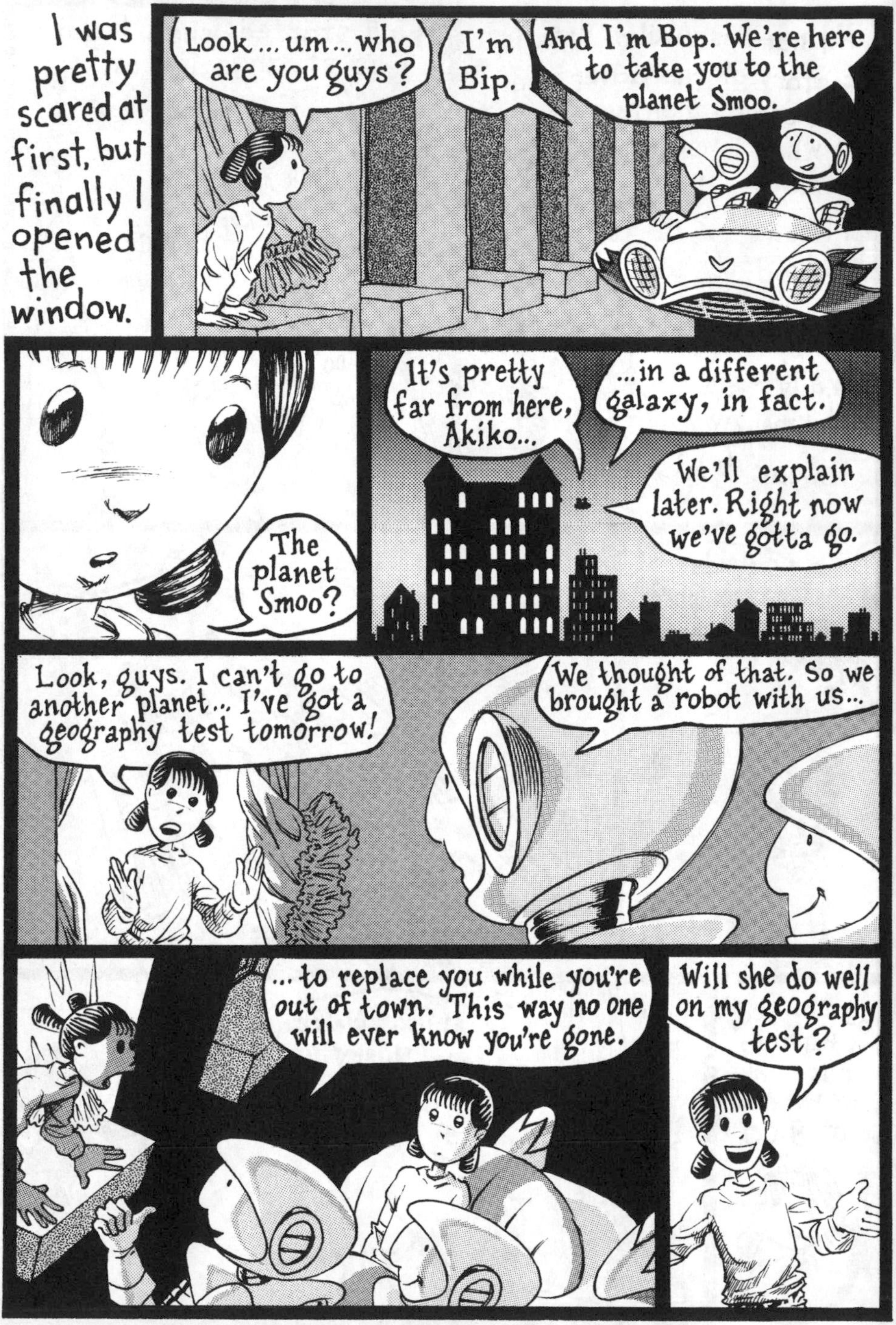
I was pretty scared at first, but finally I opened the window.
Look ... um ... who are you guys?
I'm Bip.
And I'm Bop. We're here to take you to the planet Smoo.
The planet Smoo?
It's pretty far from here, Akiko...
...in a different galaxy, in fact.
We'll explain later. Right now we've gotta go.
Look, guys. I can't go to another planet... I've got a geography test tomorrow!
We thought of that. So we brought a robot with us...
... to replace you while you're out of town. This way no one will ever know you're gone.
Will she do well on my geography test?

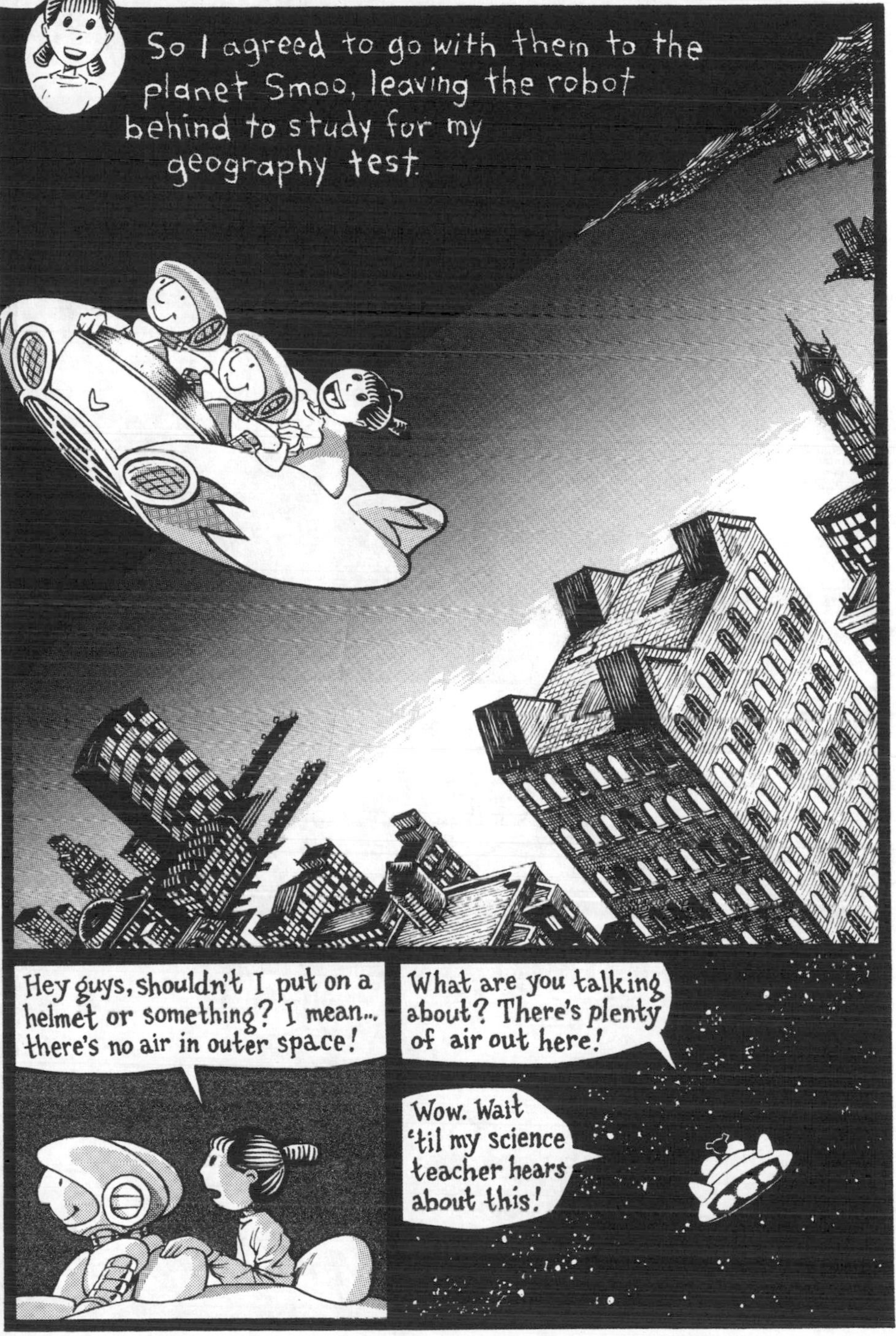
So I agreed to go with them to the planet Smoo, leaving the robot behind to study for my geography test.
Hey guys, shouldn't I put on a helmet or something? I mean... there's no air in outer space!
What are you talking about? There's plenty of air out here!
Wow. Wait 'til my science teacher hears about this!

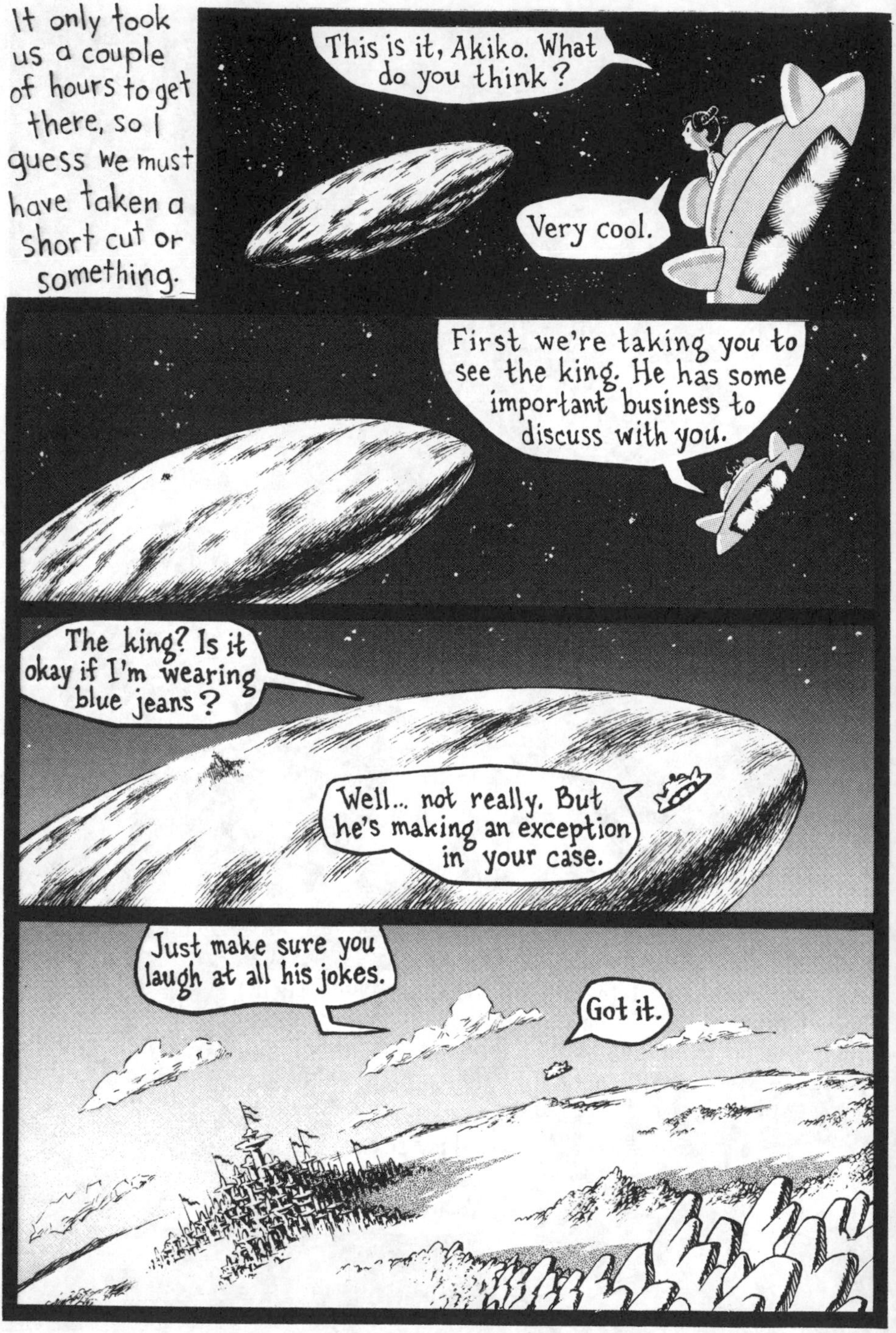
It only took us a couple of hours to get there, so I guess we must have taken a short cut or something.
This is it, Akiko. What do you think?
Very cool.
First we're taking you to see the king. He has some important business to discuss with you.
The king? Is it okay if I'm wearing blue jeans?
Well... not really. But he's making an exception in your case.
Just make sure you laugh at all his jokes.
Got it.

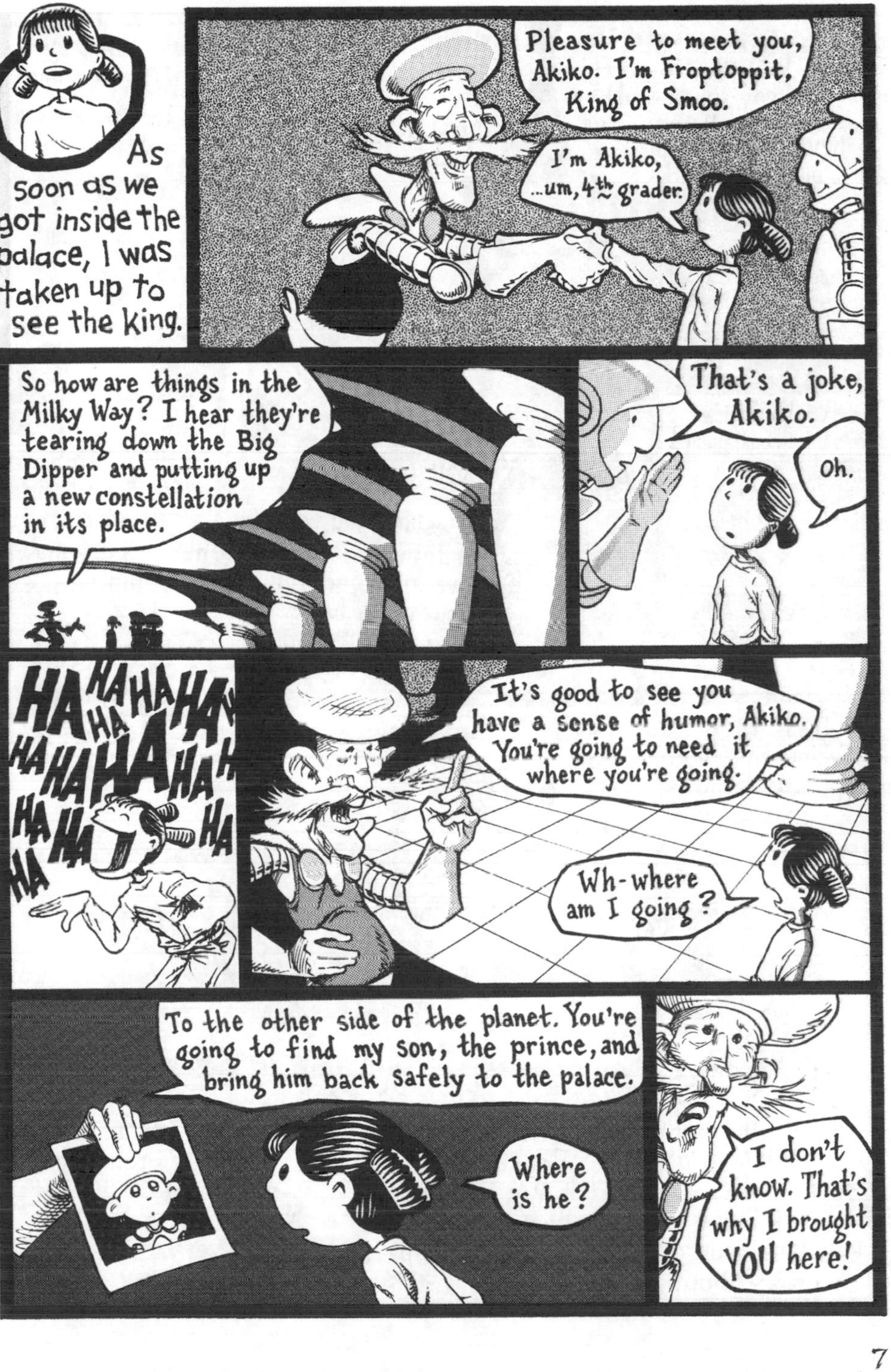
As soon as we got inside the palace, I was taken up to see the king.
Pleasure to meet you, Akiko. I'm Froptoppit, King of Smoo.
I'm Akiko, ...um, 4th grader.
So how are things in the Milky Way? I hear they're tearing down the Big Dipper and putting up a new constellation in its place.
That's a joke, Akiko.
Oh.
HA HA HA HA HA HA HA HA HA HA HA HA HA HA HA HA HA
It's good to see you have a sense of humor, Akiko. You're going to need it where you're going.
Wh-where am I going?
To the other side of the planet. You're going to find my son, the prince, and bring him back safely to the palace.
Where is he?
I don't know. That's why I brought YOU here!

Now wait a minute. How am I supposed to find somebody on the other side of a planet I've never been to before? I'm just a kid!

Don't be so modest, Akiko. You were very highly recommended to me by a gentleman in the Andromeda galaxy...

He said you were an expert in these matters!

But I don't even KNOW anyone in the Andromeda galaxy!

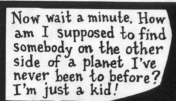

Really? Hm! Maybe I misheard him.

Well, don't worry, Akiko. I'm sure you'll do fine!

Besides, you won't be doing this alone. I've arranged for some of my best men to accompany you.

I didn't seem to have any other choice, so I said I'd give it a try. When I met my new companions, though, I started to have second thoughts.

First there was Poog, from the planet Toog. He was kind of hard to describe. →

Then there was Mr. Beeba. He'd never been to the other side of Smoo before, but he'd read a lot of books about it.

Next came Spuckler Boach. He looked like he hadn't taken a bath in about fourteen years.

Finally there was Spuckler's robot, Gax. Spuckler promised it wouldn't break down. Not very often, anyway.

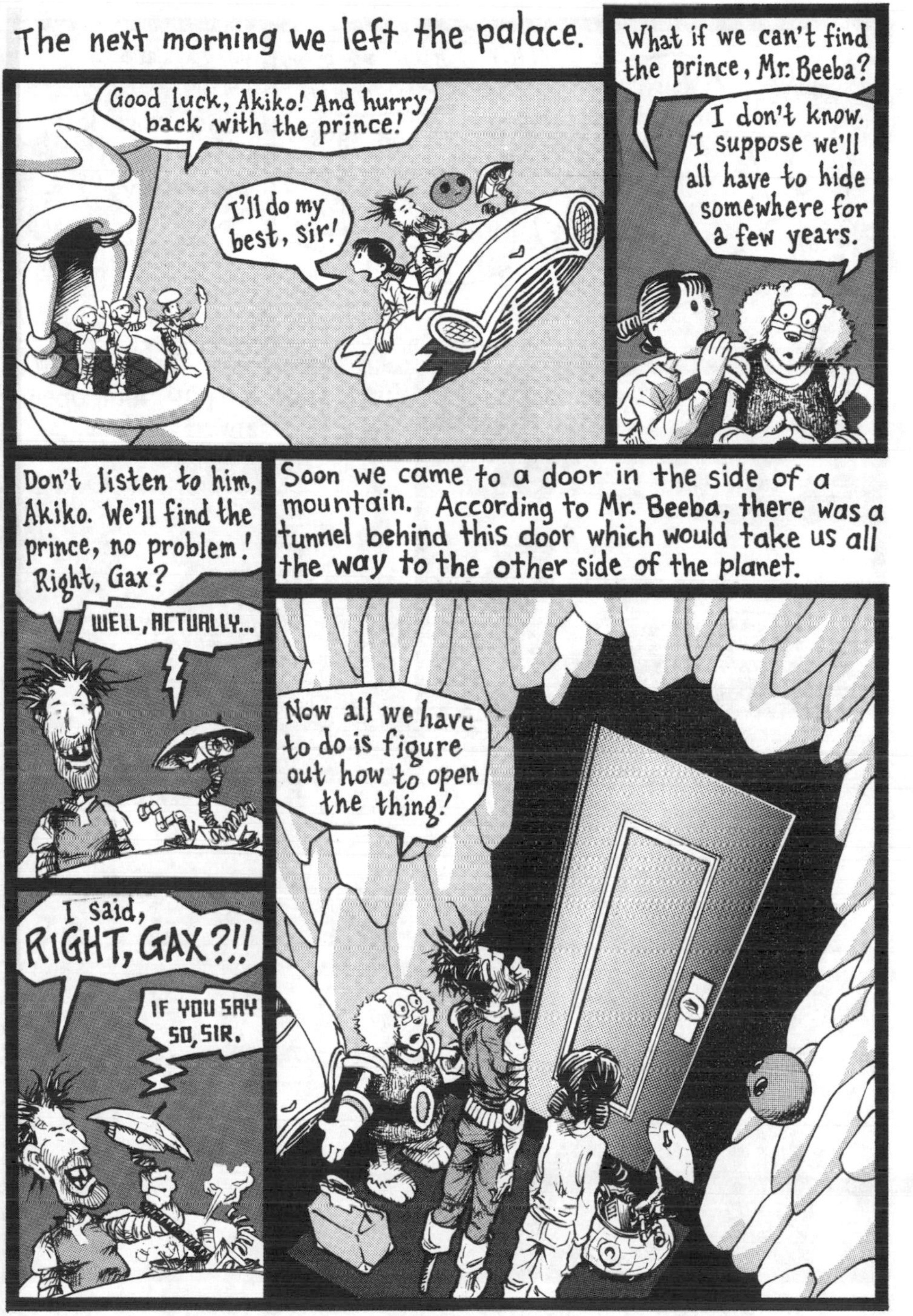

The next morning we left the palace.
Good luck, Akiko! And hurry back with the prince!
I'll do my best, sir!
What if we can't find the prince, Mr. Beeba?
I don't know. I suppose we'll all have to hide somewhere for a few years.
Don't listen to him, Akiko. We'll find the prince, no problem! Right, Gax?
WELL, ACTUALLY...
I said, RIGHT, GAX?!!
IF YOU SAY SO, SIR.
Soon we came to a door in the side of a mountain. According to Mr. Beeba, there was a tunnel behind this door which would take us all the way to the other side of the planet.
Now all we have to do is figure out how to open the thing!

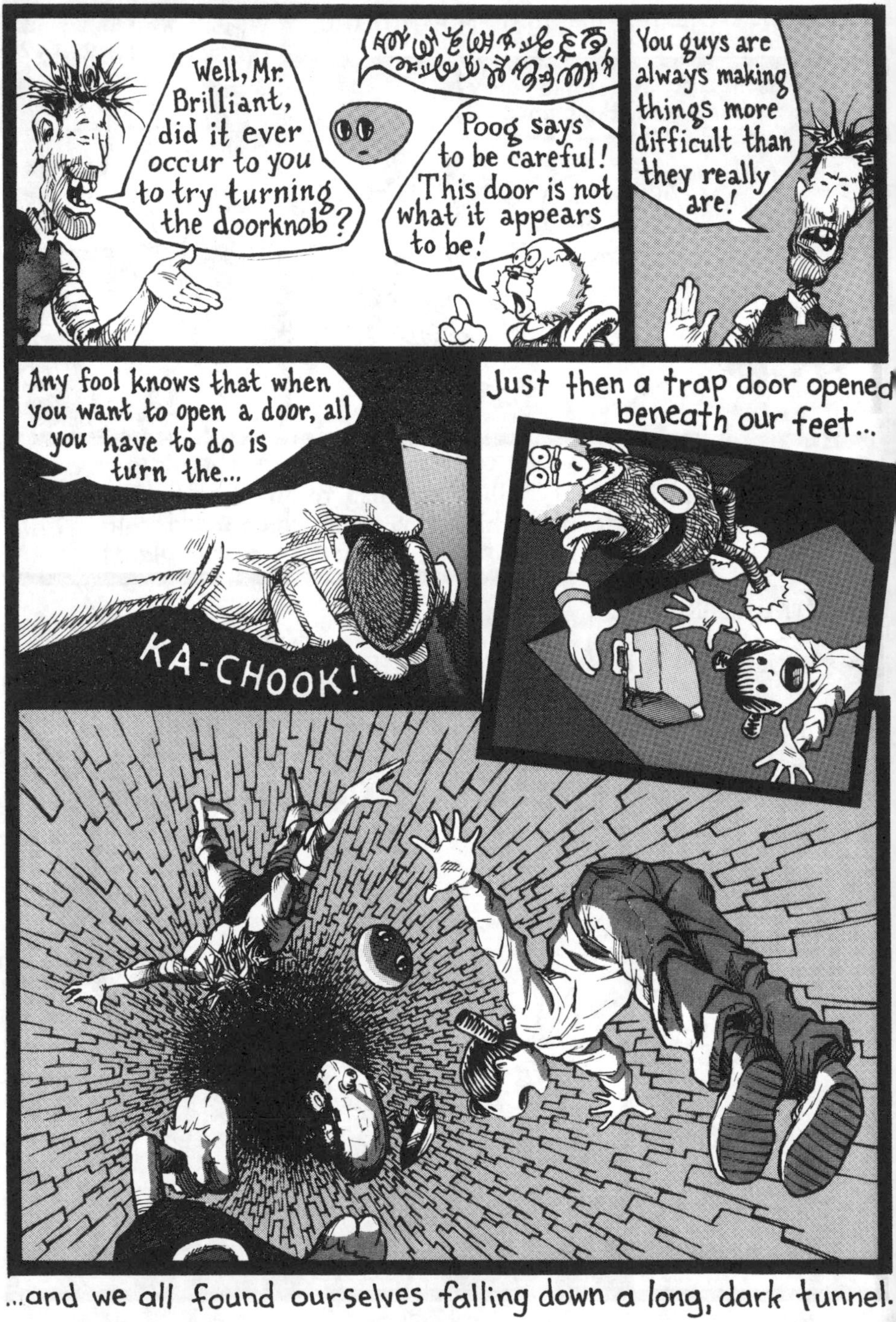
Well, Mr. Brilliant, did it ever occur to you to try turning the doorknob?
Poog says to be careful! This door is not what it appears to be!
You guys are always making things more difficult than they really are!
Any fool knows that when you want to open a door, all you have to do is turn the...
KA-CHOOK!
Just then a trap door opened beneath our feet...
...and we all found ourselves falling down a long, dark tunnel.

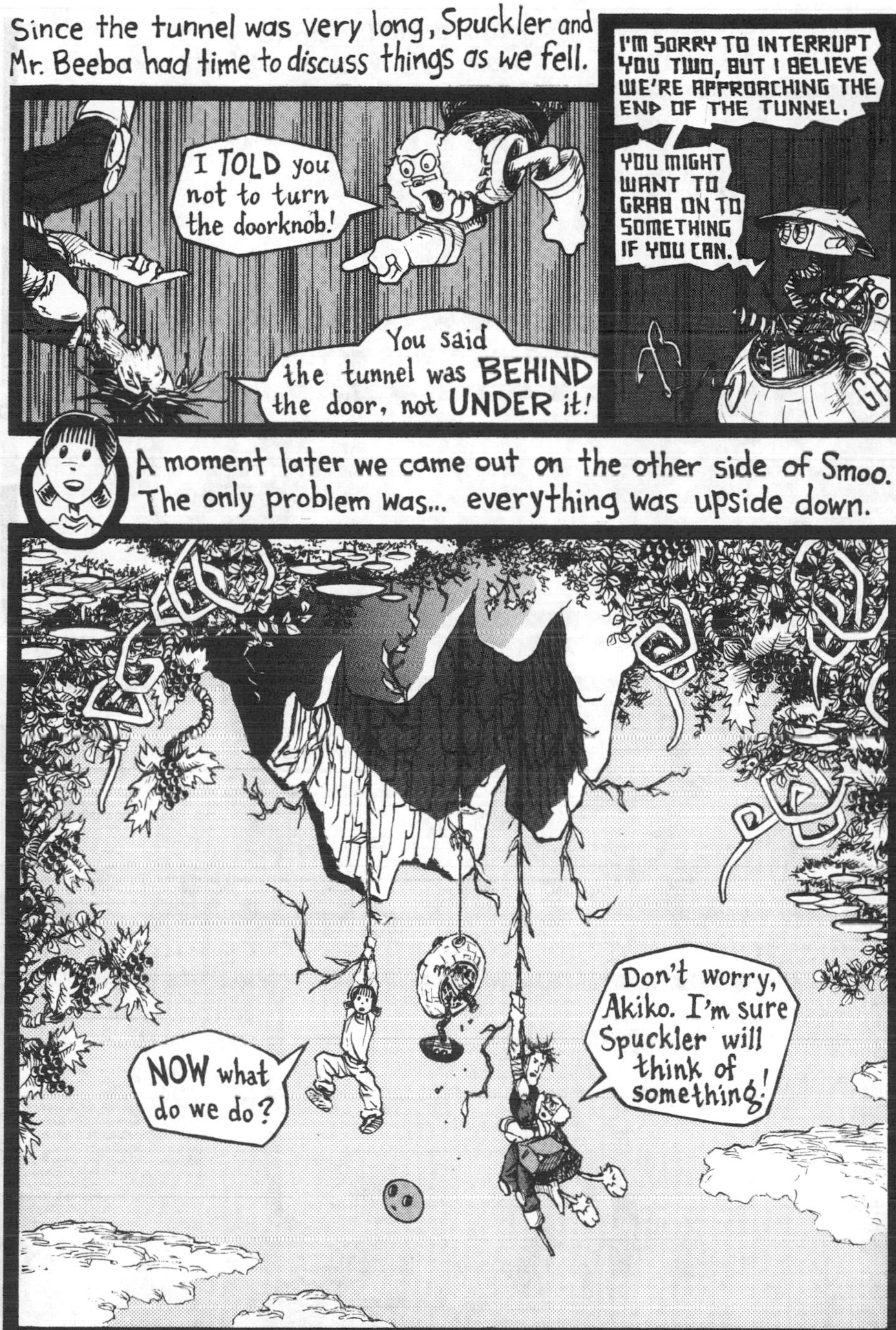
Since the tunnel was very long, Spuckler and Mr. Beeba had time to discuss things as we fell.
I TOLD you not to turn the doorknob!
You said the tunnel was BEHIND the door, not UNDER it!
I'M SORRY TO INTERRUPT YOU TWO, BUT I BELIEVE WE'RE APPROACHING THE END OF THE TUNNEL.
YOU MIGHT WANT TO GRAB ON TO SOMETHING IF YOU CAN.
A moment later we came out on the other side of Smoo. The only problem was... everything was upside down.
NOW what do we do?
Don't worry, Akiko. I'm sure Spuckler will think of something!

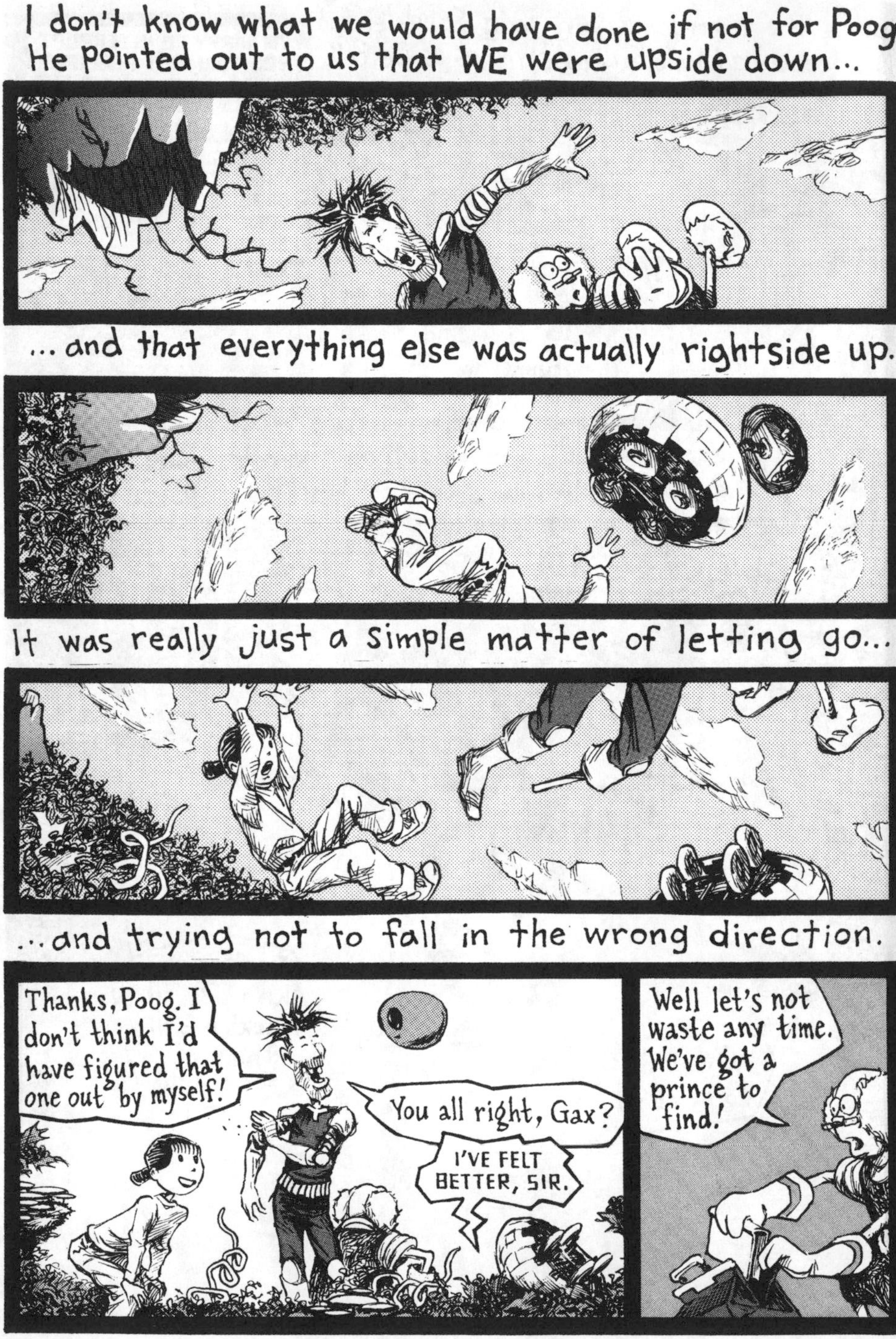
I don't know what we would have done if not for Poog.
He pointed out to us that WE were upside down...
...and that everything else was actually rightside up.
It was really just a simple matter of letting go...
...and trying not to fall in the wrong direction.
Thanks, Poog. I don't think I'd have figured that one out by myself!
You all right, Gax?
I'VE FELT BETTER, SIR.
Well let's not waste any time. We've got a prince to find!

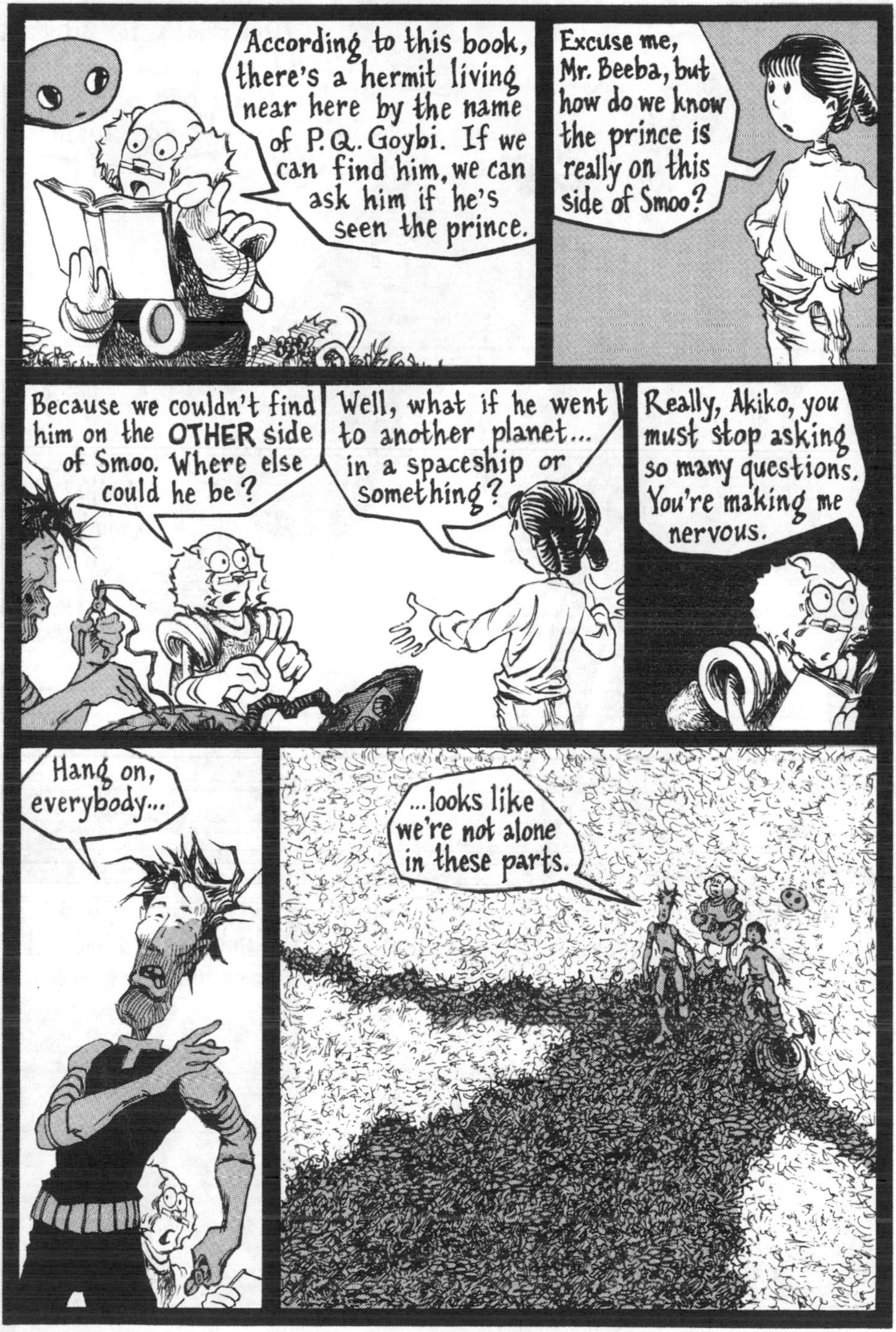
According to this book, there's a hermit living near here by the name of P.Q. Goybi. If we can find him, we can ask him if he's seen the prince.
Excuse me, Mr. Beeba, but how do we know the prince is really on this side of Smoo?
Because we couldn't find him on the OTHER side of Smoo. Where else could he be?
Well, what if he went to another planet... in a spaceship or something?
Really, Akiko, you must stop asking so many questions. You're making me nervous.
Hang on, everybody...
...looks like we're not alone in these parts.

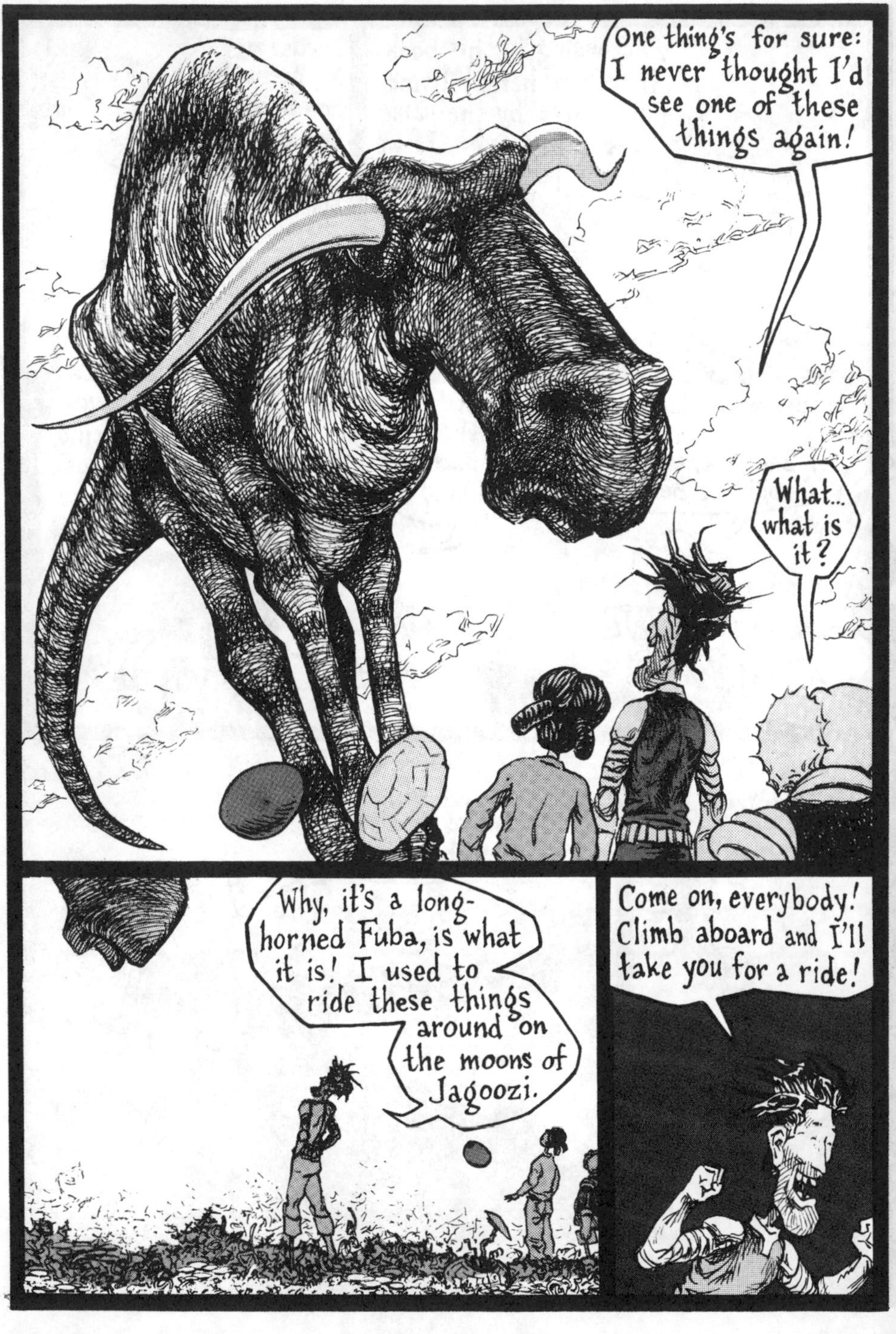
One thing's for sure: I never thought I'd see one of these things again!
What... what is it?
Why, it's a long-horned Fuba, is what it is! I used to ride these things around on the moons of Jagoozi.
Come on, everybody! Climb aboard and I'll take you for a ride!

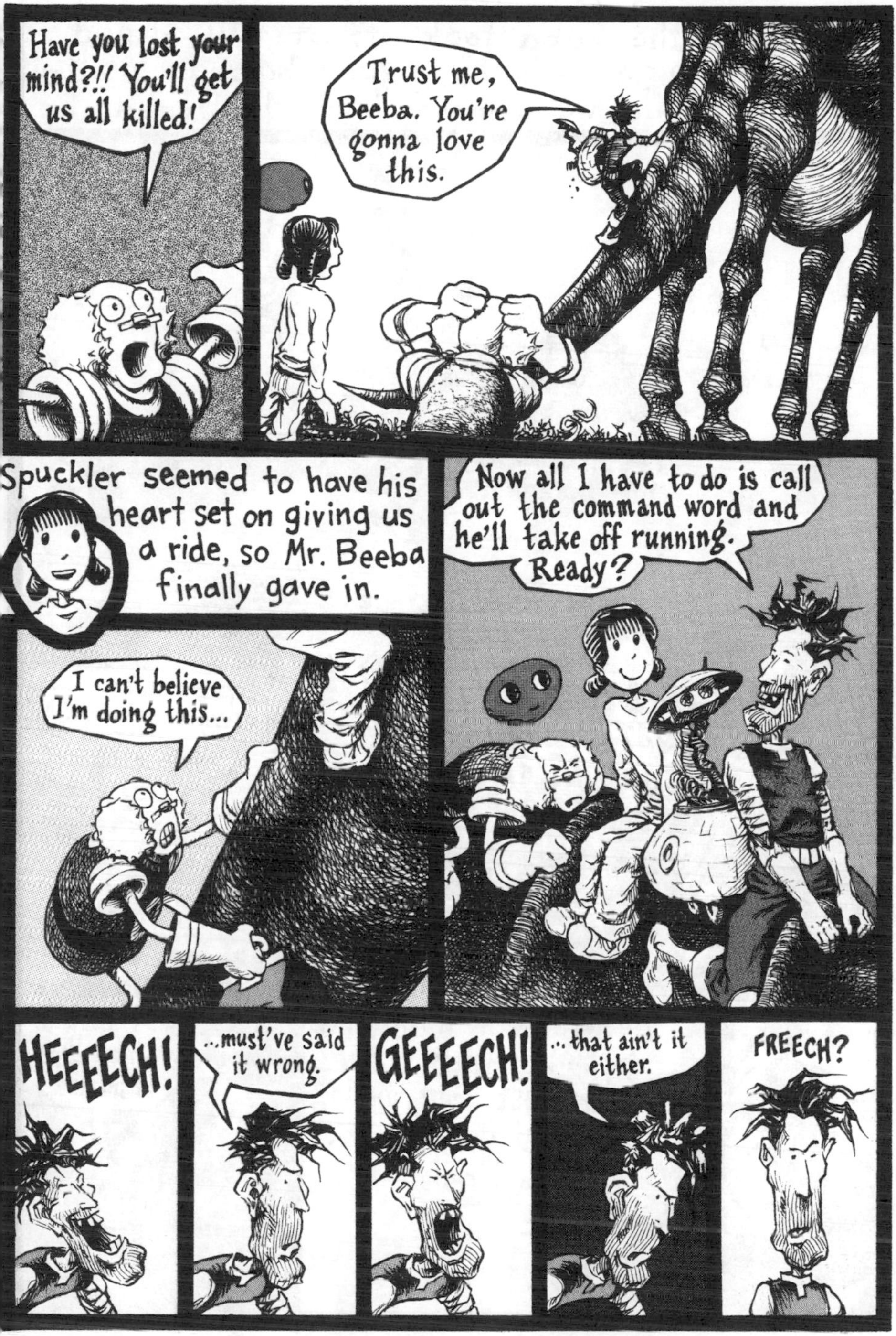
Have you lost your mind?!! You'll get us all killed!
Trust me, Beeba. You're gonna love this.
Spuckler seemed to have his heart set on giving us a ride, so Mr. Beeba finally gave in.
Now all I have to do is call out the command word and he'll take off running. Ready?
I can't believe I'm doing this...
HEEEECH!
...must've said it wrong.
GEEEECH!
...that ain't it either.
FREECH?

With that, the Fuba took off at full speed. I managed to get a pretty good hold on his back, but I'm afraid we almost lost Mr. Beeba.

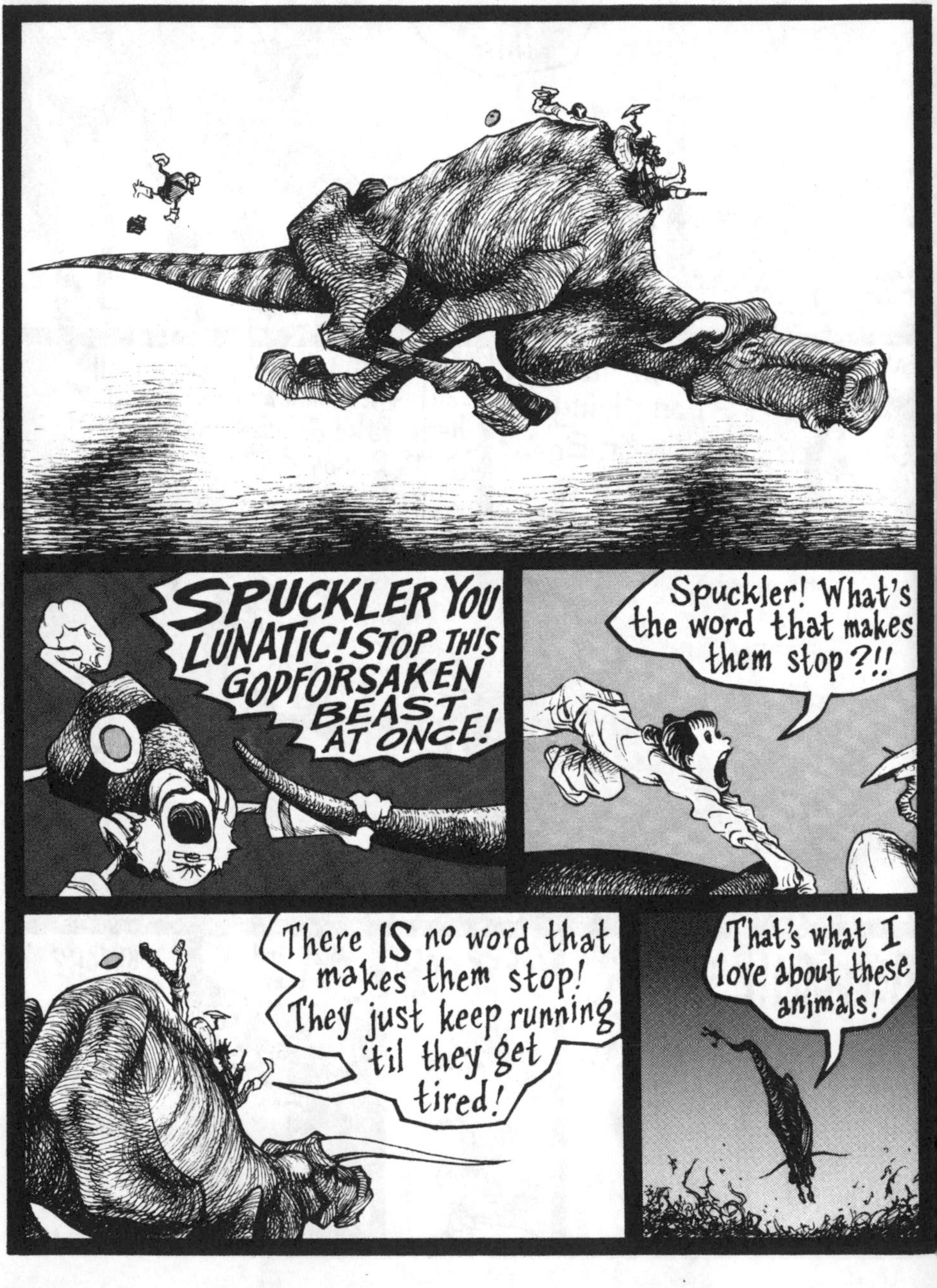
SPUCKLER YOU LUNATIC! STOP THIS GODFORSAKEN BEAST AT ONCE!
Spuckler! What's the word that makes them stop?!!
There IS no word that makes them stop! They just keep running 'til they get tired!
That's what I love about these animals!

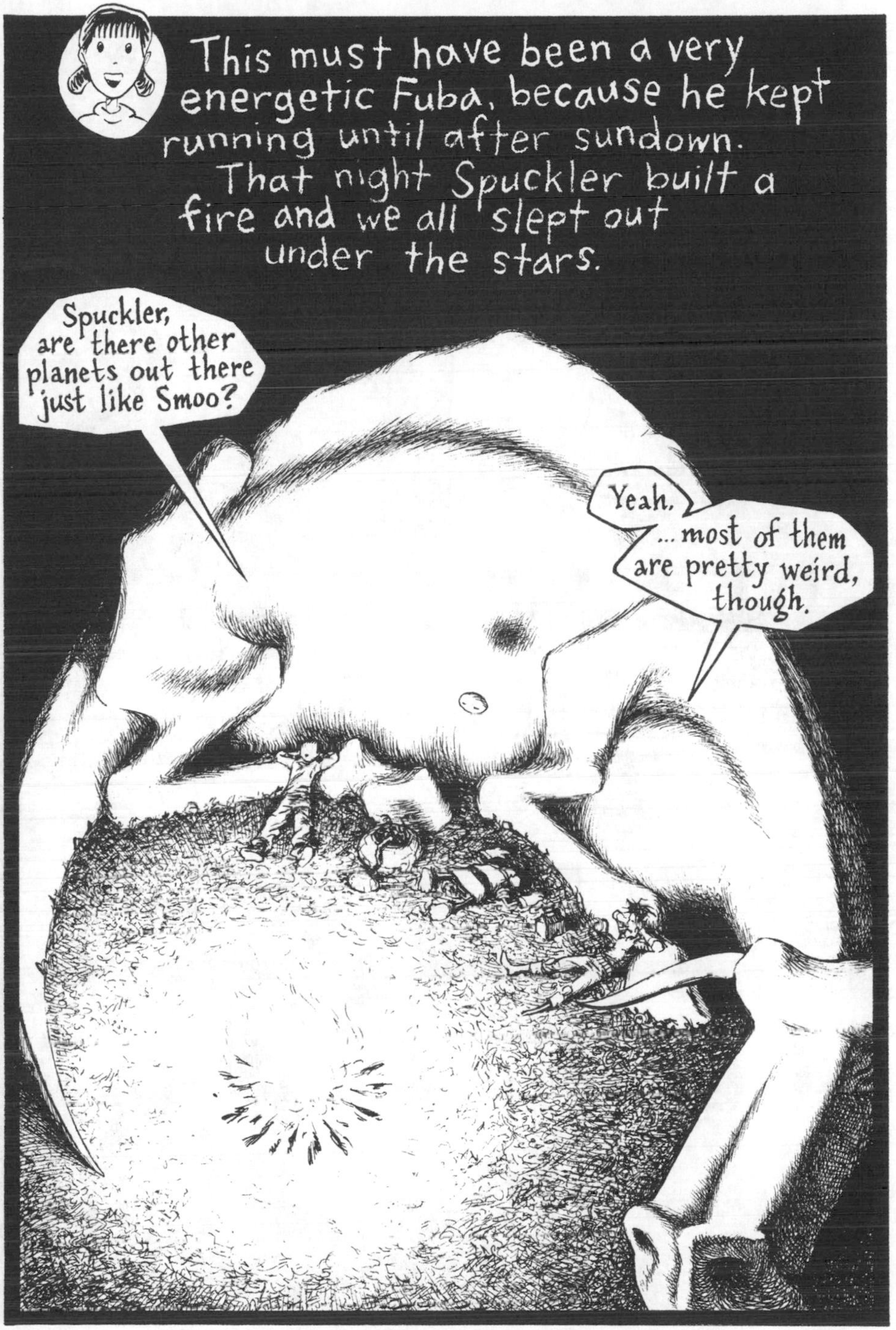
This must have been a very energetic Fuba, because he kept running until after sundown. That night Spuckler built a fire and we all slept out under the stars.
Spuckler, are there other planets out there just like Smoo?
Yeah.
...most of them are pretty weird, though.

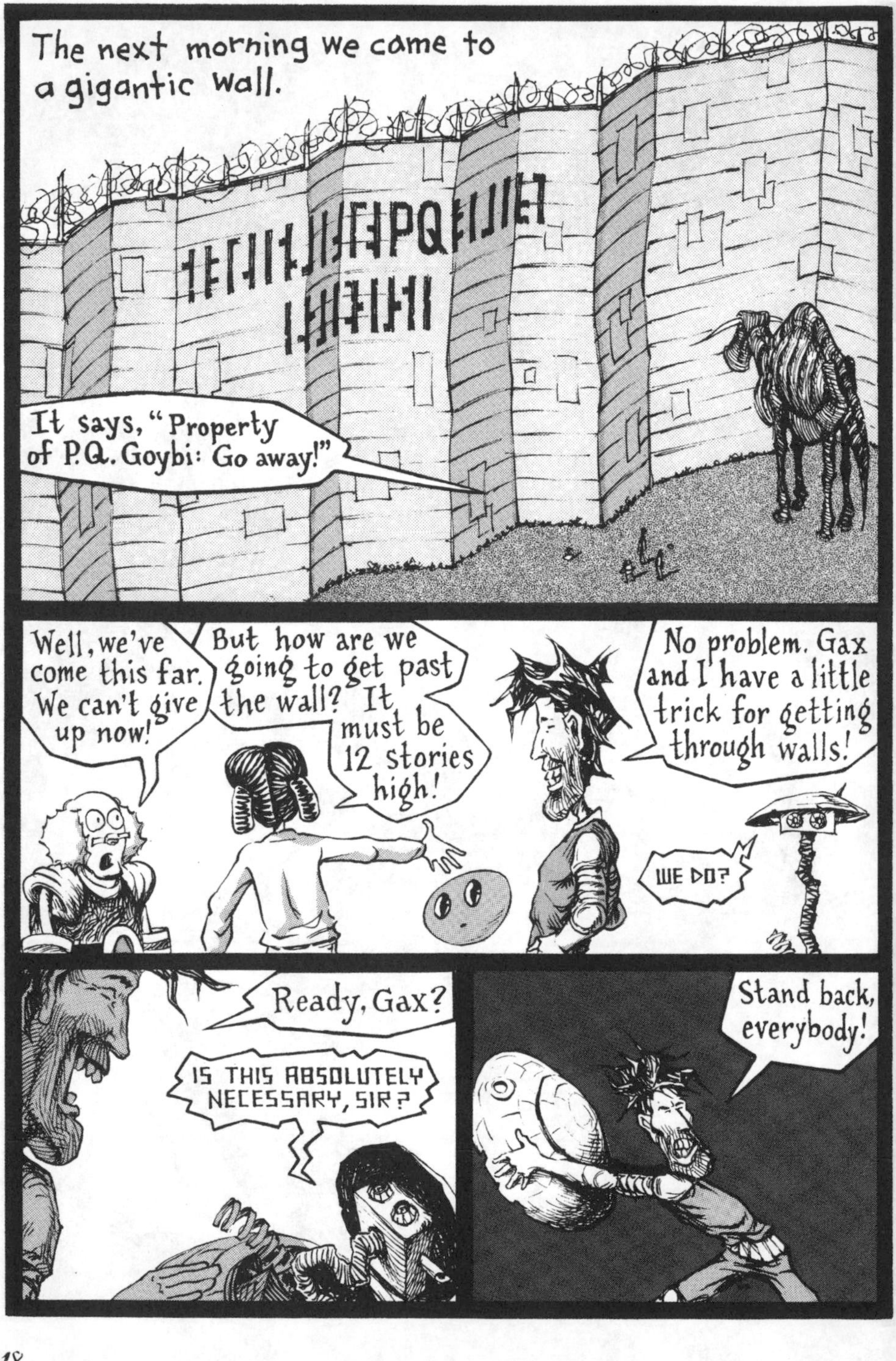
The next morning we came to a gigantic wall.
It says, "Property of P.Q. Goybi: Go away!"
Well, we've come this far. We can't give up now!
But how are we going to get past the wall? It must be 12 stories high!
No problem. Gax and I have a little trick for getting through walls!
WE DO?
Ready, Gax?
IS THIS ABSOLUTELY NECESSARY, SIR?
Stand back, everybody!

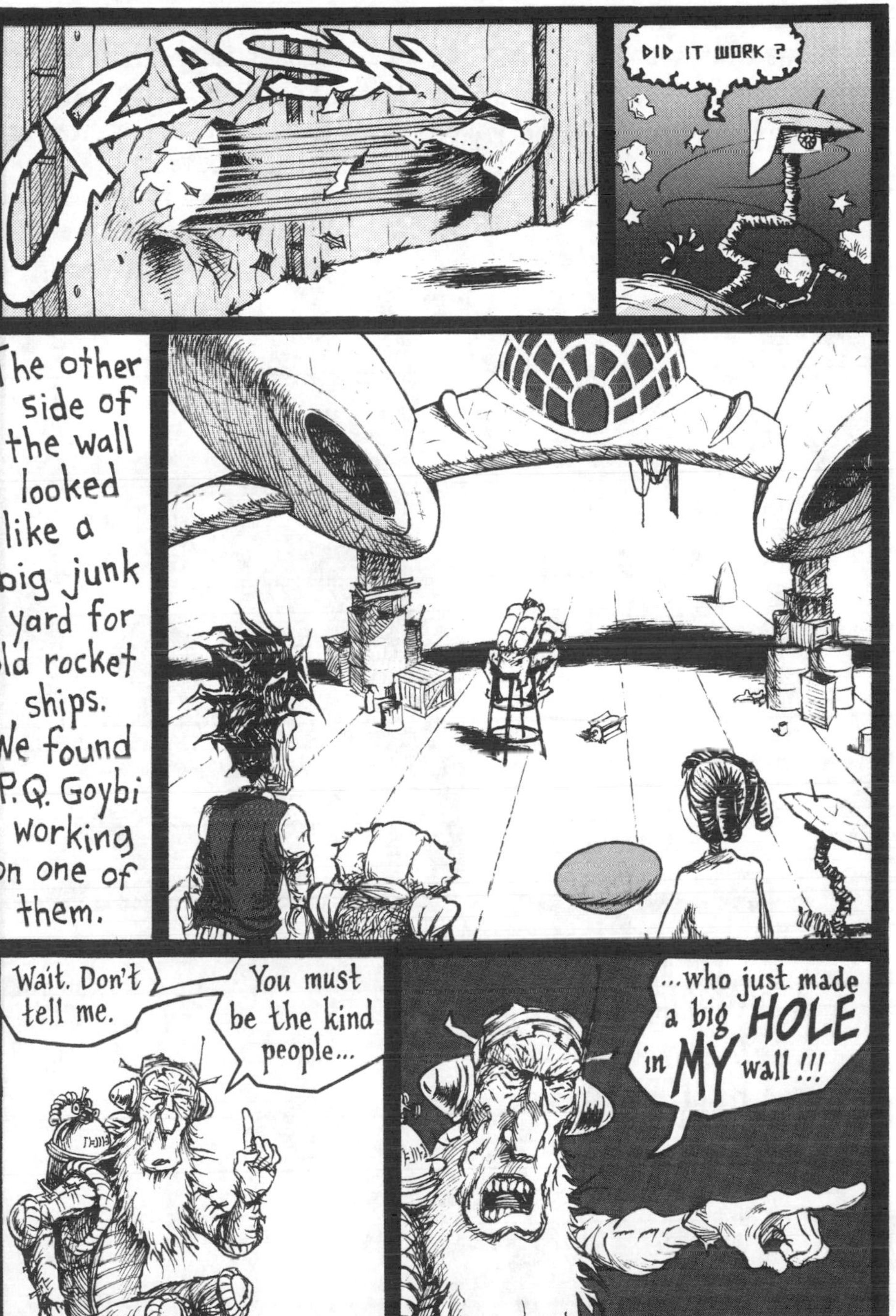
CRASH
DID IT WORK ?
The other side of the wall looked like a big junk yard for old rocket ships. We found P.Q. Goybi working on one of them.
Wait. Don't tell me.
You must be the kind people...
...who just made a big HOLE in MY wall !!!

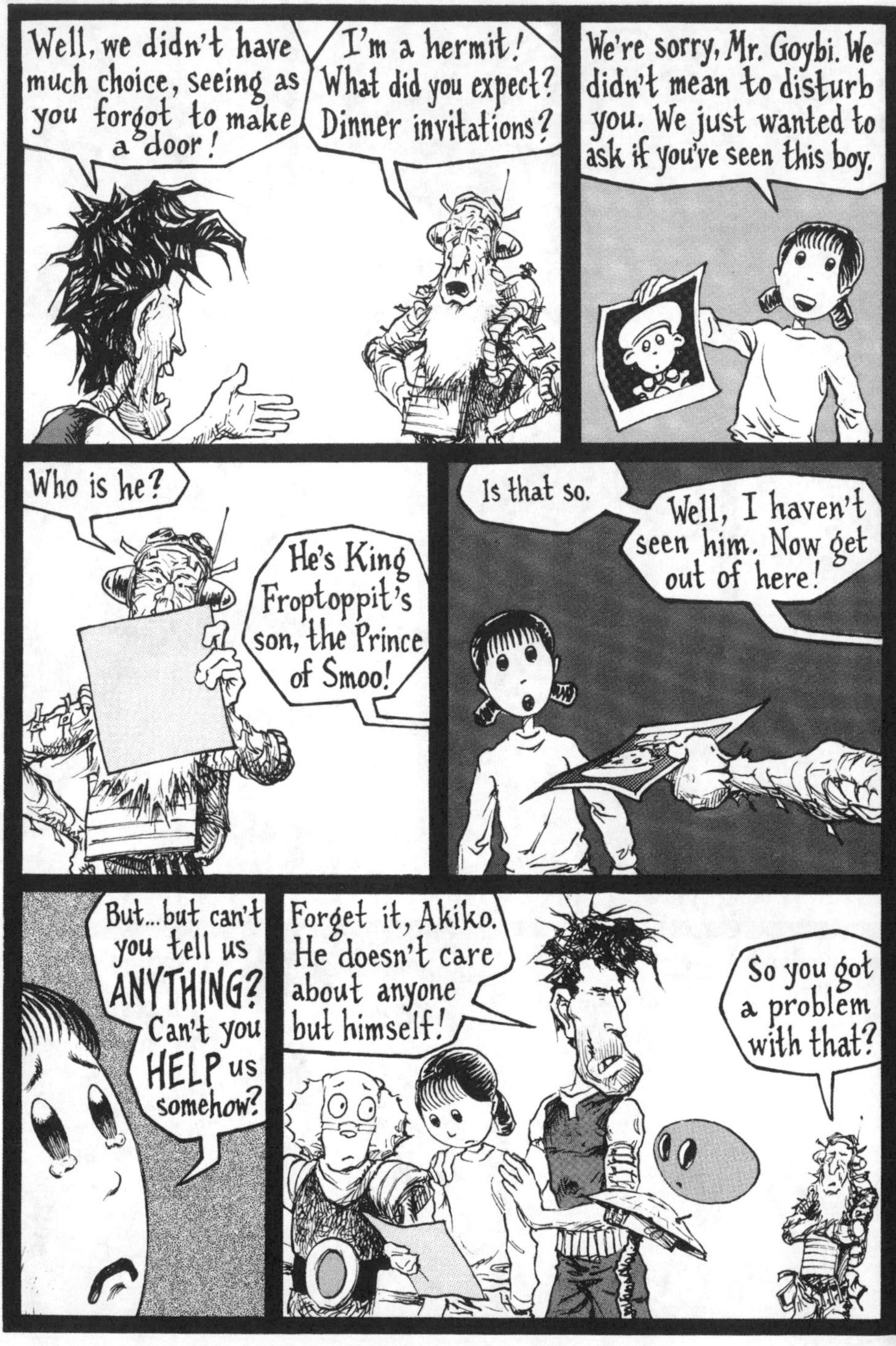
Well, we didn't have much choice, seeing as you forgot to make a door!
I'm a hermit! What did you expect? Dinner invitations?
We're sorry, Mr. Goybi. We didn't mean to disturb you. We just wanted to ask if you've seen this boy.
Who is he?
He's King Froptoppit's son, the Prince of Smoo!
Is that so.
Well, I haven't seen him. Now get out of here!
But...but can't you tell us ANYTHING? Can't you HELP us somehow?
Forget it, Akiko. He doesn't care about anyone but himself!
So you got a problem with that?

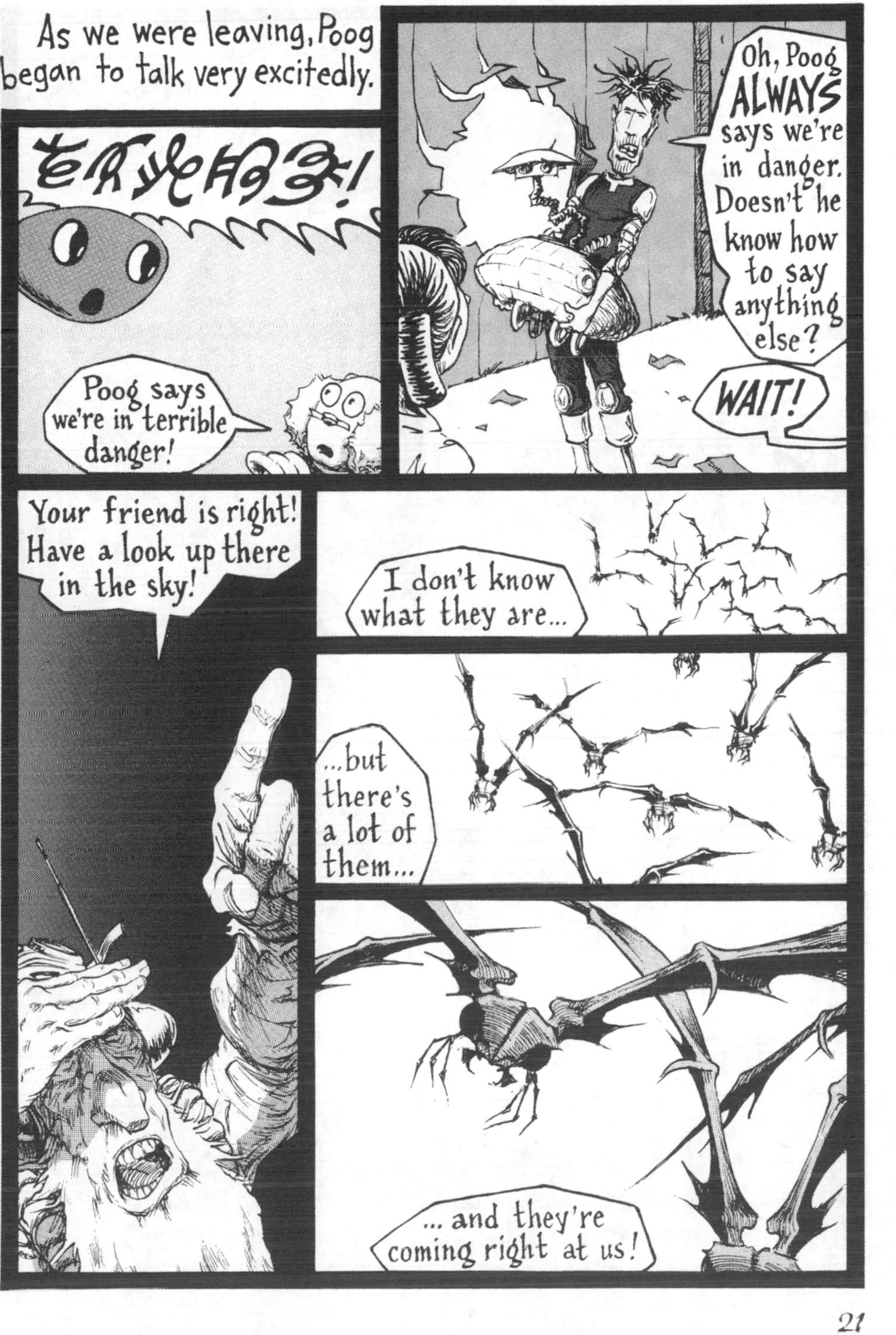
As we were leaving, Poog began to talk very excitedly.
Poog says we're in terrible danger!
Oh, Poog ALWAYS says we're in danger. Doesn't he know how to say anything else?
WAIT!
Your friend is right! Have a look up there in the sky!
I don't know what they are...
...but there's a lot of them...
... and they're coming right at us!

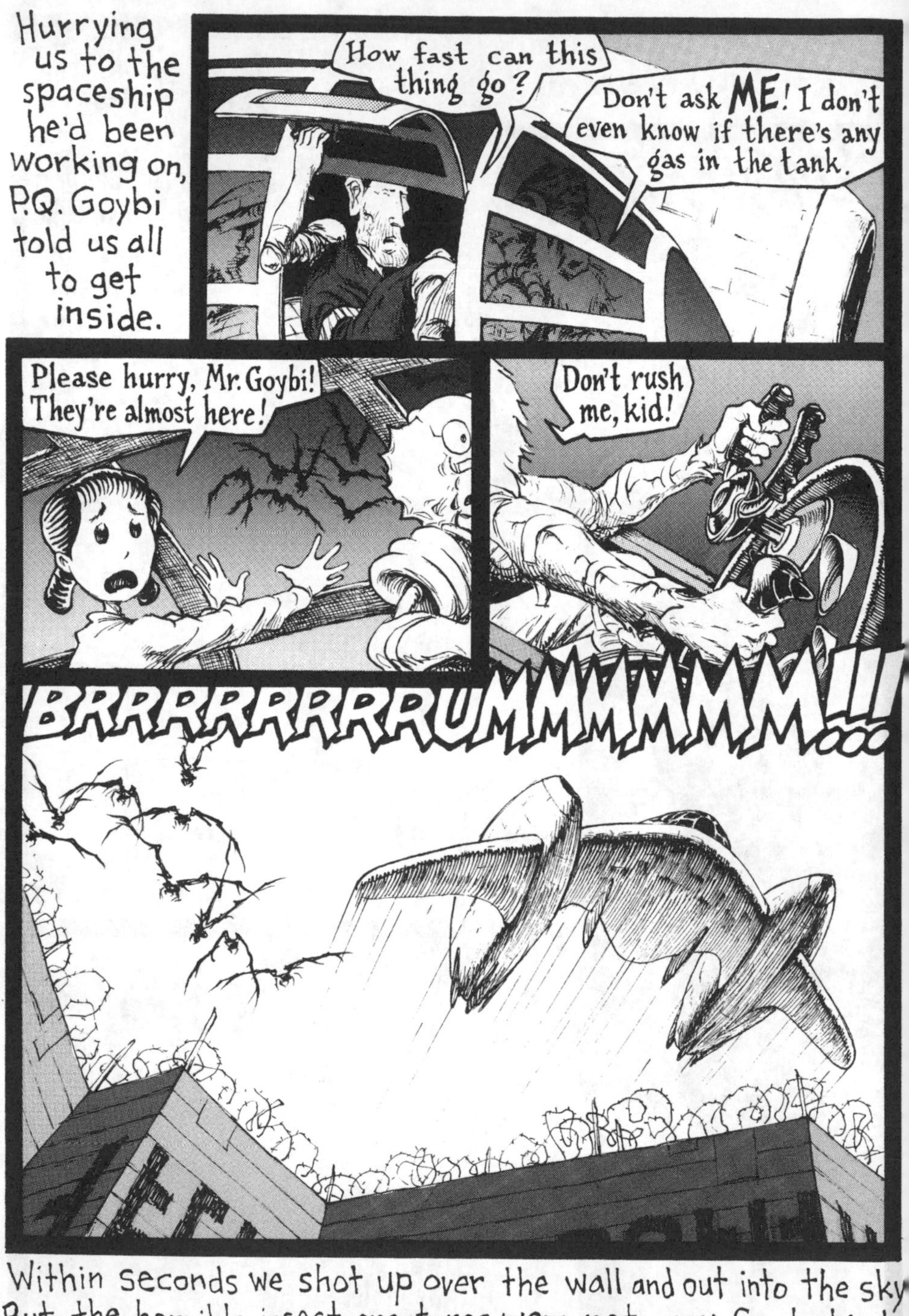
Hurrying us to the spaceship he'd been working on, P.Q. Goybi told us all to get inside.
How fast can this thing go?
Don't ask ME! I don't even know if there's any gas in the tank.
Please hurry, Mr. Goybi! They're almost here!
Don't rush me, kid!
BRRRRRRRRUMMMMMMMM!!...
Within seconds we shot up over the wall and out into the sky
But the horrible insect creatures were not very far behind.

Just then P.Q. Goybi suddenly changed course, and it looked as if we would crash into the side of a stony cliff.

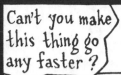

Can't you make this thing go any faster?

I bought this clunker from an old woman in Alpha Centauri. It was not intended for racing purposes!

They're gaining on us, Mr. Goybi!

Hang on, everyone. This might be a little bit frightening.

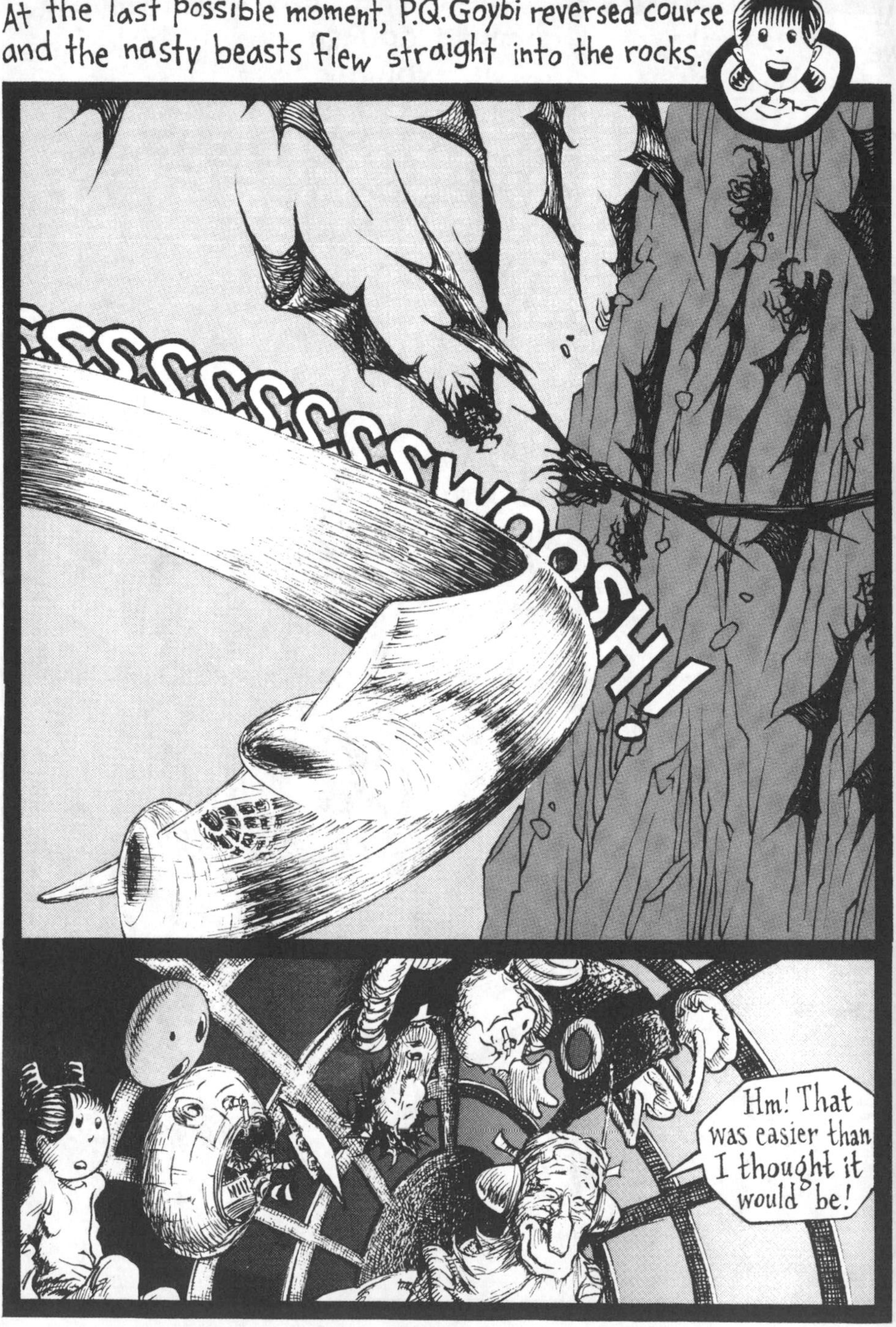
At the last possible moment, P.Q. Goybi reversed course and the nasty beasts flew straight into the rocks.
SSSSSSSSSSSWOOSH!
Hm! That was easier than I thought it would be!

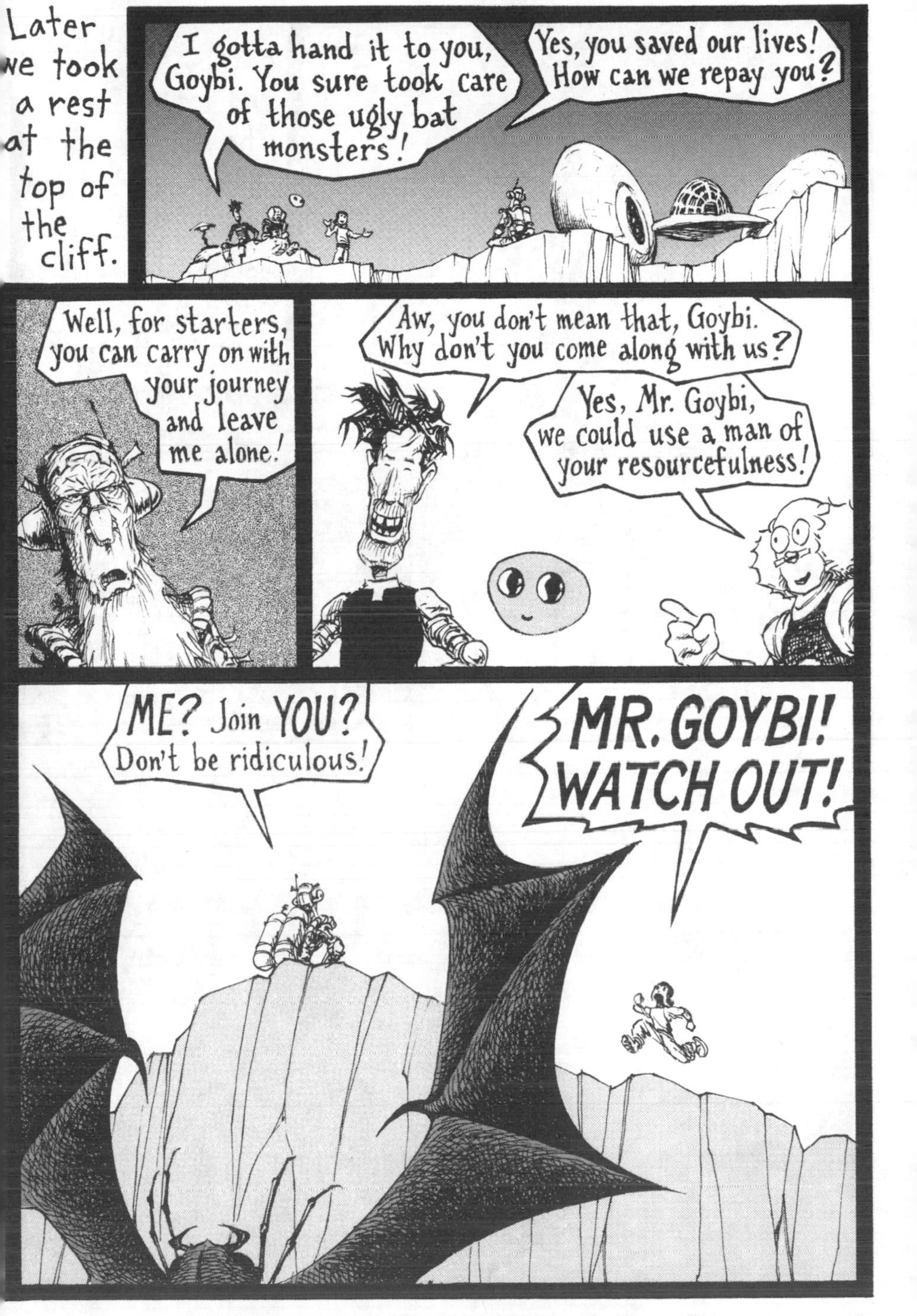
Later we took a rest at the top of the cliff.
I gotta hand it to you, Goybi. You sure took care of those ugly bat monsters!
Yes, you saved our lives! How can we repay you?
Well, for starters, you can carry on with your journey and leave me alone!
Aw, you don't mean that, Goybi. Why don't you come along with us?
Yes, Mr. Goybi, we could use a man of your resourcefulness!
ME? Join YOU? Don't be ridiculous!
MR. GOYBI! WATCH OUT!

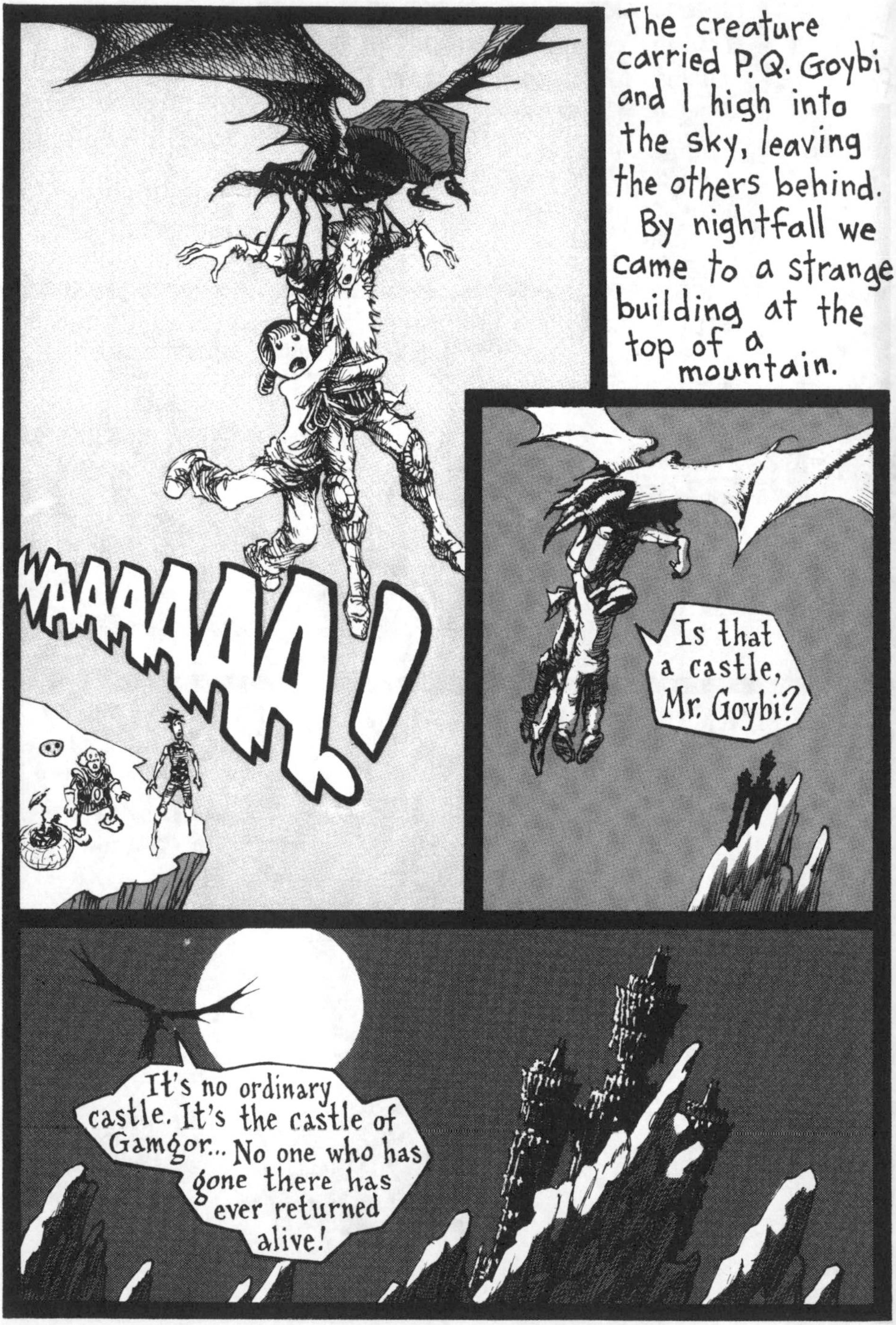
The creature carried P.Q. Goybi and I high into the sky, leaving the others behind. By nightfall we came to a strange building at the top of a mountain.
WAAAAAA!
Is that a castle, Mr. Goybi?
It's no ordinary castle. It's the castle of Gamgor... No one who has gone there has ever returned alive!

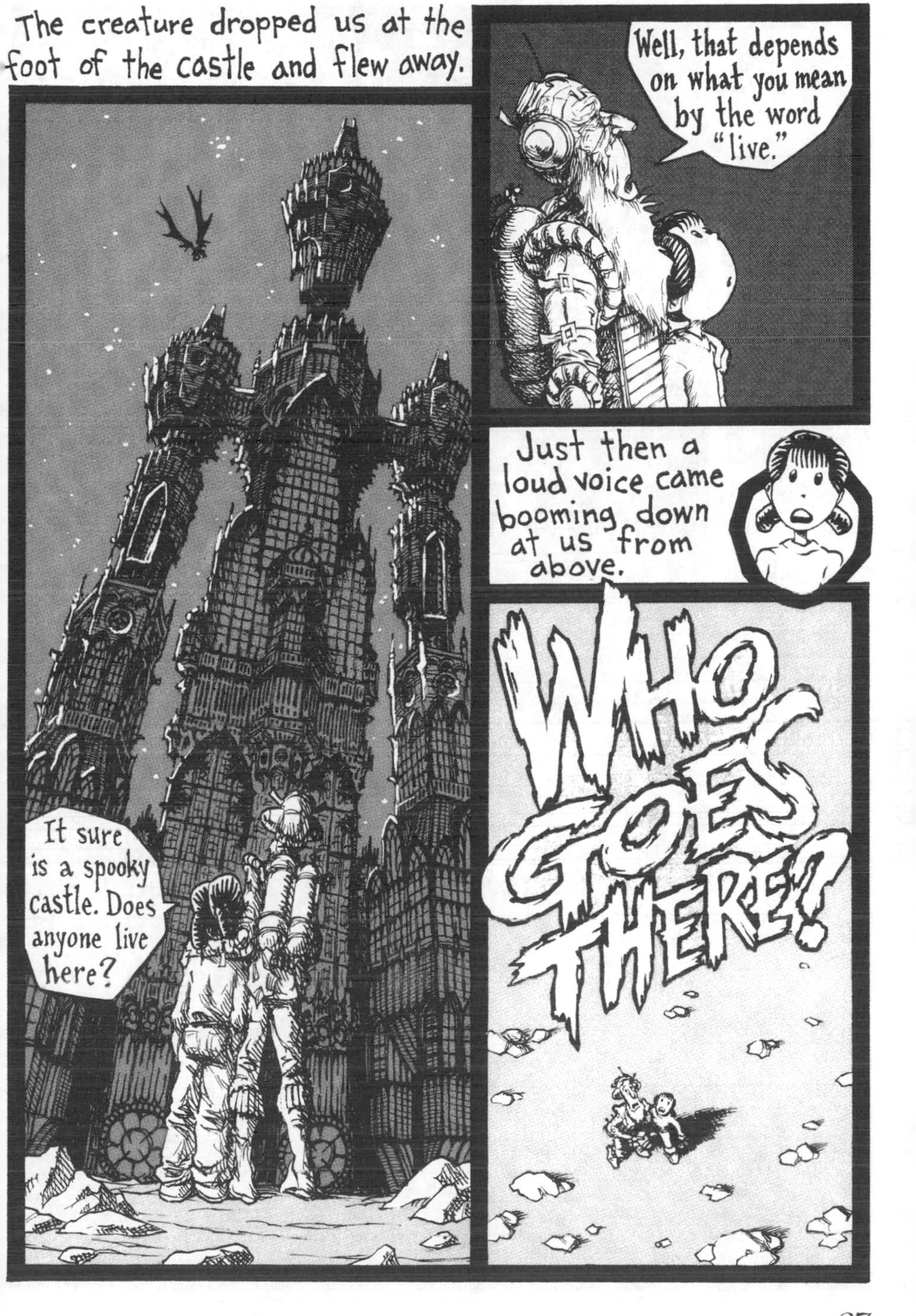
The creature dropped us at the foot of the castle and flew away.
It sure is a spooky castle. Does anyone live here?
Well, that depends on what you mean by the word "live."
Just then a loud voice came booming down at us from above.
WHO GOES THERE?

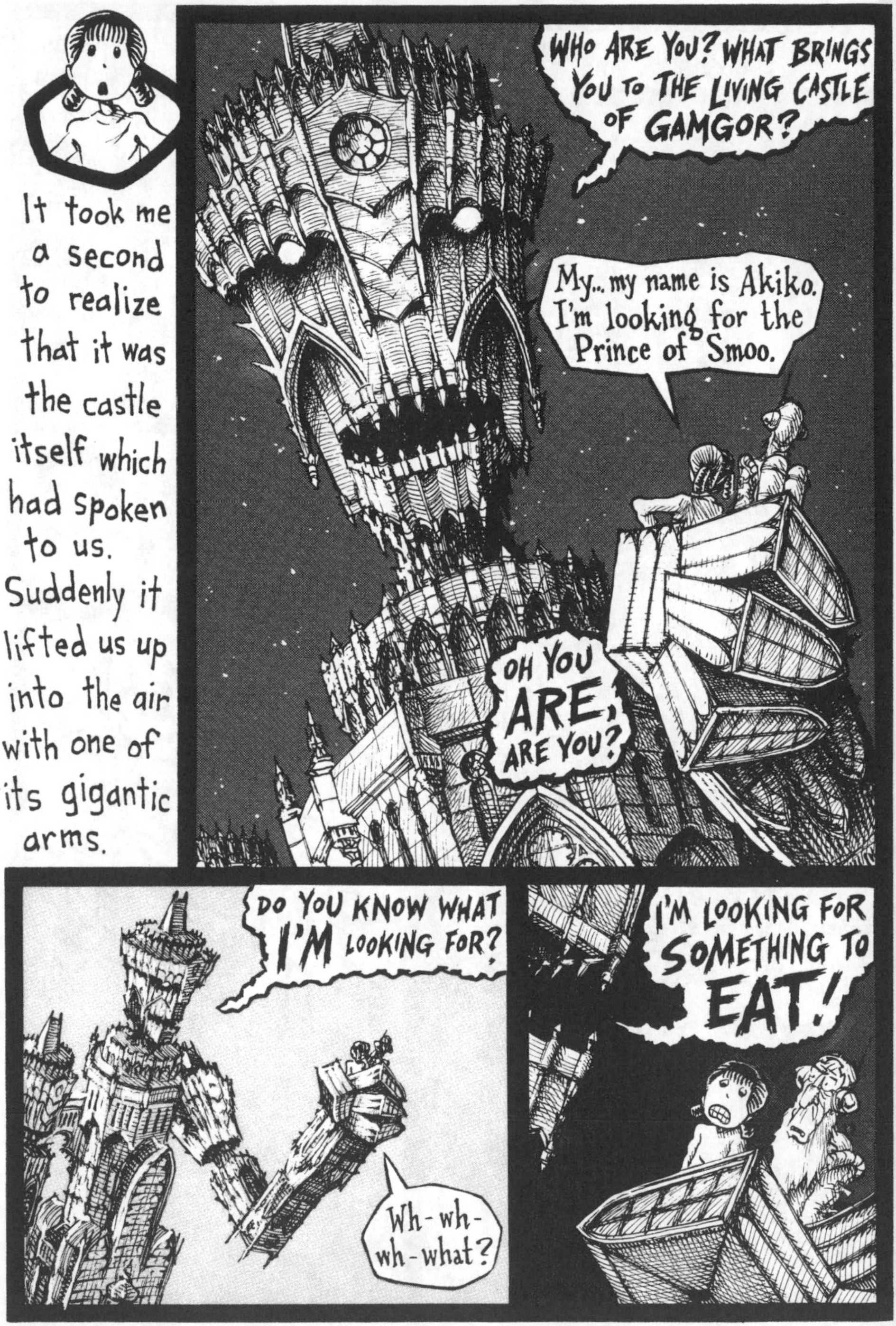
It took me a second to realize that it was the castle itself which had spoken to us. Suddenly it lifted us up into the air with one of its gigantic arms.
WHO ARE YOU? WHAT BRINGS YOU TO THE LIVING CASTLE OF GAMGOR?
My.. my name is Akiko. I'm looking for the Prince of Smoo.
OH YOU ARE, ARE YOU?
DO YOU KNOW WHAT I'M LOOKING FOR?
Wh-wh-wh-what?
I'M LOOKING FOR SOMETHING TO EAT!

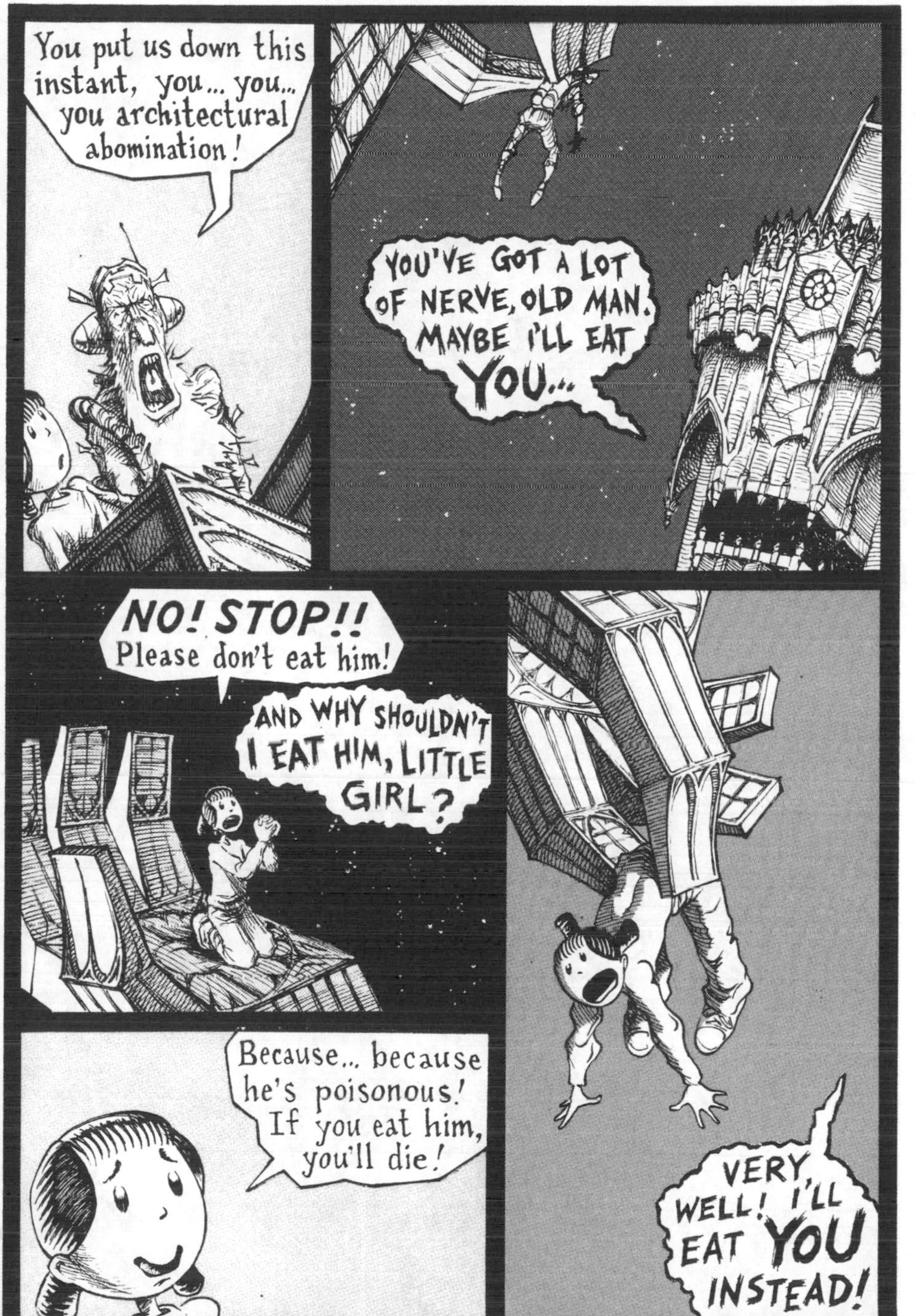
You put us down this instant, you... you... you architectural abomination!
YOU'VE GOT A LOT OF NERVE, OLD MAN. MAYBE I'LL EAT YOU...
NO! STOP!! Please don't eat him!
AND WHY SHOULDN'T I EAT HIM, LITTLE GIRL?
Because... because he's poisonous! If you eat him, you'll die!
VERY WELL! I'LL EAT YOU INSTEAD!

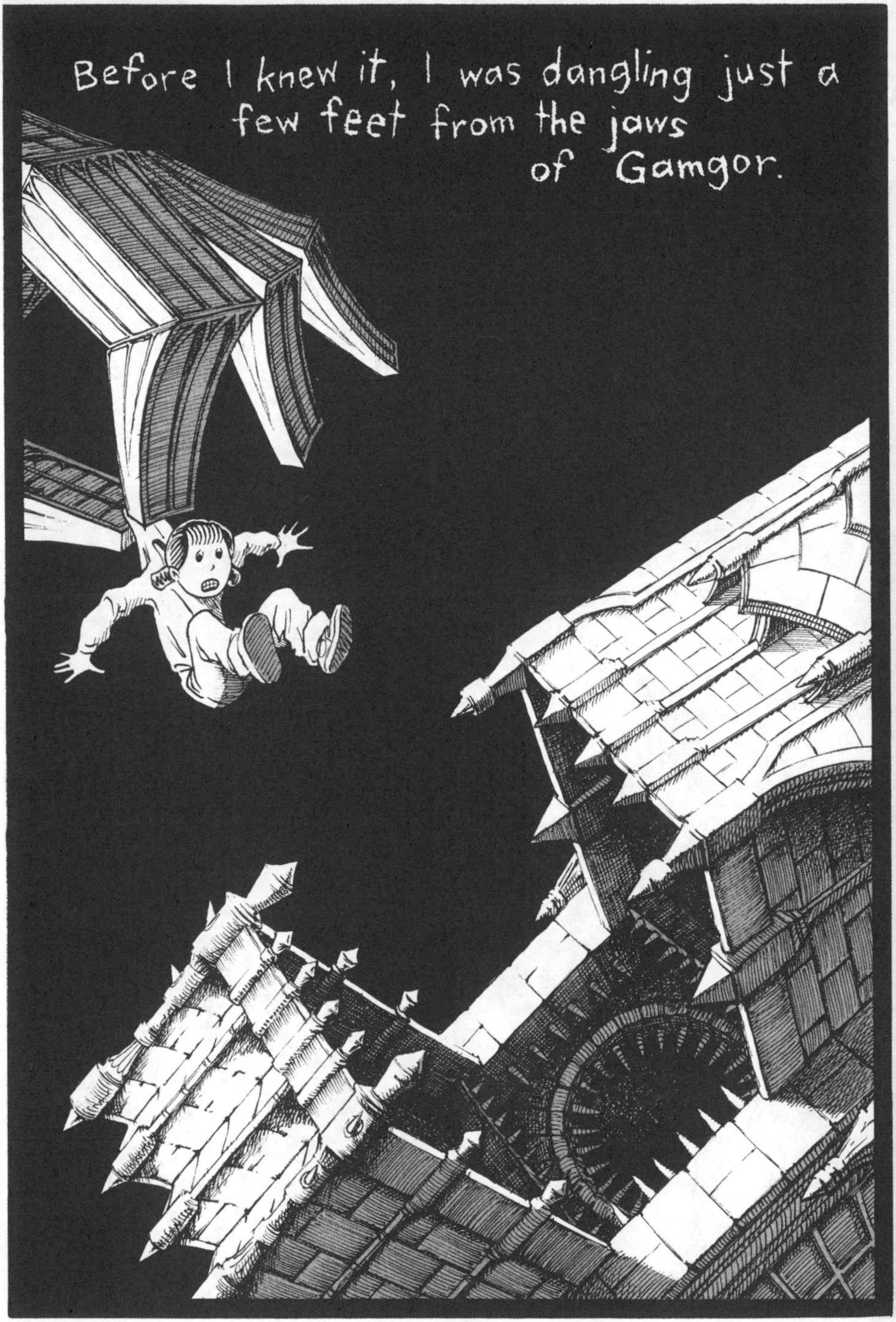
Before I knew it, I was dangling just a few feet from the jaws of Gamgor.

Just then I remembered my toothbrush. I pulled it out of my back pocket and threw it down into Gamgor's throat.

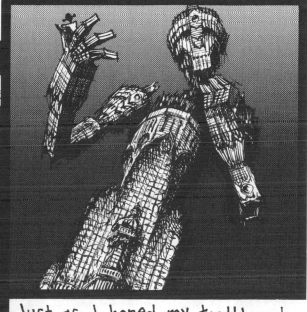

Just as I hoped, my toothbrush got stuck somewhere down in Gamgor's throat, and he started to choke. In fact...

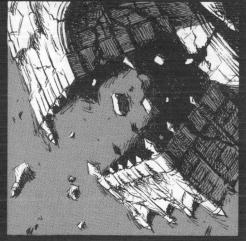

...he coughed so hard, he began to fall apart!

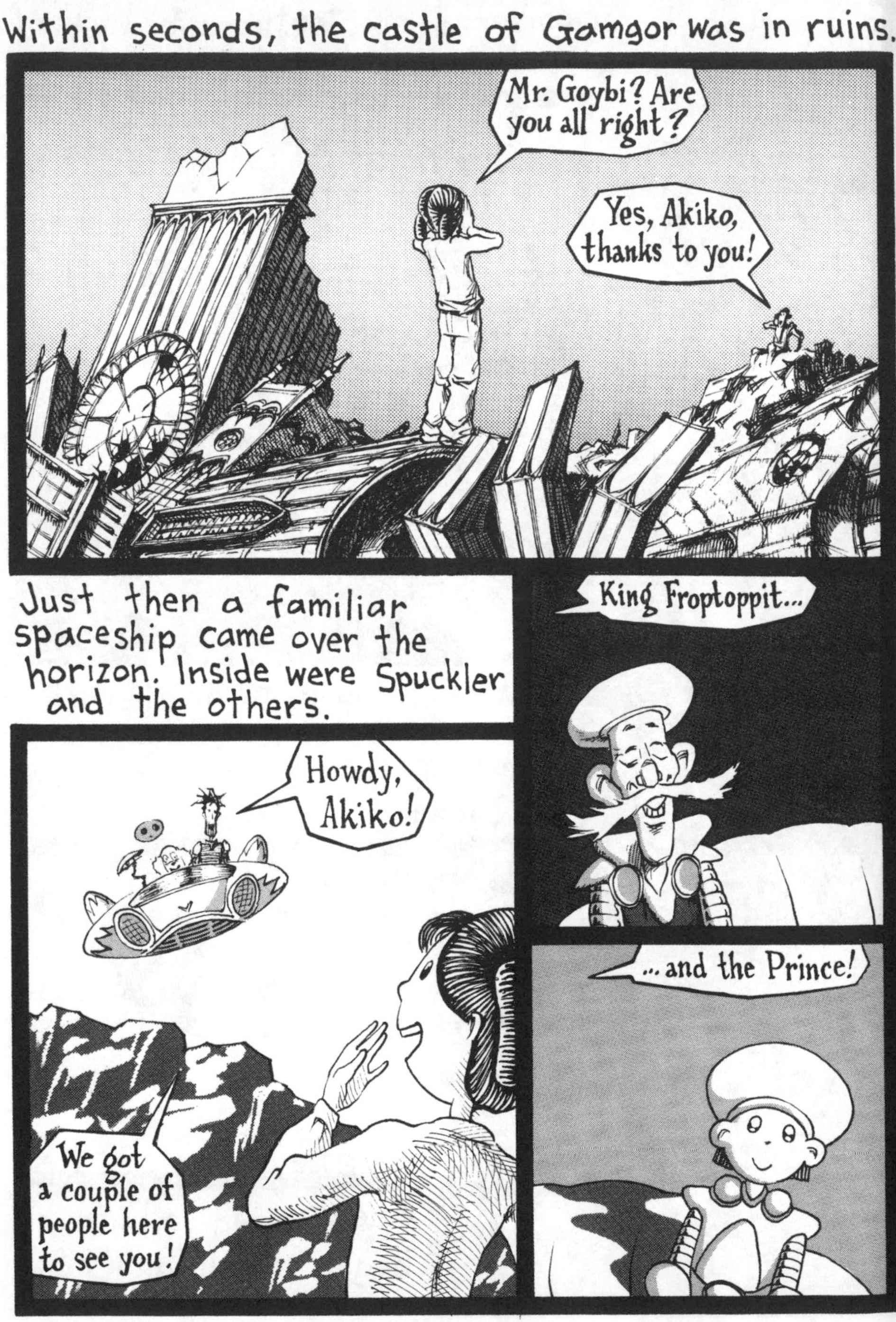
Within seconds, the castle of Gamgor was in ruins.
Mr. Goybi? Are you all right?
Yes, Akiko, thanks to you!
Just then a familiar spaceship came over the horizon. Inside were Spuckler and the others.
Howdy, Akiko!
We got a couple of people here to see you!
King Froptoppit...
...and the Prince!

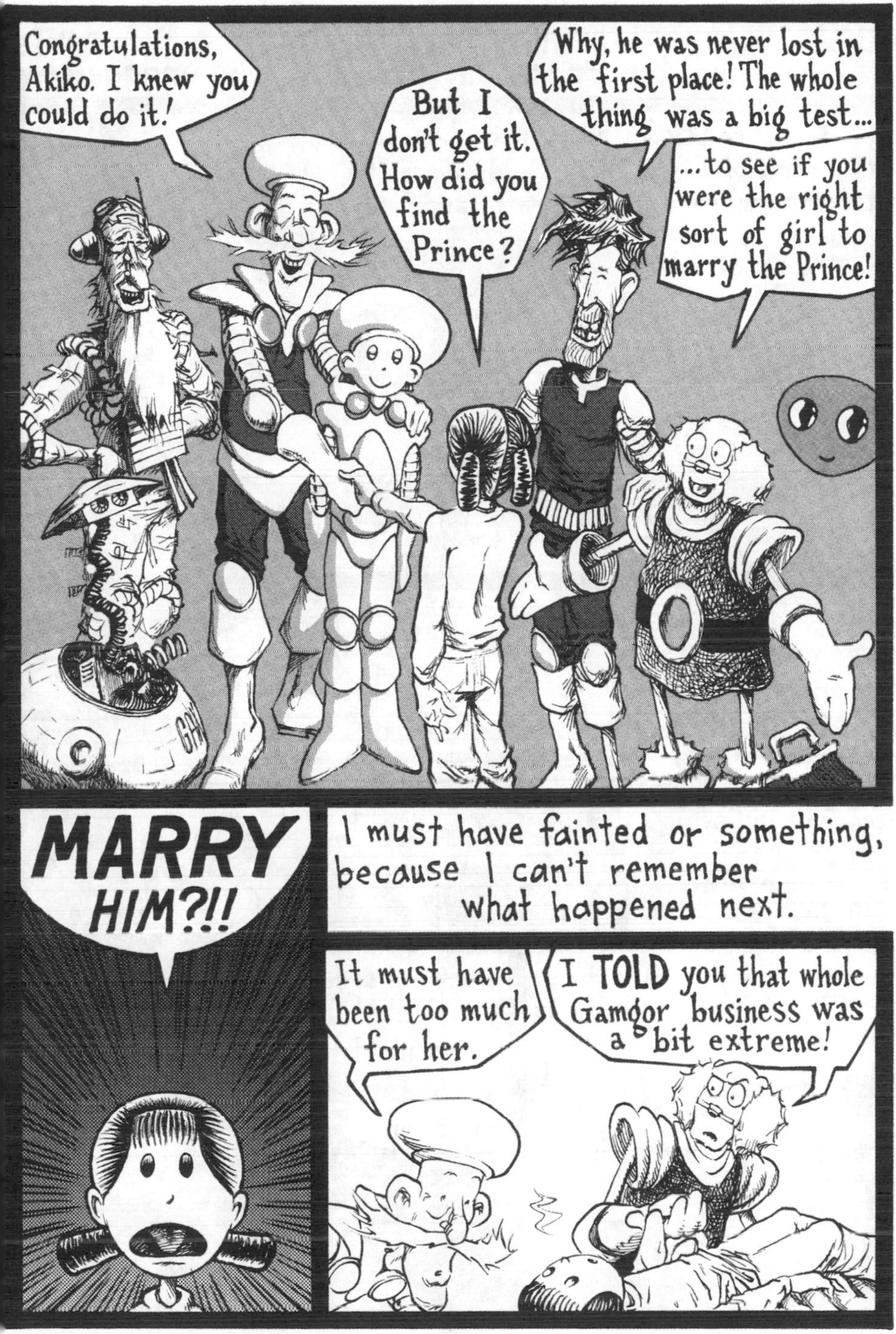
Congratulations, Akiko. I knew you could do it!
But I don't get it. How did you find the Prince?
Why, he was never lost in the first place! The whole thing was a big test...
...to see if you were the right sort of girl to marry the Prince!
MARRY HIM?!!
I must have fainted or something, because I can't remember what happened next.
It must have been too much for her.
I TOLD you that whole Gamgor business was a bit extreme!

That night at the palace they threw a big party for me and the Prince, in honor of our engagement.

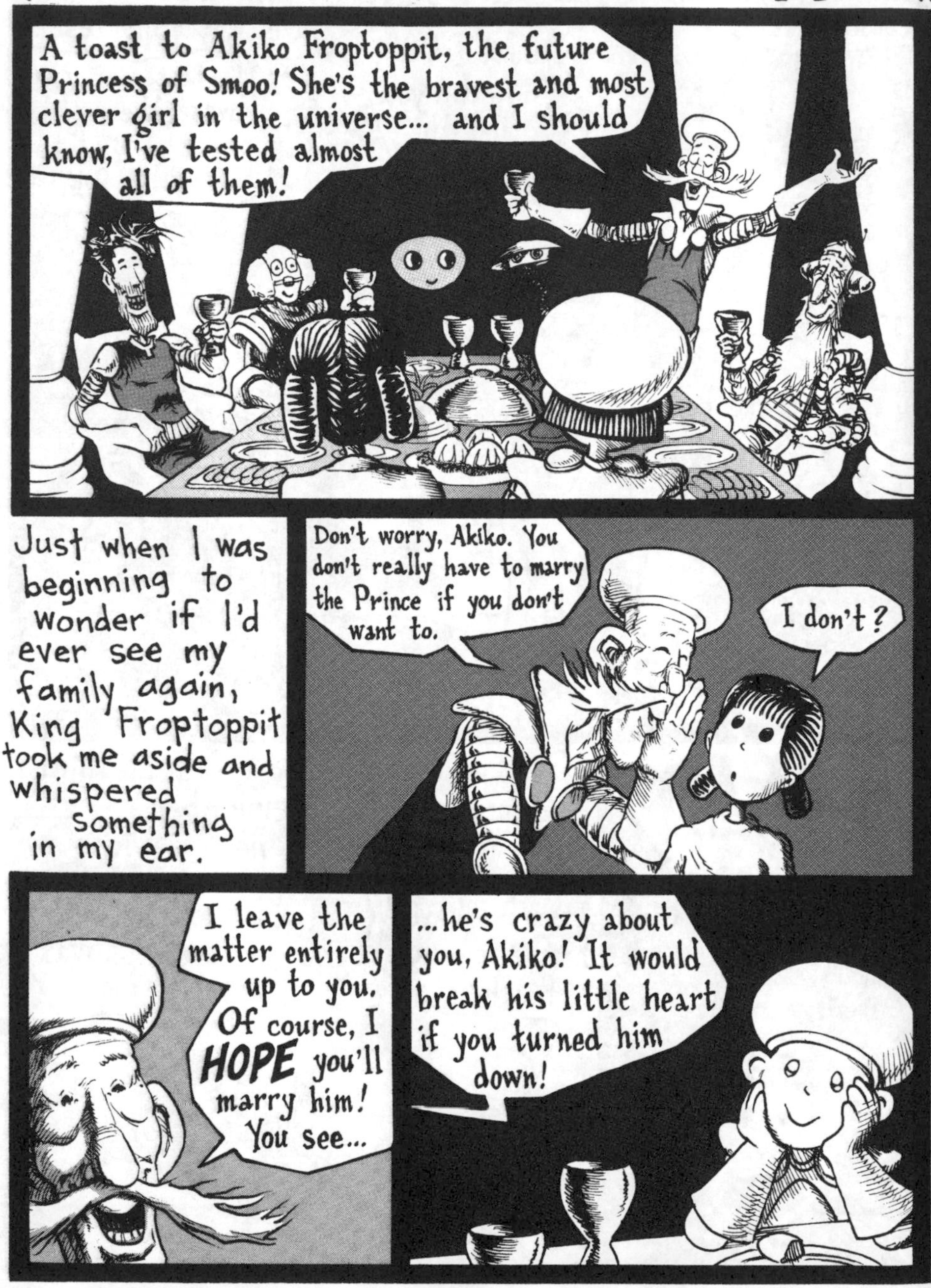
A toast to Akiko Froptoppit, the future Princess of Smoo! She's the bravest and most clever girl in the universe... and I should know, I've tested almost all of them!
Just when I was beginning to wonder if I'd ever see my family again, King Froptoppit took me aside and whispered something in my ear.
Don't worry, Akiko. You don't really have to marry the Prince if you don't want to.
I don't?
I leave the matter entirely up to you. Of course, I HOPE you'll marry him! You see...
...he's crazy about you, Akiko! It would break his little heart if you turned him down!

In the end, the King agreed to let me go back to earth and think it over for a while. I told him I at least want to finish the 6th grade before I consider any marriage proposals.

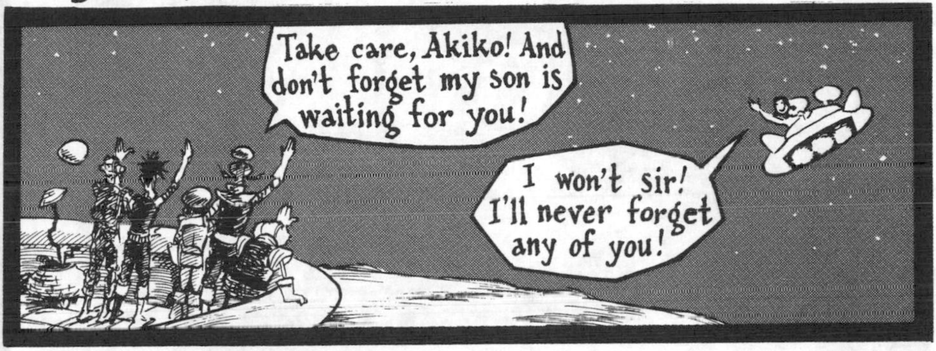
Take care, Akiko! And don't forget my son is waiting for you!
I won't sir! I'll never forget any of you!

Life has been pretty quiet since then. I sort of miss Spuckler and Mr. Beeba and Poog and Gax and everybody. They're a lot more interesting than most of the kids in the 4th grade.

But I still can't decide whether I'm going to marry the Prince or not. I mean, spending the rest of my life on another planet could be difficult.

But then again, if I stay here on earth, I think the chances of me marrying a prince are pretty slim.

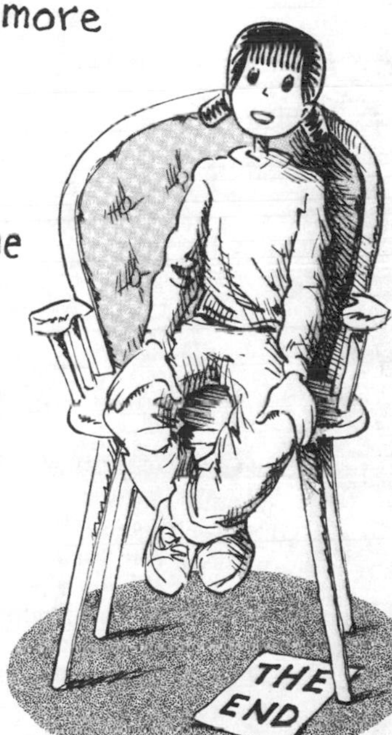
THE END

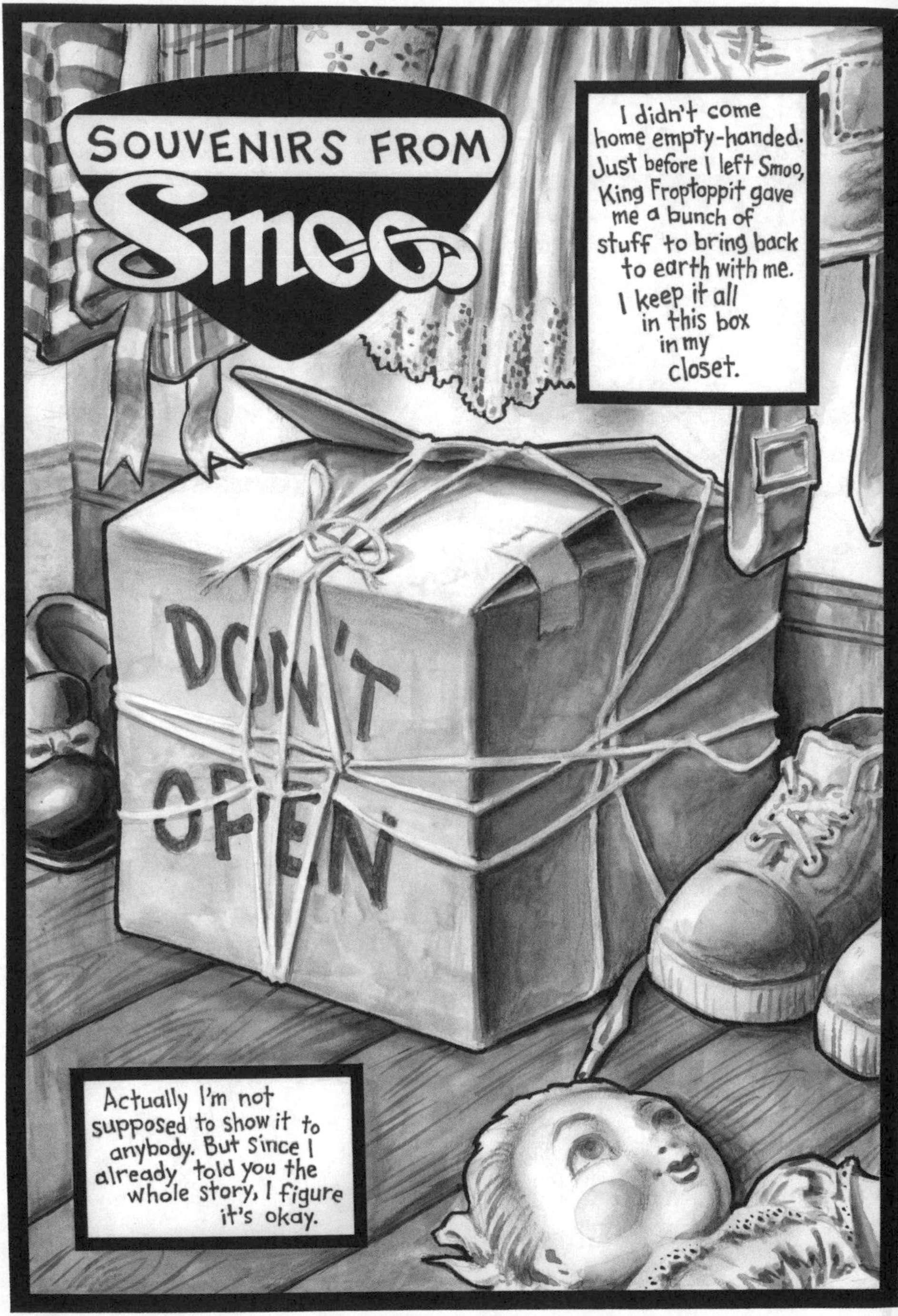
SOUVENIRS FROM
Smoo
I didn't come home empty-handed. Just before I left Smoo, King Froptoppit gave me a bunch of stuff to bring back to earth with me. I keep it all in this box in my closet.
DON'T OPEN
Actually I'm not supposed to show it to anybody. But since I already told you the whole story, I figure it's okay.

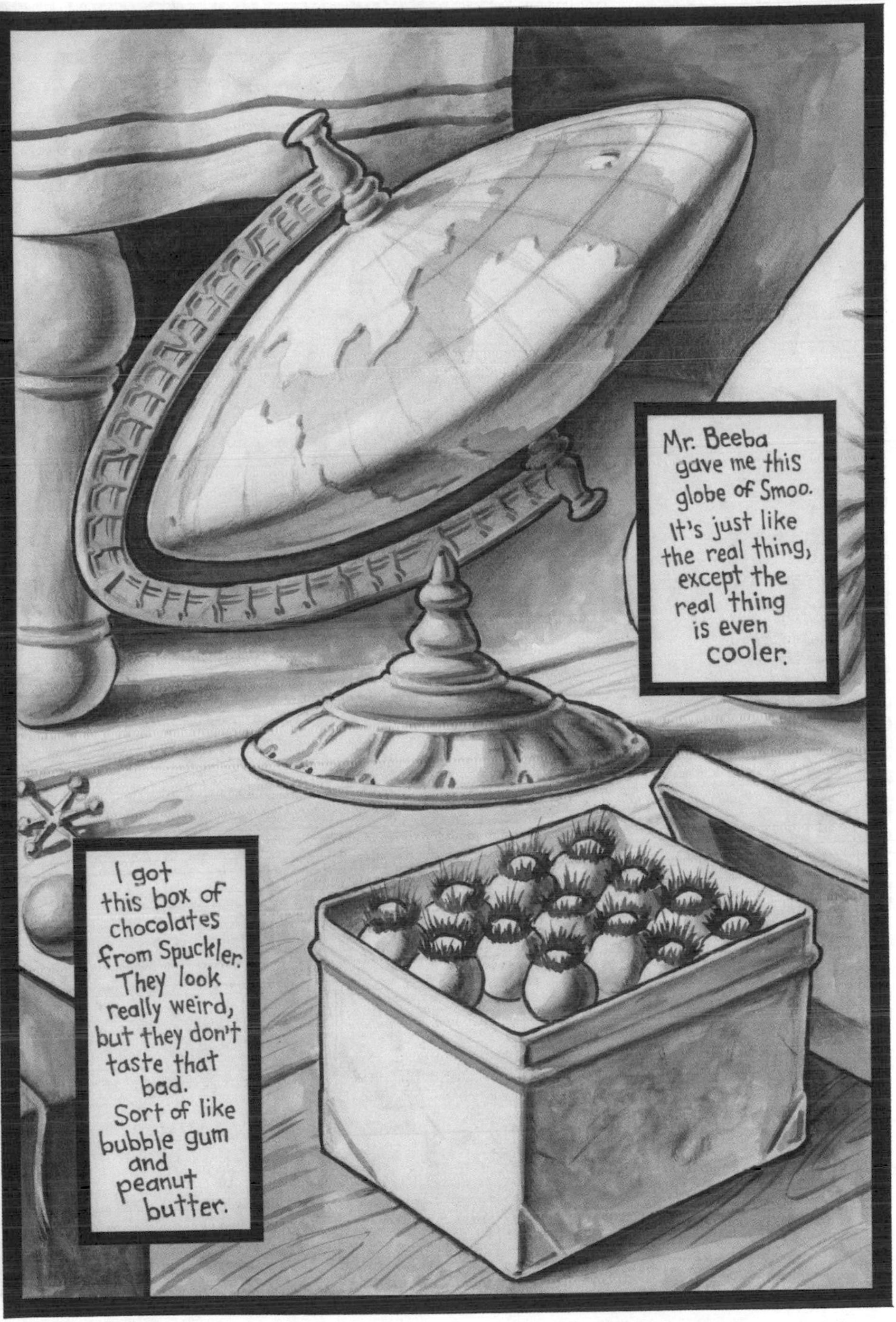
Mr. Beeba gave me this globe of Smoo. It's just like the real thing, except the real thing is even cooler.
I got this box of chocolates from Spuckler. They look really weird, but they don't taste that bad. Sort of like bubble gum and peanut butter.

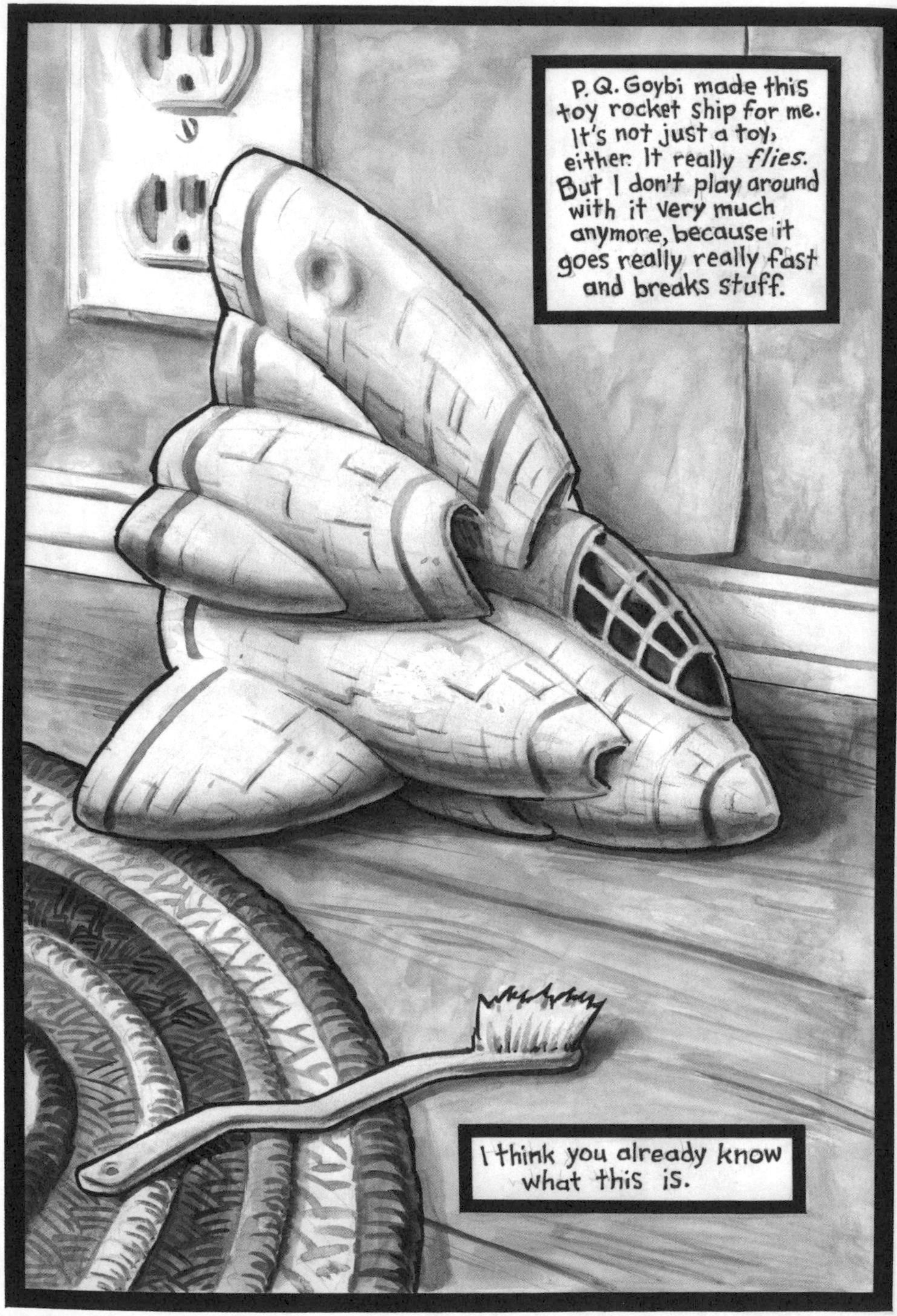
P. Q. Goybi made this toy rocket ship for me. It's not just a toy, either. It really *flies.* But I don't play around with it very much anymore, because it goes really really fast and breaks stuff.
I think you already know what this is.

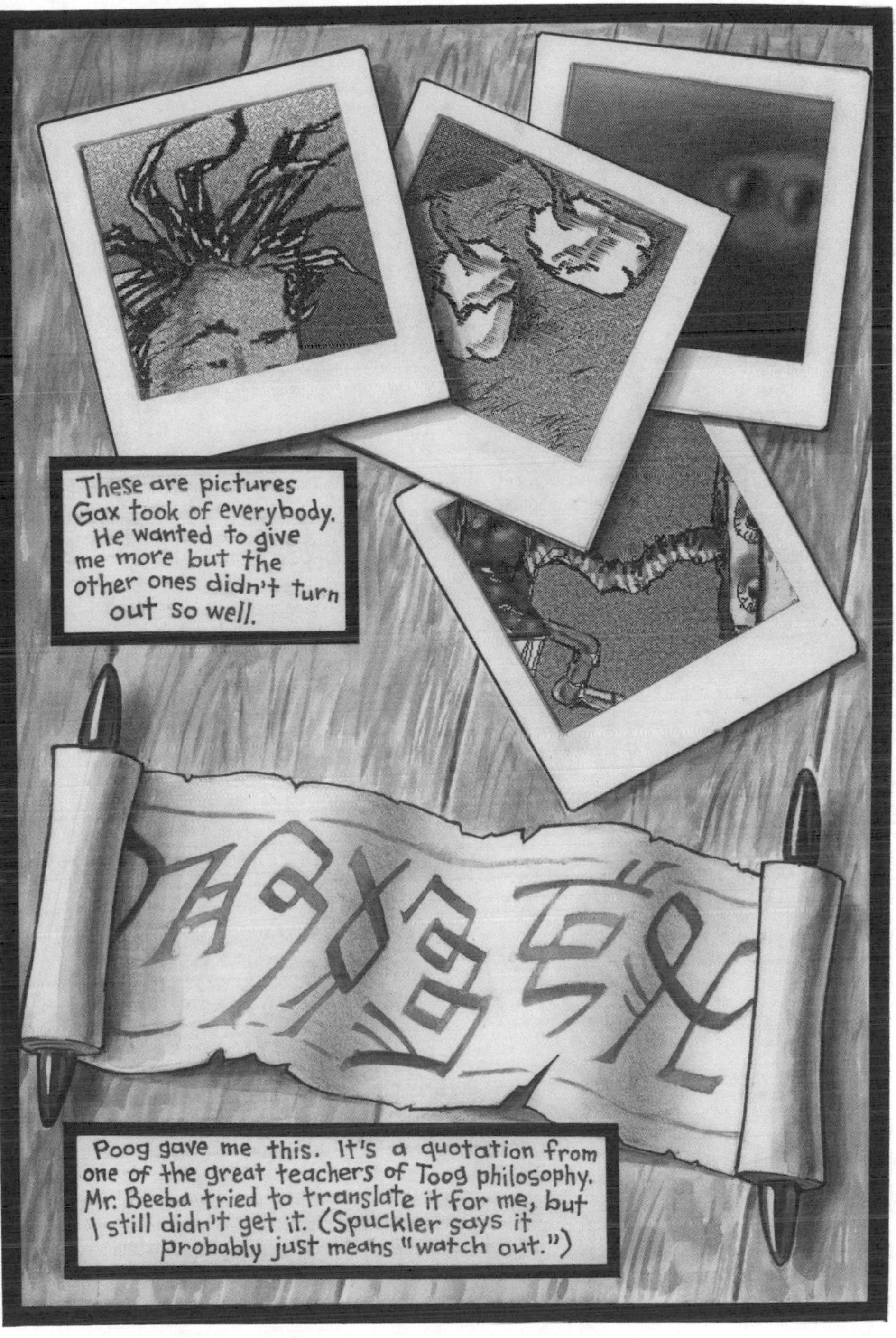

These are pictures Gax took of everybody. He wanted to give me more but the other ones didn't turn out so well.
Poog gave me this. It's a quotation from one of the great teachers of Toog philosophy. Mr. Beeba tried to translate it for me, but I still didn't get it. (Spuckler says it probably just means "watch out.")

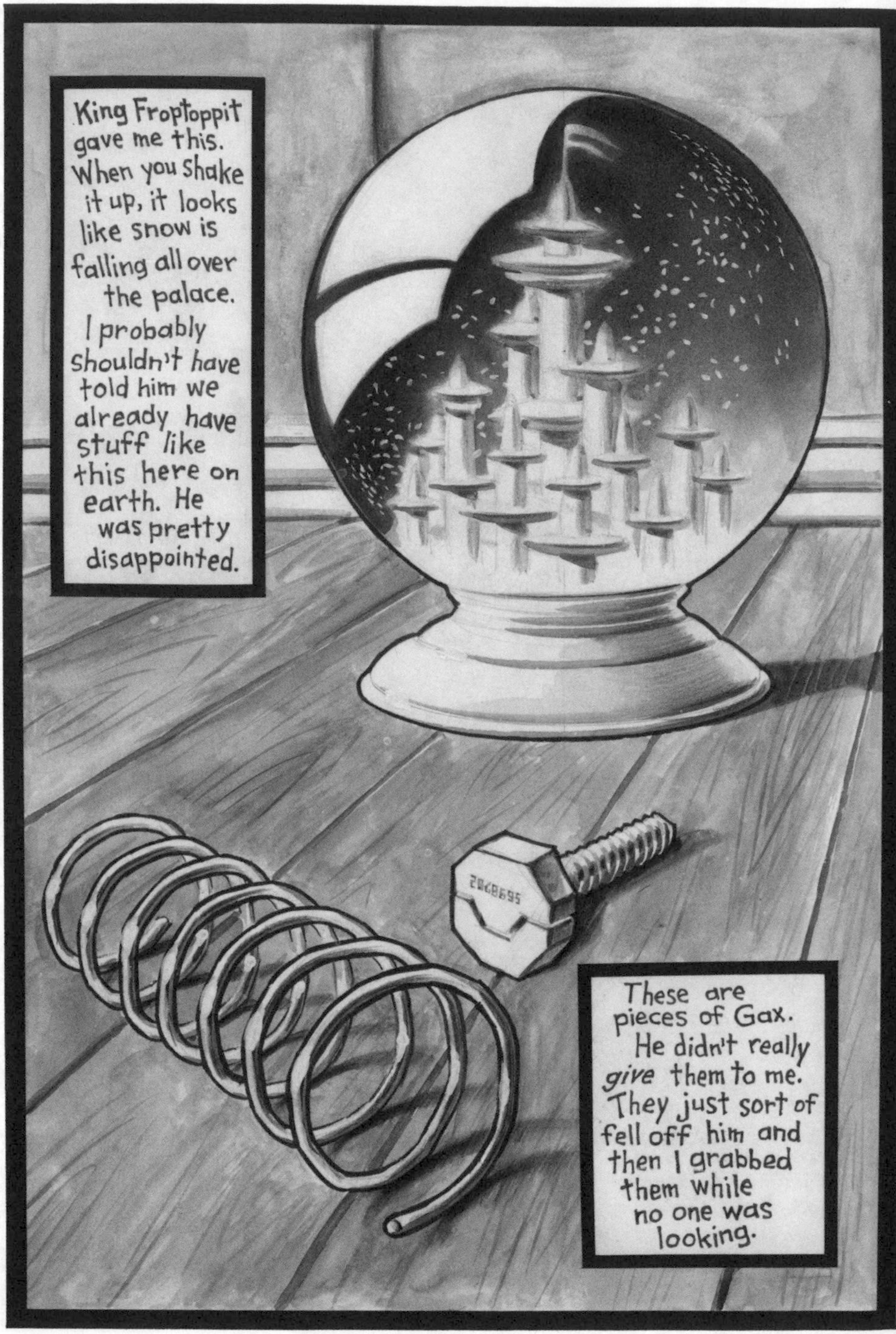
King Froptoppit gave me this. When you shake it up, it looks like snow is falling all over the palace. I probably shouldn't have told him we already have stuff like this here on earth. He was pretty disappointed.
These are pieces of Gax. He didn't really *give* them to me. They just sort of fell off him and then I grabbed them while no one was looking.

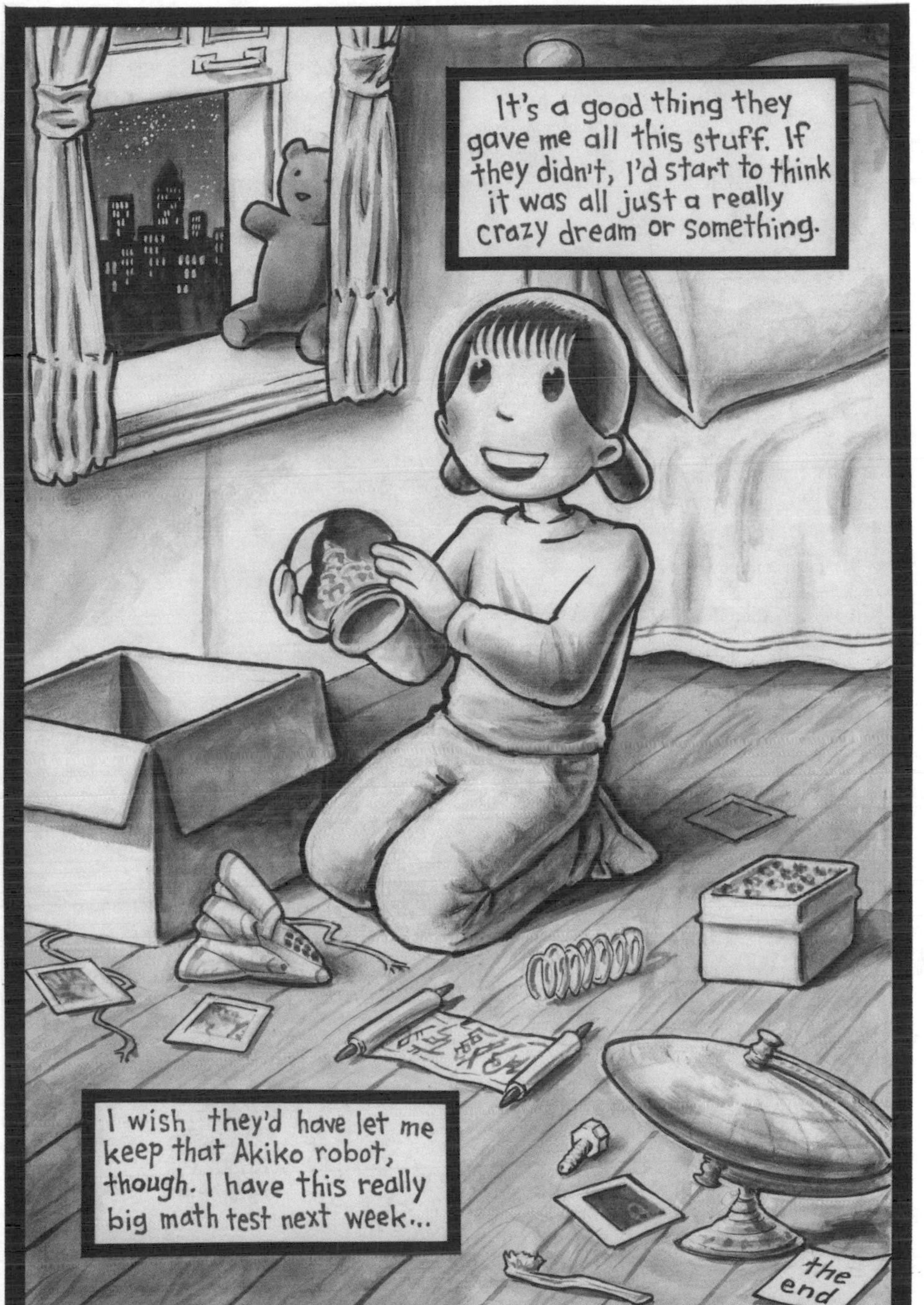
It's a good thing they gave me all this stuff. If they didn't, I'd start to think it was all just a really crazy dream or something.
I wish they'd have let me keep that Akiko robot, though. I have this really big math test next week...
the end

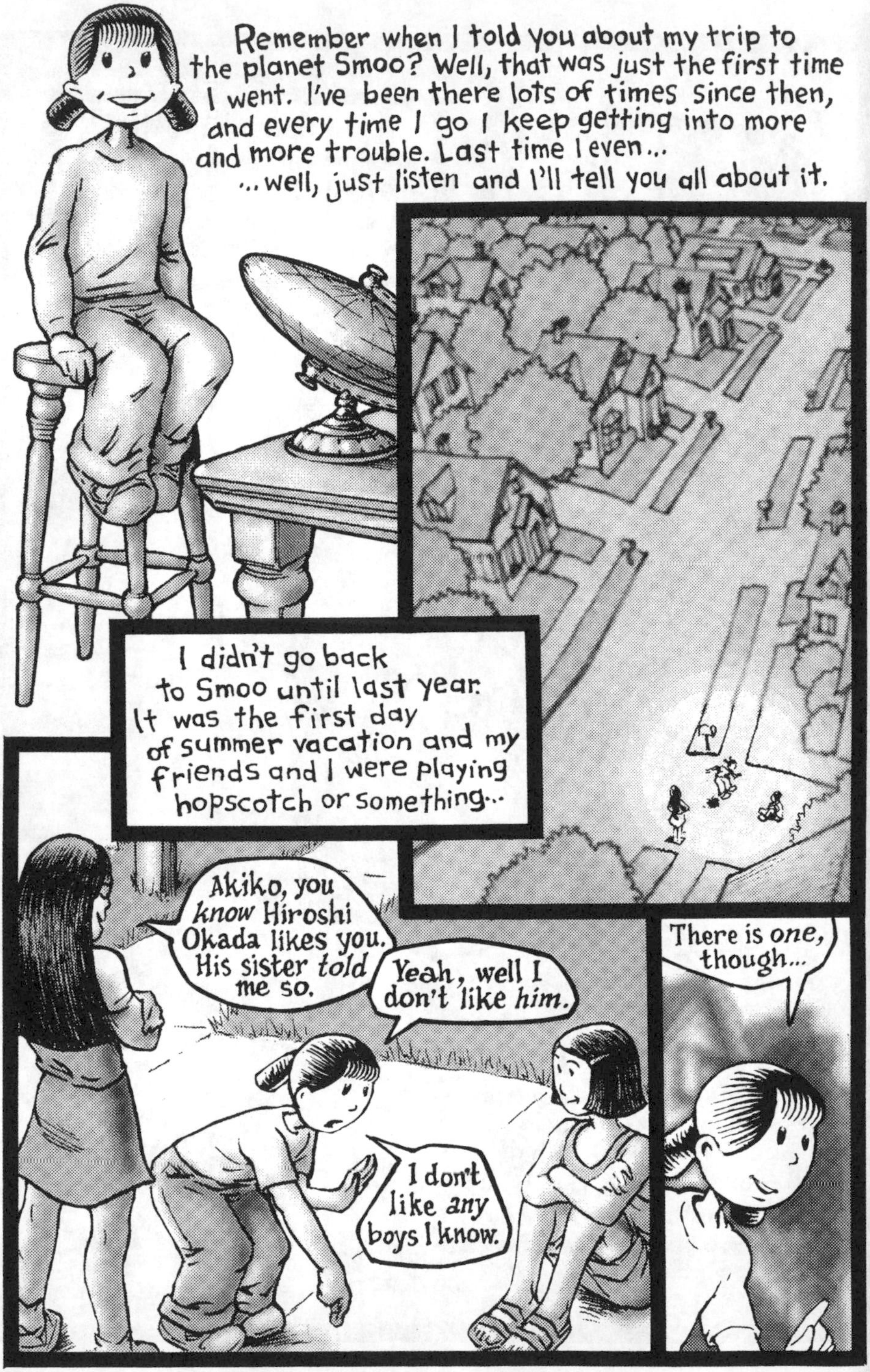
Remember when I told you about my trip to the planet Smoo? Well, that was just the first time I went. I've been there lots of times since then, and every time I go I keep getting into more and more trouble. Last time I even...
...well, just listen and I'll tell you all about it.
I didn't go back to Smoo until last year. It was the first day of summer vacation and my friends and I were playing hopscotch or something...
Akiko, you *know* Hiroshi Okada likes you. His sister *told* me so.
Yeah, well I don't like *him*.
I don't like *any* boys I know.
There is *one*, though...

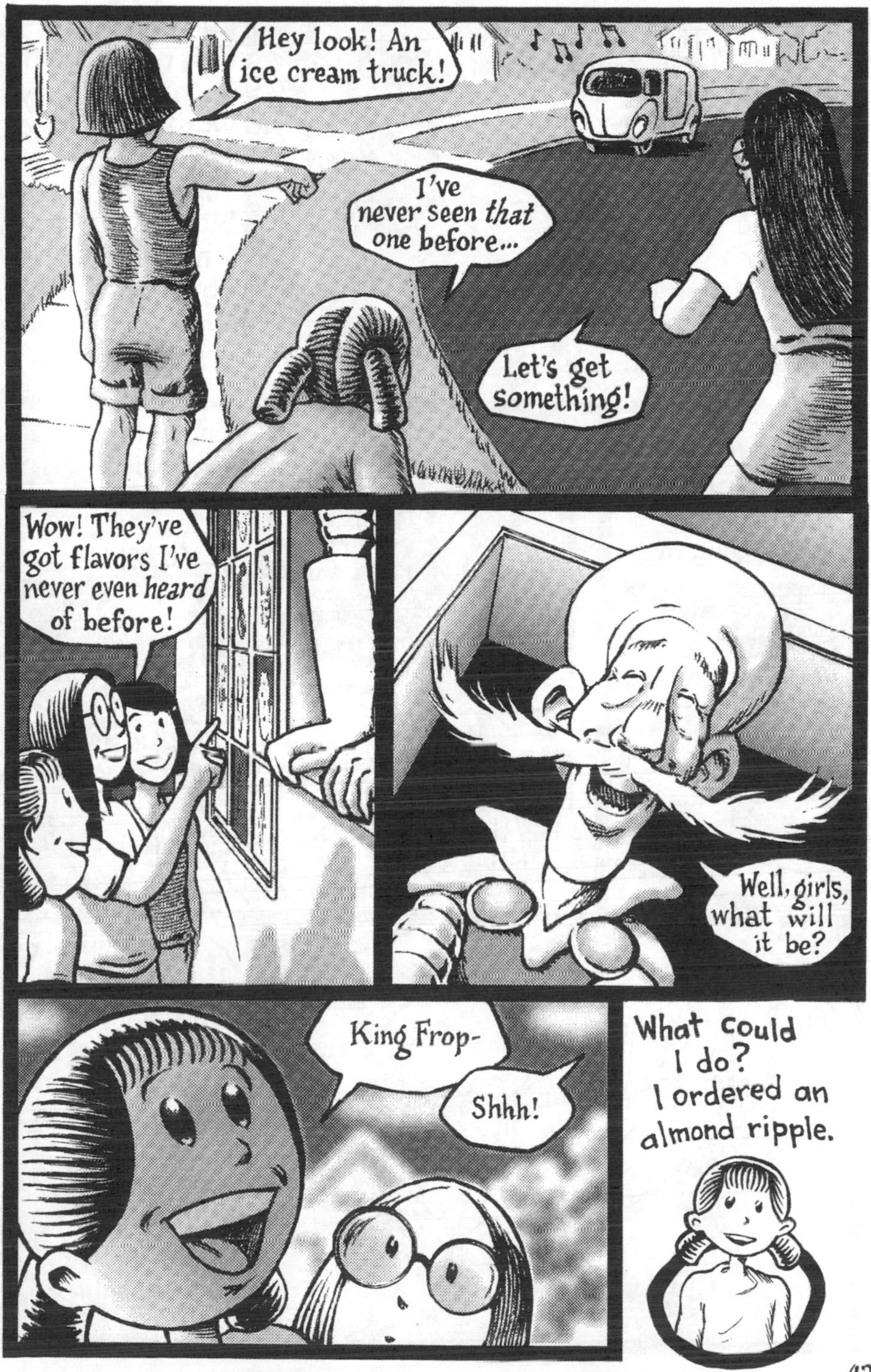
Hey look! An ice cream truck!
I've never seen *that* one before...
Let's get something!
Wow! They've got flavors I've never even *heard* of before!
Well, girls, what will it be?
King Frop-
Shhh!
What could I do? I ordered an almond ripple.

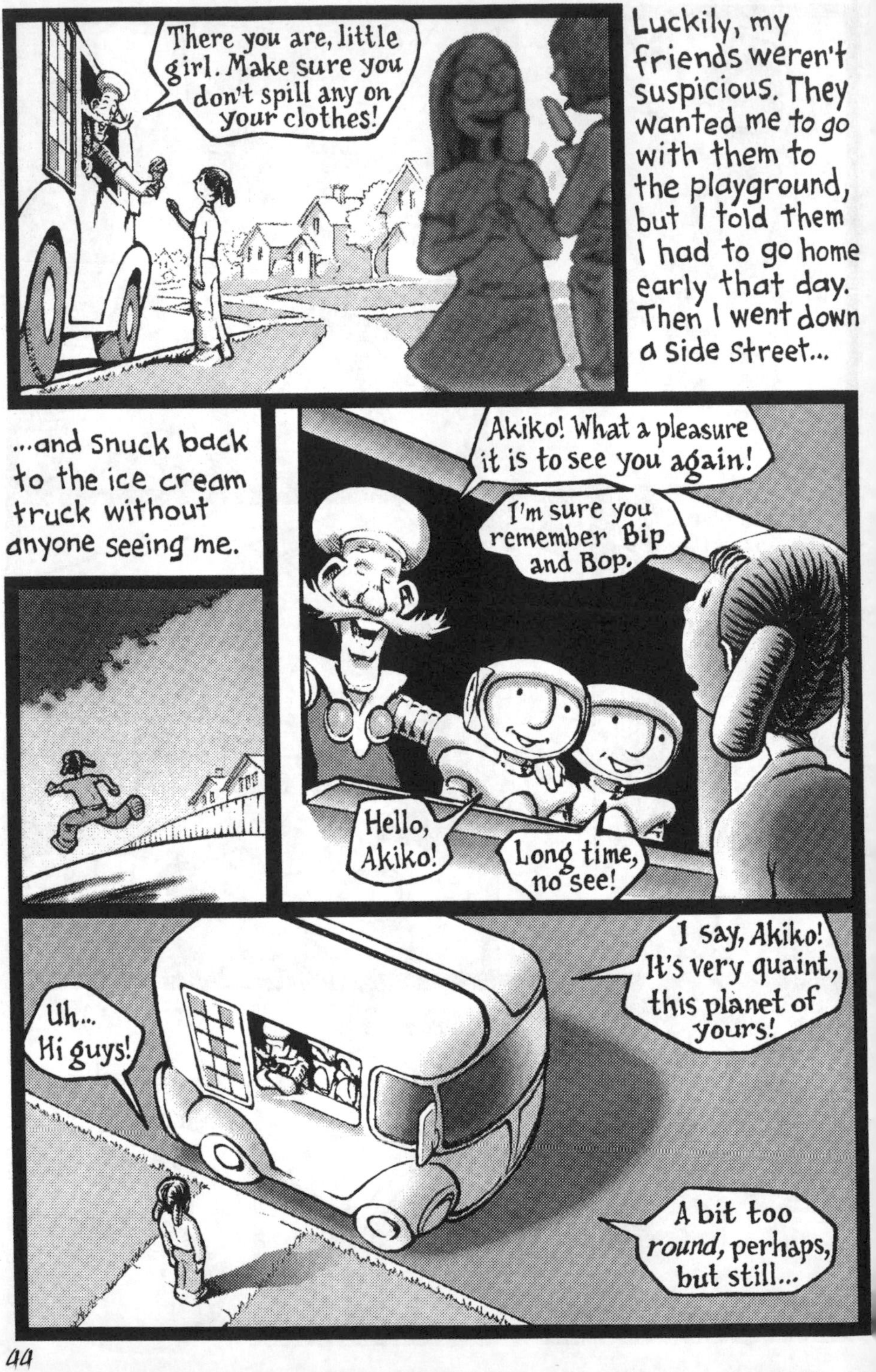
There you are, little girl. Make sure you don't spill any on your clothes!
Luckily, my friends weren't suspicious. They wanted me to go with them to the playground, but I told them I had to go home early that day. Then I went down a side street...
...and snuck back to the ice cream truck without anyone seeing me.
Akiko! What a pleasure it is to see you again!
I'm sure you remember Bip and Bop.
Hello, Akiko!
Long time, no see!
Uh... Hi guys!
I say, Akiko! It's very quaint, this planet of yours!
A bit too round, perhaps, but still...

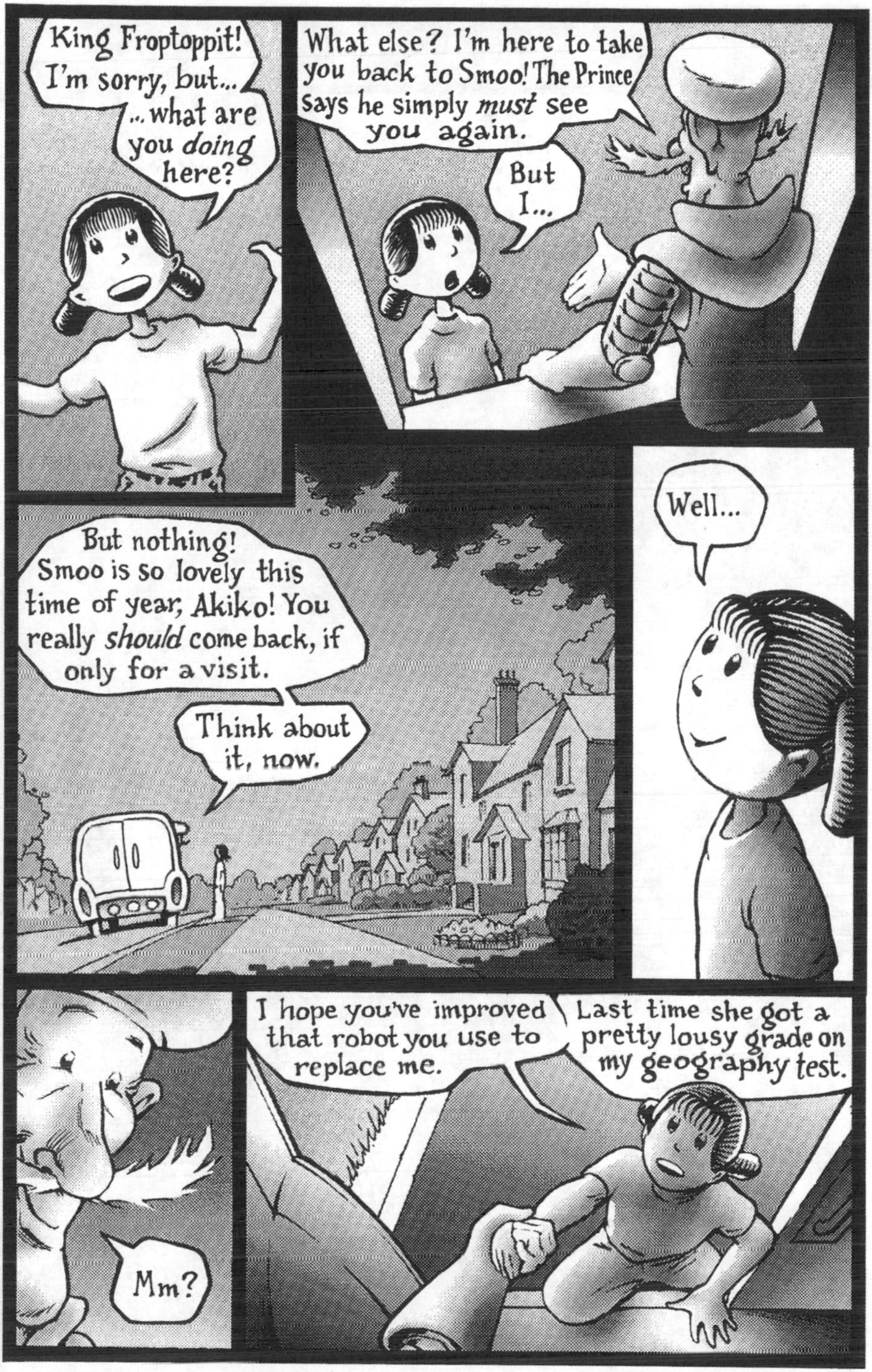
King Froptoppit! I'm sorry, but...
...what are you *doing* here?
What else? I'm here to take you back to Smoo! The Prince says he simply *must* see you again.
But I...
But nothing! Smoo is so lovely this time of year, Akiko! You really *should* come back, if only for a visit.
Think about it, now.
Well...
Mm?
I hope you've improved that robot you use to replace me.
Last time she got a pretty lousy grade on my geography test.

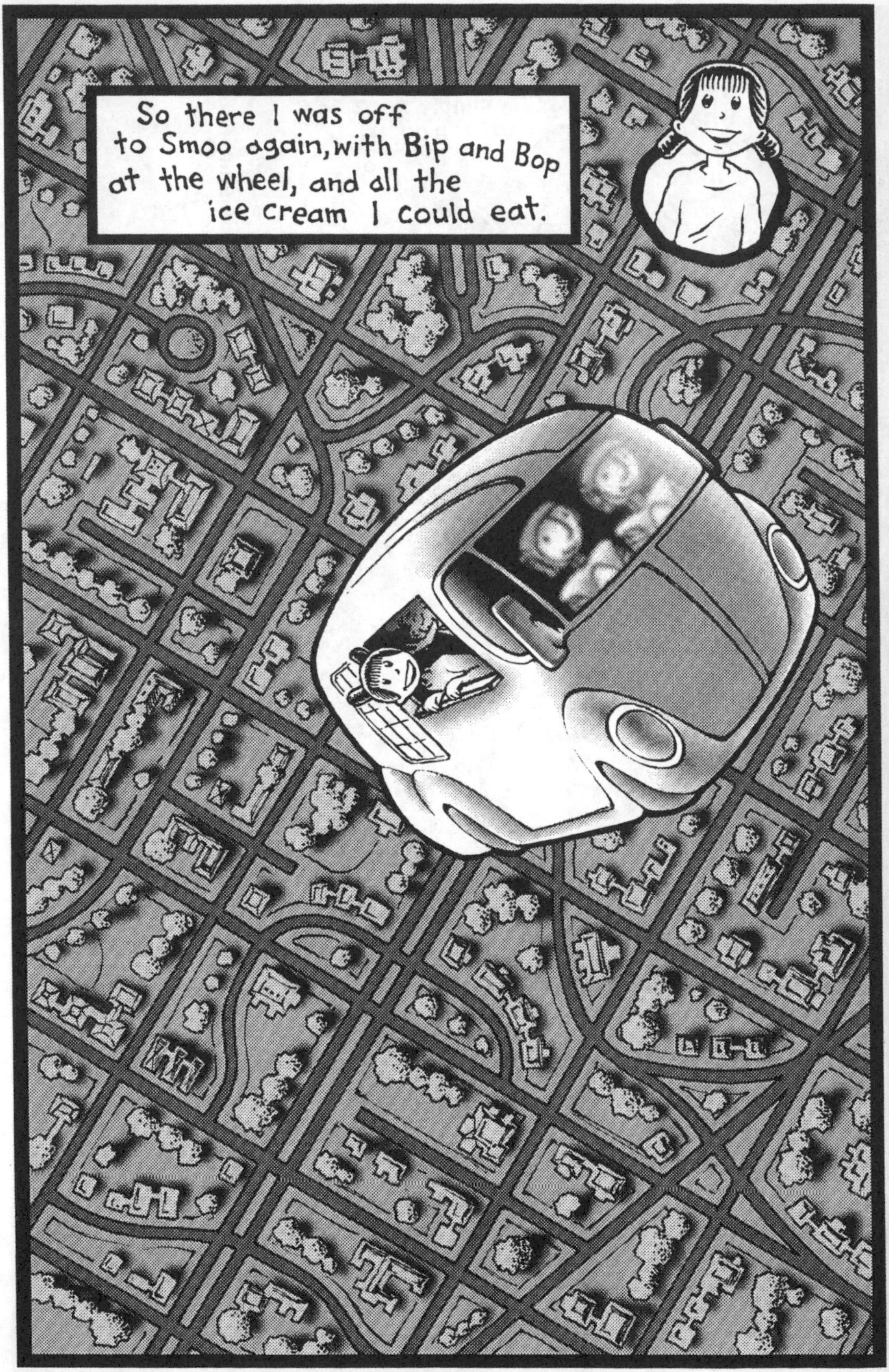
So there I was off to Smoo again, with Bip and Bop at the wheel, and all the ice cream I could eat.

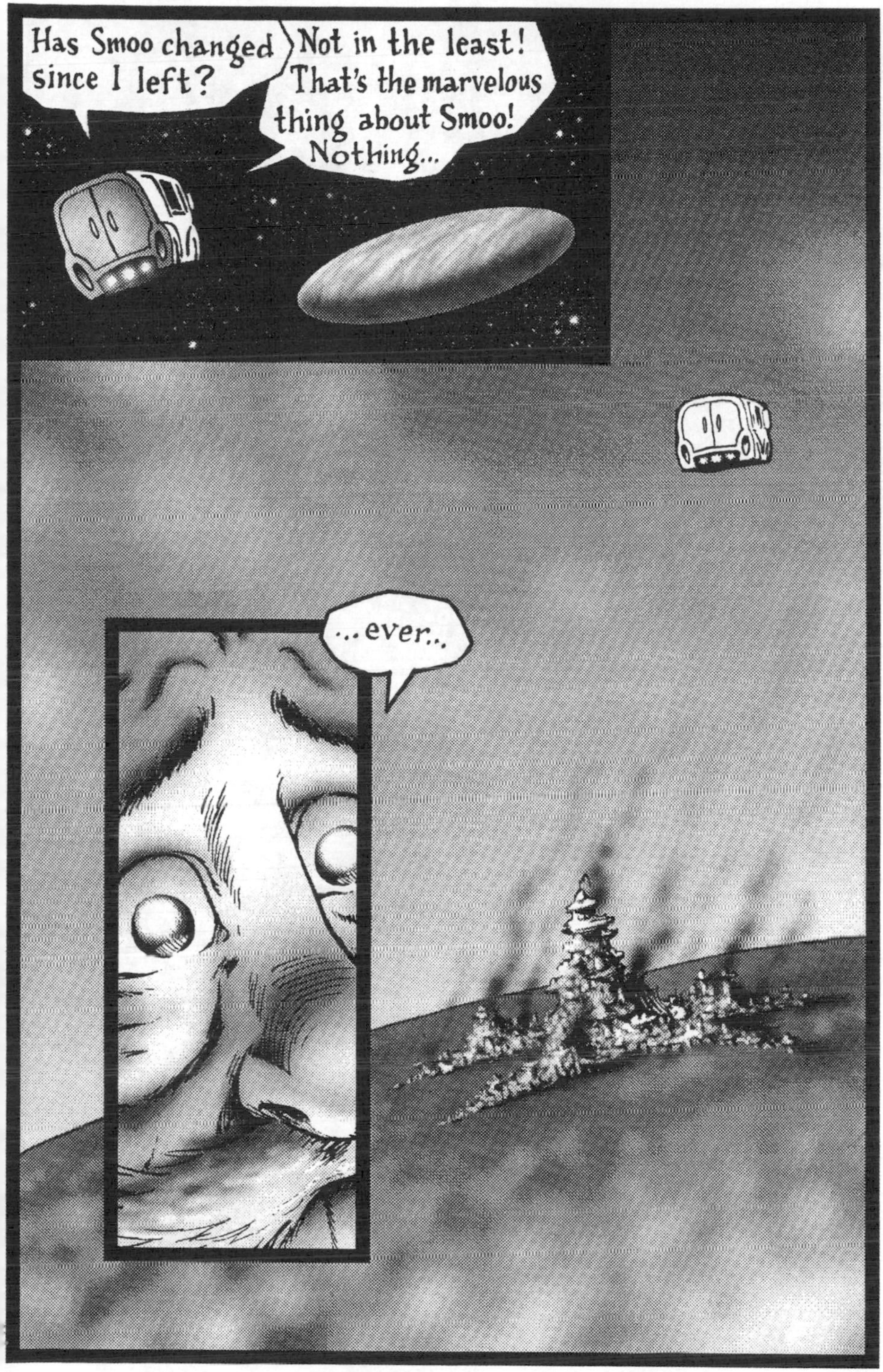
Has Smoo changed since I left?
Not in the least! That's the marvelous thing about Smoo! Nothing...
...ever...

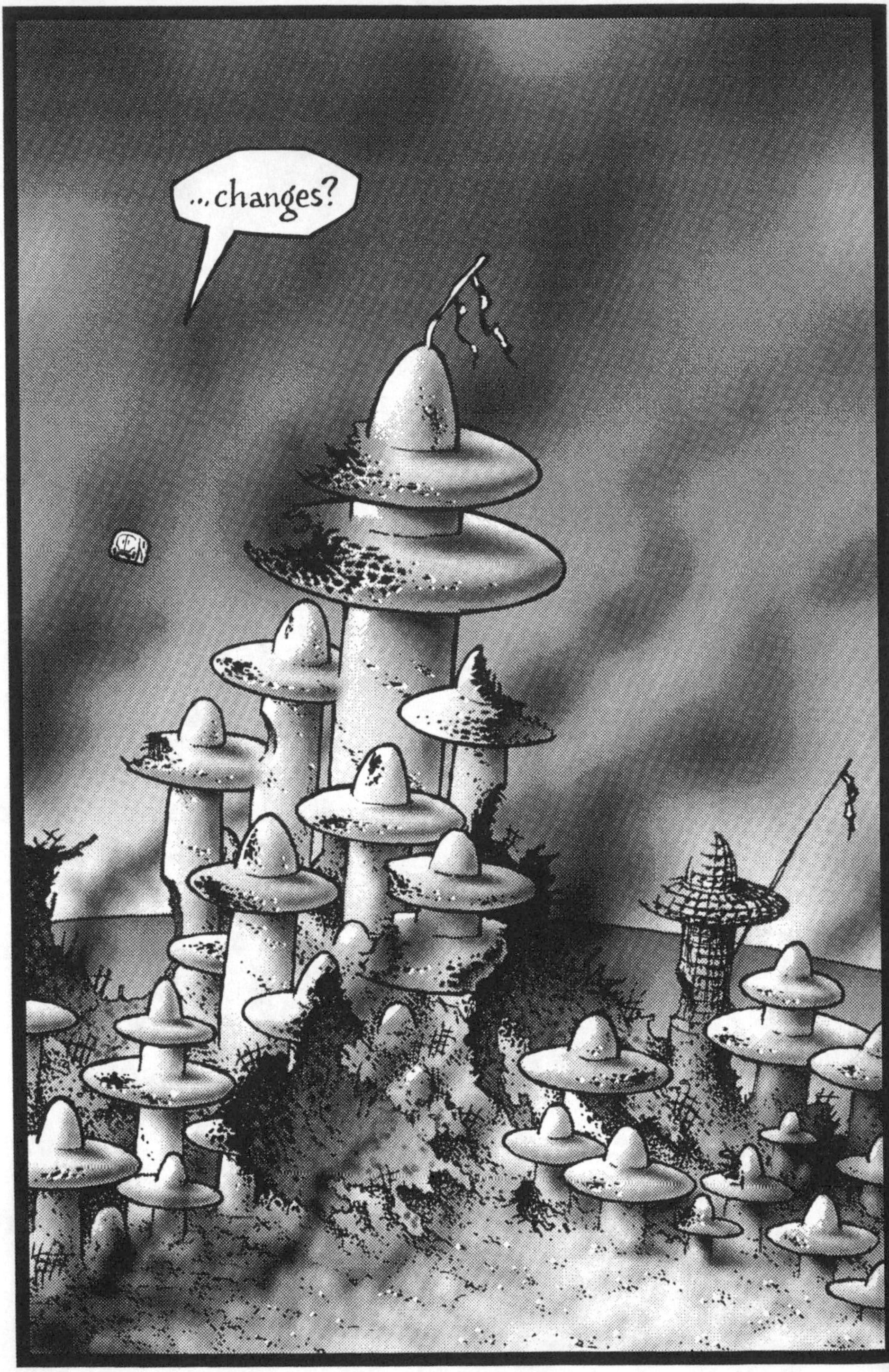
...changes?

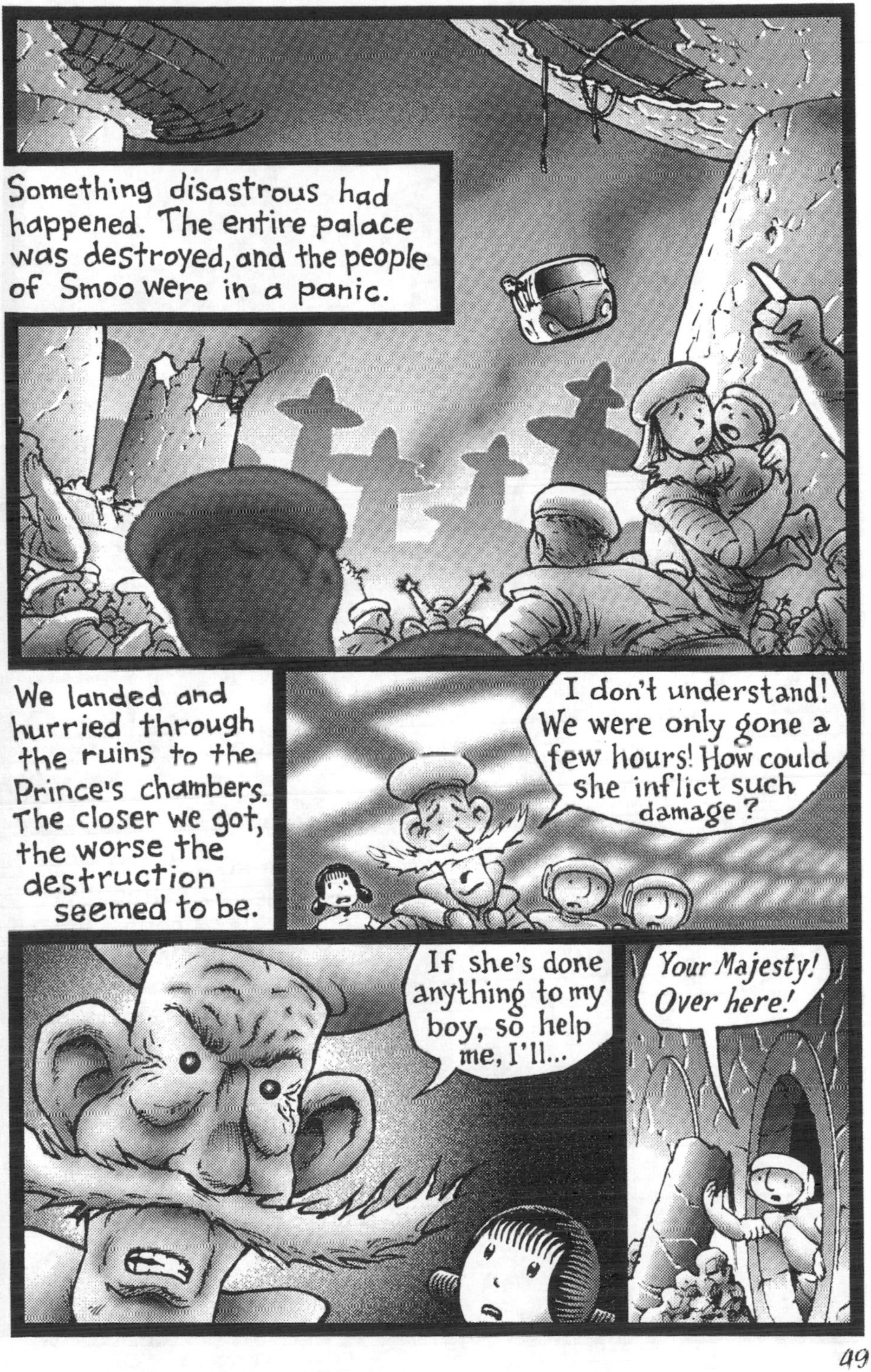
Something disastrous had happened. The entire palace was destroyed, and the people of Smoo were in a panic.
We landed and hurried through the ruins to the Prince's chambers. The closer we got, the worse the destruction seemed to be.
I don't understand! We were only gone a few hours! How could she inflict such damage?
If she's done anything to my boy, so help me, I'll...
Your Majesty! Over here!

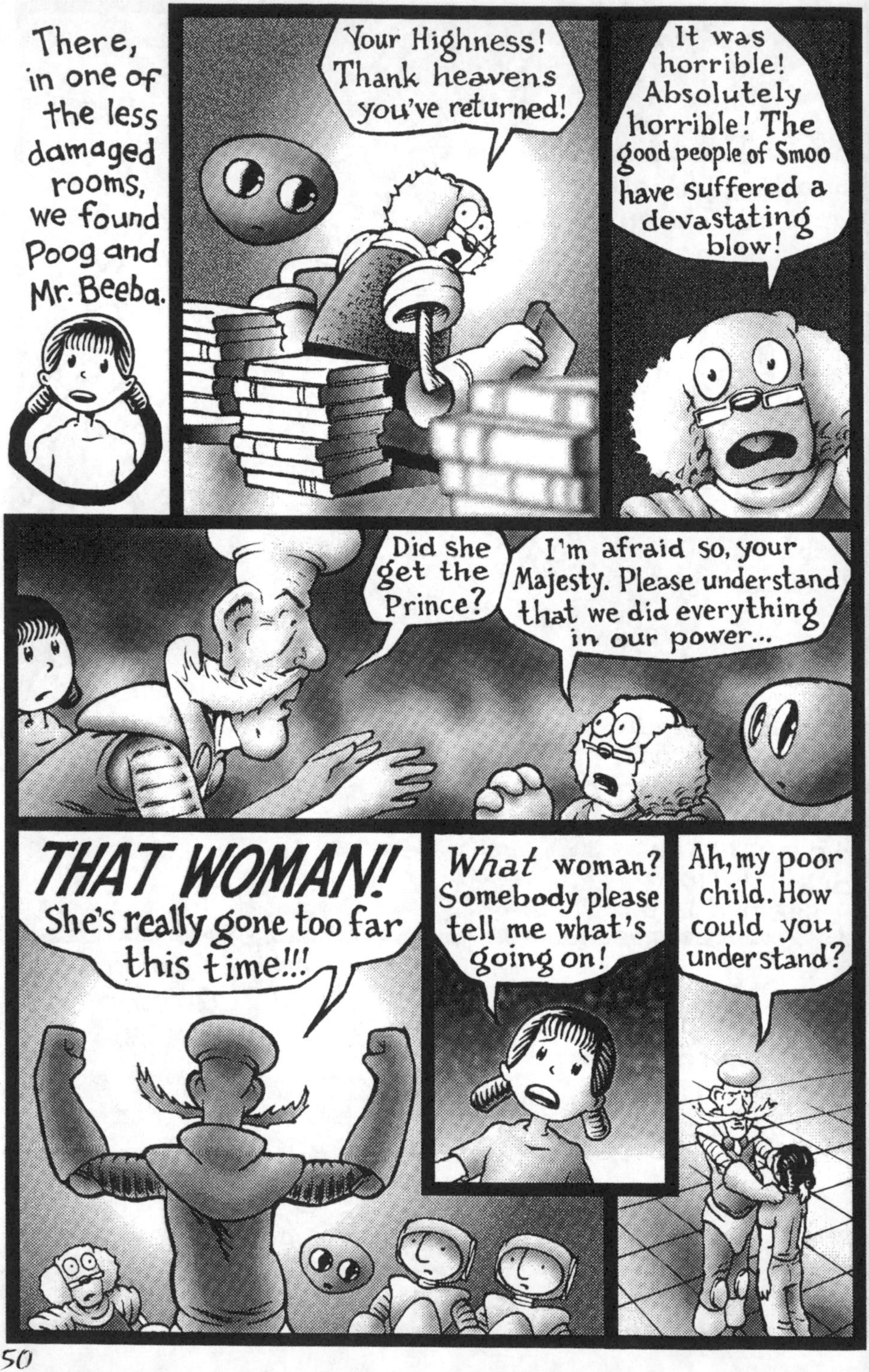
There, in one of the less damaged rooms, we found Poog and Mr. Beeba.
Your Highness! Thank heavens you've returned!
It was horrible! Absolutely horrible! The good people of Smoo have suffered a devastating blow!
Did she get the Prince?
I'm afraid so, your Majesty. Please understand that we did everything in our power...
THAT WOMAN! She's really gone too far this time!!!
What woman? Somebody please tell me what's going on!
Ah, my poor child. How could you understand?

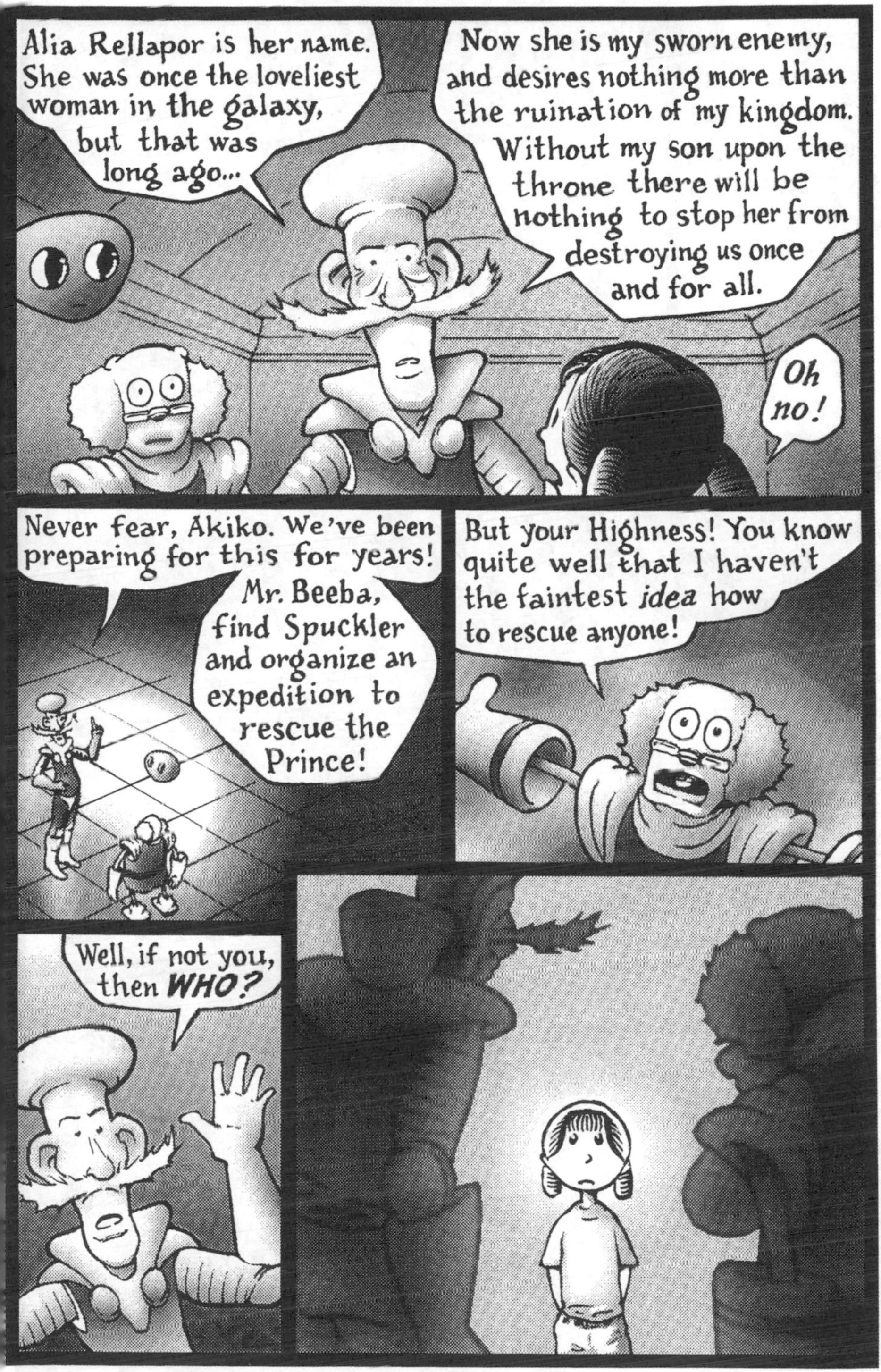
Alia Rellapor is her name. She was once the loveliest woman in the galaxy, but that was long ago...
Now she is my sworn enemy, and desires nothing more than the ruination of my kingdom. Without my son upon the throne there will be nothing to stop her from destroying us once and for all.
Oh no!
Never fear, Akiko. We've been preparing for this for years!
Mr. Beeba, find Spuckler and organize an expedition to rescue the Prince!
But your Highness! You know quite well that I haven't the faintest *idea* how to rescue anyone!
Well, if not you, then ***WHO?***

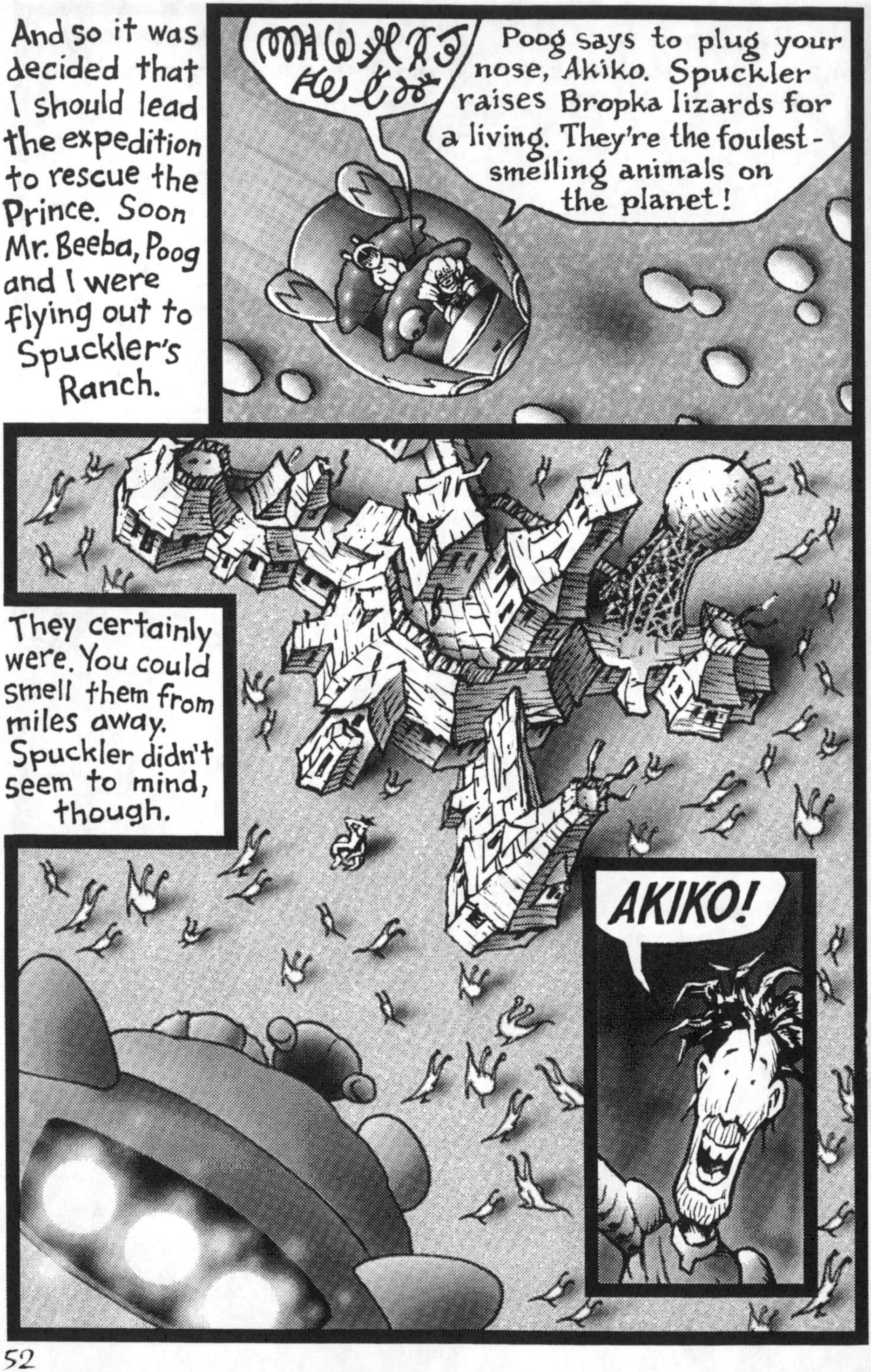
And so it was decided that I should lead the expedition to rescue the Prince. Soon Mr. Beeba, Poog and I were flying out to Spuckler's Ranch.
Poog says to plug your nose, Akiko. Spuckler raises Bropka lizards for a living. They're the foulest-smelling animals on the planet!
They certainly were. You could smell them from miles away. Spuckler didn't seem to mind, though.
AKIKO!

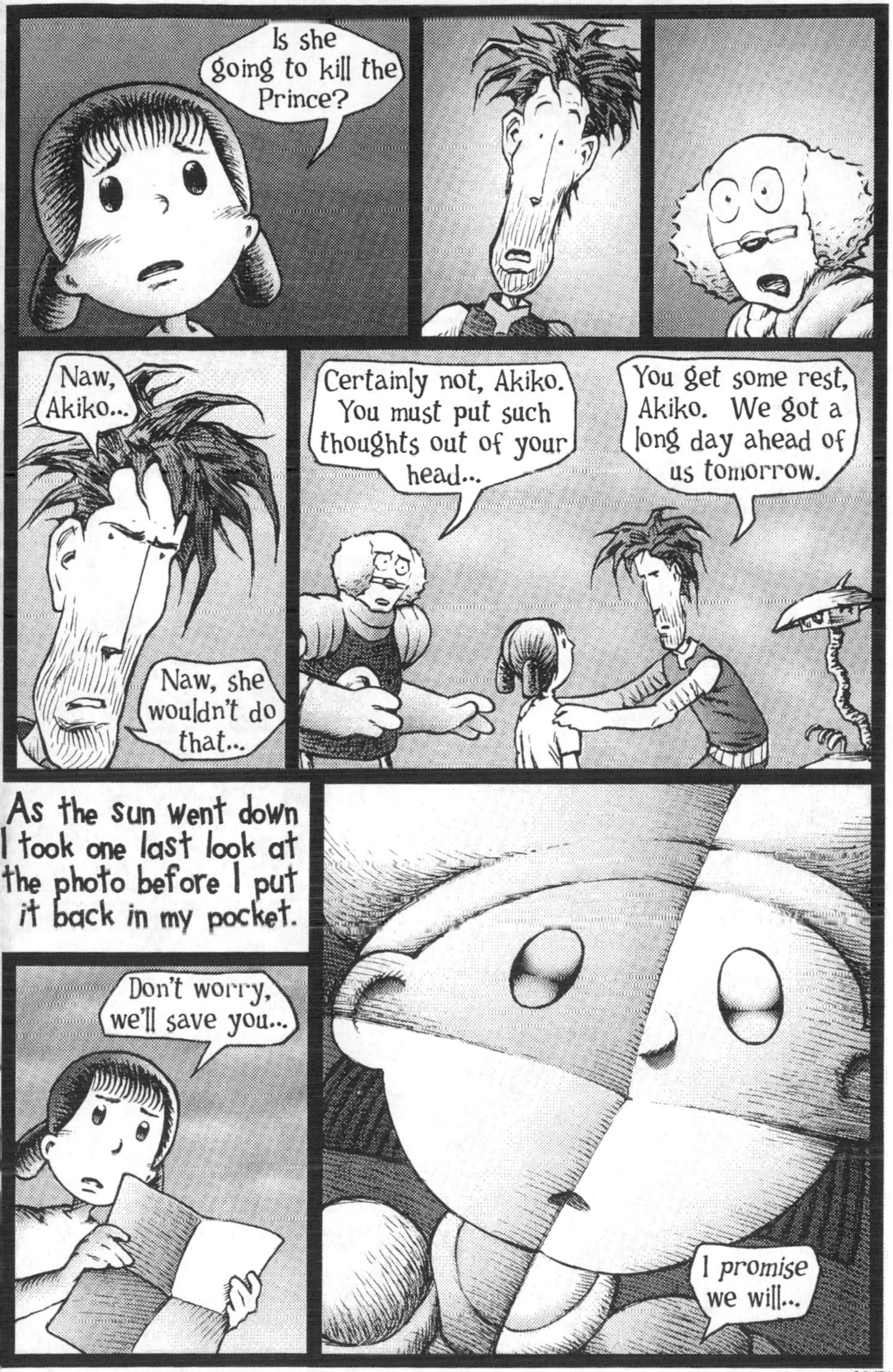
Is she going to kill the Prince?
Naw, Akiko...
Naw, she wouldn't do that...
Certainly not, Akiko. You must put such thoughts out of your head...
You get some rest, Akiko. We got a long day ahead of us tomorrow.
As the sun went down I took one last look at the photo before I put it back in my pocket.
Don't worry, we'll save you...
I *promise* we will...

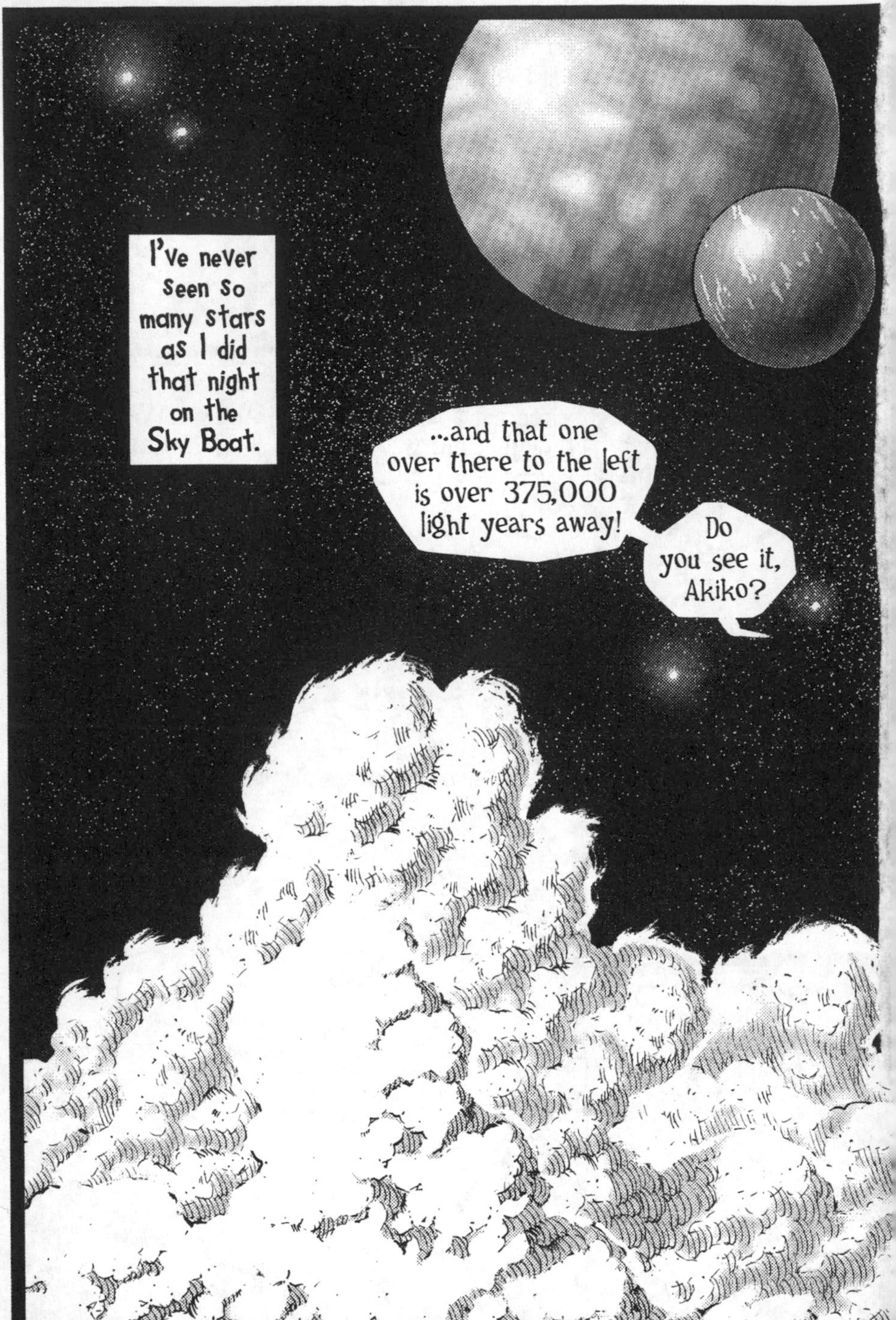
I've never seen so many stars as I did that night on the Sky Boat.
...and that one over there to the left is over 375,000 light years away!
Do you see it, Akiko?

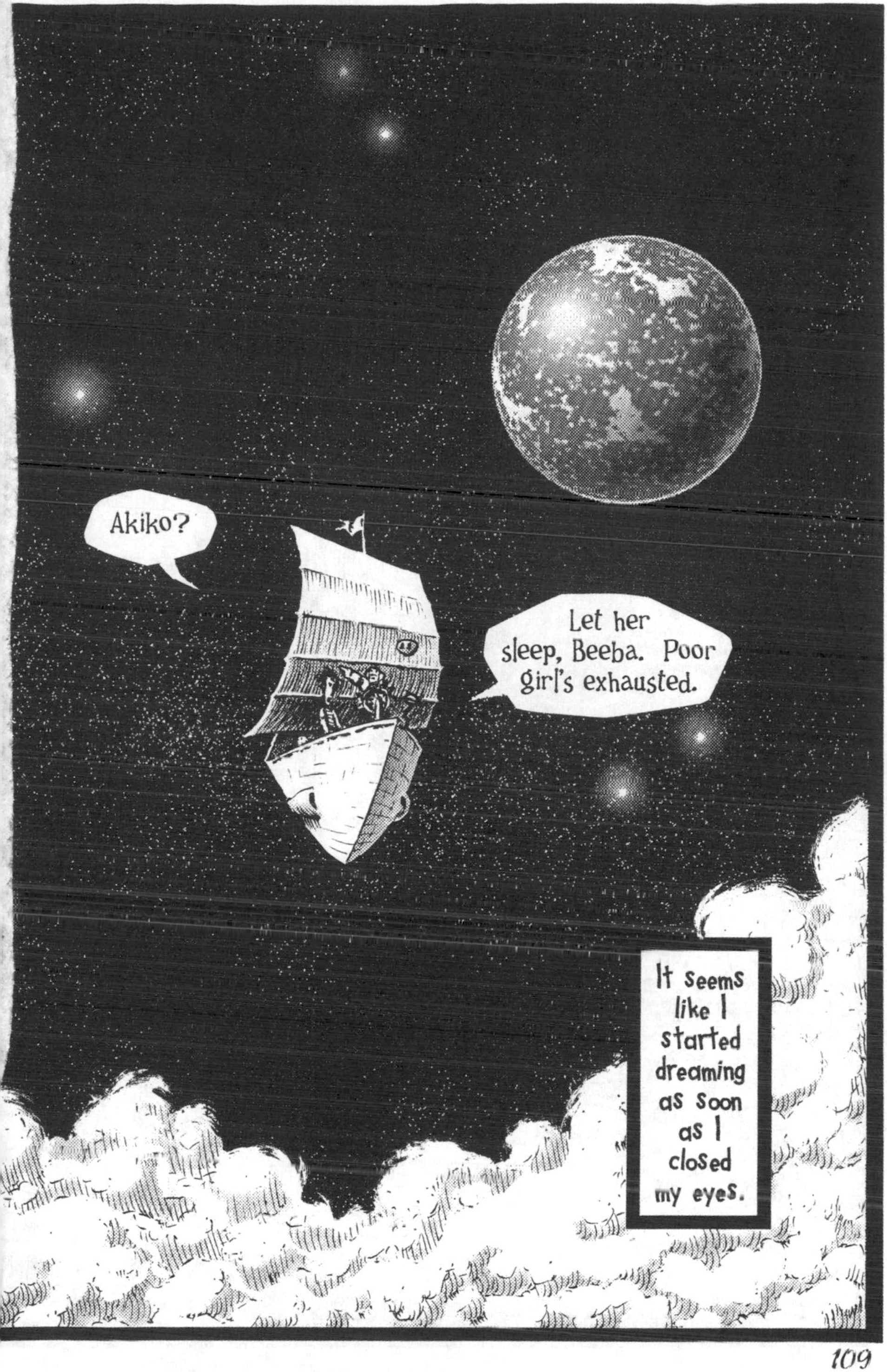
Akiko?
Let her sleep, Beeba. Poor girl's exhausted.
It seems like I started dreaming as soon as I closed my eyes.

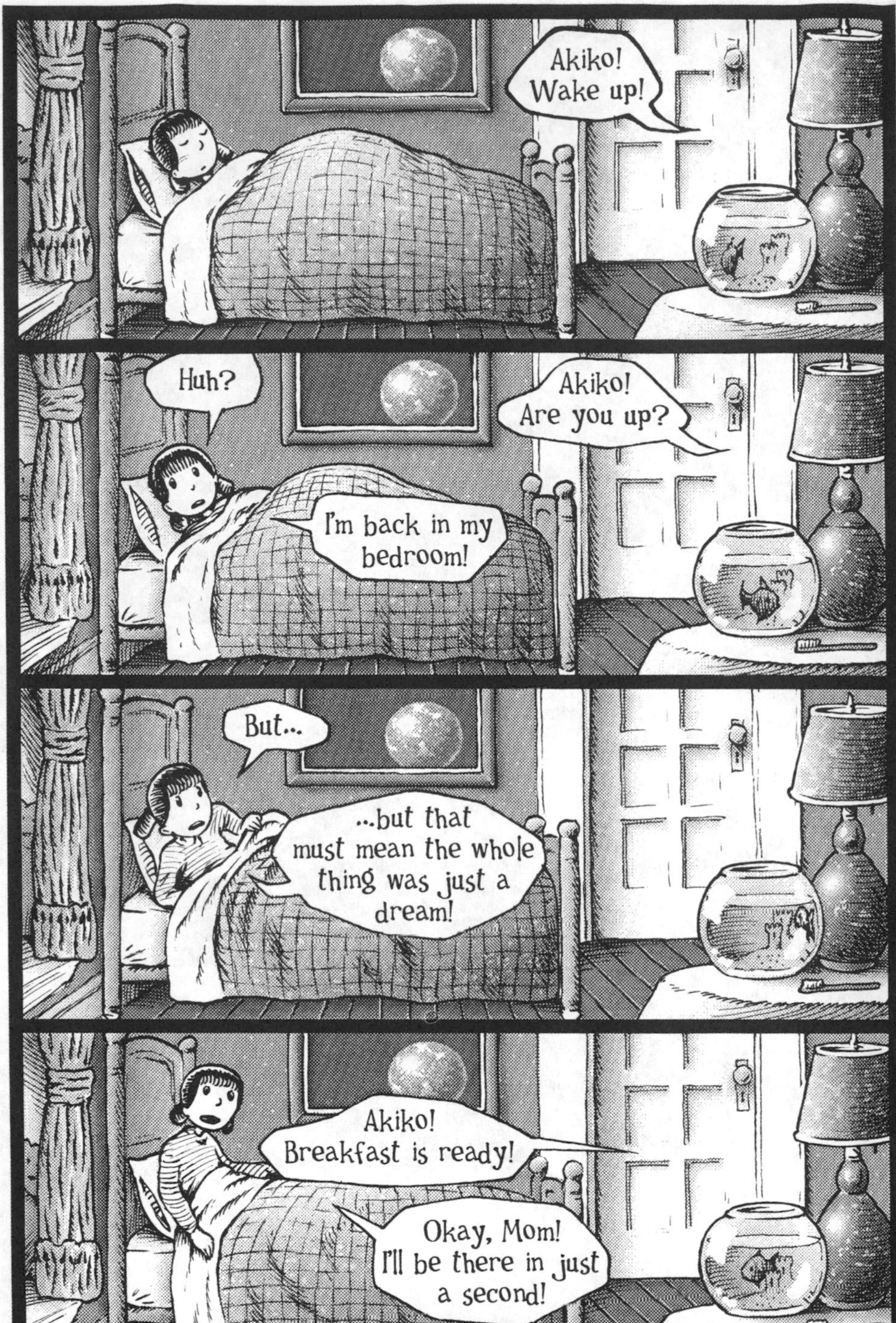
Akiko! Wake up!
Huh?
Akiko! Are you up?
I'm back in my bedroom!
But...
...but that must mean the whole thing was just a dream!
Akiko! Breakfast is ready!
Okay, Mom! I'll be there in just a second!

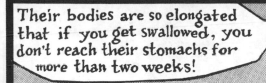

Their bodies are so elongated that if you get swallowed, you don't reach their stomachs for more than two weeks!

Beeba! For cryin' out loud!

Oh dear!

Now let me guess, Poog's predicting doom and gloom again!

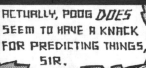

ACTUALLY, POOG *DOES* SEEM TO HAVE A KNACK FOR PREDICTING THINGS, SIR.

Shut up, Gax.

As a matter of fact, Poog says that we are heading directly into the domain of a band of Sky Pirates!

PIRATES?!

Well, there's no turnin' back now...

55

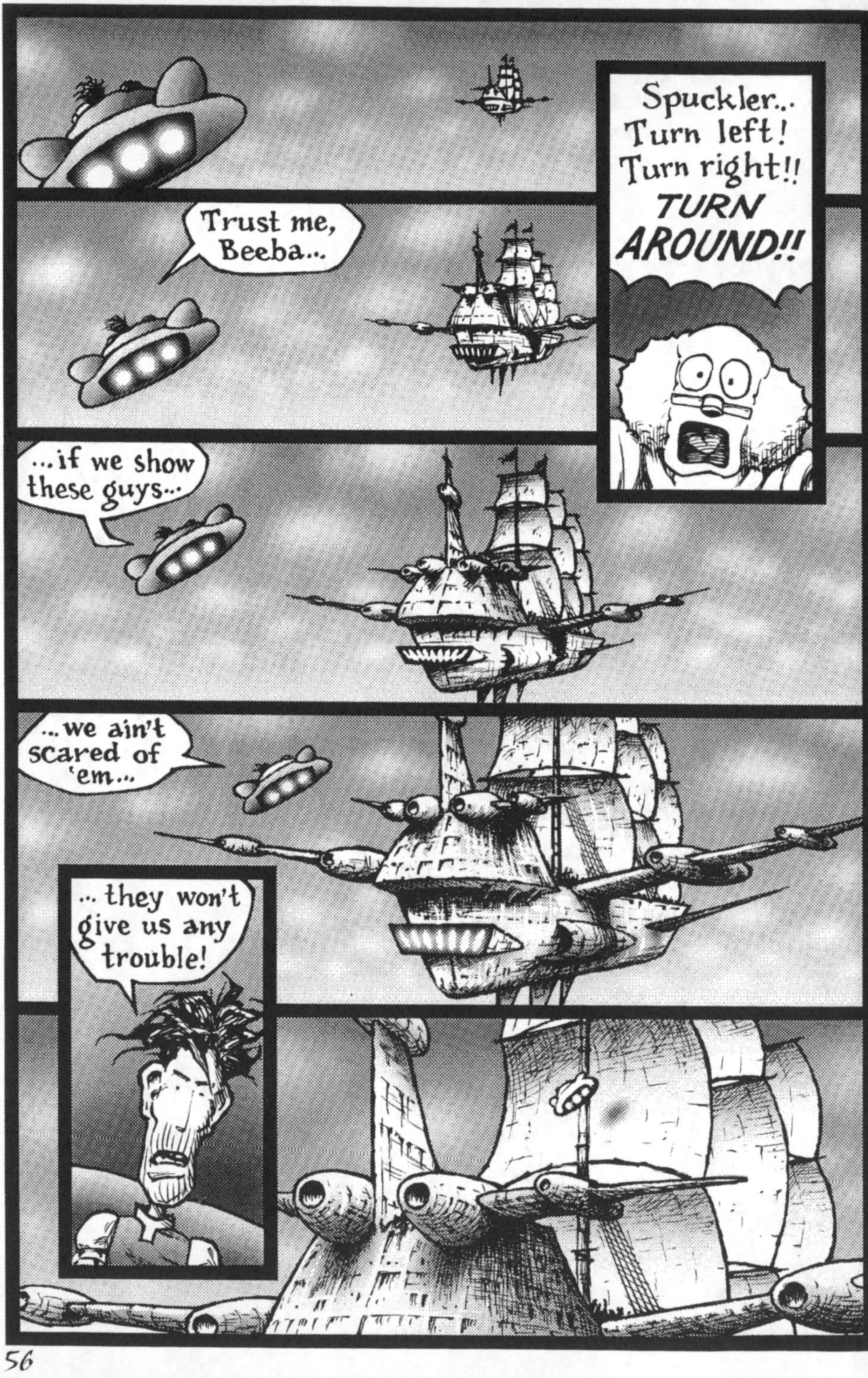
Spuckler.. Turn left! Turn right!! TURN AROUND!!
Trust me, Beeba...
...if we show these guys...
...we ain't scared of 'em...
...they won't give us any trouble!

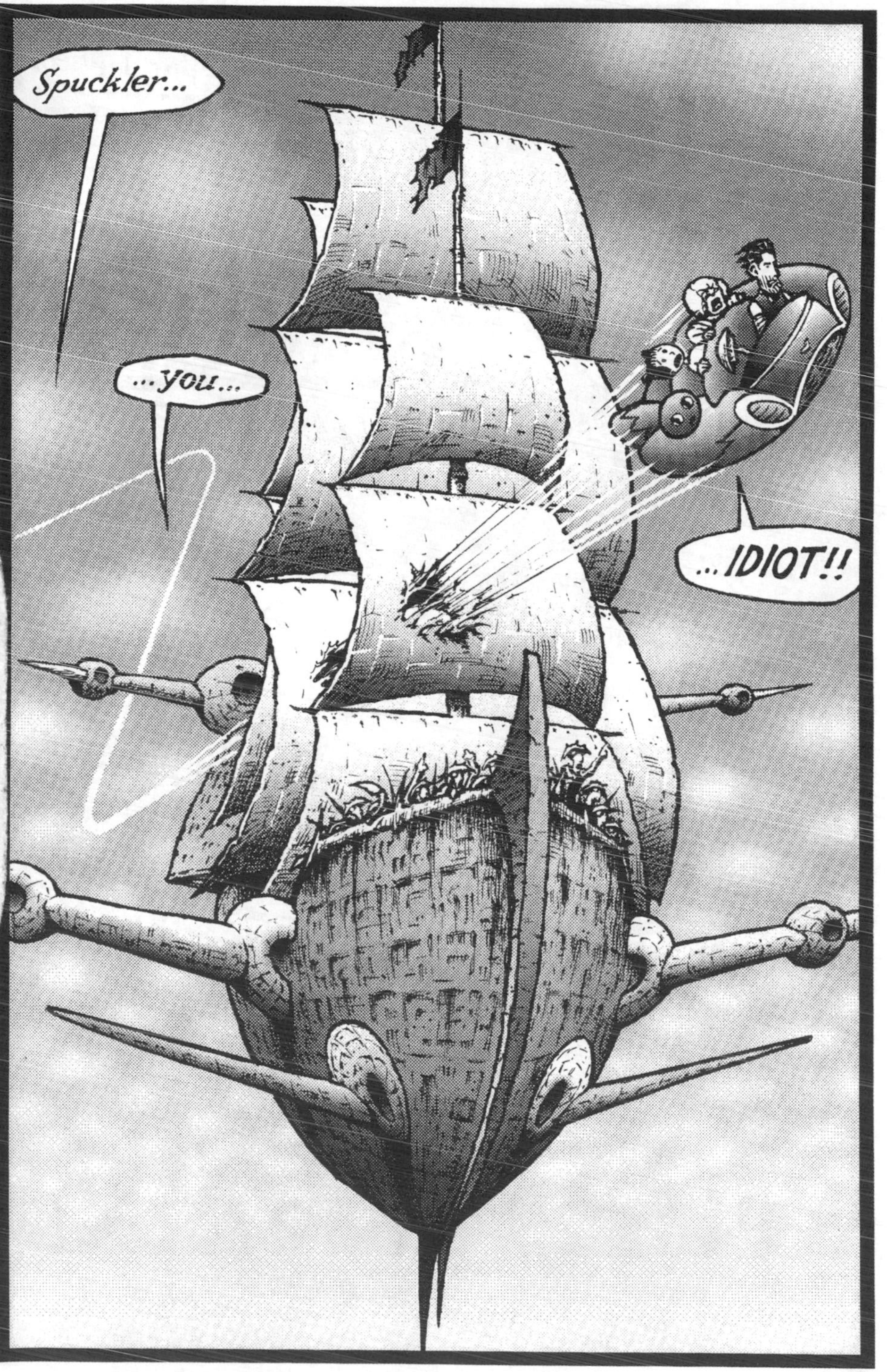
Spuckler...
...you...
...IDIOT!!

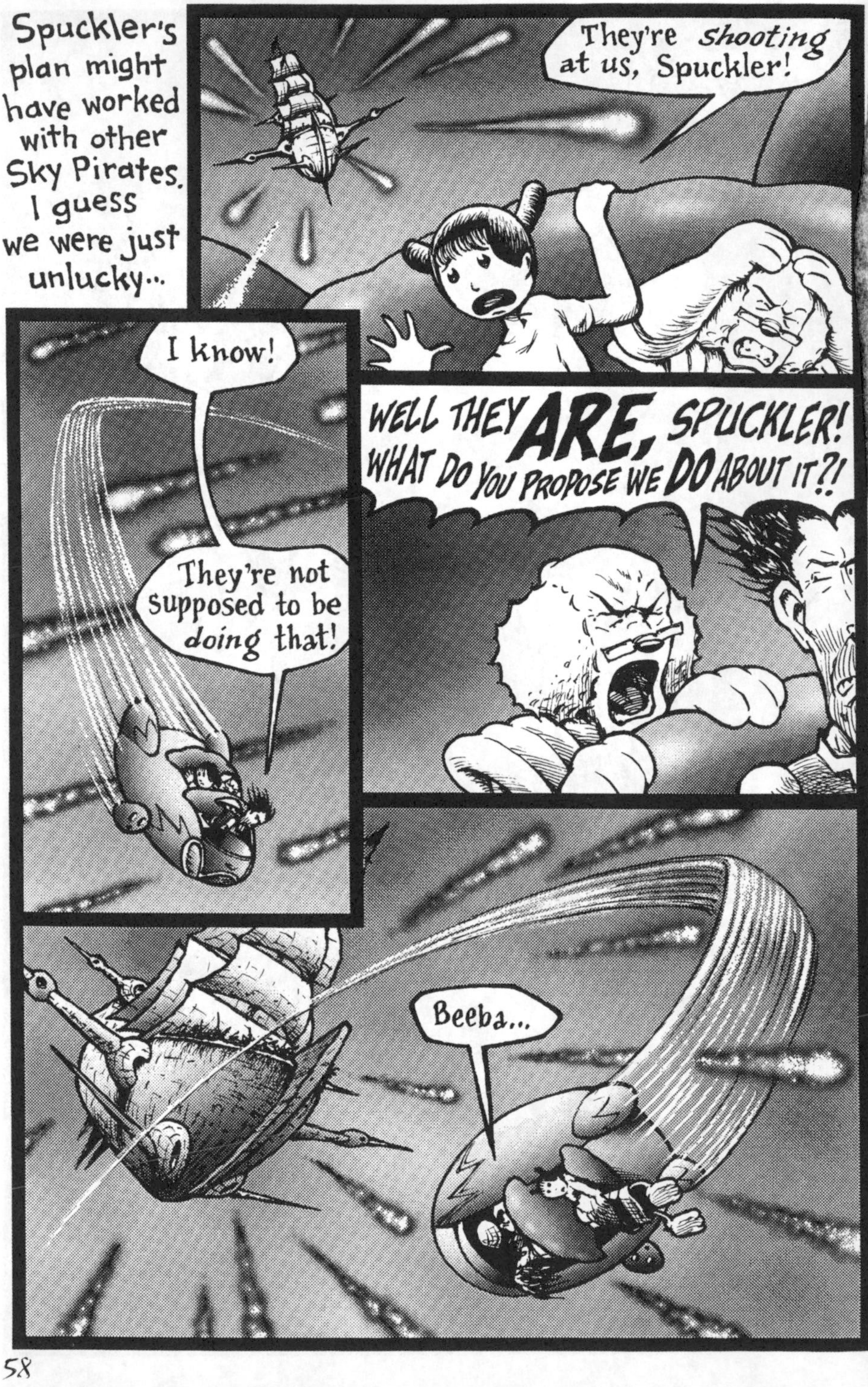
Spuckler's plan might have worked with other Sky Pirates. I guess we were just unlucky...
They're *shooting* at us, Spuckler!
I know!
They're not supposed to be *doing* that!
WELL THEY **ARE**, SPUCKLER! WHAT DO YOU PROPOSE WE **DO** ABOUT IT?!
Beeba...

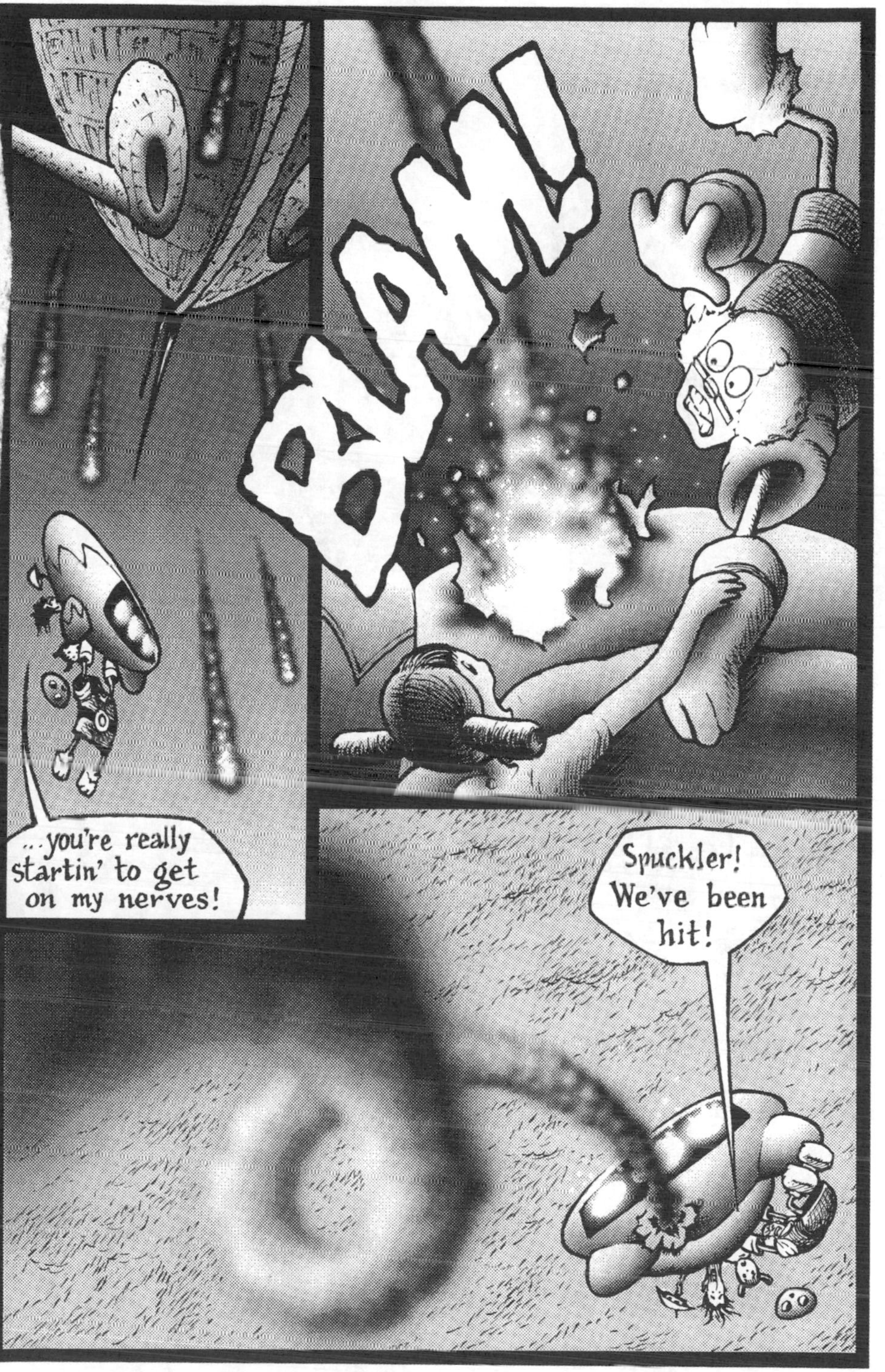

BLAM!
...you're really startin' to get on my nerves!
Spuckler! We've been hit!

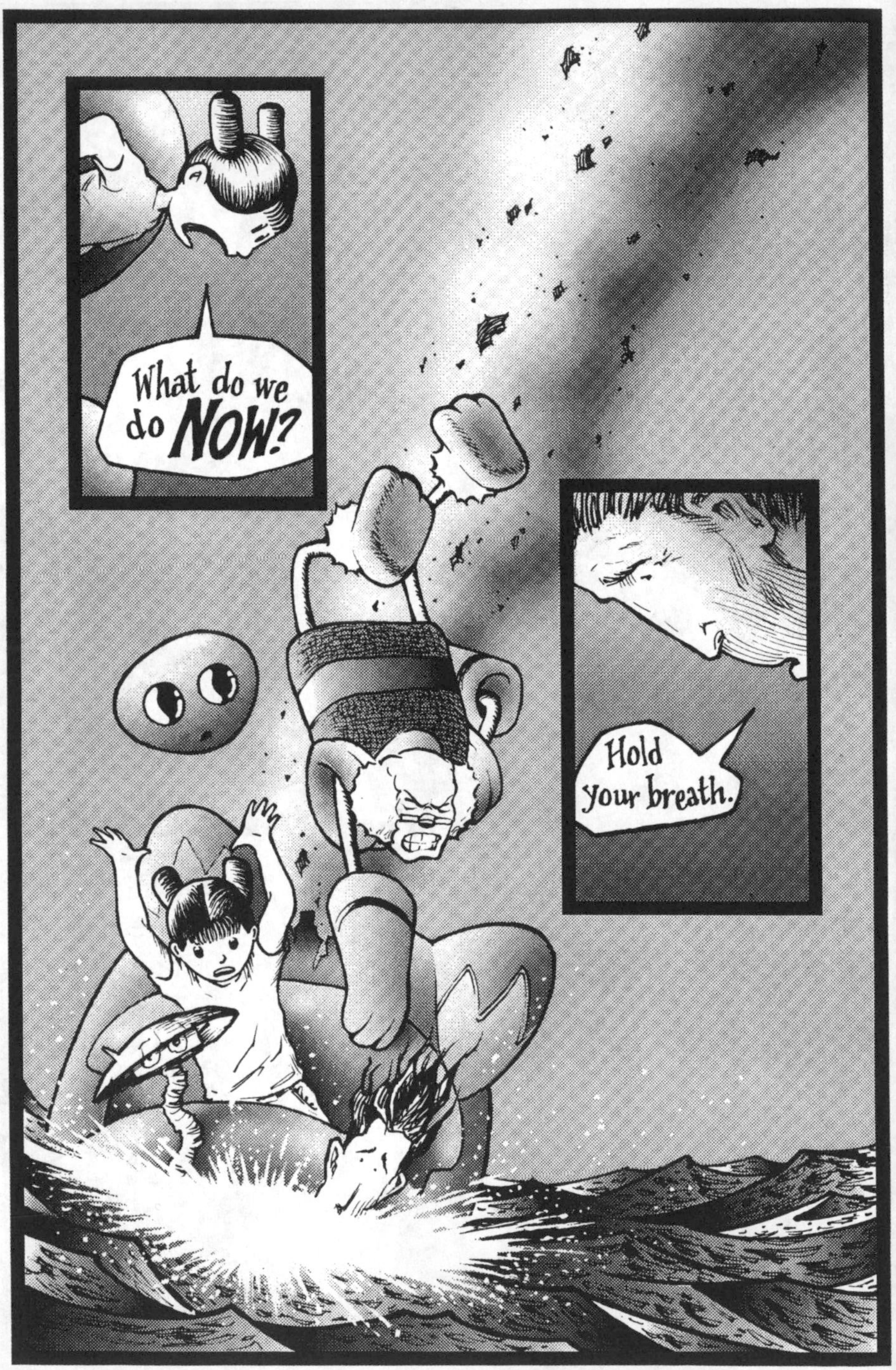
What do we do NOW?
Hold your breath.

Next Issue: "Captives of the Sky Pirates"

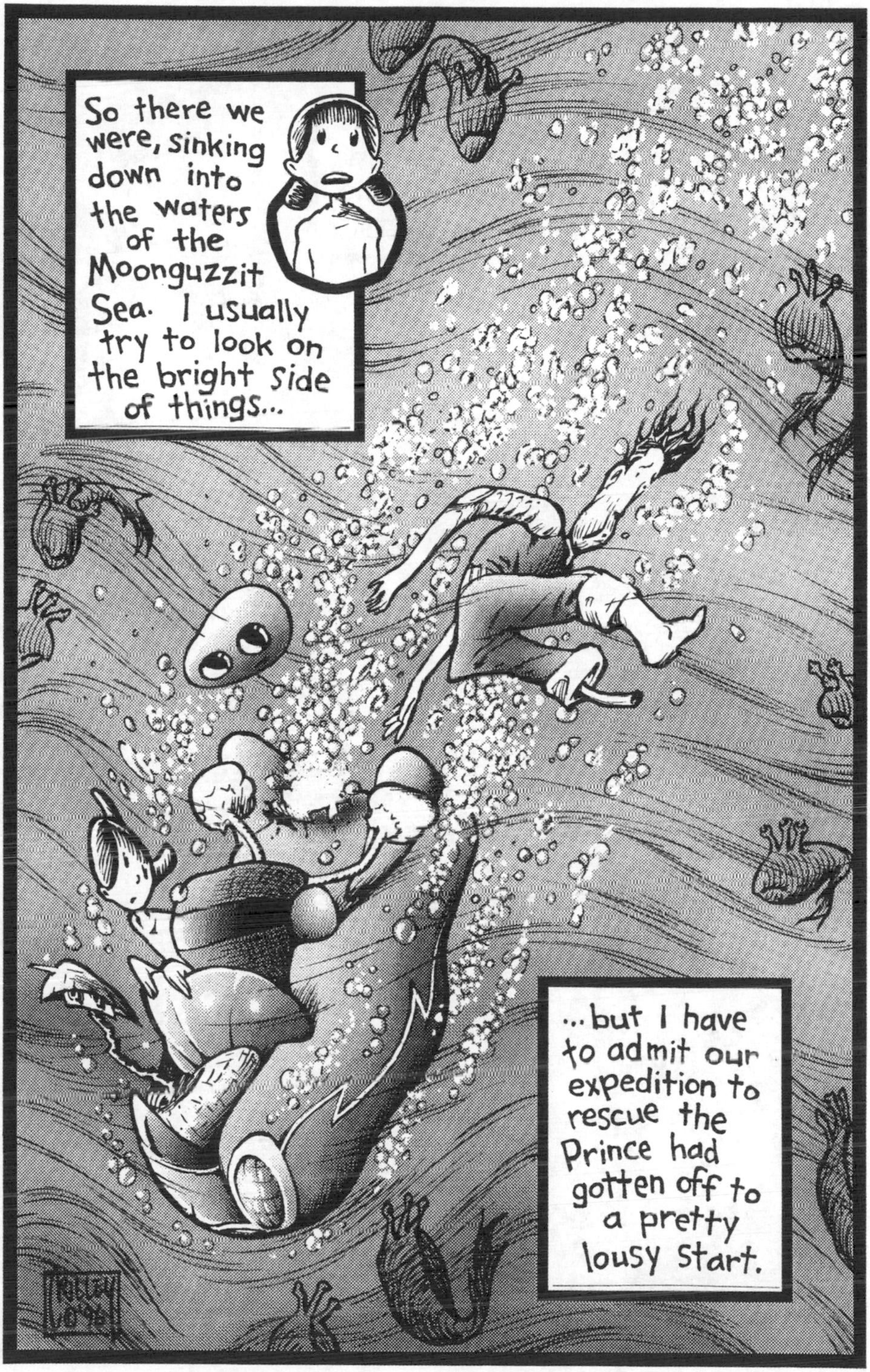
So there we were, sinking down into the waters of the Moonguzzit Sea. I usually try to look on the bright side of things...
...but I have to admit our expedition to rescue the Prince had gotten off to a pretty lousy start.
RIDLEY '96

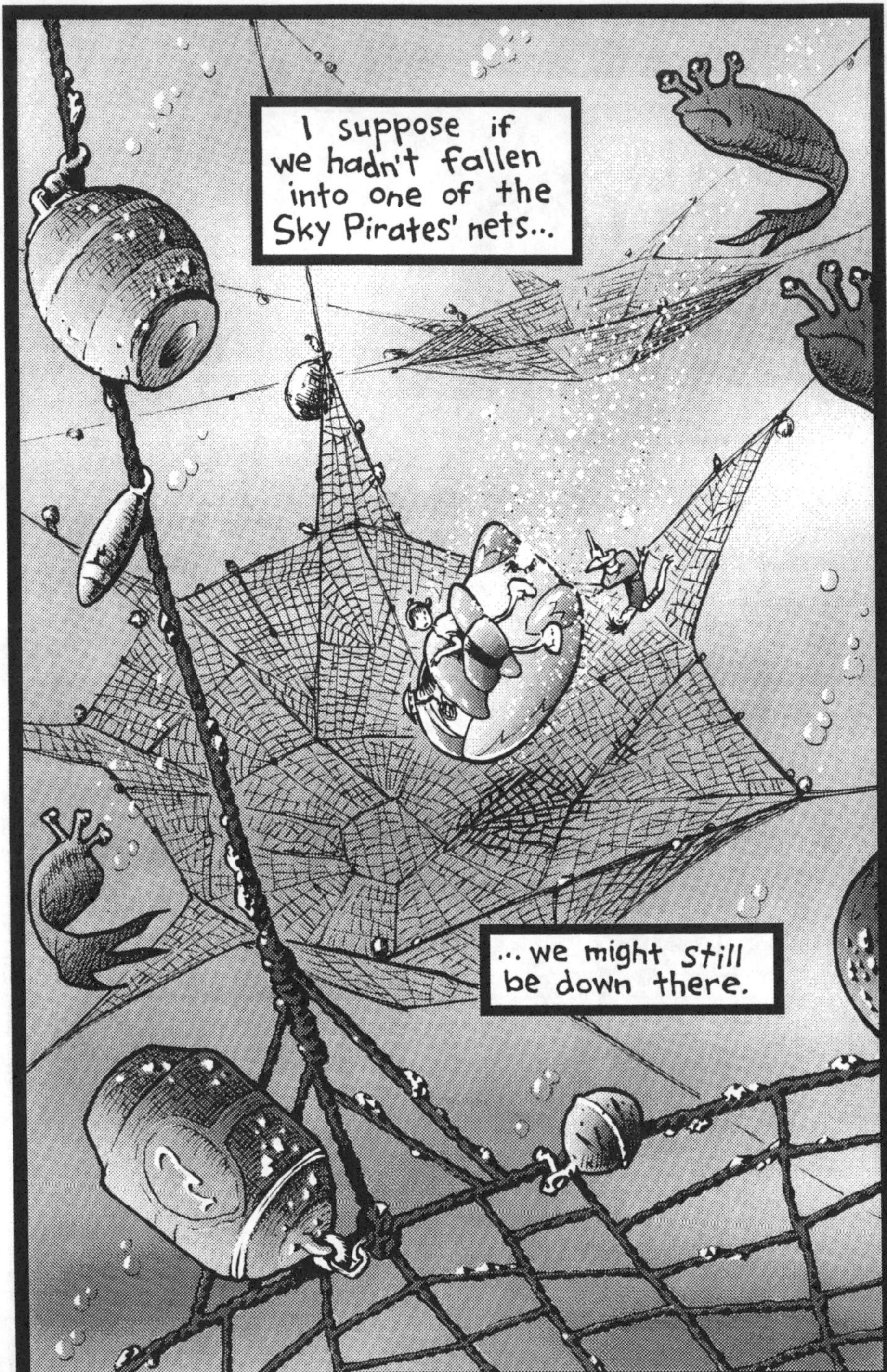
I suppose if we hadn't fallen into one of the Sky Pirates' nets...
...we might *still* be down there.

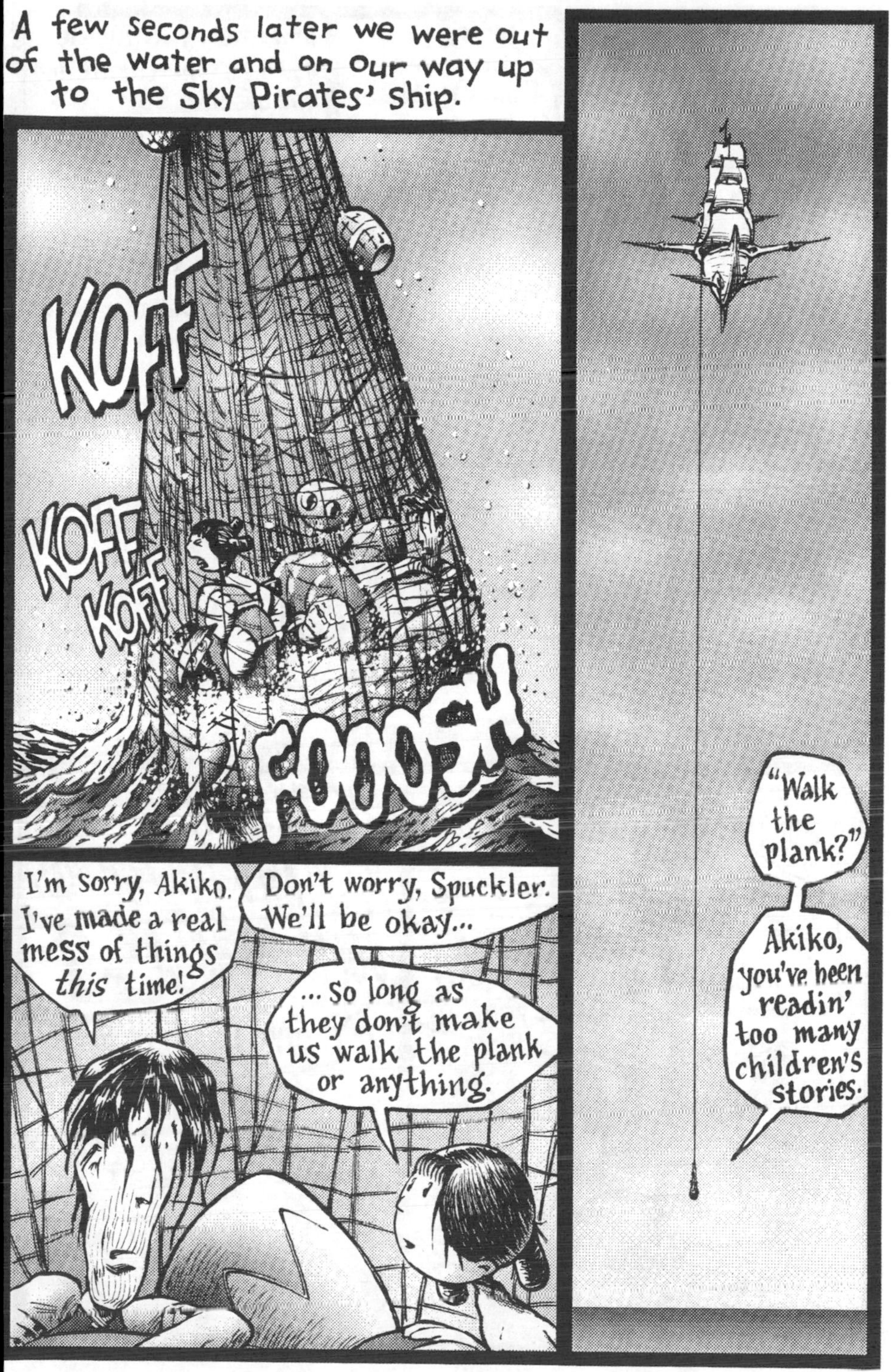
A few seconds later we were out of the water and on our way up to the Sky Pirates' ship.
KOFF
KOFF KOFF KOFF
FOOOSH
I'm sorry, Akiko. I've made a real mess of things *this* time!
Don't worry, Spuckler. We'll be okay...
... So long as they don't make us walk the plank or anything.
"Walk the plank?"
Akiko, you've been readin' too many children's stories.

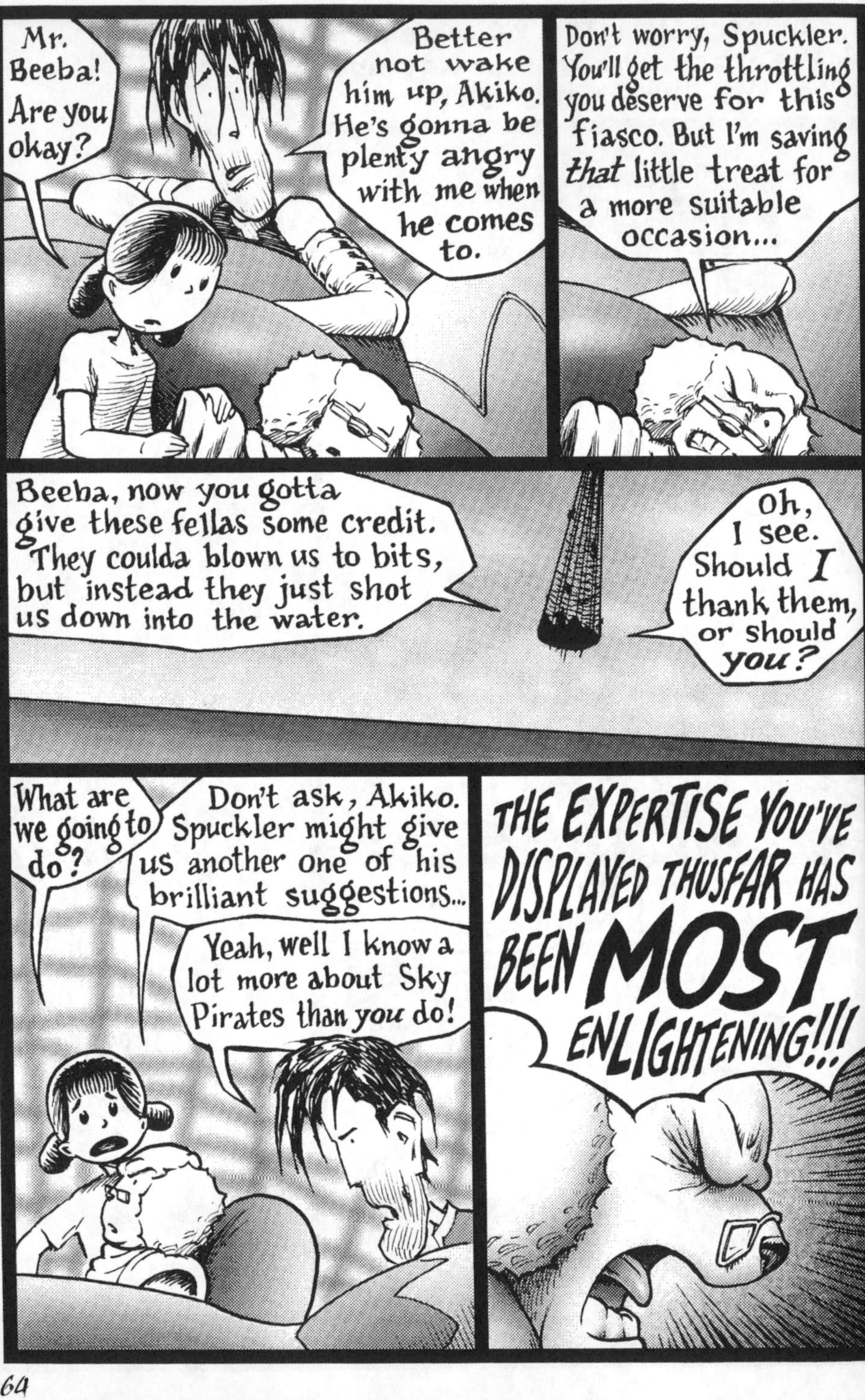
Mr. Beeba! Are you okay?
Better not wake him up, Akiko. He's gonna be plenty angry with me when he comes to.
Don't worry, Spuckler. You'll get the throttling you deserve for this fiasco. But I'm saving *that* little treat for a more suitable occasion...
Beeba, now you gotta give these fellas some credit. They coulda blown us to bits, but instead they just shot us down into the water.
Oh, I see. Should *I* thank them, or should *you*?
What are we going to do?
Don't ask, Akiko. Spuckler might give us another one of his brilliant suggestions...
Yeah, well I know a lot more about Sky Pirates than *you* do!
THE EXPERTISE YOU'VE DISPLAYED THUSFAR HAS BEEN **MOST** ENLIGHTENING!!!

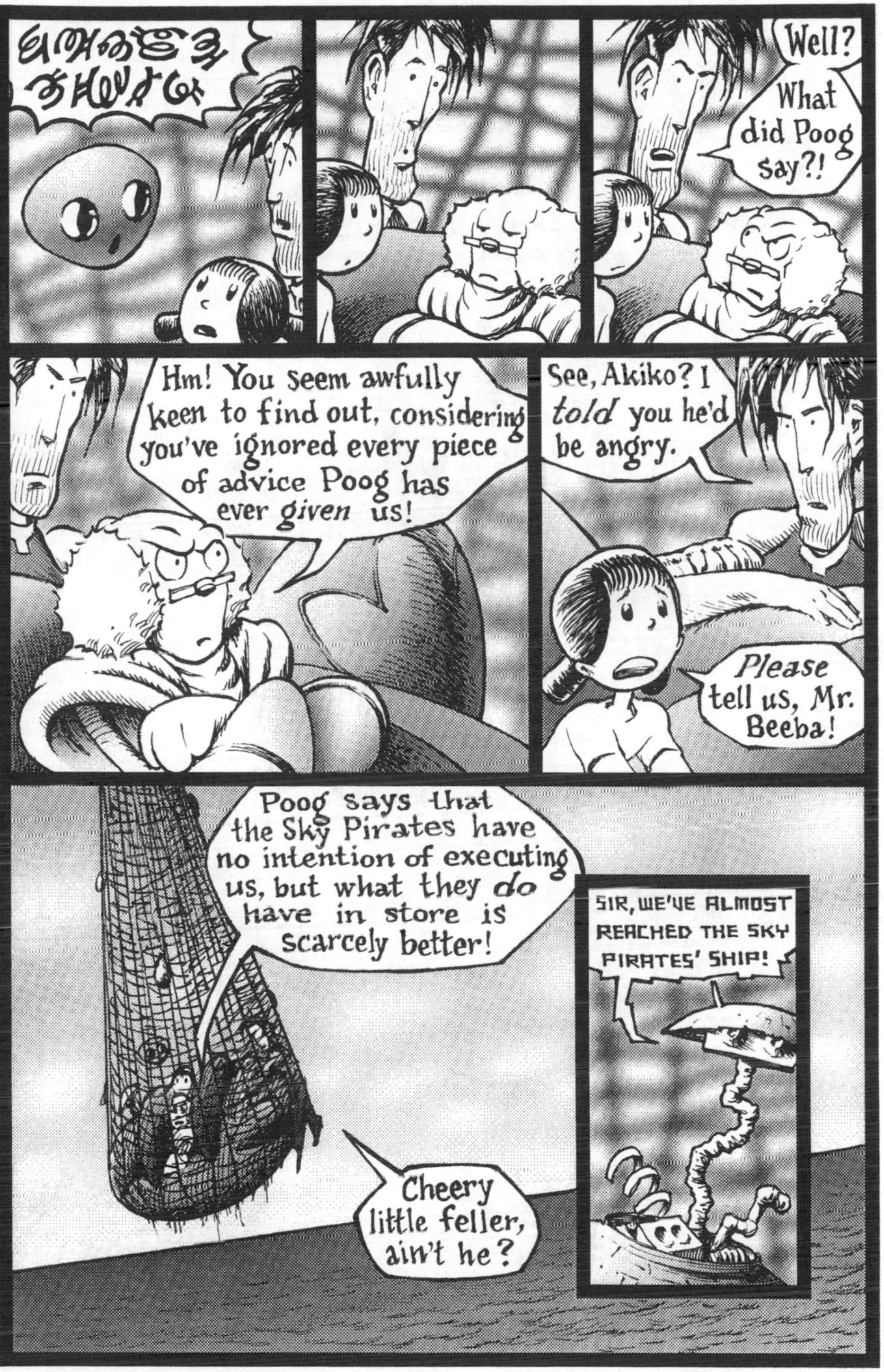
Well?
What did Poog say?!
Hm! You seem awfully keen to find out, considering you've ignored every piece of advice Poog has ever *given* us!
See, Akiko? I *told* you he'd be angry.
Please tell us, Mr. Beeba!
Poog says that the Sky Pirates have no intention of executing us, but what they *do* have in store is scarcely better!
SIR, WE'VE ALMOST REACHED THE SKY PIRATES' SHIP!
Cheery little feller, ain't he?

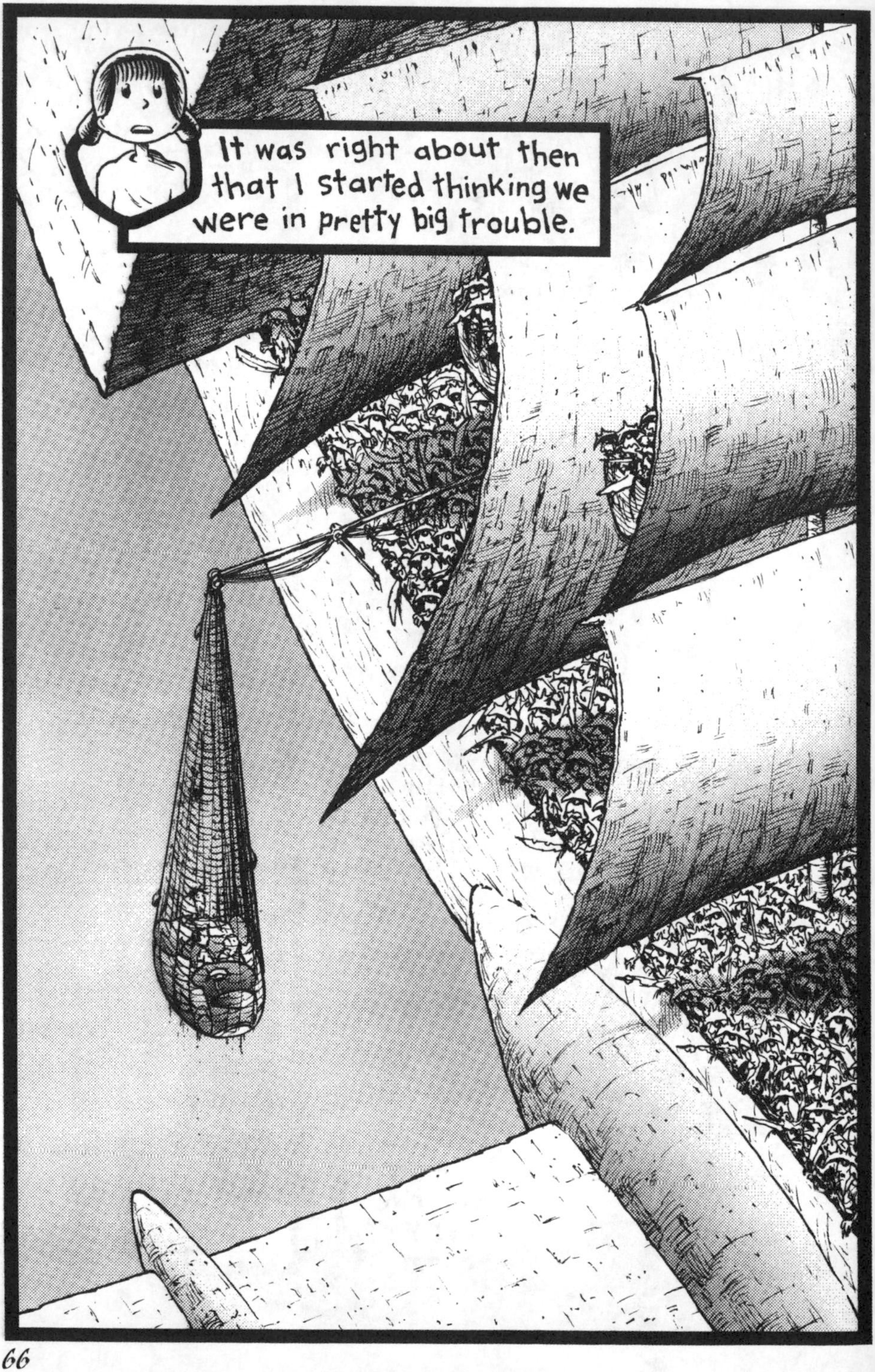
It was right about then that I started thinking we were in pretty big trouble.

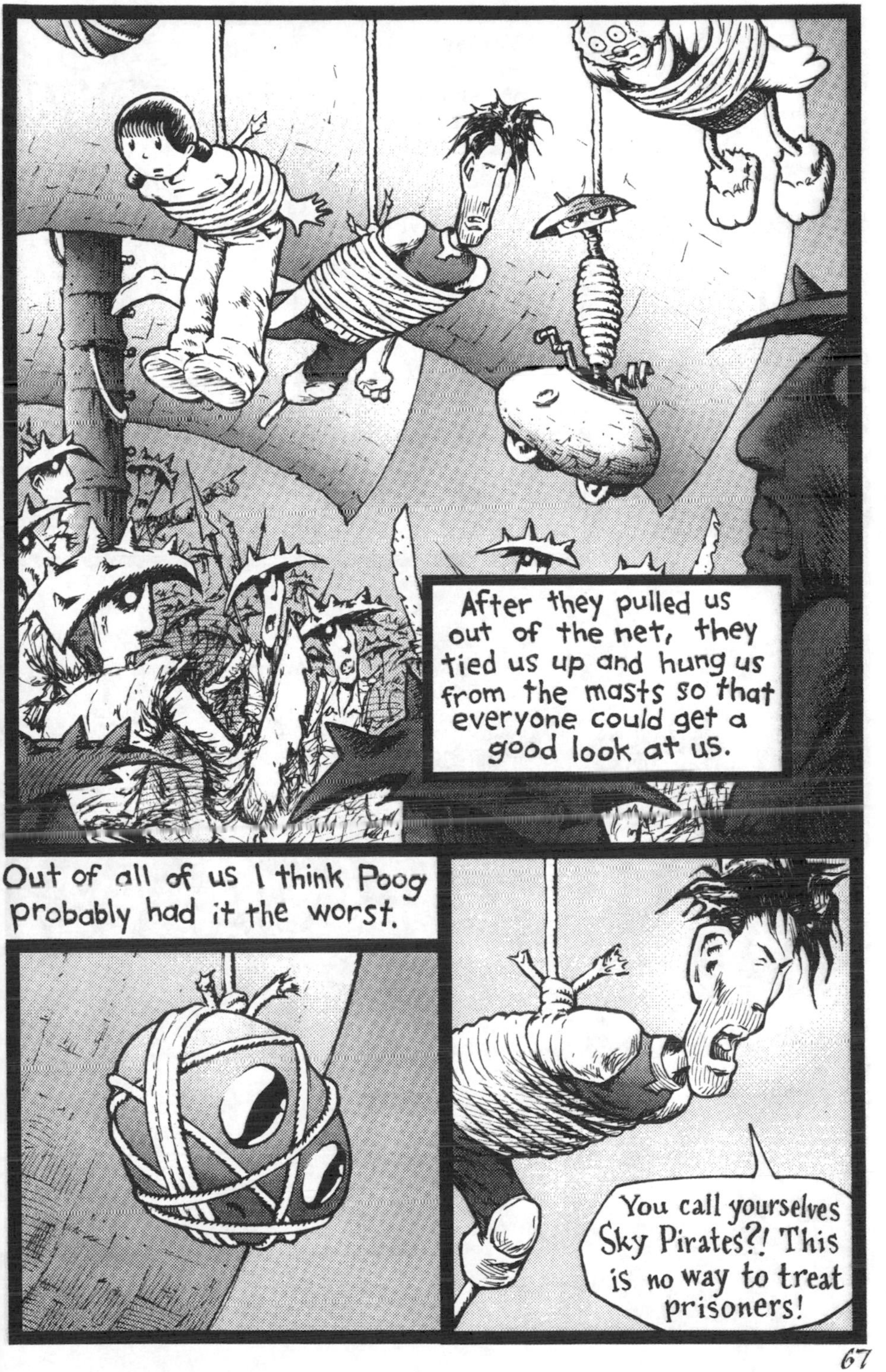
After they pulled us out of the net, they tied us up and hung us from the masts so that everyone could get a good look at us.
Out of all of us I think Poog probably had it the worst.
You call yourselves Sky Pirates?! This is no way to treat prisoners!

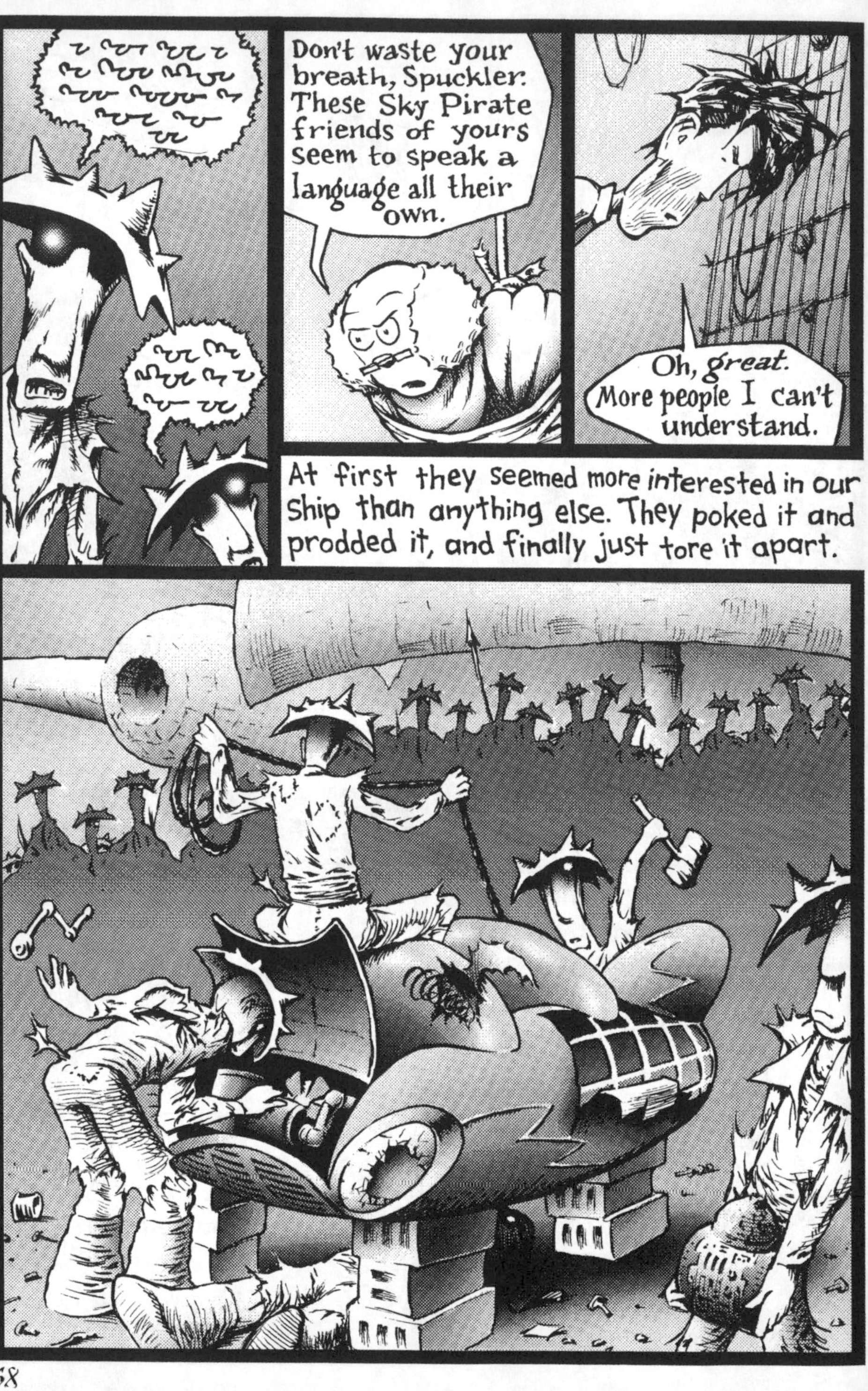
Don't waste your breath, Spuckler. These Sky Pirate friends of yours seem to speak a language all their own.
Oh, *great*. More people I can't understand.
At first they seemed more interested in our Ship than anything else. They poked it and prodded it, and finally just tore it apart.

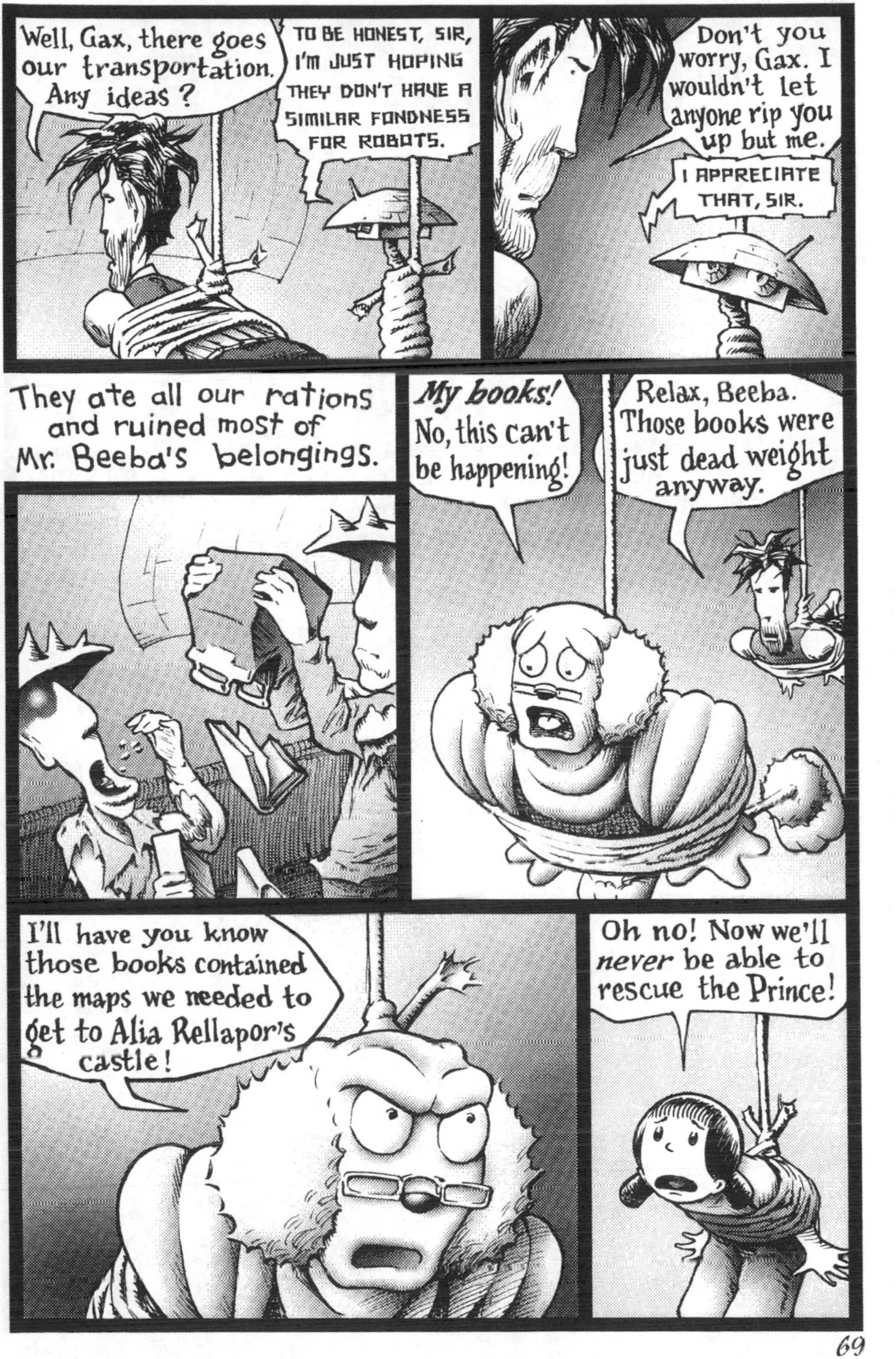

Well, Gax, there goes our transportation. Any ideas?
TO BE HONEST, SIR, I'M JUST HOPING THEY DON'T HAVE A SIMILAR FONDNESS FOR ROBOTS.
Don't you worry, Gax. I wouldn't let anyone rip you up but me.
I APPRECIATE THAT, SIR.
They ate all our rations and ruined most of Mr. Beeba's belongings.
My books! No, this can't be happening!
Relax, Beeba. Those books were just dead weight anyway.
I'll have you know those books contained the maps we needed to get to Alia Rellapor's castle!
Oh no! Now we'll *never* be able to rescue the Prince!

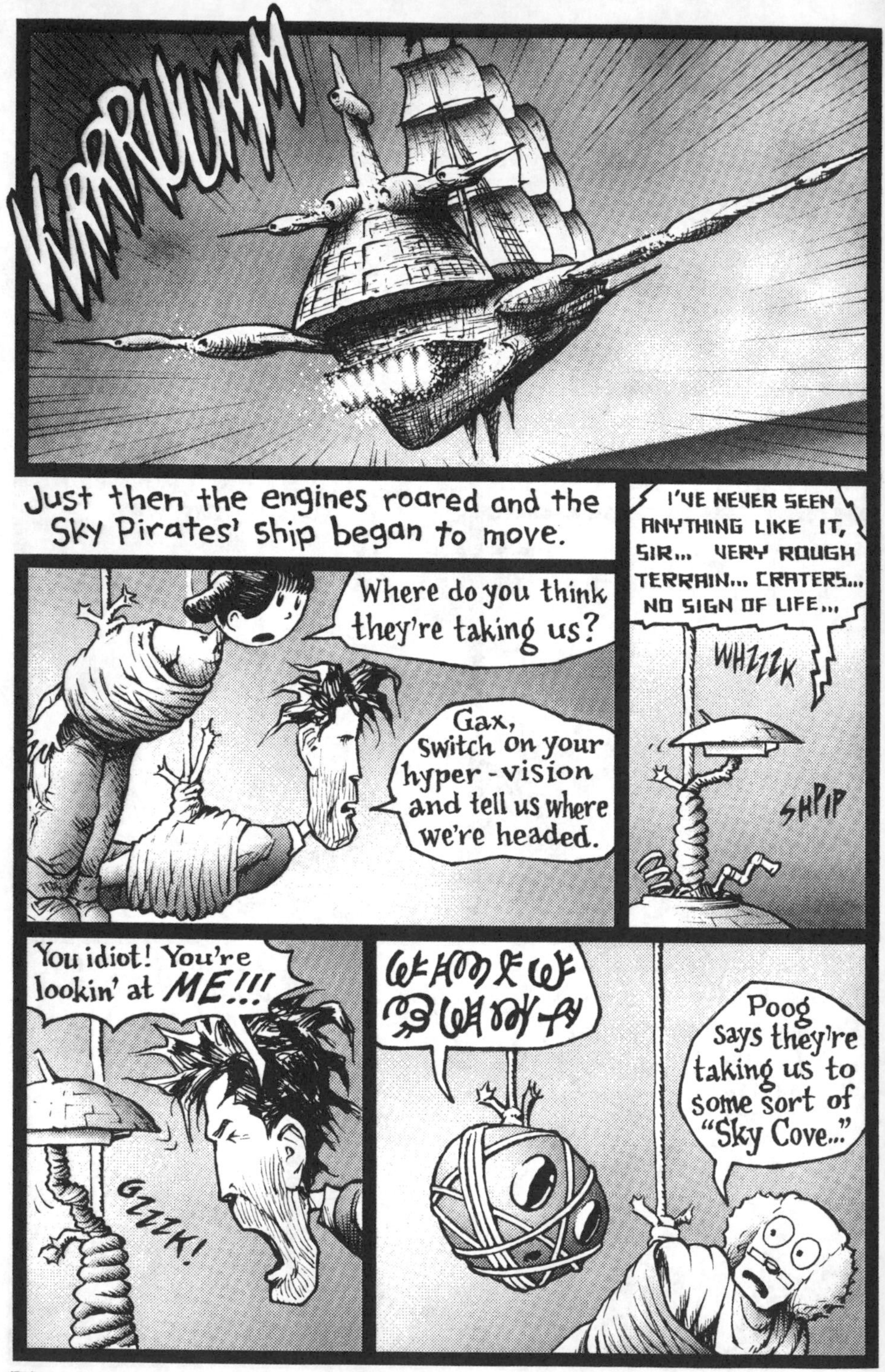
WRRRUUMM
Just then the engines roared and the Sky Pirates' ship began to move.
Where do you think they're taking us?
Gax, Switch on your hyper-vision and tell us where we're headed.
I'VE NEVER SEEN ANYTHING LIKE IT, SIR... VERY ROUGH TERRAIN... CRATERS... NO SIGN OF LIFE...
WHZZZK
SHPIP
You idiot! You're lookin' at ME!!!
GZZZK!
Poog says they're taking us to some sort of "Sky Cove..."

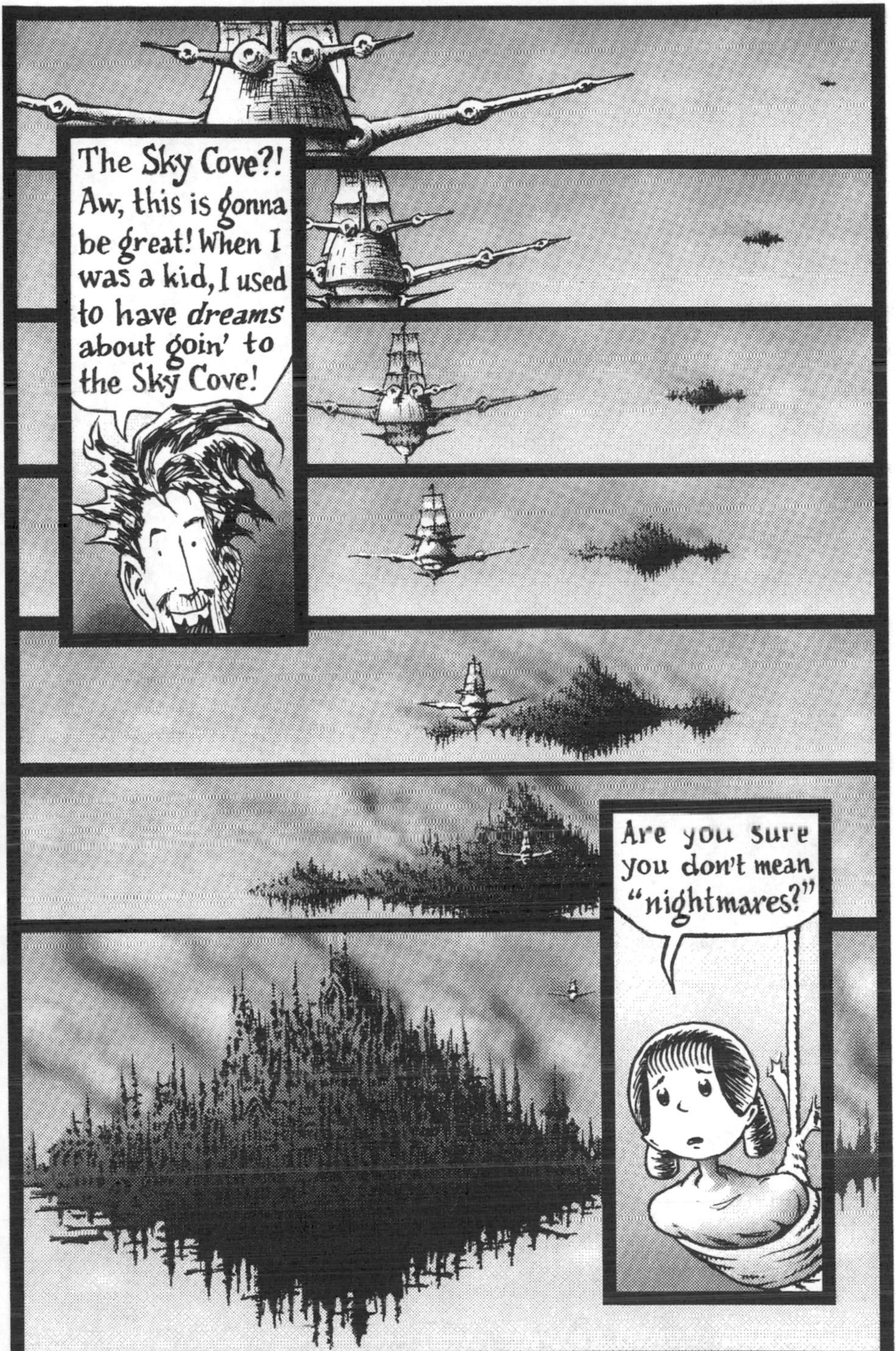
The Sky Cove?! Aw, this is gonna be great! When I was a kid, I used to have *dreams* about goin' to the Sky Cove!
Are you sure you don't mean "nightmares?"

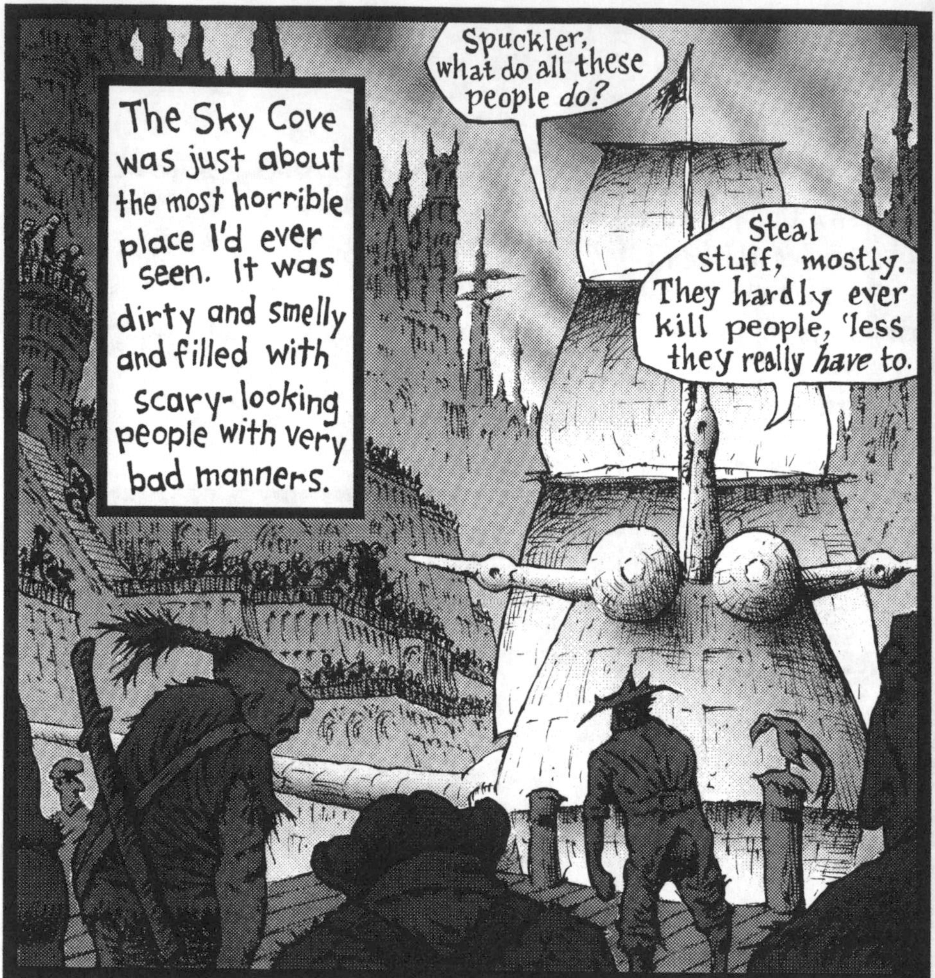
The Sky Cove was just about the most horrible place I'd ever seen. It was dirty and smelly and filled with scary-looking people with very bad manners.
Spuckler, what do all these people *do?*
Steal stuff, mostly. They hardly ever kill people, 'less they really *have* to.

When the ship was docked, some wealthy-looking men came aboard. Then they began discussing something with the Sky Pirates.

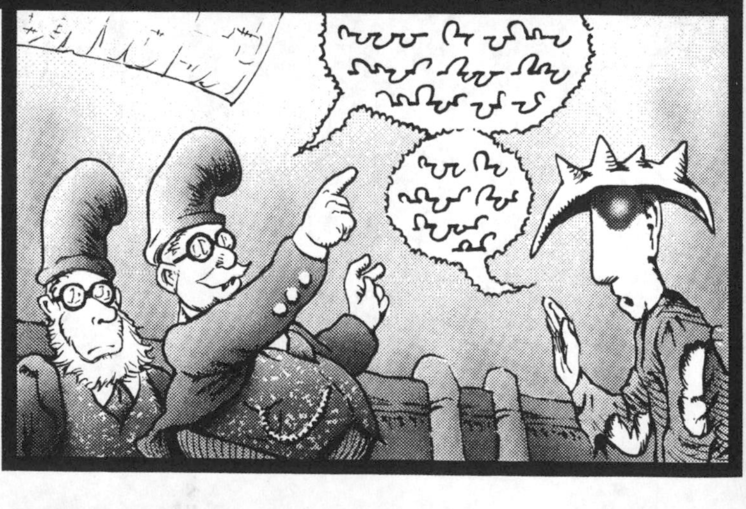

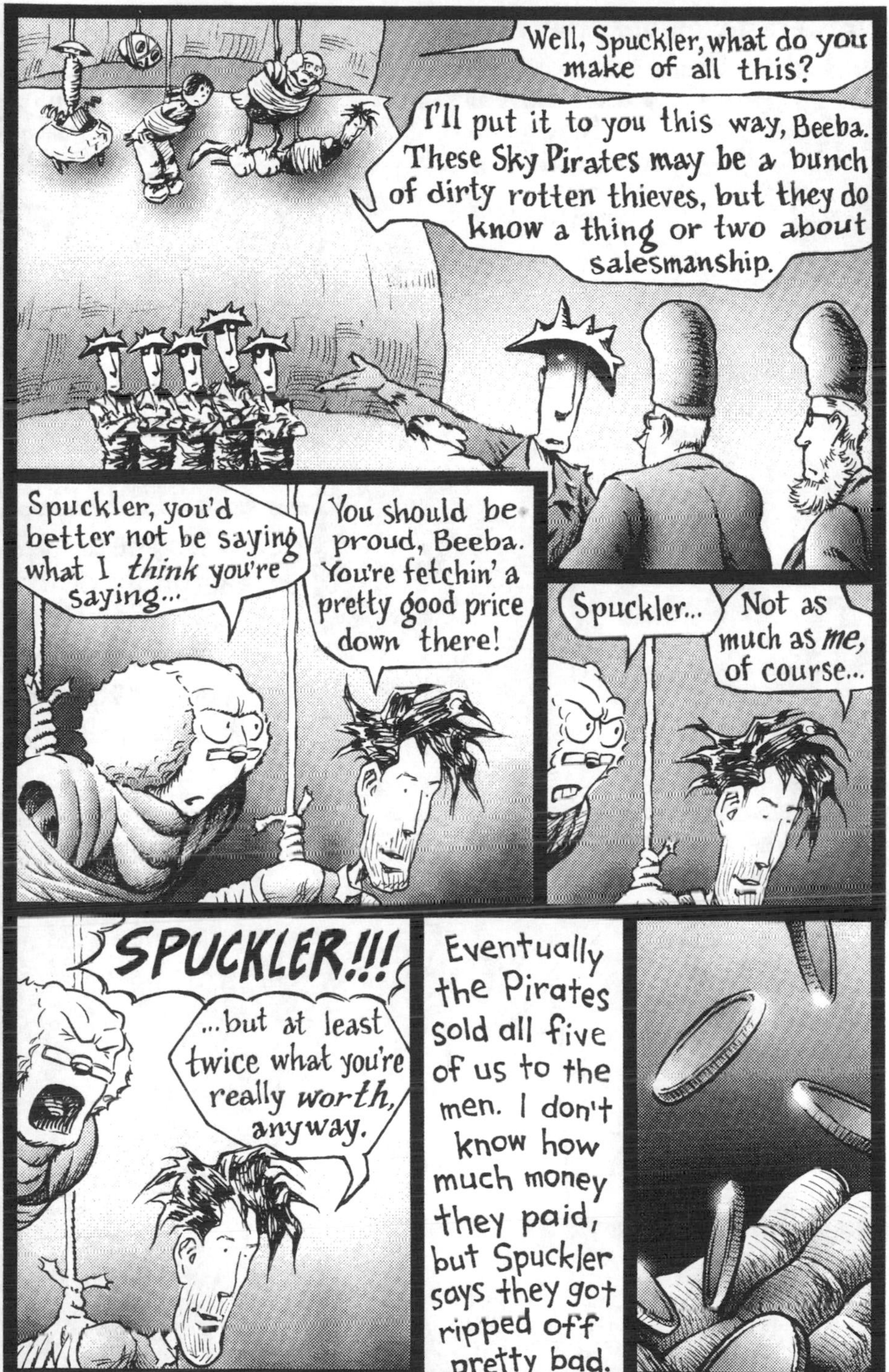
Well, Spuckler, what do you make of all this?
I'll put it to you this way, Beeba. These Sky Pirates may be a bunch of dirty rotten thieves, but they do know a thing or two about salesmanship.
Spuckler, you'd better not be saying what I *think* you're saying...
You should be proud, Beeba. You're fetchin' a pretty good price down there!
Spuckler...
Not as much as *me*, of course...
SPUCKLER!!!
...but at least twice what you're really *worth*, anyway.
Eventually the Pirates sold all five of us to the men. I don't know how much money they paid, but Spuckler says they got ripped off pretty bad.

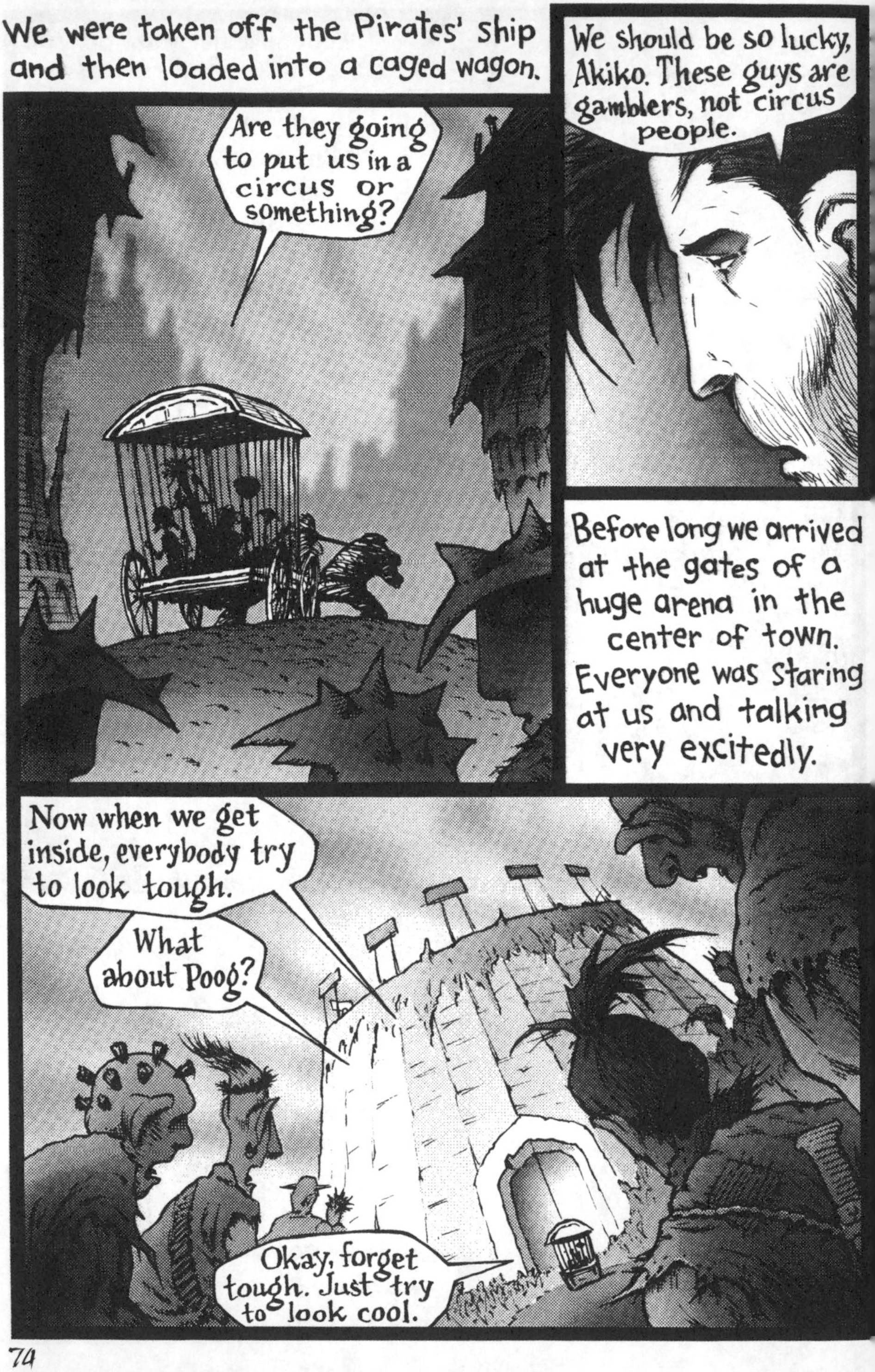
We were taken off the Pirates' ship and then loaded into a caged wagon.
Are they going to put us in a circus or something?
We should be so lucky, Akiko. These guys are gamblers, not circus people.
Before long we arrived at the gates of a huge arena in the center of town. Everyone was staring at us and talking very excitedly.
Now when we get inside, everybody try to look tough.
What about Poog?
Okay, forget tough. Just try to look cool.

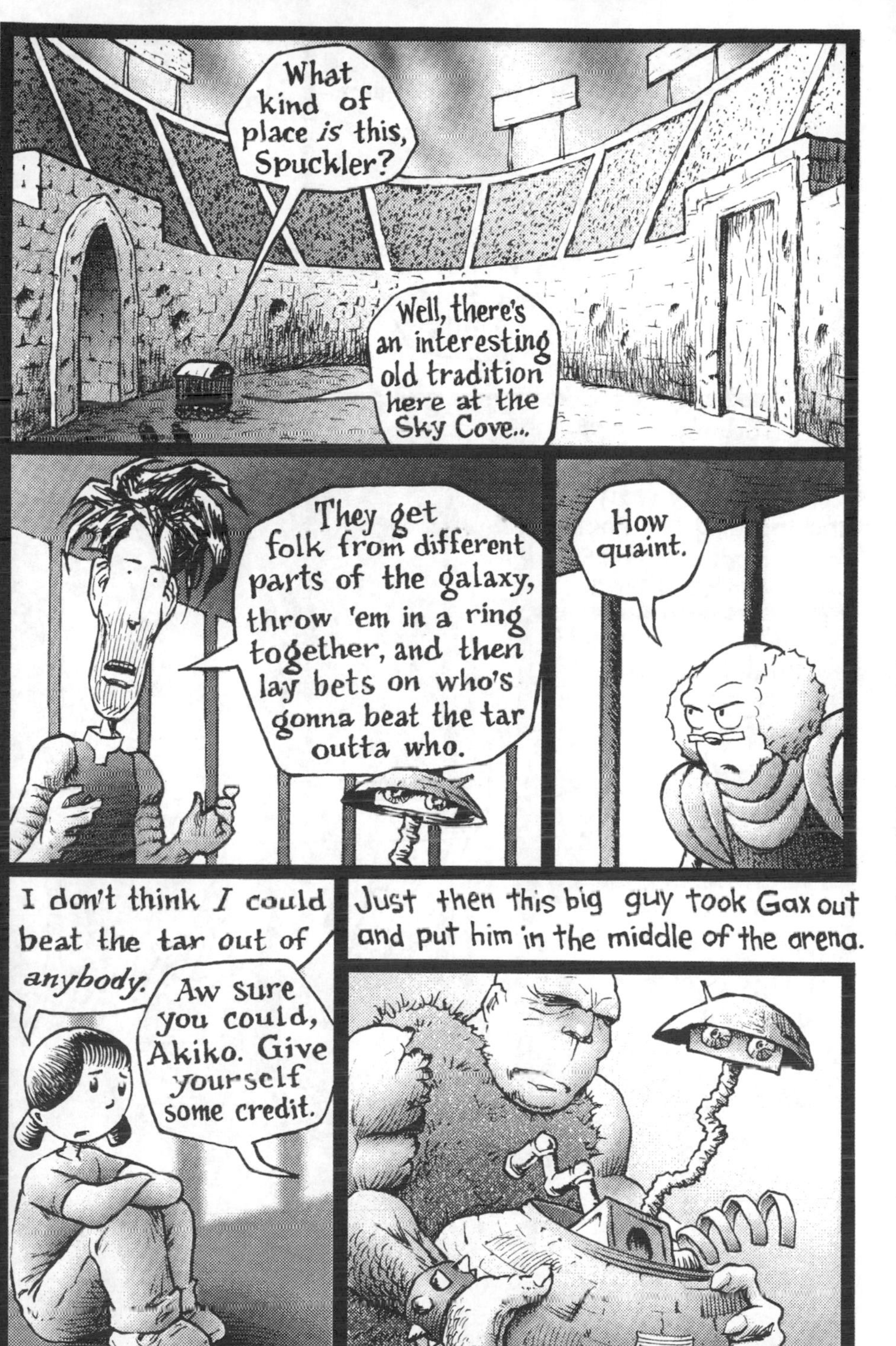
What kind of place *is* this, Spuckler?
Well, there's an interesting old tradition here at the Sky Cove...
They get folk from different parts of the galaxy, throw 'em in a ring together, and then lay bets on who's gonna beat the tar outta who.
How quaint.
I don't think *I* could beat the tar out of *anybody.*
Aw sure you could, Akiko. Give yourself some credit.
Just then this big guy took Gax out and put him in the middle of the arena.

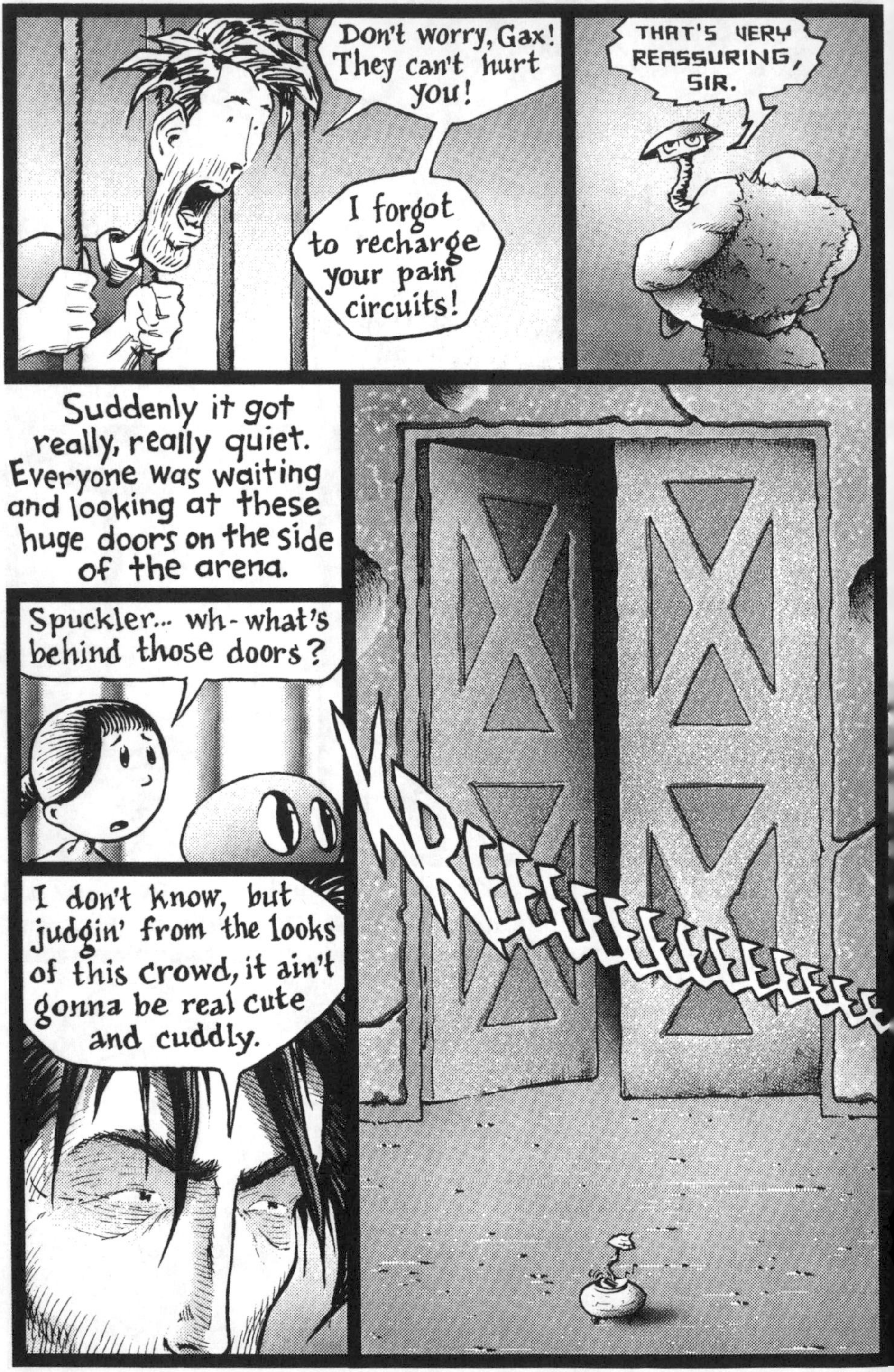

Don't worry, Gax! They can't hurt you!
I forgot to recharge your pain circuits!
THAT'S VERY REASSURING, SIR.
Suddenly it got really, really quiet. Everyone was waiting and looking at these huge doors on the side of the arena.
Spuckler... wh-what's behind those doors?
I don't know, but judgin' from the looks of this crowd, it ain't gonna be real cute and cuddly.
KREEEEEEEEEEEEEEEEE

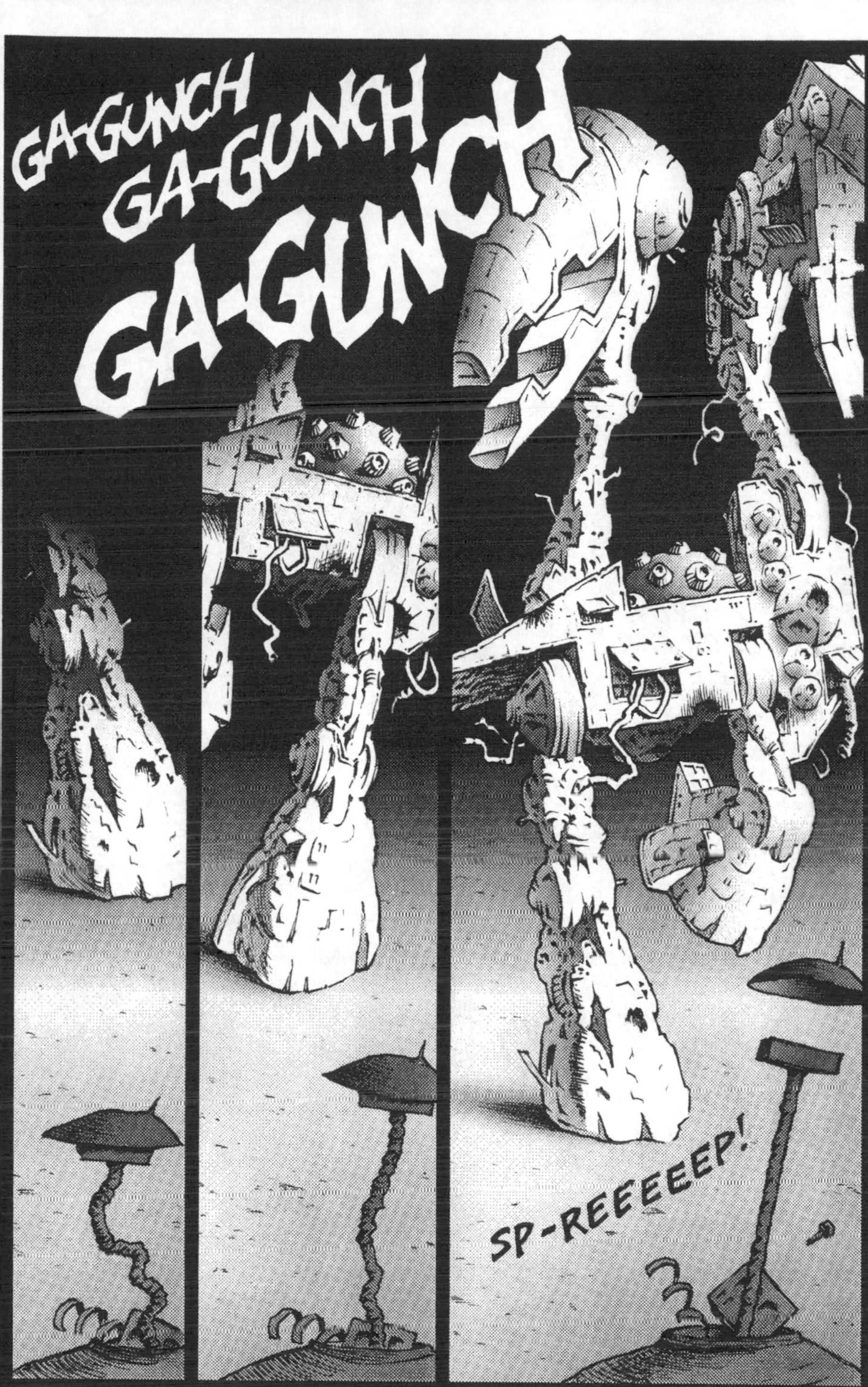
GA-GUNCH
GA-GUNCH
GA-GUNCH
SP-REEEEEEP!

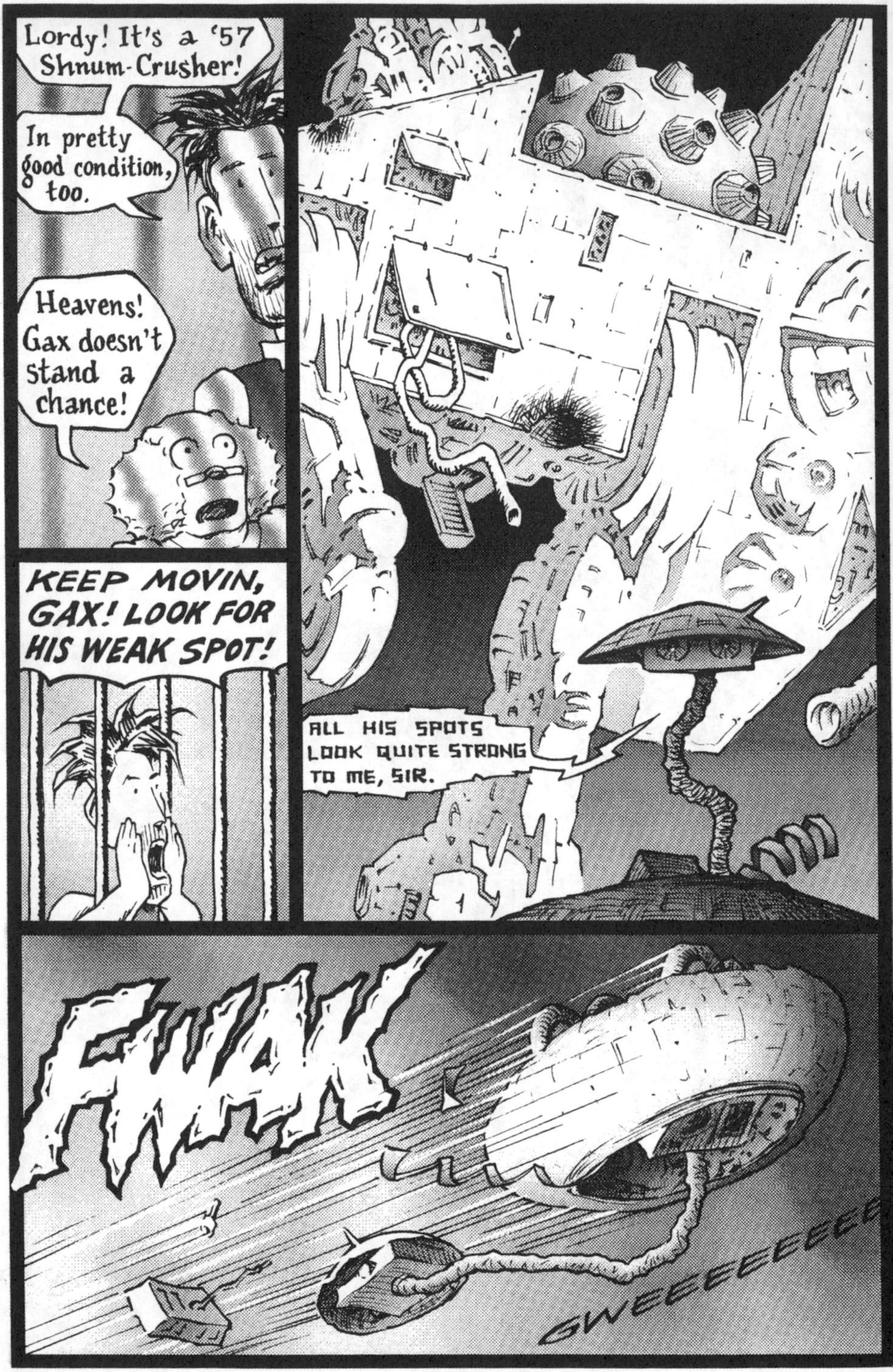
Lordy! It's a '57 Shnum-Crusher!
In pretty good condition, too.
Heavens! Gax doesn't stand a chance!
KEEP MOVIN, GAX! LOOK FOR HIS WEAK SPOT!
ALL HIS SPOTS LOOK QUITE STRONG TO ME, SIR.
FWAK
GWEEEEEEEEE

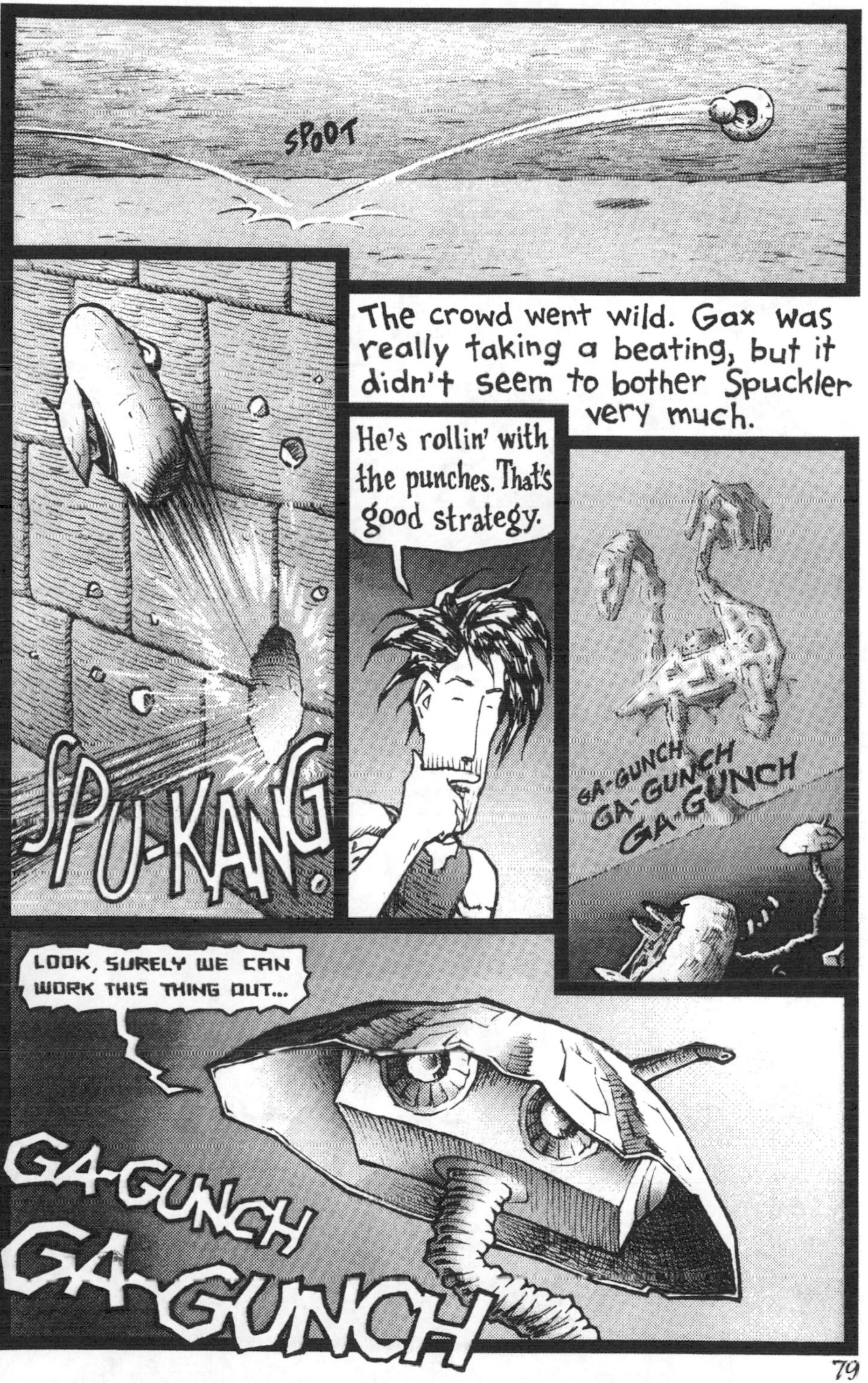
SPOOT
SPU-KANG
The crowd went wild. Gax was really taking a beating, but it didn't seem to bother Spuckler very much.
He's rollin' with the punches. That's good strategy.
GA-GUNCH GA-GUNCH GA-GUNCH
LOOK, SURELY WE CAN WORK THIS THING OUT...
GA-GUNCH
GA-GUNCH

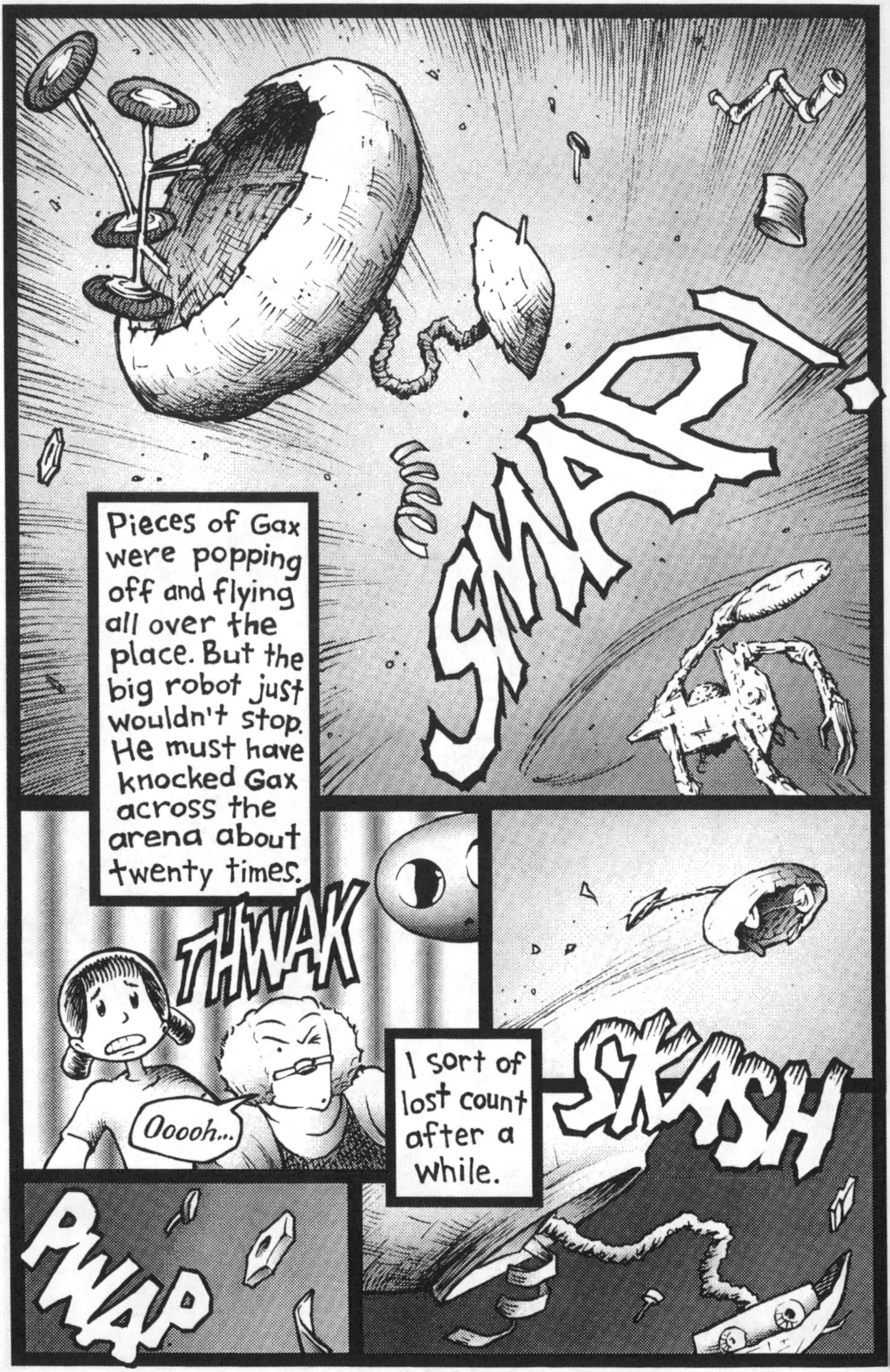
SMAP!
Pieces of Gax were popping off and flying all over the place. But the big robot just wouldn't stop. He must have knocked Gax across the arena about twenty times.
THWAK
Ooooh...
I sort of lost count after a while.
SKASH
PWAP

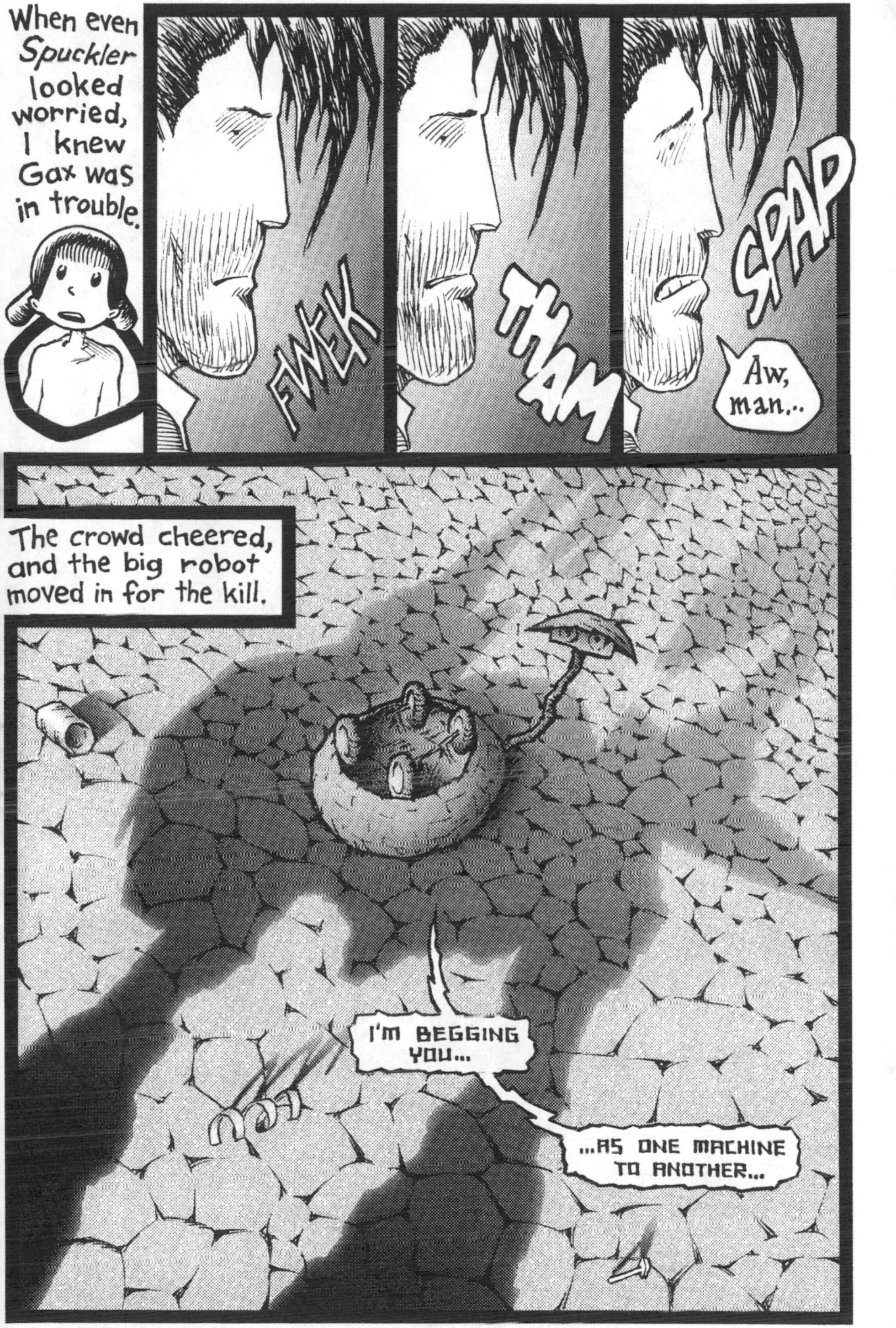
When even Spuckler looked worried, I knew Gax was in trouble.
FWEK
THAM
SPAP
Aw, man...
The crowd cheered, and the big robot moved in for the kill.
I'M BEGGING YOU...
...AS ONE MACHINE TO ANOTHER...

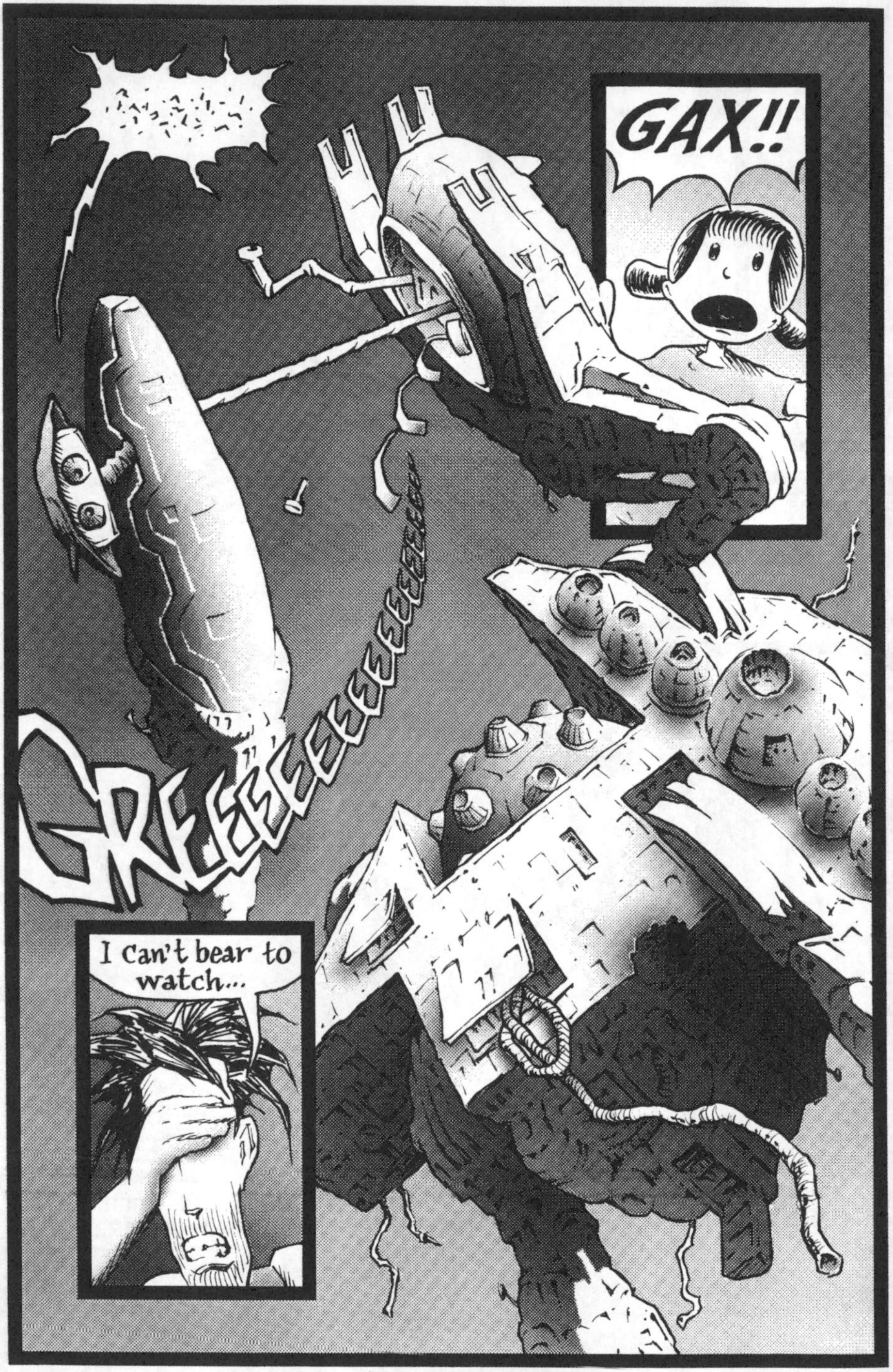
GAX!!
GREEEEEEEEEEEEEEEEE
I can't bear to watch...

Next Issue: "Mistaken Identity"

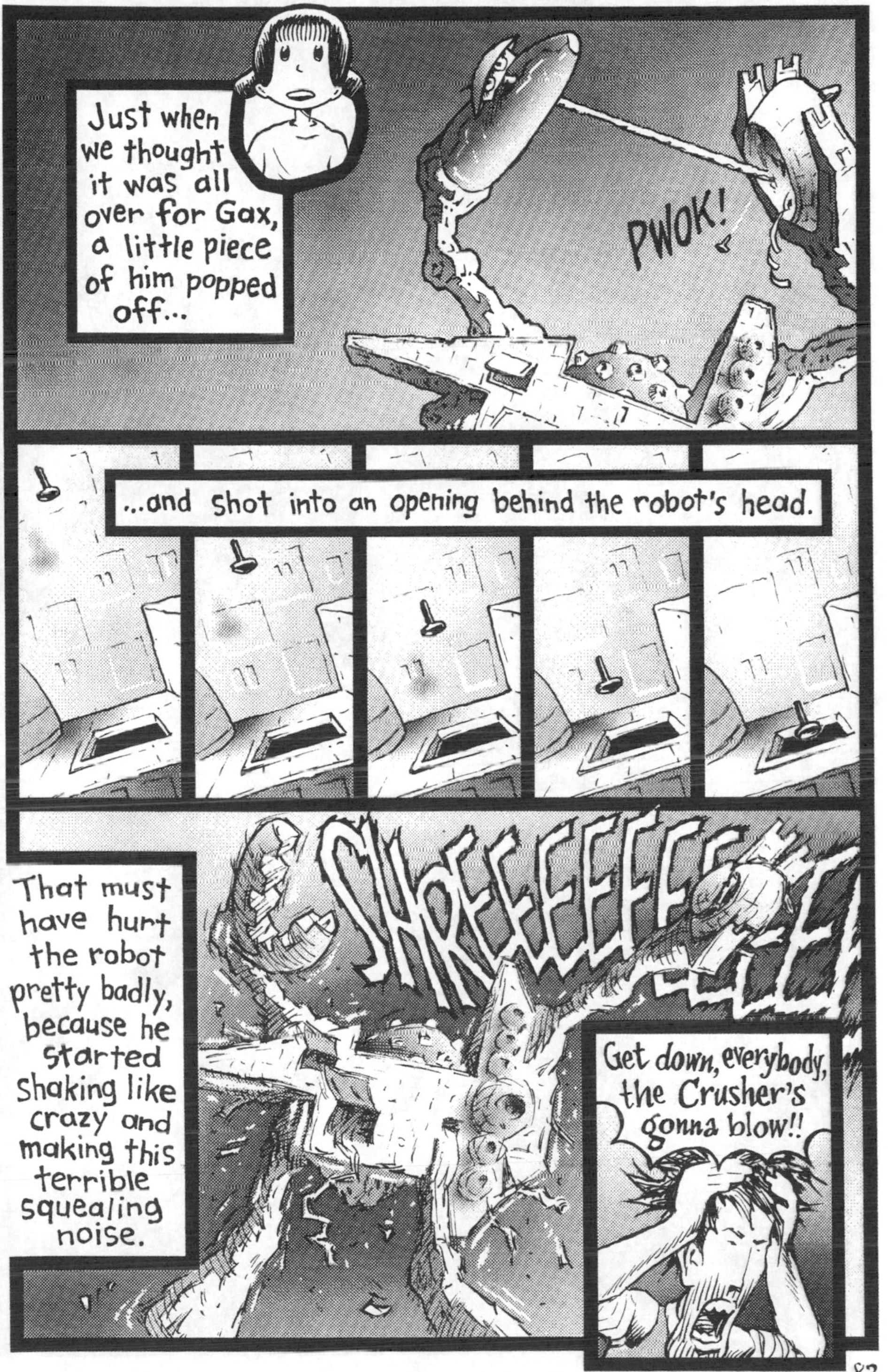

Just when we thought it was all over for Gax, a little piece of him popped off...
PWOK!
...and shot into an opening behind the robot's head.
That must have hurt the robot pretty badly, because he started shaking like crazy and making this terrible squealing noise.
SHREEEEEEEEE
Get down, everybody, the Crusher's gonna blow!!

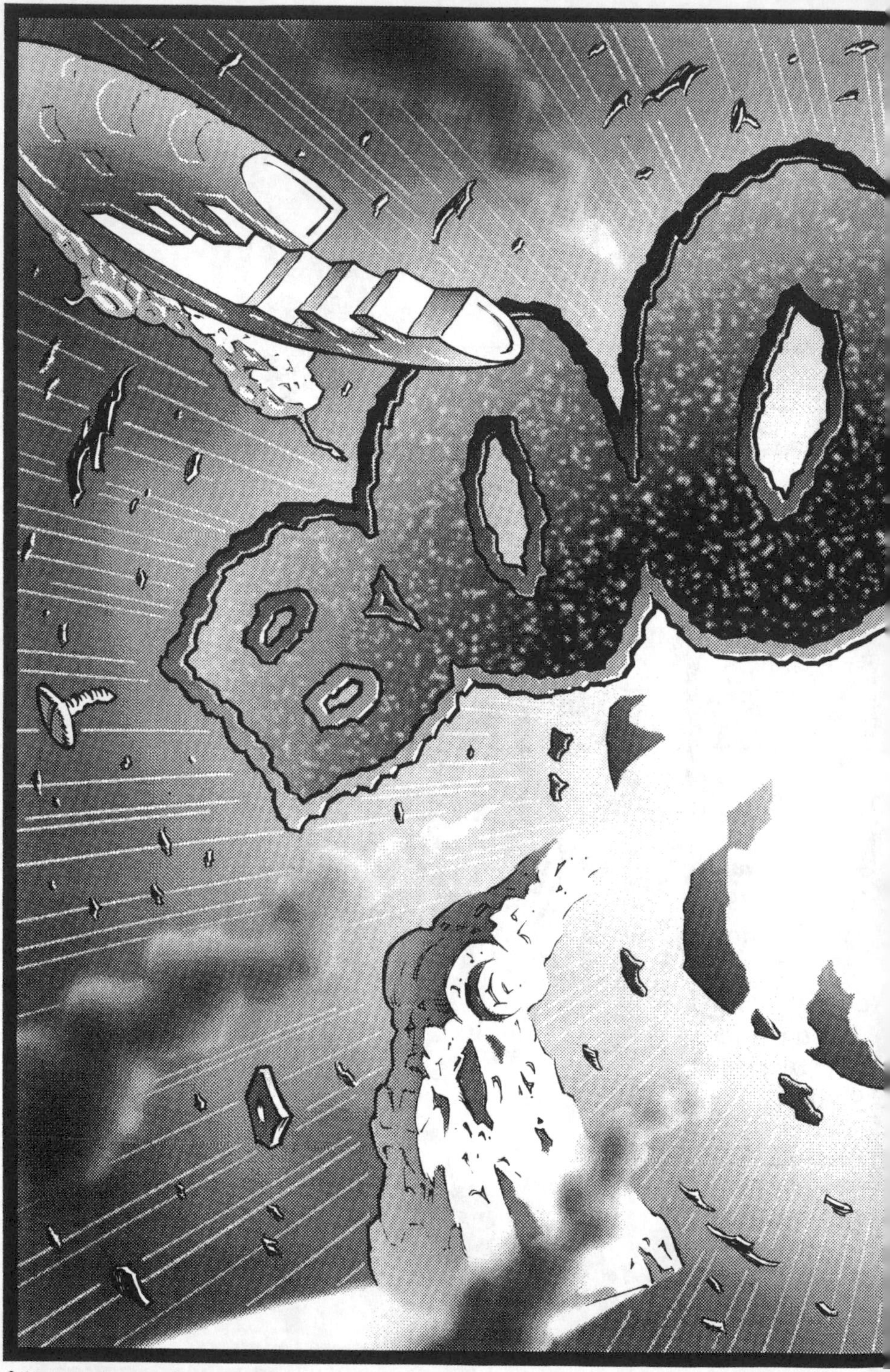
BOO

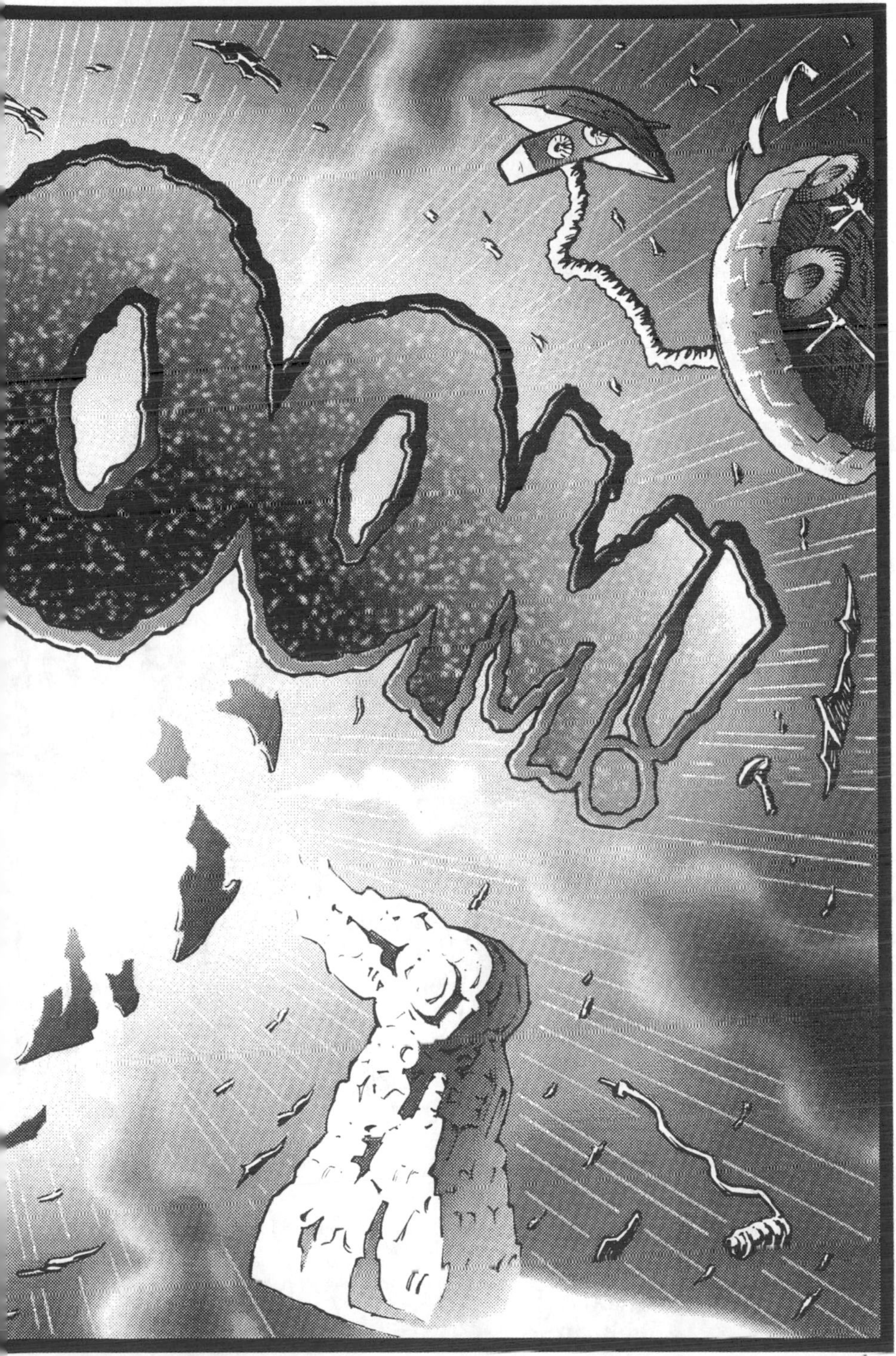

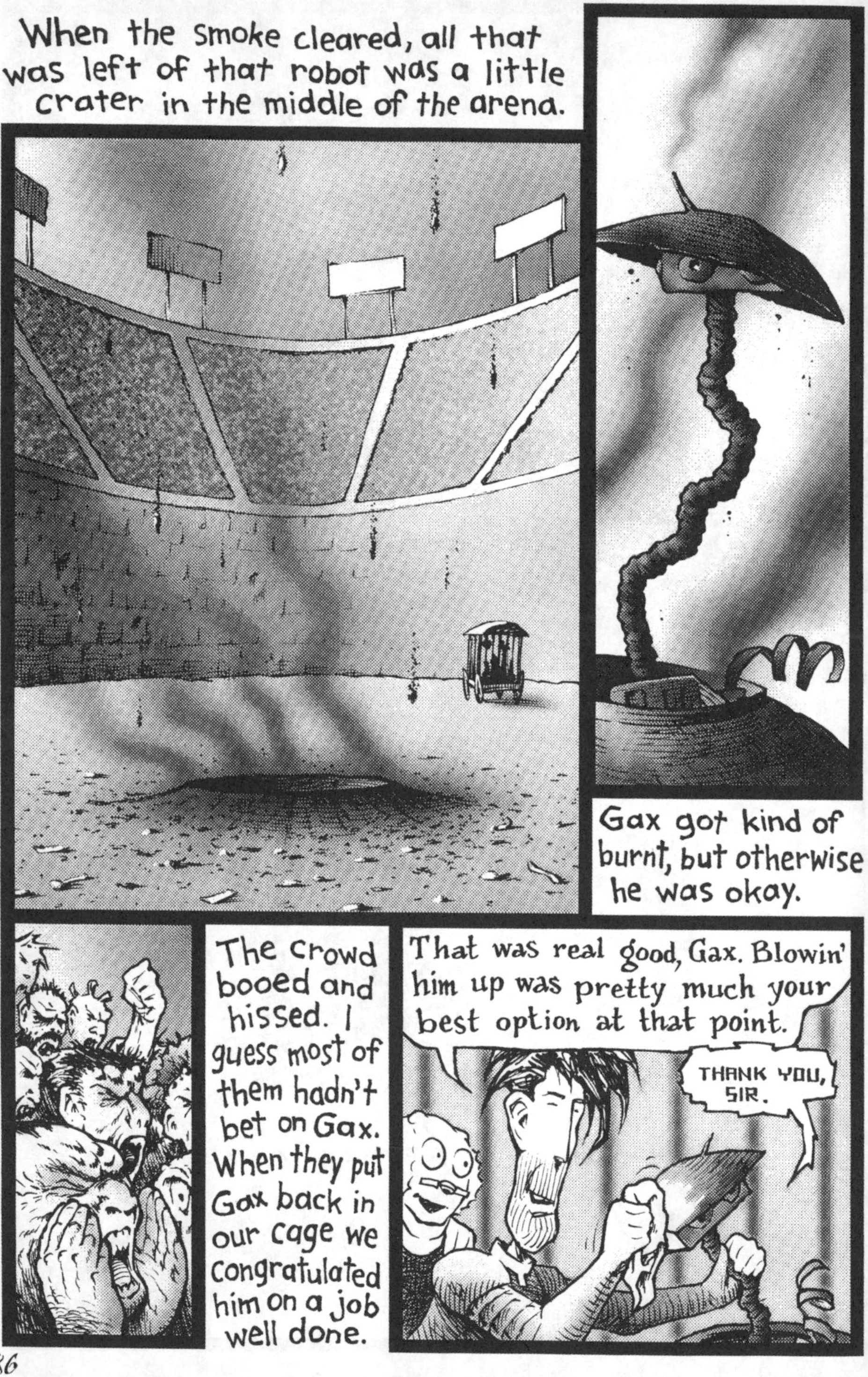

When the smoke cleared, all that was left of that robot was a little crater in the middle of the arena.
Gax got kind of burnt, but otherwise he was okay.
The crowd booed and hissed. I guess most of them hadn't bet on Gax. When they put Gax back in our cage we congratulated him on a job well done.
That was real good, Gax. Blowin' him up was pretty much your best option at that point.
THANK YOU, SIR.

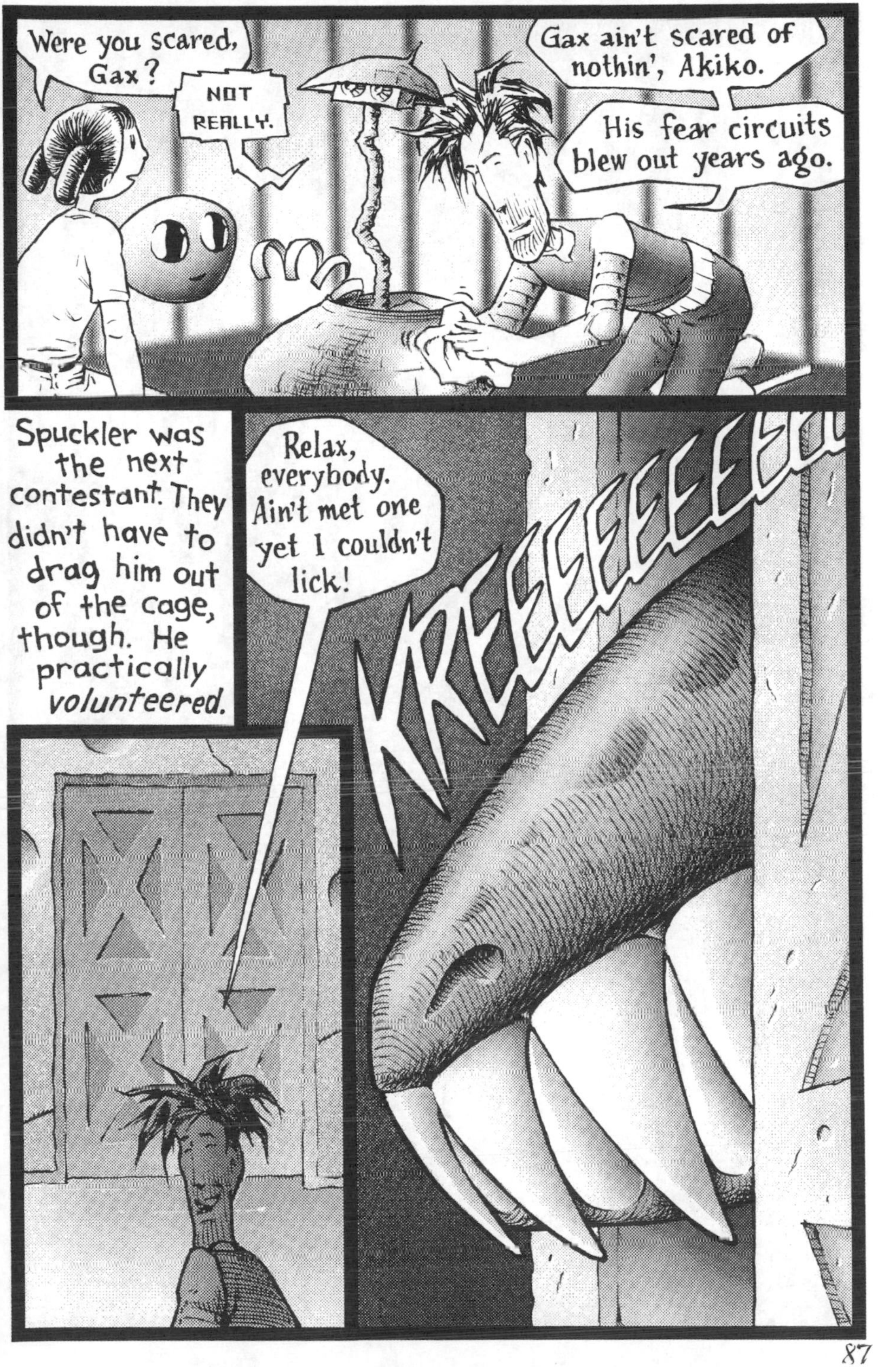

Were you scared, Gax?
NOT REALLY.
Gax ain't scared of nothin', Akiko.
His fear circuits blew out years ago.
Spuckler was the next contestant. They didn't have to drag him out of the cage, though. He practically *volunteered.*
Relax, everybody. Ain't met one yet I couldn't lick!
KREEEEEEEEEE

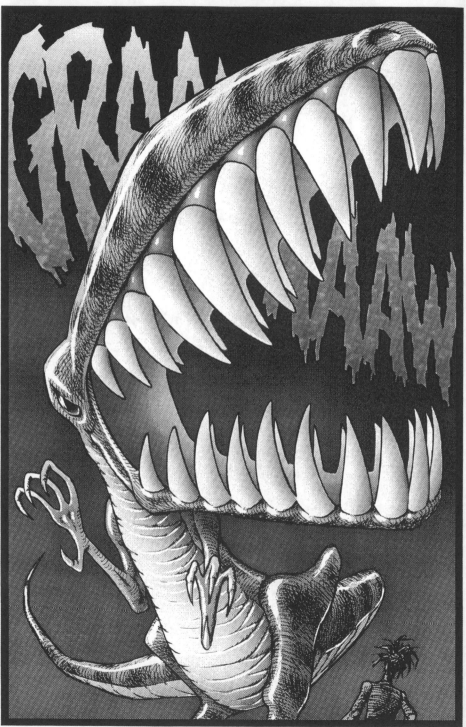

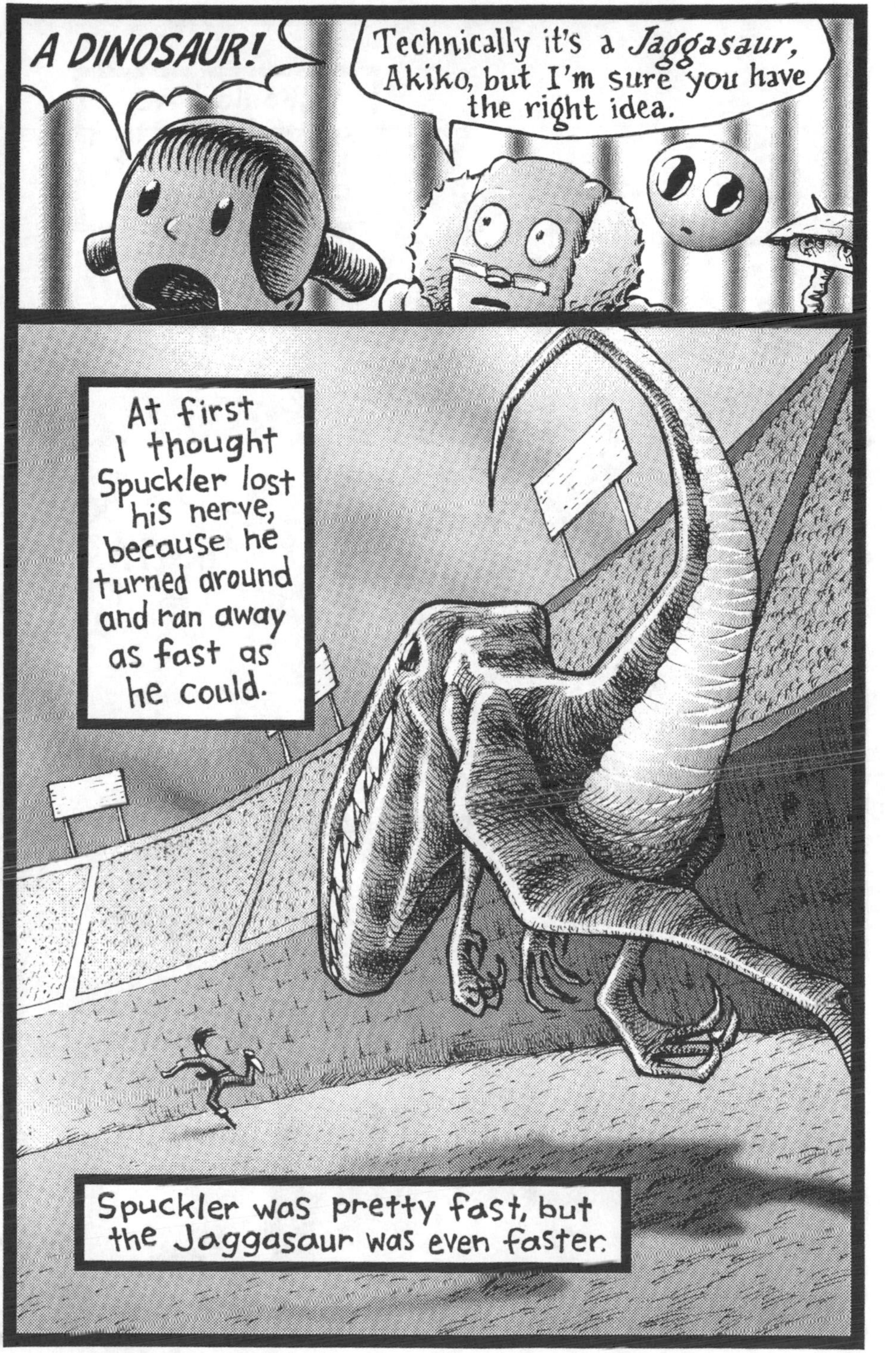
A DINOSAUR!
Technically it's a *Jaggasaur*, Akiko, but I'm sure you have the right idea.
At first I thought Spuckler lost his nerve, because he turned around and ran away as fast as he could.
Spuckler was pretty fast, but the Jaggasaur was even faster.

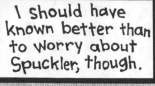

I should have known better than to worry about Spuckler, though.

GROOK?

FFFFWAP!

He knew what he was doing.

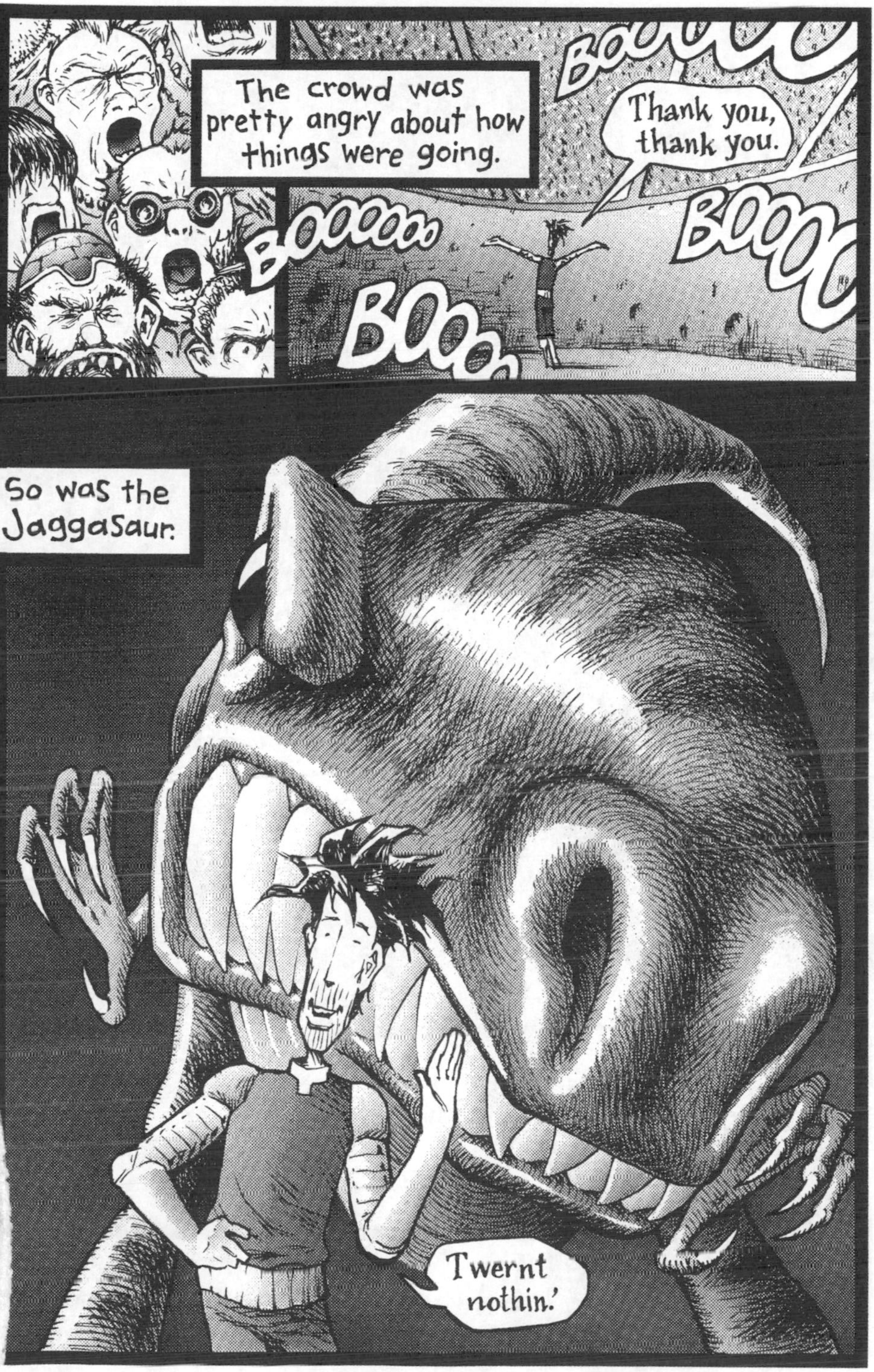
The crowd was pretty angry about how things were going.
BOOOOOO
BOOO
Thank you, thank you.
BOOO
BOOOO
So was the Jaggasaur.
Twernt nothin.'

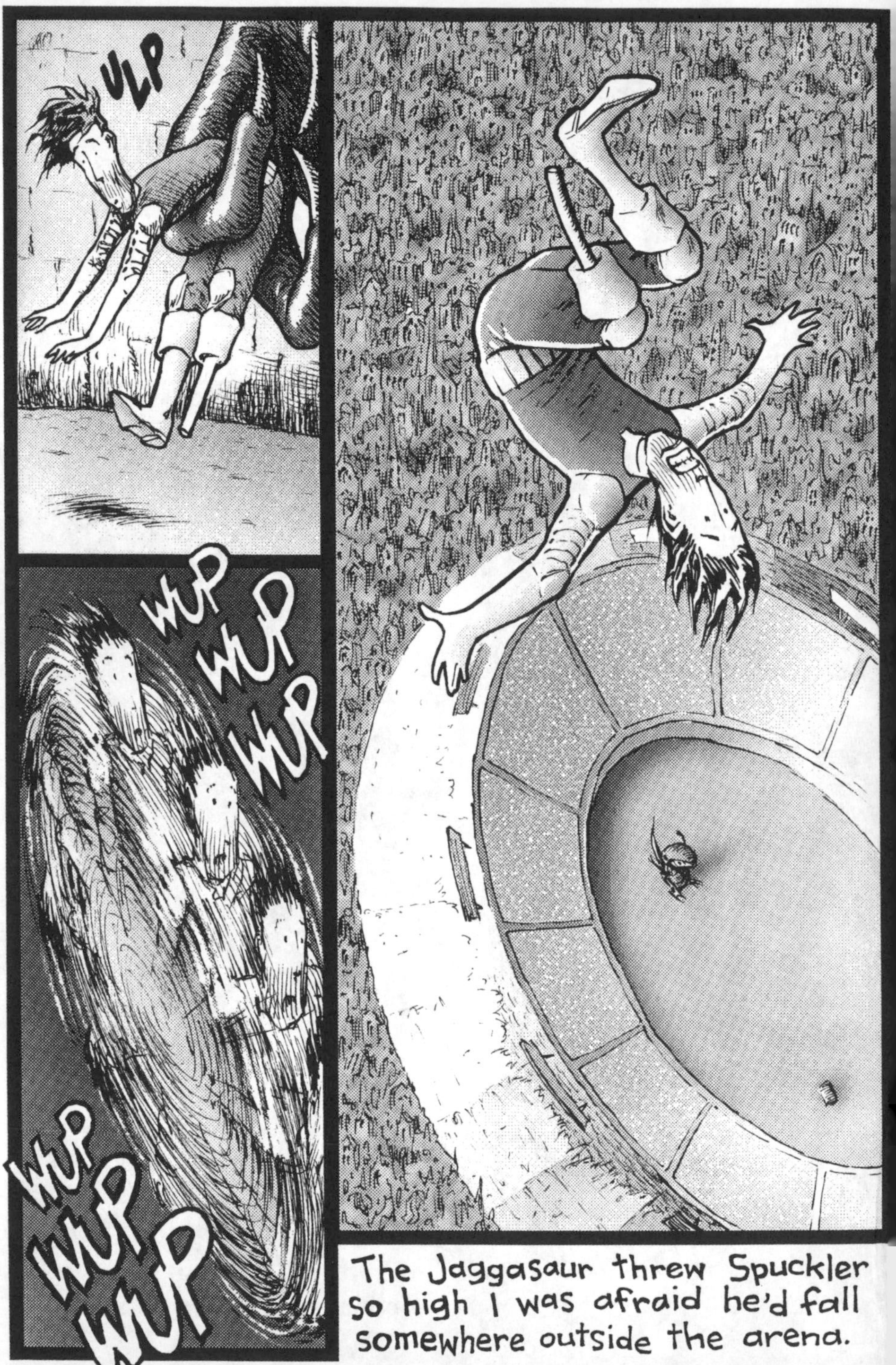
ULP
WUP
WUP
WUP
WUP
WUP
WUP

The Jaggasaur threw Spuckler so high I was afraid he'd fall somewhere outside the arena.

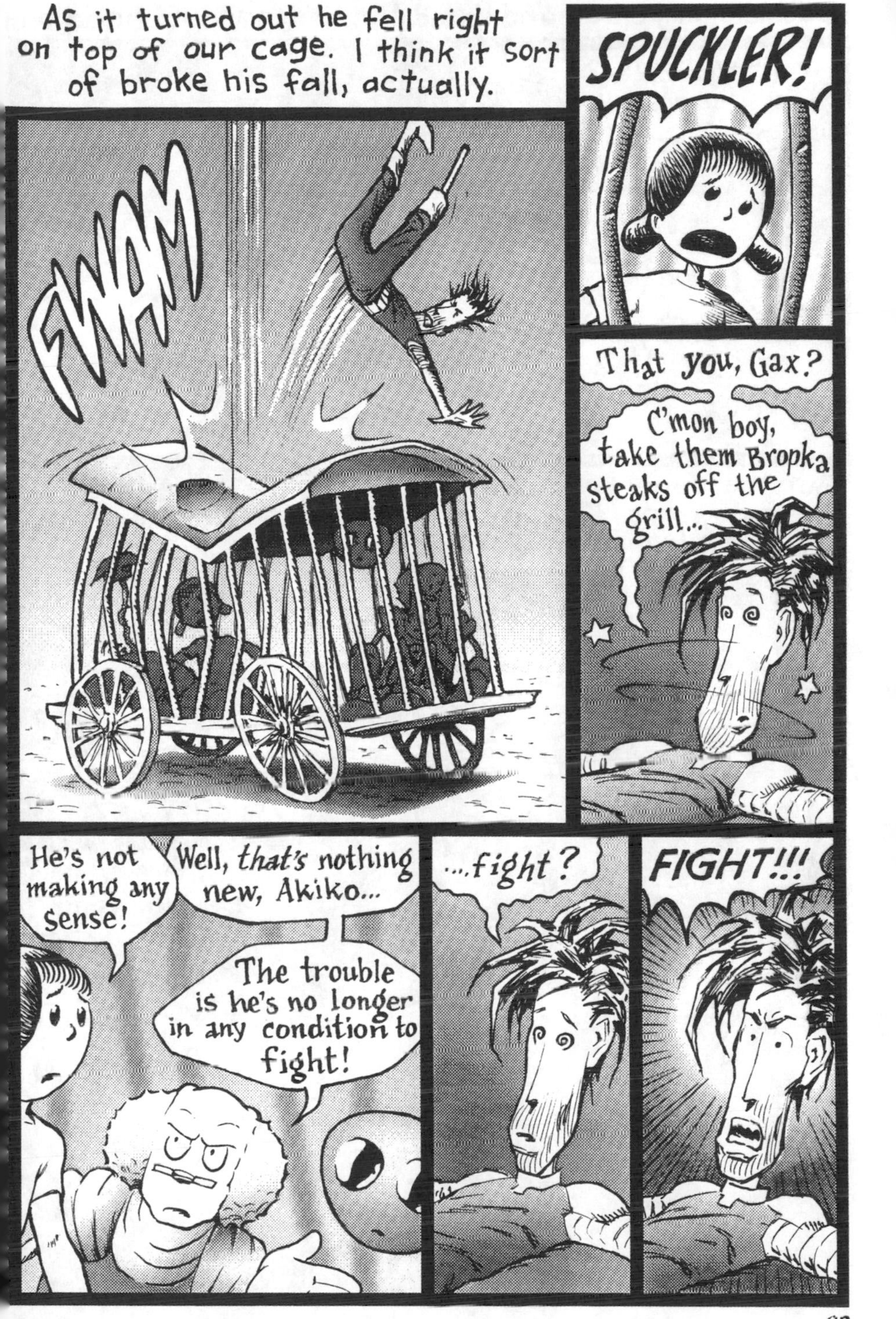
As it turned out he fell right on top of our cage. I think it sort of broke his fall, actually.
FWAM
SPUCKLER!
That you, Gax?
C'mon boy, take them Bropka steaks off the grill...
He's not making any sense!
Well, that's nothing new, Akiko...
The trouble is he's no longer in any condition to fight!
....fight?
FIGHT!!!

Spuckler jumped up and faced the Jaggasaur head on.

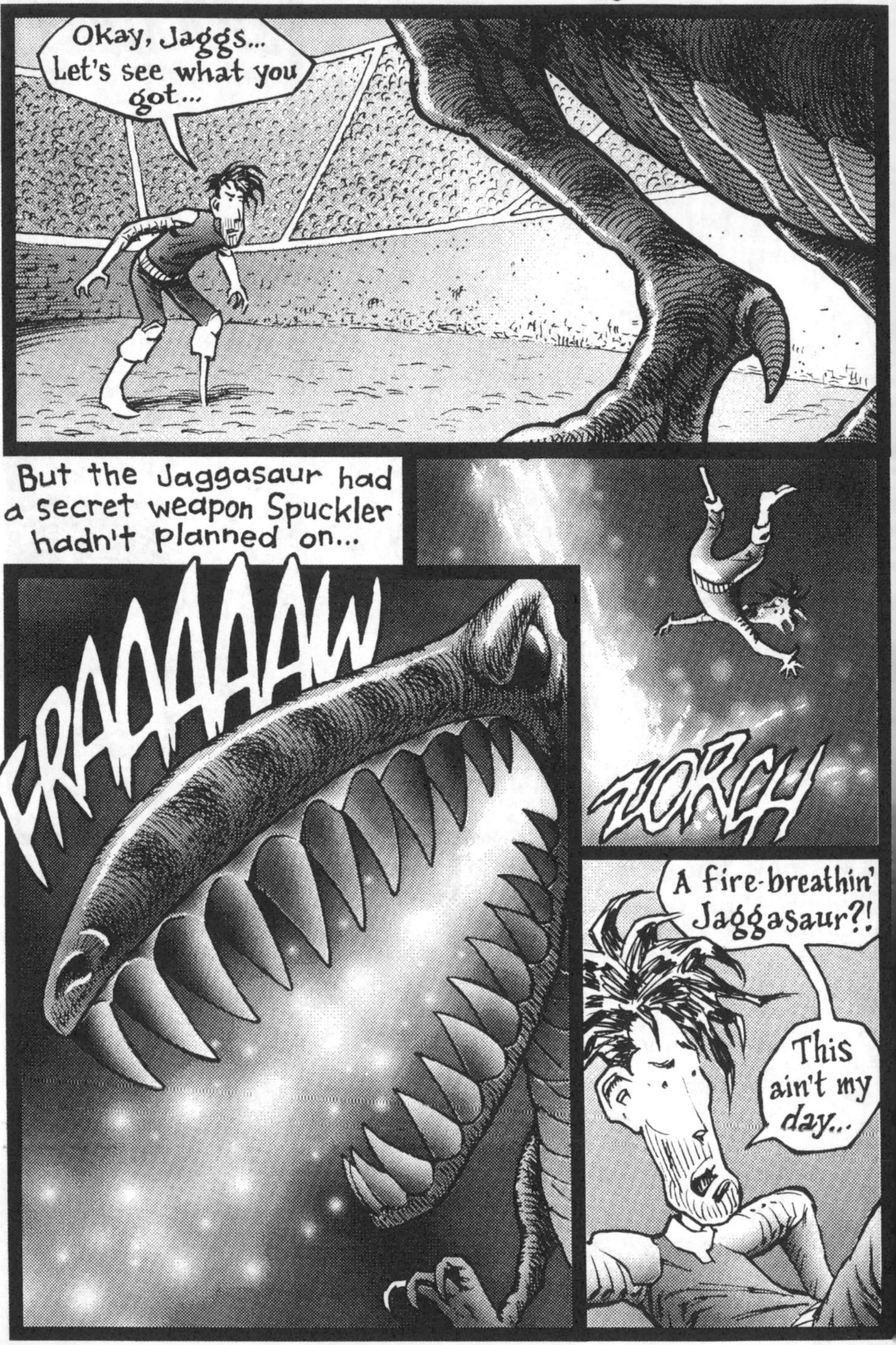
Okay, Jaggs... Let's see what you got...
But the Jaggasaur had a secret weapon Spuckler hadn't planned on...
GRAAAAAW
ZORCH
A fire-breathin' Jaggasaur?!
This ain't my day...

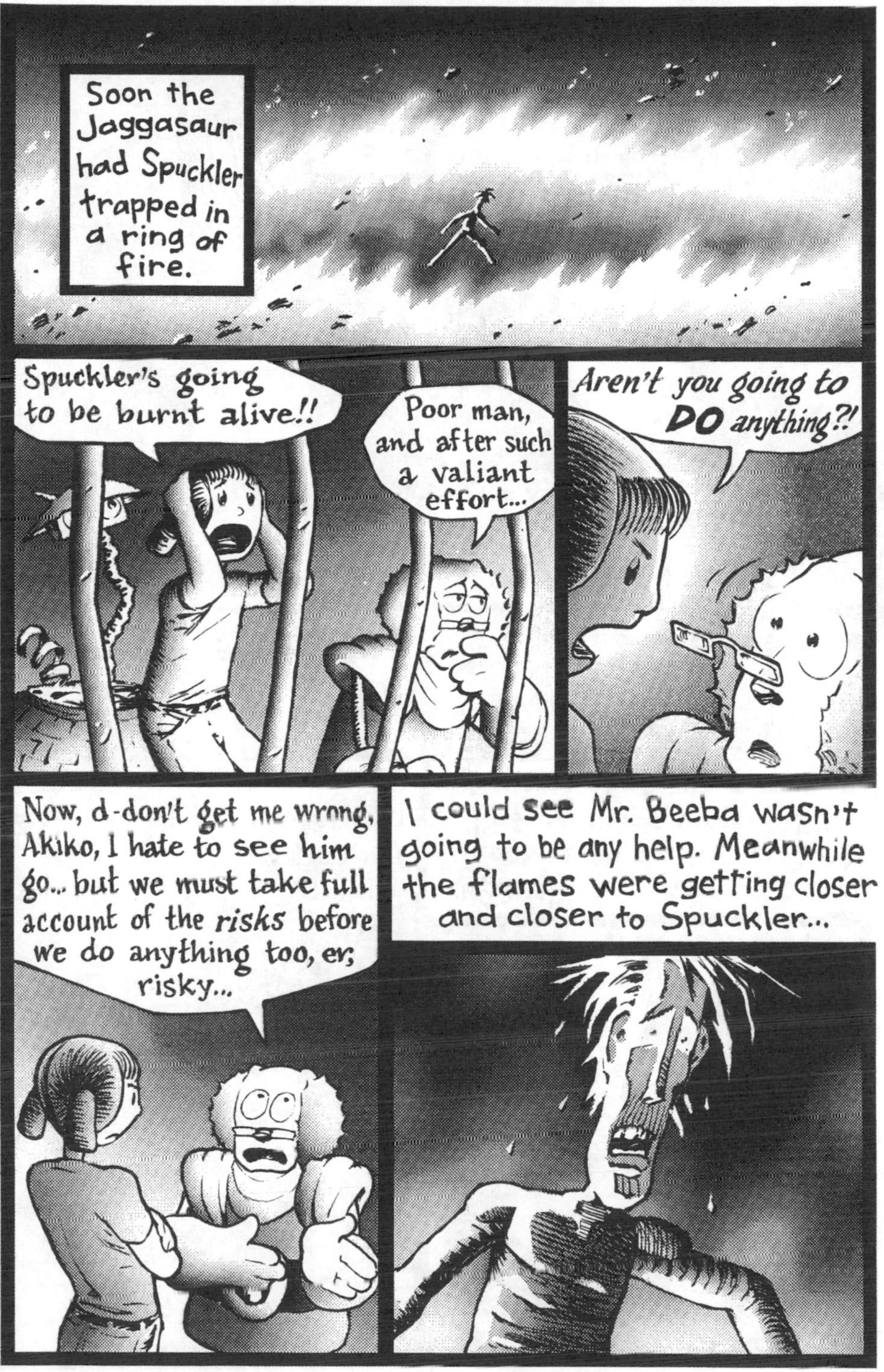
Soon the Jaggasaur had Spuckler trapped in a ring of fire.
Spuckler's going to be burnt alive!!
Poor man, and after such a valiant effort...
Aren't you going to DO anything?!
Now, d-don't get me wrong, Akiko, I hate to see him go... but we must take full account of the risks before we do anything too, er, risky...
I could see Mr. Beeba wasn't going to be any help. Meanwhile the flames were getting closer and closer to Spuckler...

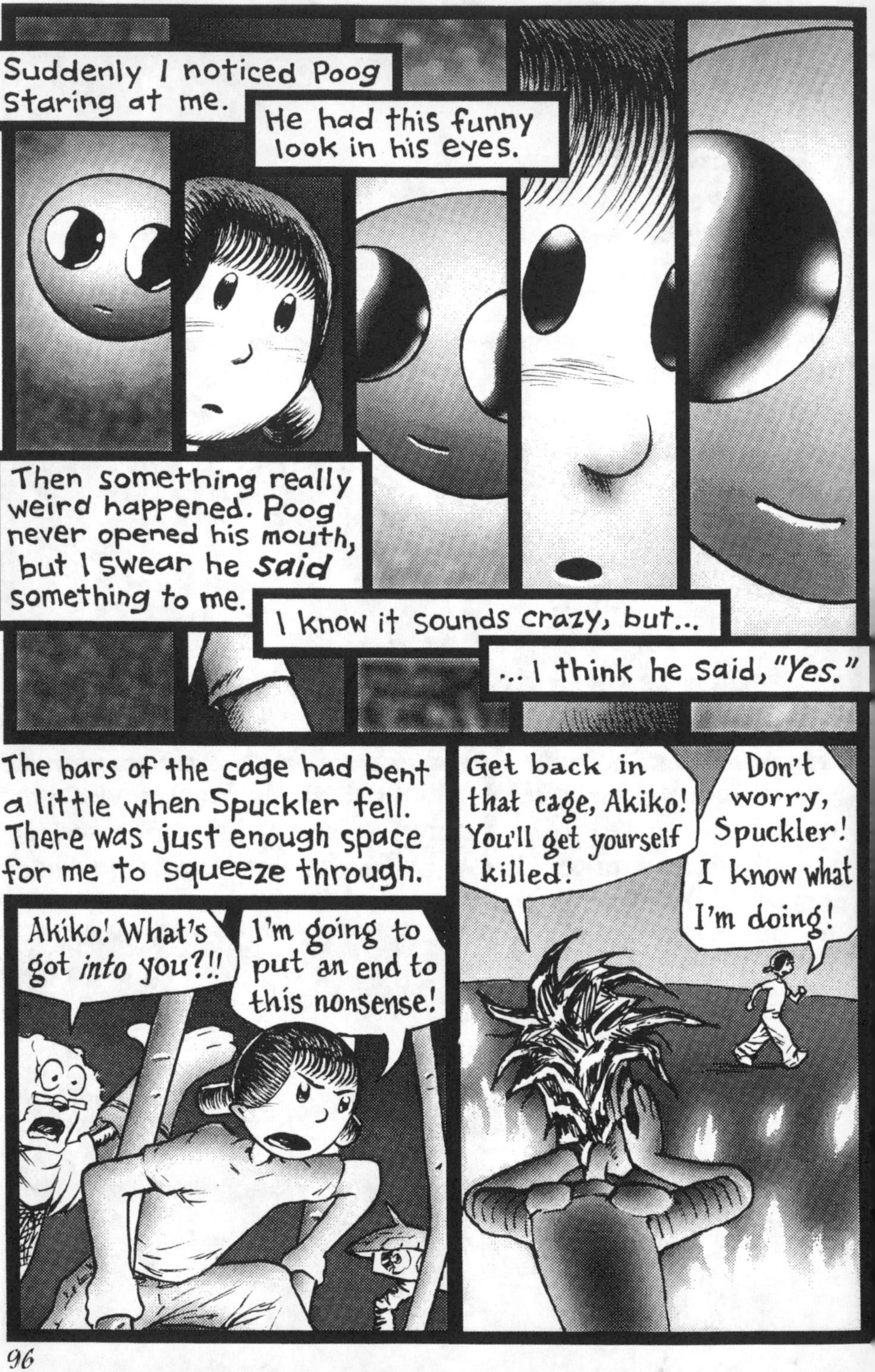
Suddenly I noticed Poog staring at me.
He had this funny look in his eyes.
Then something really weird happened. Poog never opened his mouth, but I swear he *said* something to me.
I know it sounds crazy, but...
...I think he said, "*Yes.*"
The bars of the cage had bent a little when Spuckler fell. There was just enough space for me to squeeze through.
Akiko! What's got *into* you?!!
I'm going to put an end to this nonsense!
Get back in that cage, Akiko! You'll get yourself killed!
Don't worry, Spuckler! I know what I'm doing!

I walked up to that Jaggasaur and gave him a good scolding. I figure he had it coming to him.

"Scrawny?"

Just then I saw two big guys sneaking up from behind to stop me from interrupting the fight. That was when I got a little out of control...

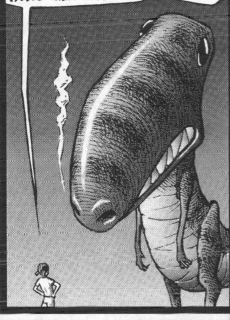

You should be *ashamed* of yourself, bullying a scrawny little man like that!

Pick on someone your *own* size!

Don't touch me or you'll be sorry! Who do you think you *are* anyway?!

*I DON'T HAVE TIME TO MESS **AROUND** WITH YOU CRAZY PEOPLE! I'VE GOT A **PRINCE** TO RESCUE! I'VE GOT TO FIND **ALIA RELLAPOR** AND...*

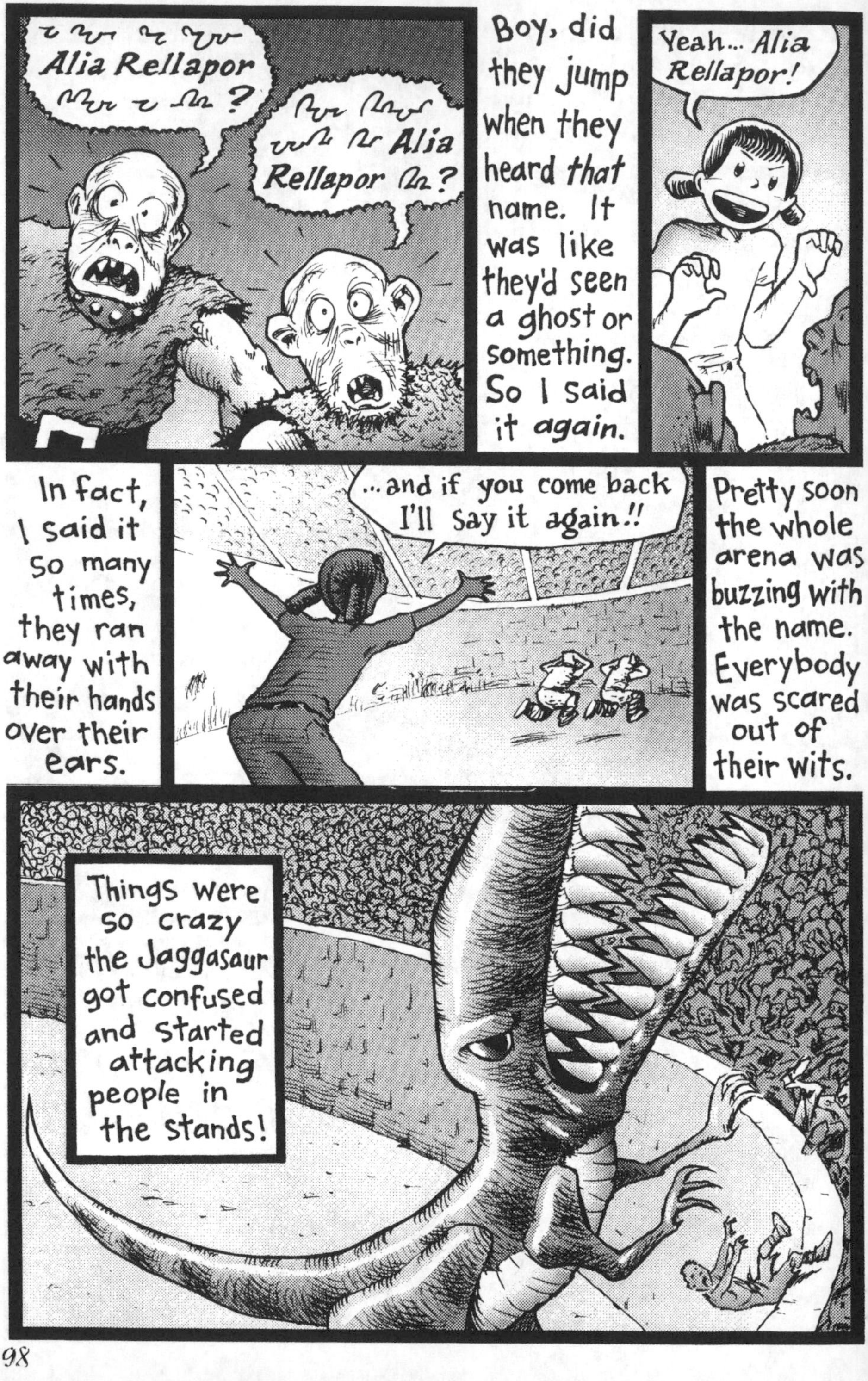
Alia Rellapor ?
Alia Rellapor ?
Boy, did they jump when they heard *that* name. It was like they'd seen a ghost or something. So I said it *again*.
Yeah... *Alia Rellapor!*
In fact, I said it so many times, they ran away with their hands over their ears.
...and if you come back I'll say it again!!
Pretty soon the whole arena was buzzing with the name. Everybody was scared out of their wits.
Things were so crazy the Jaggasaur got confused and started attacking people in the stands!

Finally they just had to tie him up...

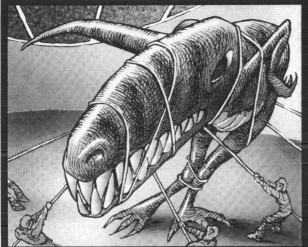

FROONK!

...and drag him out of the arena.

It was right about then that I noticed my feet were getting wet.

FOOOOSH

It was like a miracle! Water was pouring into the arena...

...just in time to save Spuckler from the fire!

SSSSSSS

99

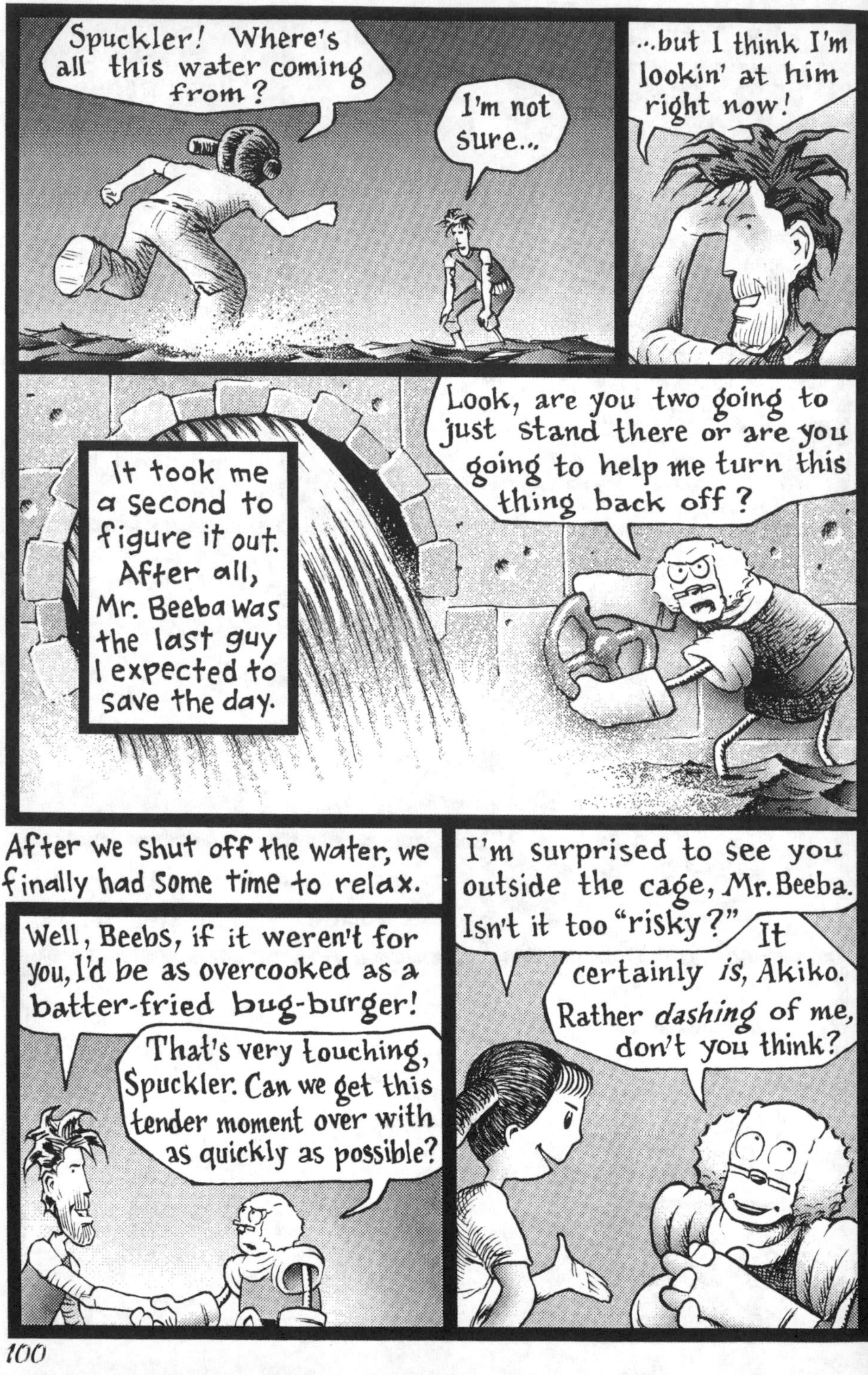
Spuckler! Where's all this water coming from?
I'm not sure...
...but I think I'm lookin' at him right now!
It took me a second to figure it out. After all, Mr. Beeba was the last guy I expected to save the day.
Look, are you two going to just stand there or are you going to help me turn this thing back off?
After we shut off the water, we finally had some time to relax.
Well, Beebs, if it weren't for you, I'd be as overcooked as a batter-fried bug-burger!
That's very touching, Spuckler. Can we get this tender moment over with as quickly as possible?
I'm surprised to see you outside the cage, Mr. Beeba. Isn't it too "risky?"
It certainly *is*, Akiko. Rather *dashing* of me, don't you think?

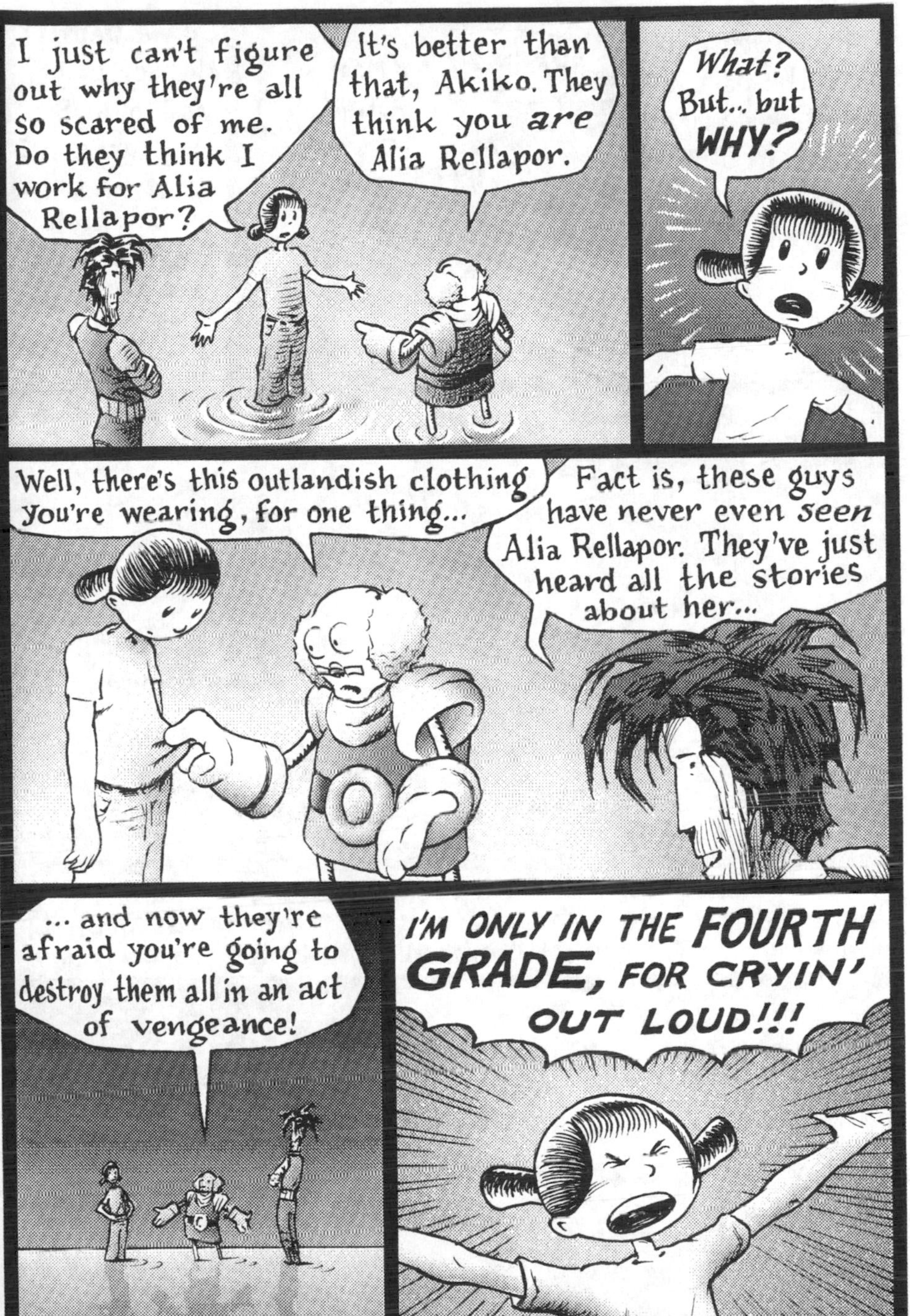
I just can't figure out why they're all so scared of me. Do they think I work for Alia Rellapor?
It's better than that, Akiko. They think you *are* Alia Rellapor.
What? But... but **WHY?**
Well, there's this outlandish clothing you're wearing, for one thing...
Fact is, these guys have never even *seen* Alia Rellapor. They've just heard all the stories about her...
... and now they're afraid you're going to destroy them all in an act of vengeance!
I'M ONLY IN THE FOURTH GRADE, FOR CRYIN' OUT LOUD!!!

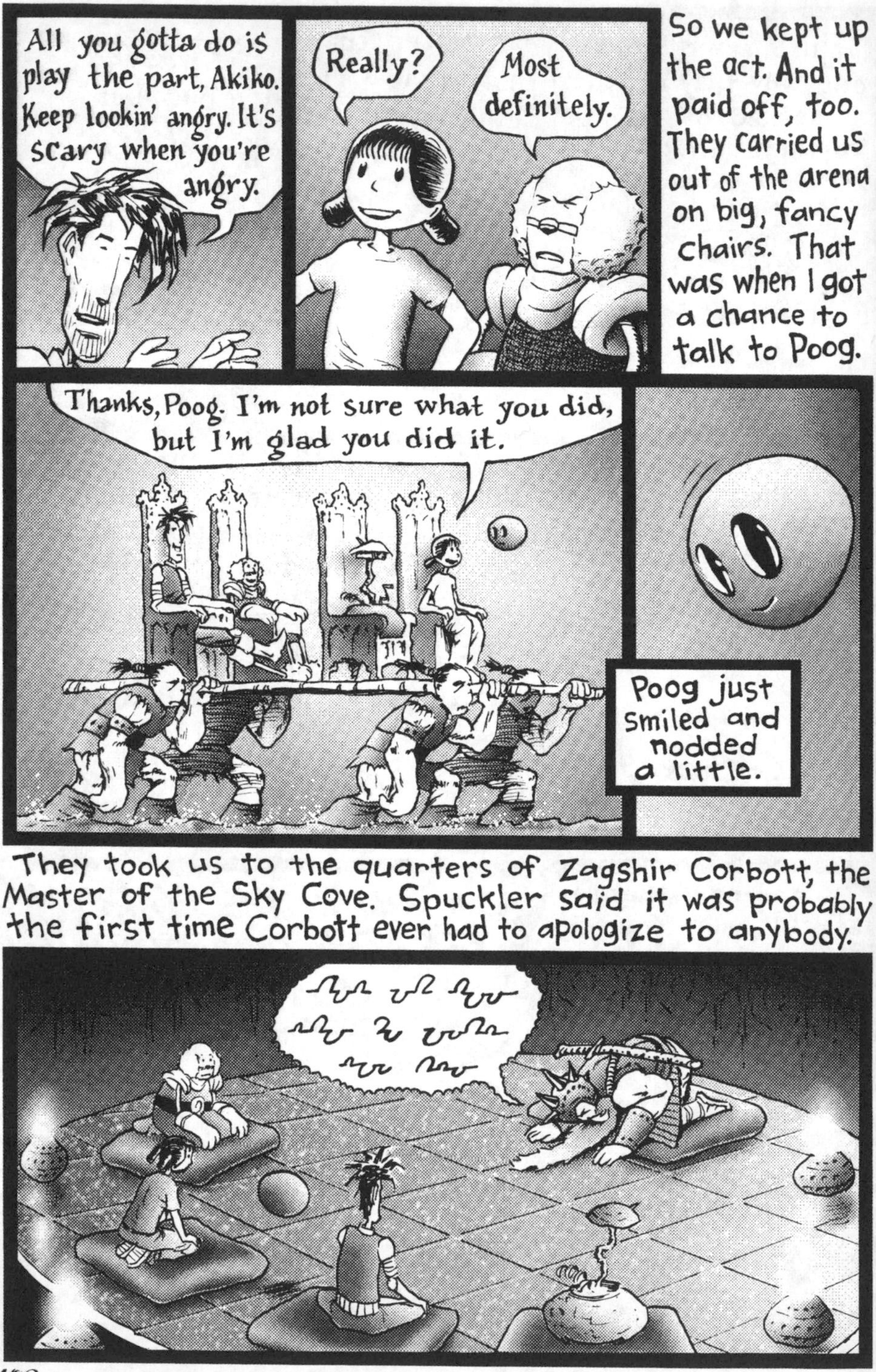
All you gotta do is play the part, Akiko. Keep lookin' angry. It's scary when you're angry.
Really?
Most definitely.
So we kept up the act. And it paid off, too. They carried us out of the arena on big, fancy chairs. That was when I got a chance to talk to Poog.
Thanks, Poog. I'm not sure what you did, but I'm glad you did it.
Poog just smiled and nodded a little.
They took us to the quarters of Zagshir Corbott, the Master of the Sky Cove. Spuckler said it was probably the first time Corbott ever had to apologize to anybody.

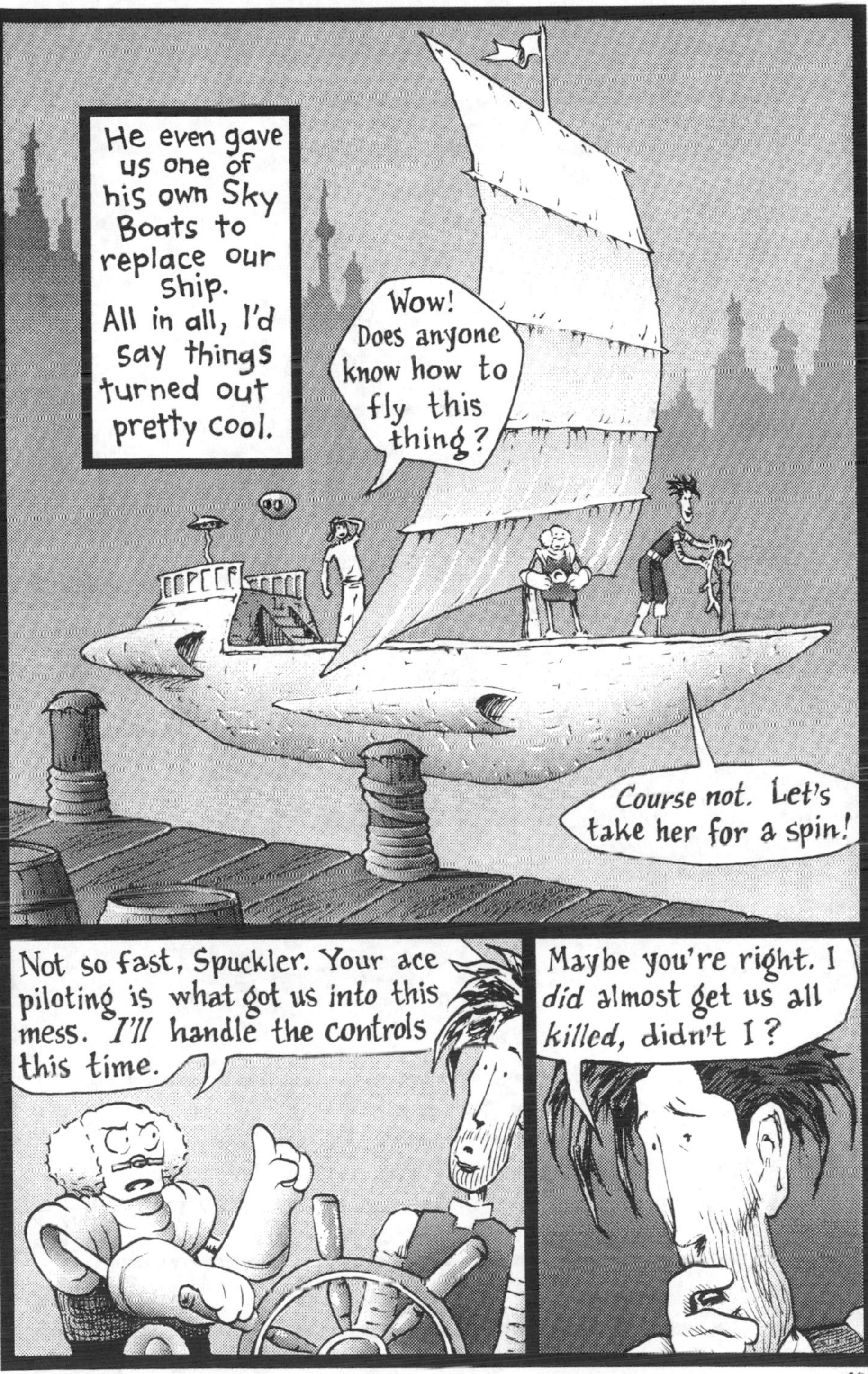
He even gave us one of his own Sky Boats to replace our ship. All in all, I'd say things turned out pretty cool.
Wow! Does anyone know how to fly this thing?
Course not. Let's take her for a spin!
Not so fast, Spuckler. Your ace piloting is what got us into this mess. *I'll* handle the controls this time.
Maybe you're right. I *did* almost get us all *killed*, didn't I?

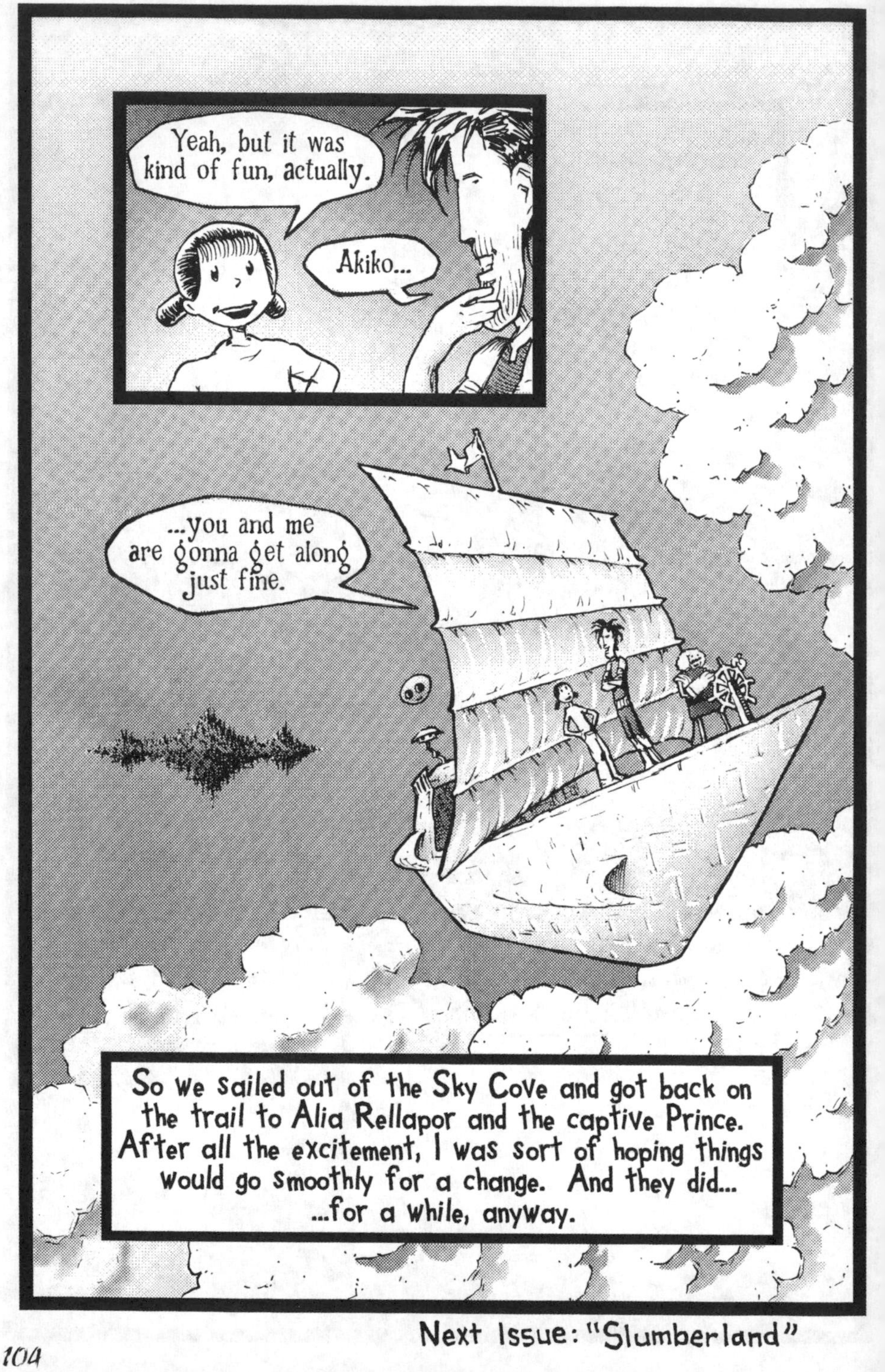
Yeah, but it was kind of fun, actually.
Akiko...
...you and me are gonna get along just fine.
So we sailed out of the Sky Cove and got back on the trail to Alia Rellapor and the captive Prince. After all the excitement, I was sort of hoping things would go smoothly for a change. And they did...
...for a while, anyway.

Next Issue: "Slumberland"

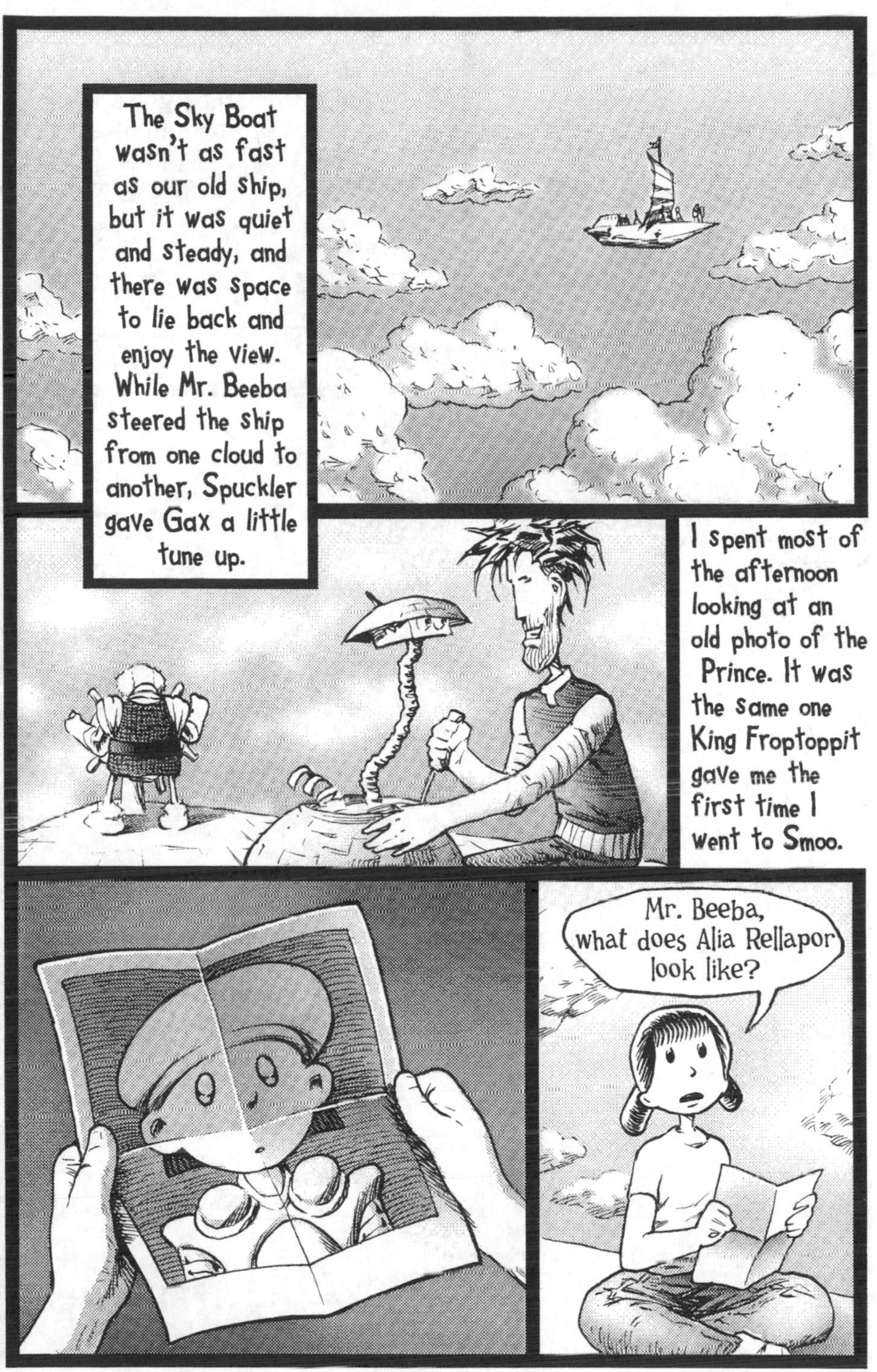
The Sky Boat wasn't as fast as our old ship, but it was quiet and steady, and there was space to lie back and enjoy the view. While Mr. Beeba steered the ship from one cloud to another, Spuckler gave Gax a little tune up.
I spent most of the afternoon looking at an old photo of the Prince. It was the same one King Froptoppit gave me the first time I went to Smoo.
Mr. Beeba, what does Alia Rellapor look like?

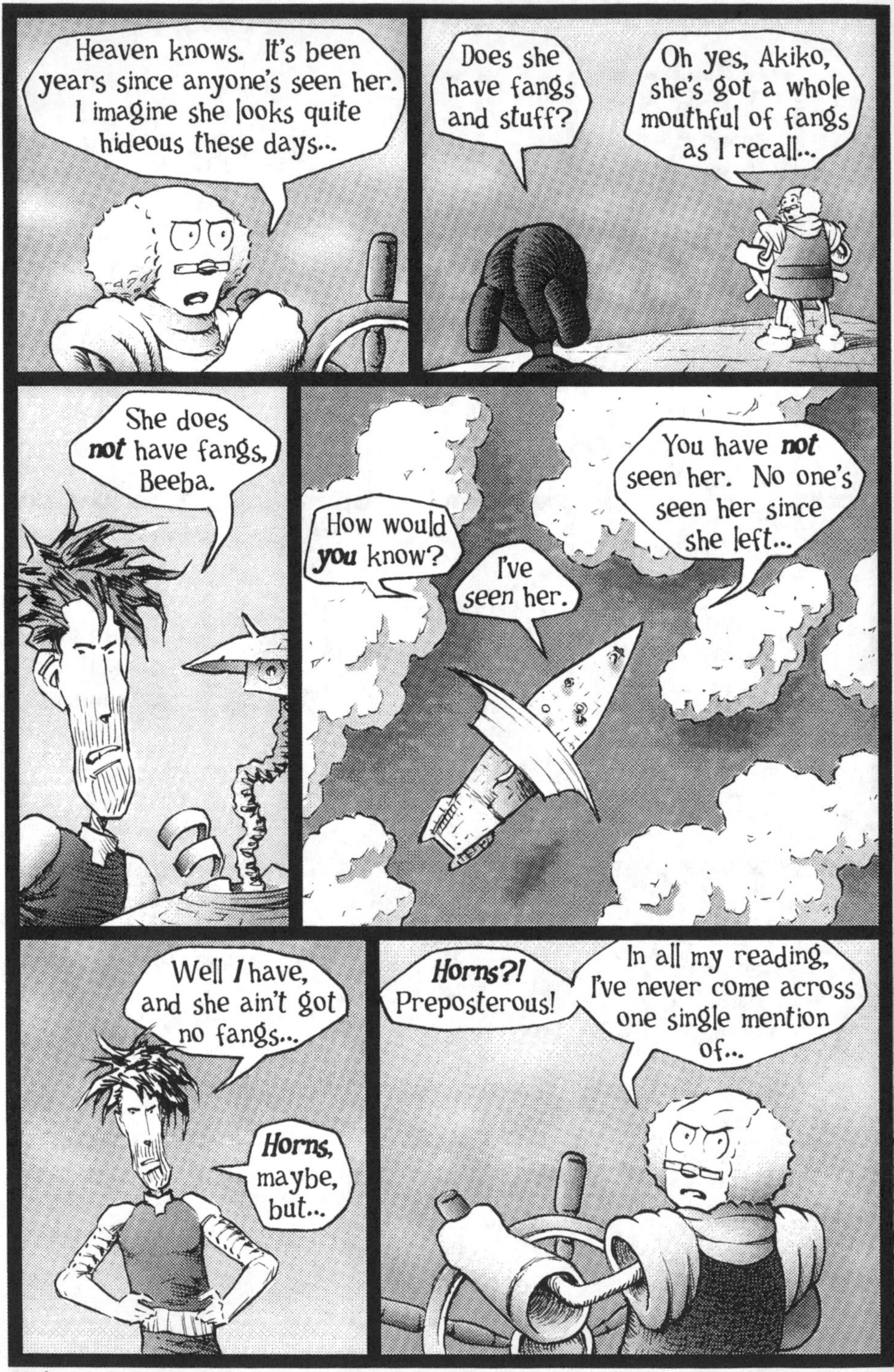
Heaven knows. It's been years since anyone's seen her. I imagine she looks quite hideous these days...
Does she have fangs and stuff?
Oh yes, Akiko, she's got a whole mouthful of fangs as I recall...
She does *not* have fangs, Beeba.
How would *you* know?
I've *seen* her.
You have *not* seen her. No one's seen her since she left...
Well *I* have, and she ain't got no fangs...
Horns, maybe, but...
Horns?! Preposterous!
In all my reading, I've never come across one single mention of...

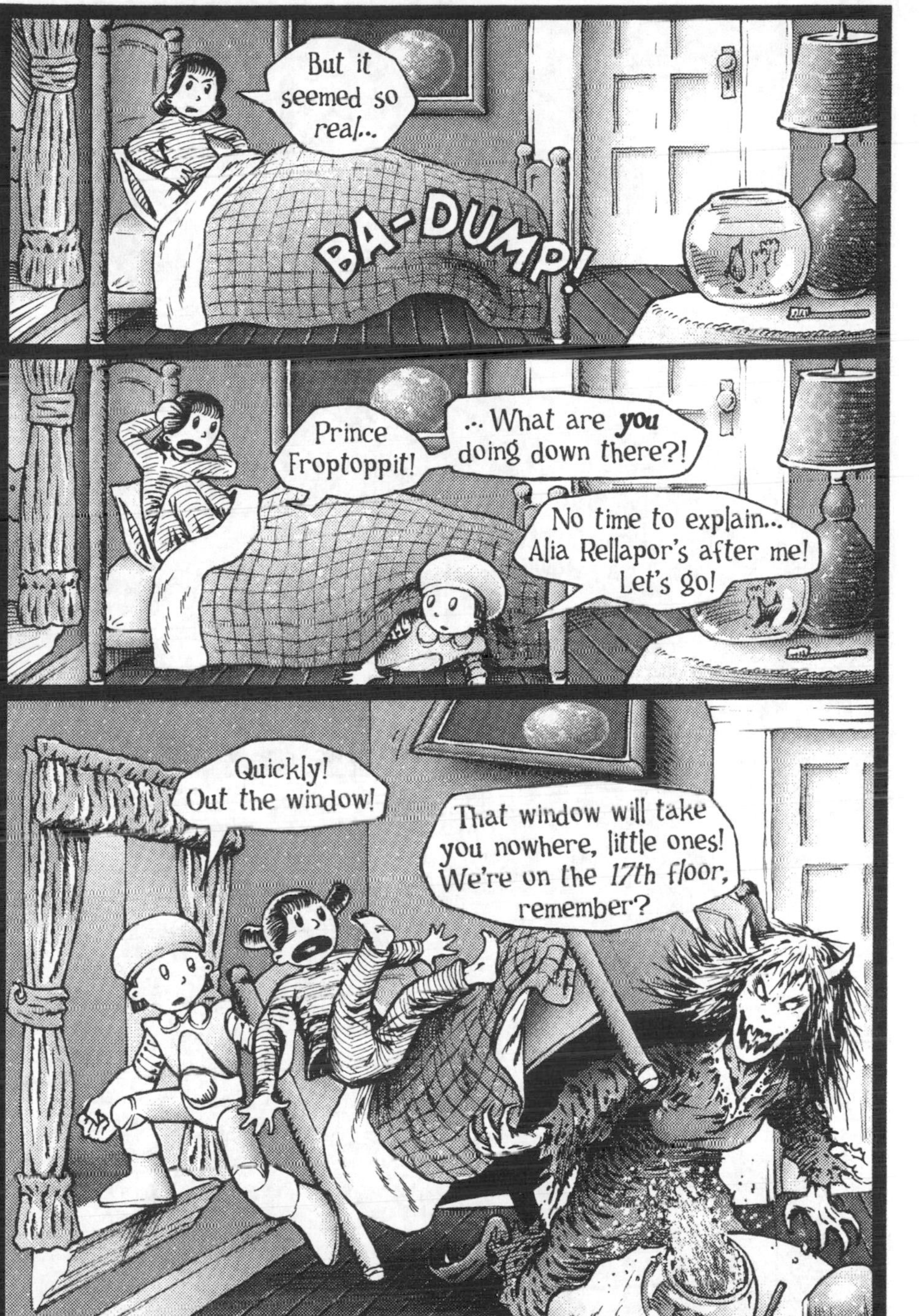
But it seemed so real...
BA-DUMP!
Prince Froptoppit!
... What are you doing down there?!
No time to explain... Alia Rellapor's after me! Let's go!
Quickly! Out the window!
That window will take you nowhere, little ones! We're on the 17th floor, remember?

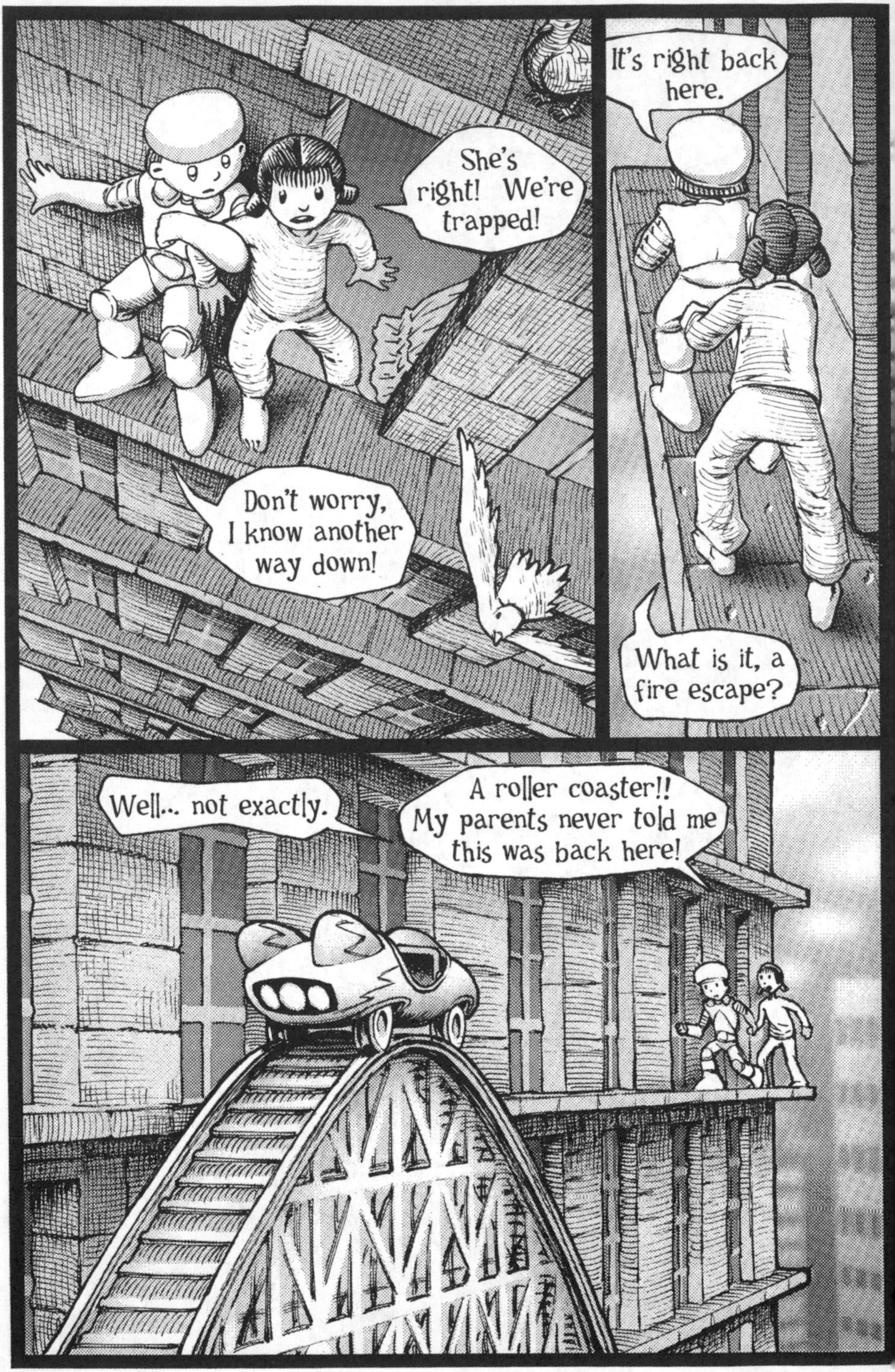
She's right! We're trapped!
Don't worry, I know another way down!
It's right back here.
What is it, a fire escape?
Well... not exactly.
A roller coaster!! My parents never told me this was back here!

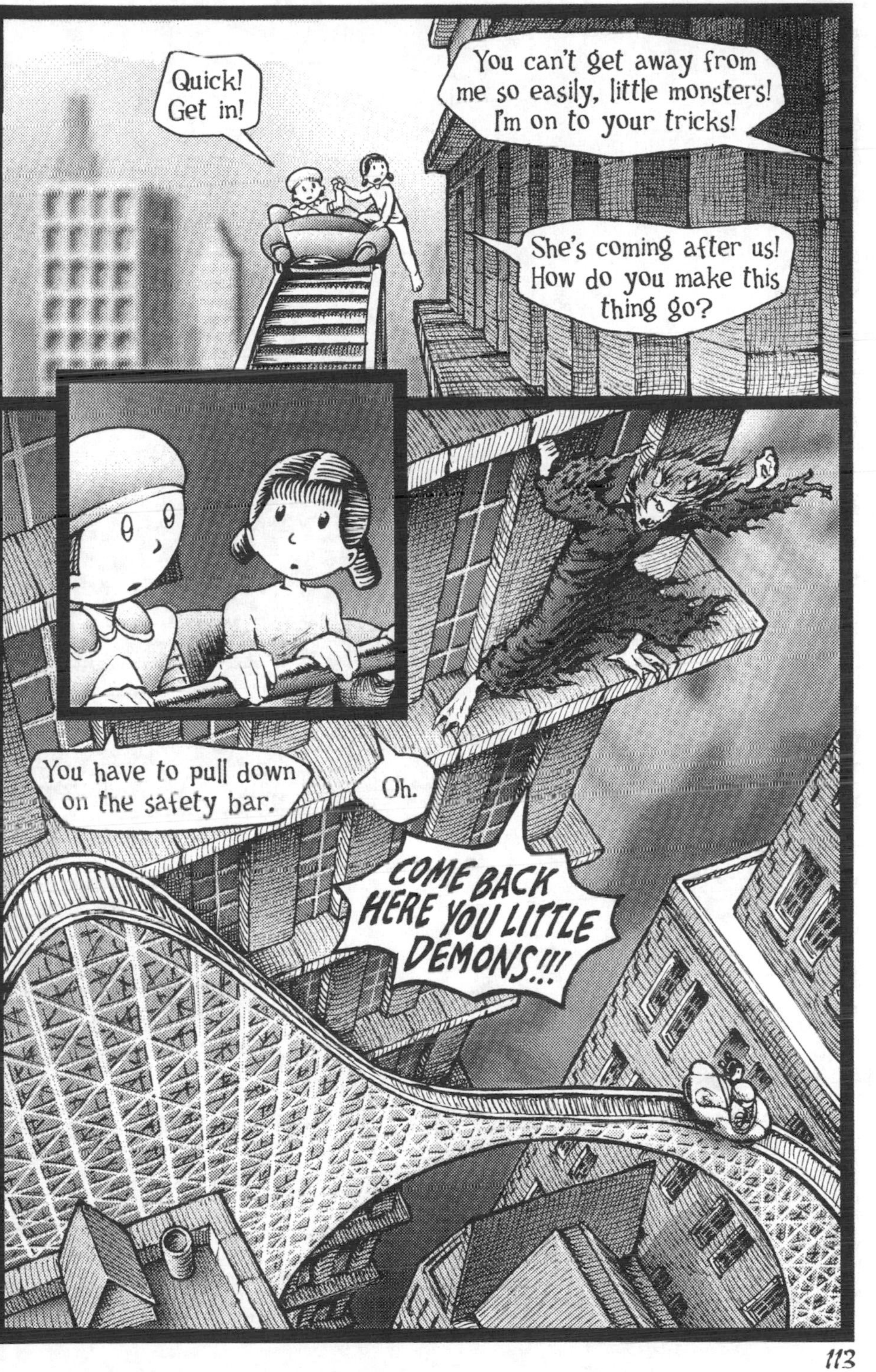
Quick! Get in!
You can't get away from me so easily, little monsters! I'm on to your tricks!
She's coming after us! How do you make this thing go?
You have to pull down on the safety bar.
Oh.
COME BACK HERE YOU LITTLE DEMONS!!!

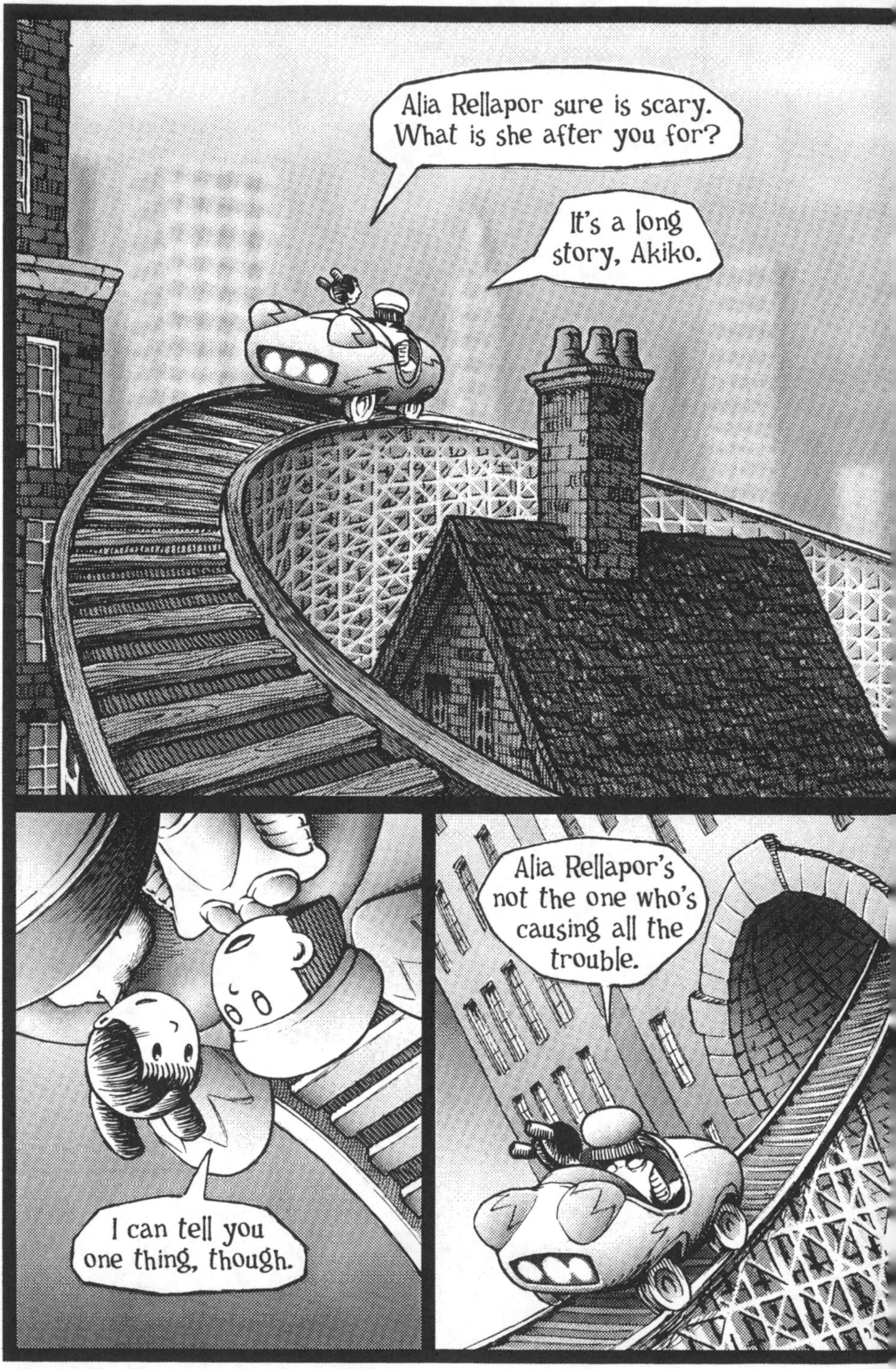
Alia Rellapor sure is scary. What is she after you for?
It's a long story, Akiko.
I can tell you one thing, though.
Alia Rellapor's not the one who's causing all the trouble.

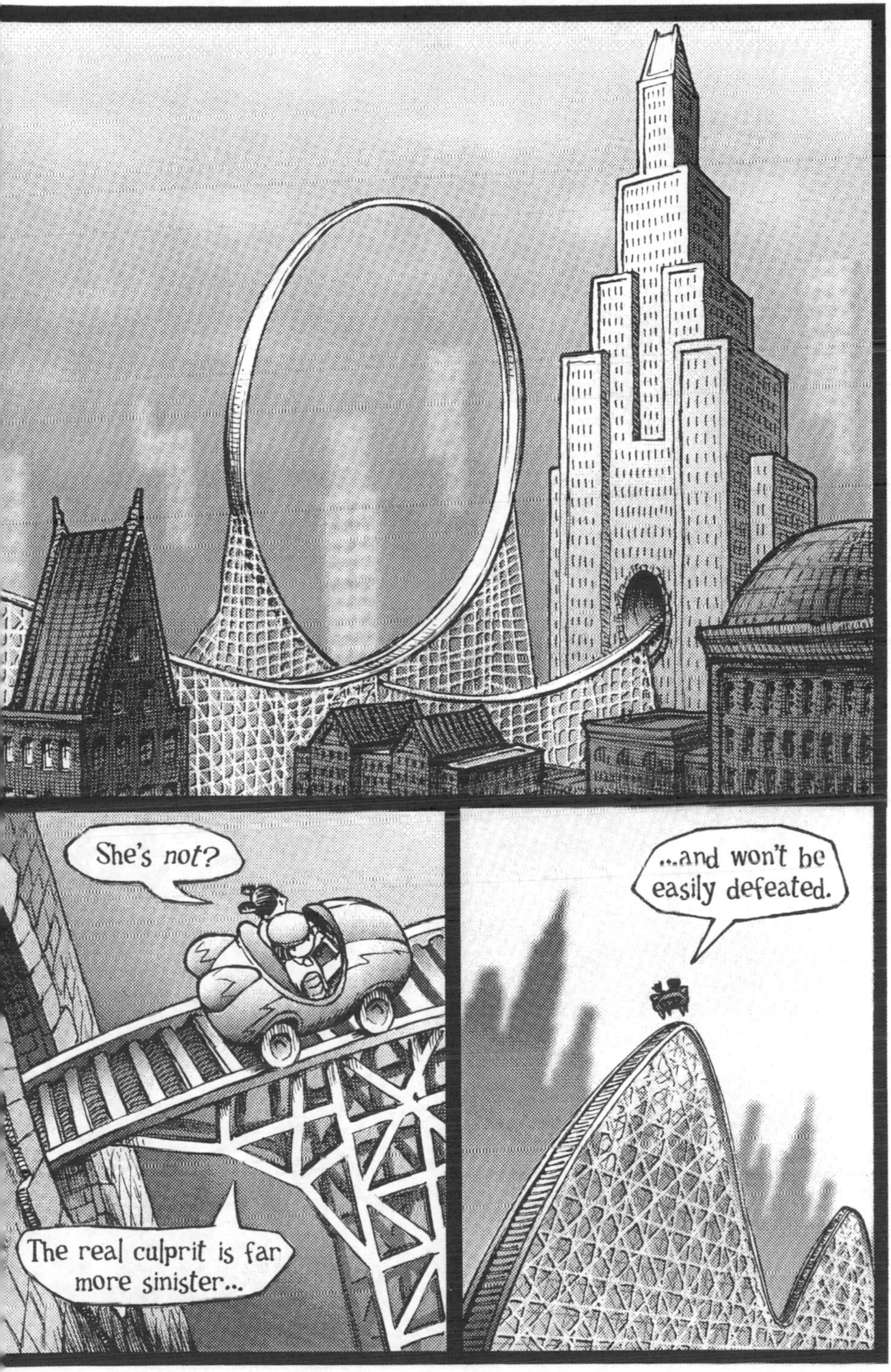
She's *not?*
The real culprit is far more sinister...
...and won't be easily defeated.

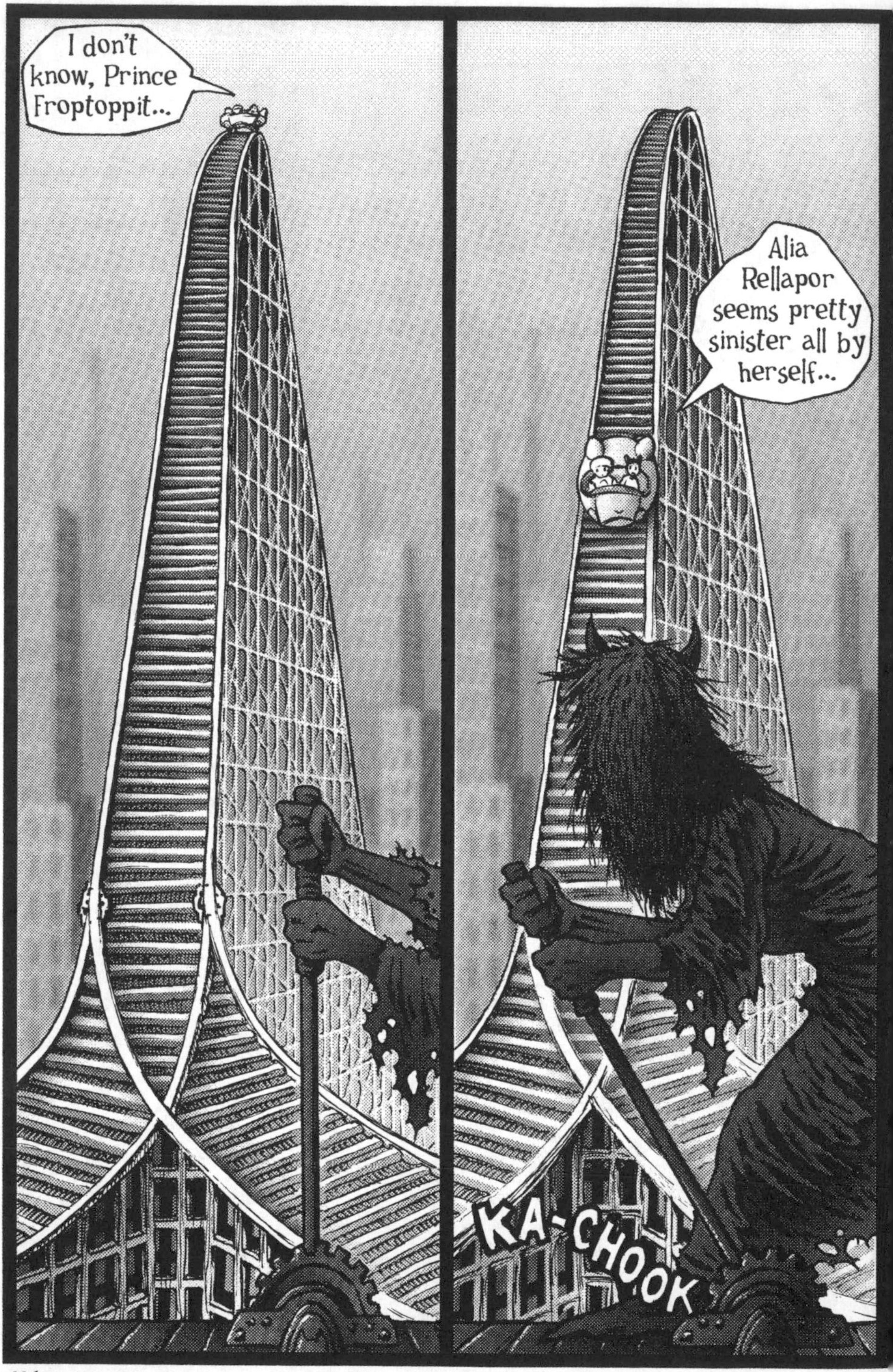
I don't know, Prince Froptoppit...
Alia Rellapor seems pretty sinister all by herself...
KA-CHOOK

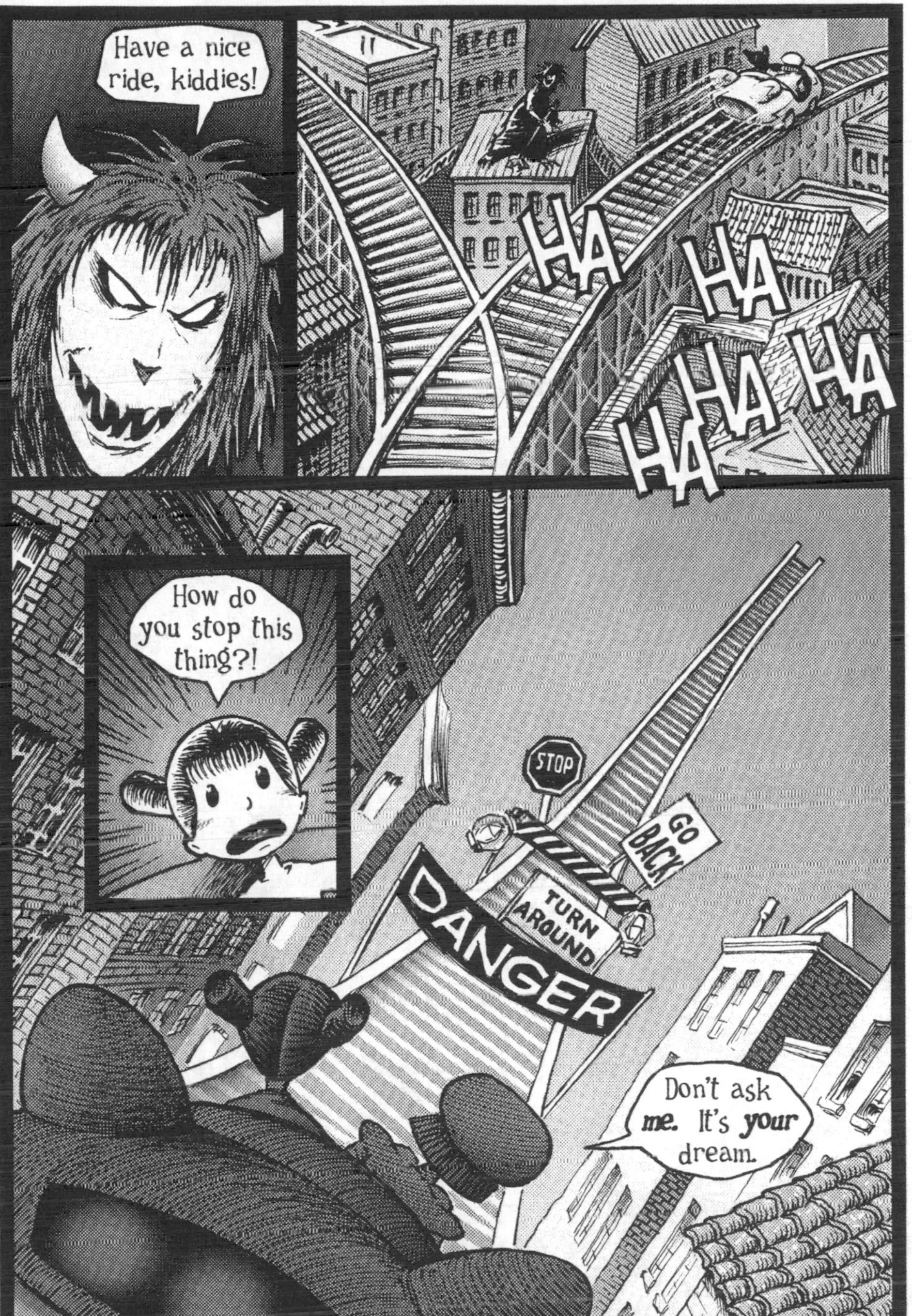
Have a nice ride, kiddies!
HA HA HA HA HA HA
How do you stop this thing?!
STOP
GO BACK
TURN AROUND
DANGER
Don't ask **me.** It's ***your*** dream.

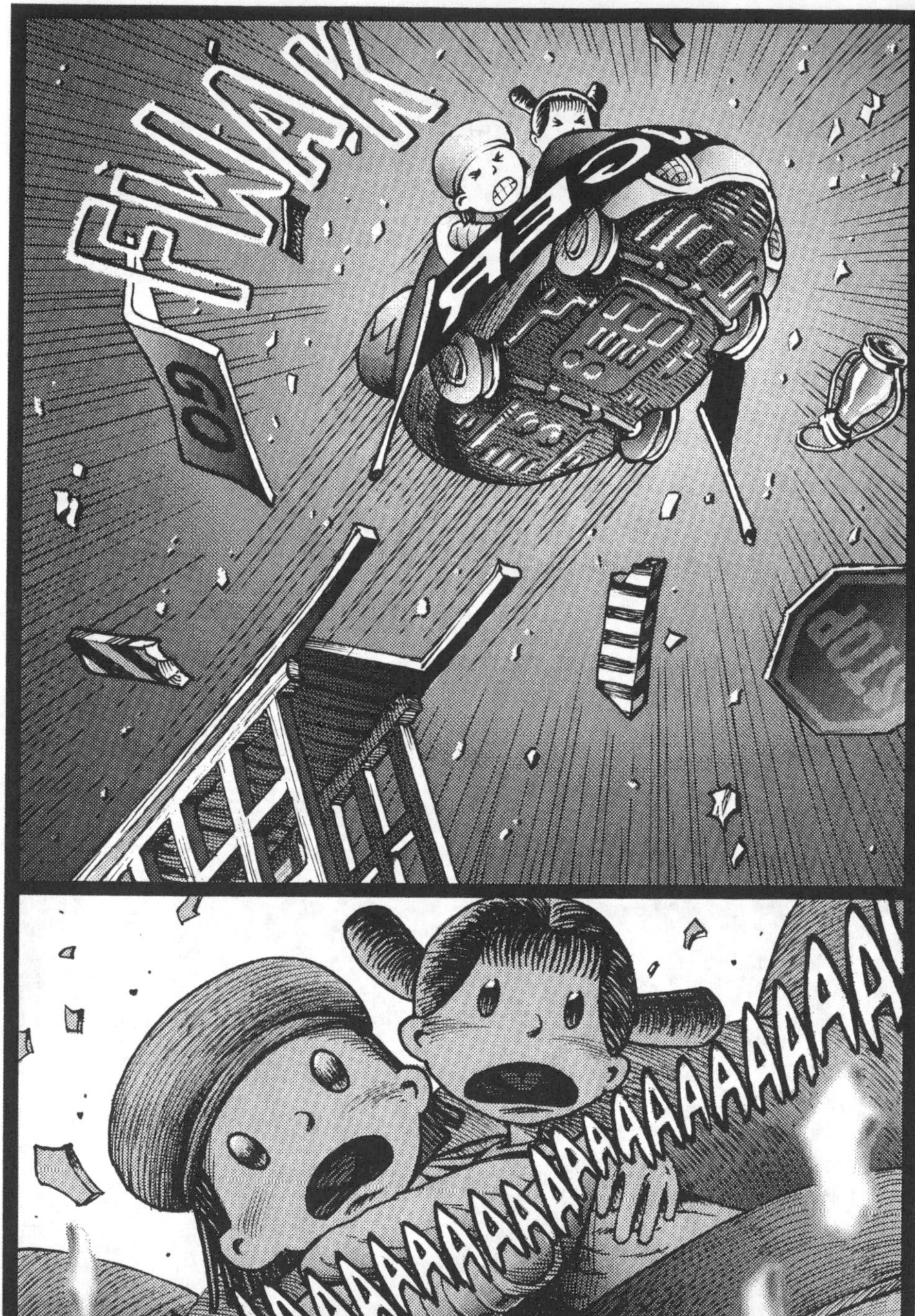
FWAK
GO
WAAAAAAAAAAAAAAAAAAAAAAA

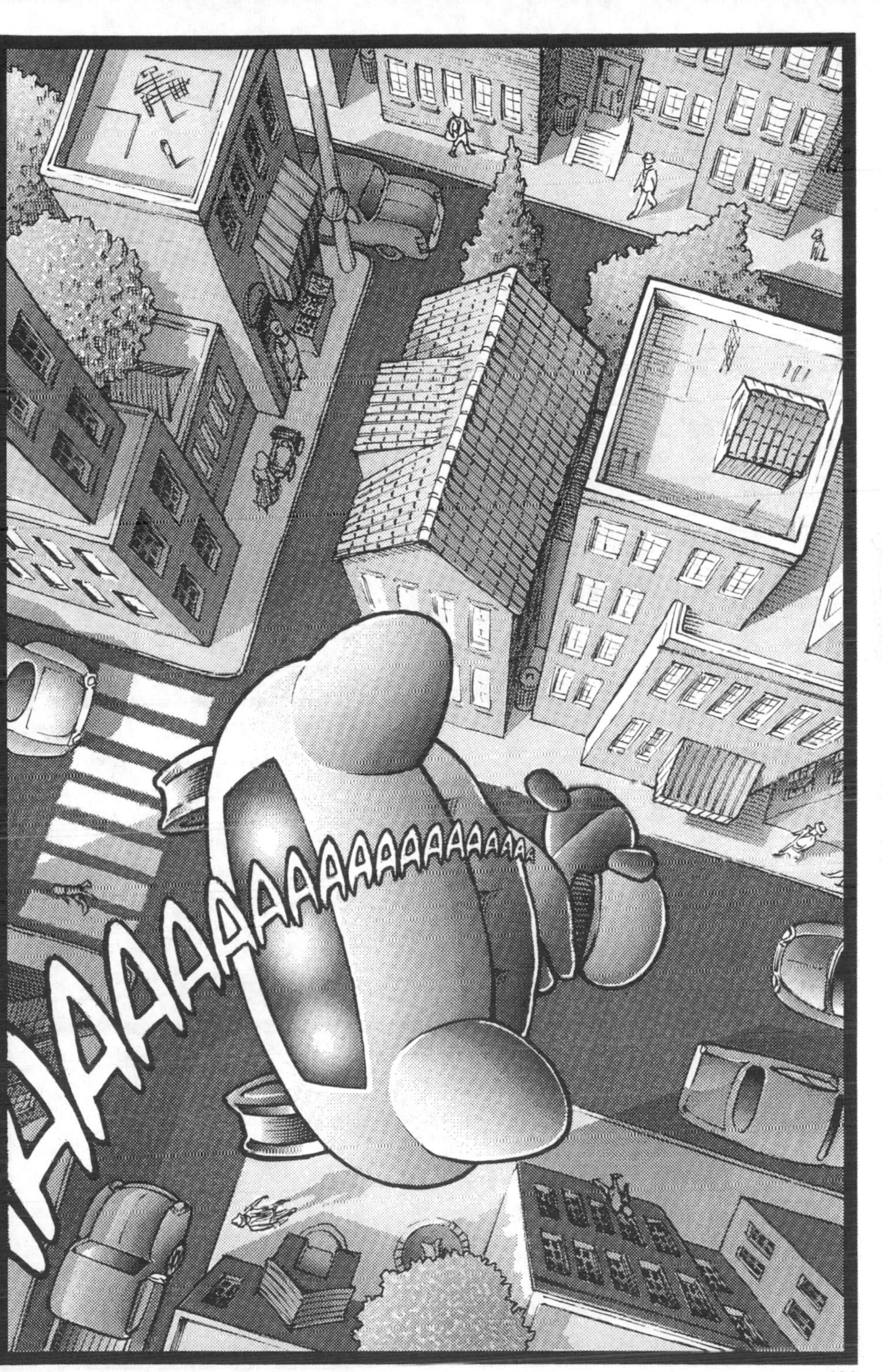
AAAAAAAAAAAAAAAAAAaaa

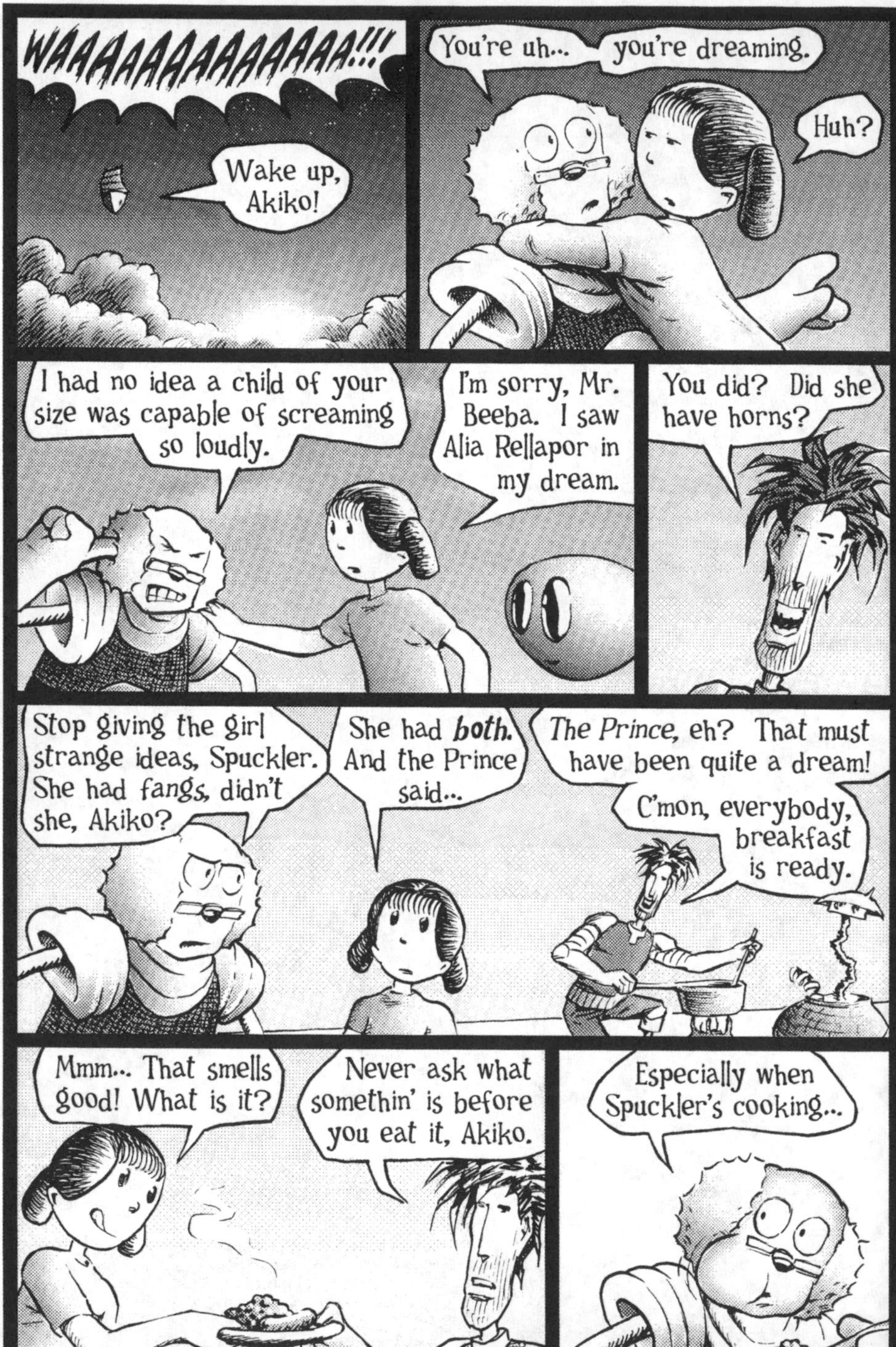
WAAAAAAAAAAAAAA!!!
Wake up, Akiko!
You're uh...
you're dreaming.
Huh?
I had no idea a child of your size was capable of screaming so loudly.
I'm sorry, Mr. Beeba. I saw Alia Rellapor in my dream.
You did? Did she have horns?
Stop giving the girl strange ideas, Spuckler. She had fangs, didn't she, Akiko?
She had both. And the Prince said...
The Prince, eh? That must have been quite a dream!
C'mon, everybody, breakfast is ready.
Mmm... That smells good! What is it?
Never ask what somethin' is before you eat it, Akiko.
Especially when Spuckler's cooking...

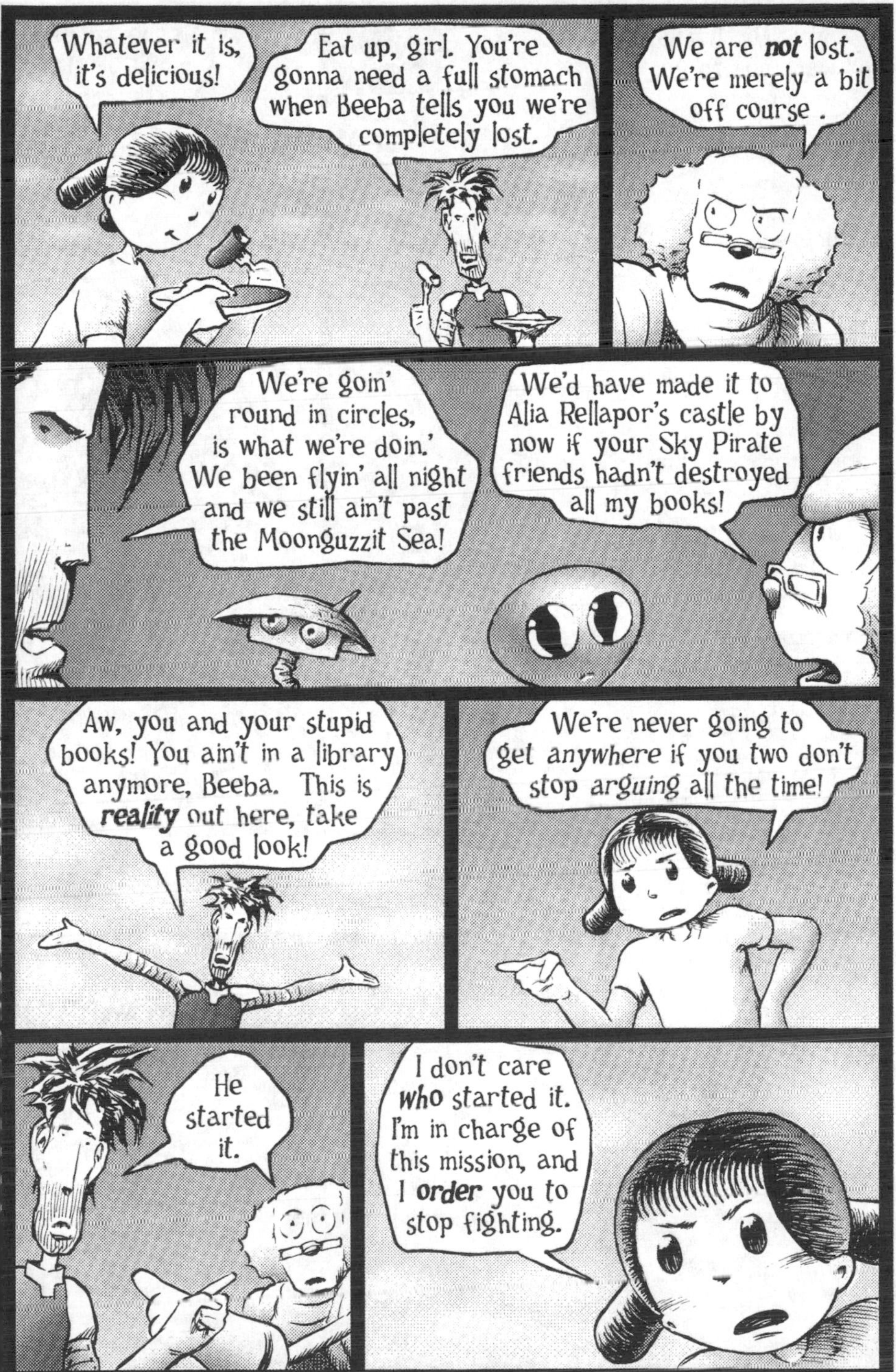
Whatever it is, it's delicious!
Eat up, girl. You're gonna need a full stomach when Beeba tells you we're completely lost.
We are **not** lost. We're merely a bit off course .
We're goin' round in circles, is what we're doin.' We been flyin' all night and we still ain't past the Moonguzzit Sea!
We'd have made it to Alia Rellapor's castle by now if your Sky Pirate friends hadn't destroyed all my books!
Aw, you and your stupid books! You ain't in a library anymore, Beeba. This is ***reality*** out here, take a good look!
We're never going to get *anywhere* if you two don't stop *arguing* all the time!
He started it.
I don't care **who** started it. I'm in charge of this mission, and I **order** you to stop fighting.

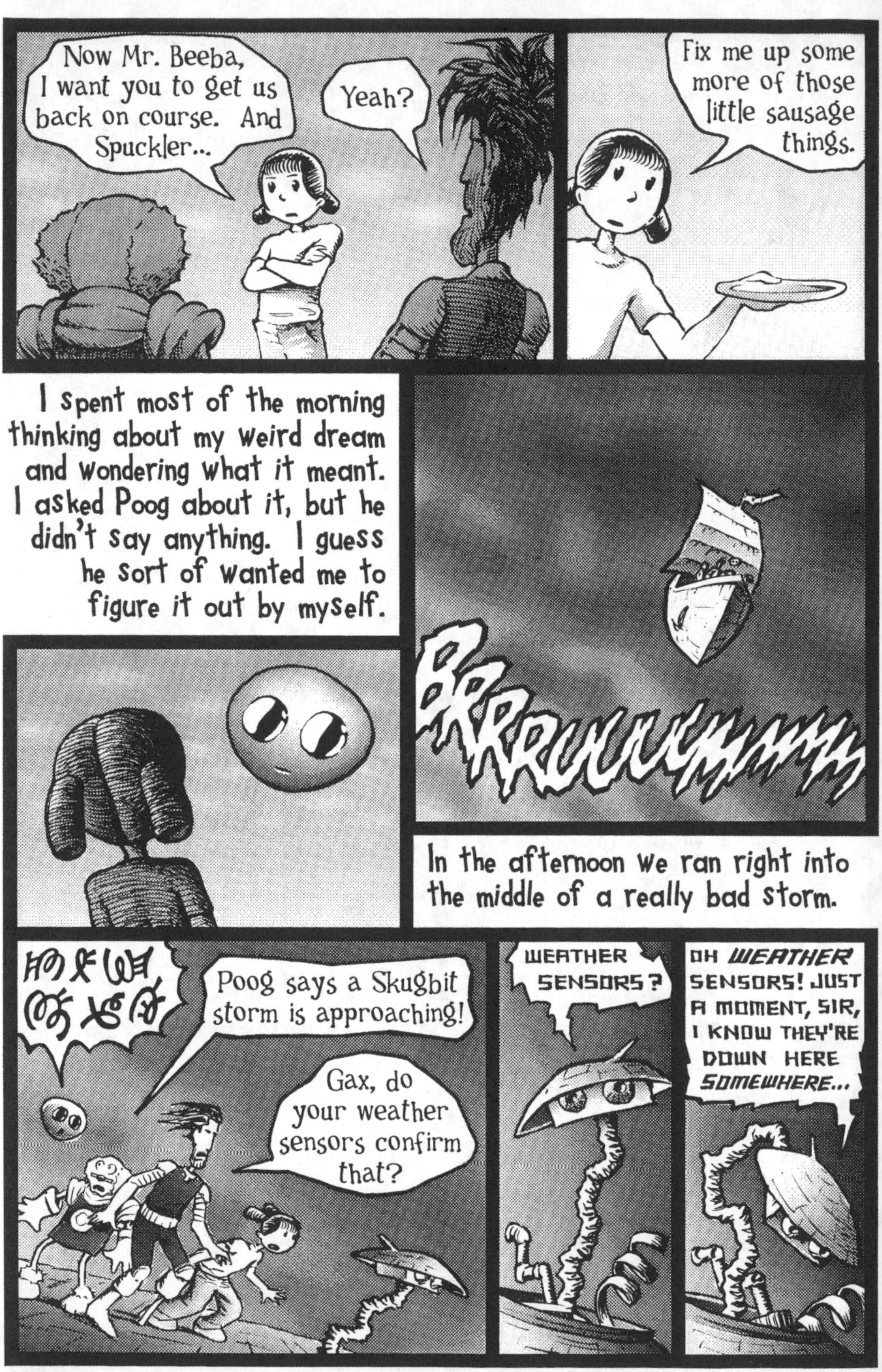
Now Mr. Beeba, I want you to get us back on course. And Spuckler...
Yeah?
Fix me up some more of those little sausage things.
I spent most of the morning thinking about my weird dream and wondering what it meant. I asked Poog about it, but he didn't say anything. I guess he sort of wanted me to figure it out by myself.
BRRRUUUMMMM
In the afternoon we ran right into the middle of a really bad storm.
Poog says a Skugbit storm is approaching!
Gax, do your weather sensors confirm that?
WEATHER SENSORS?
OH WEATHER SENSORS! JUST A MOMENT, SIR, I KNOW THEY'RE DOWN HERE SOMEWHERE...

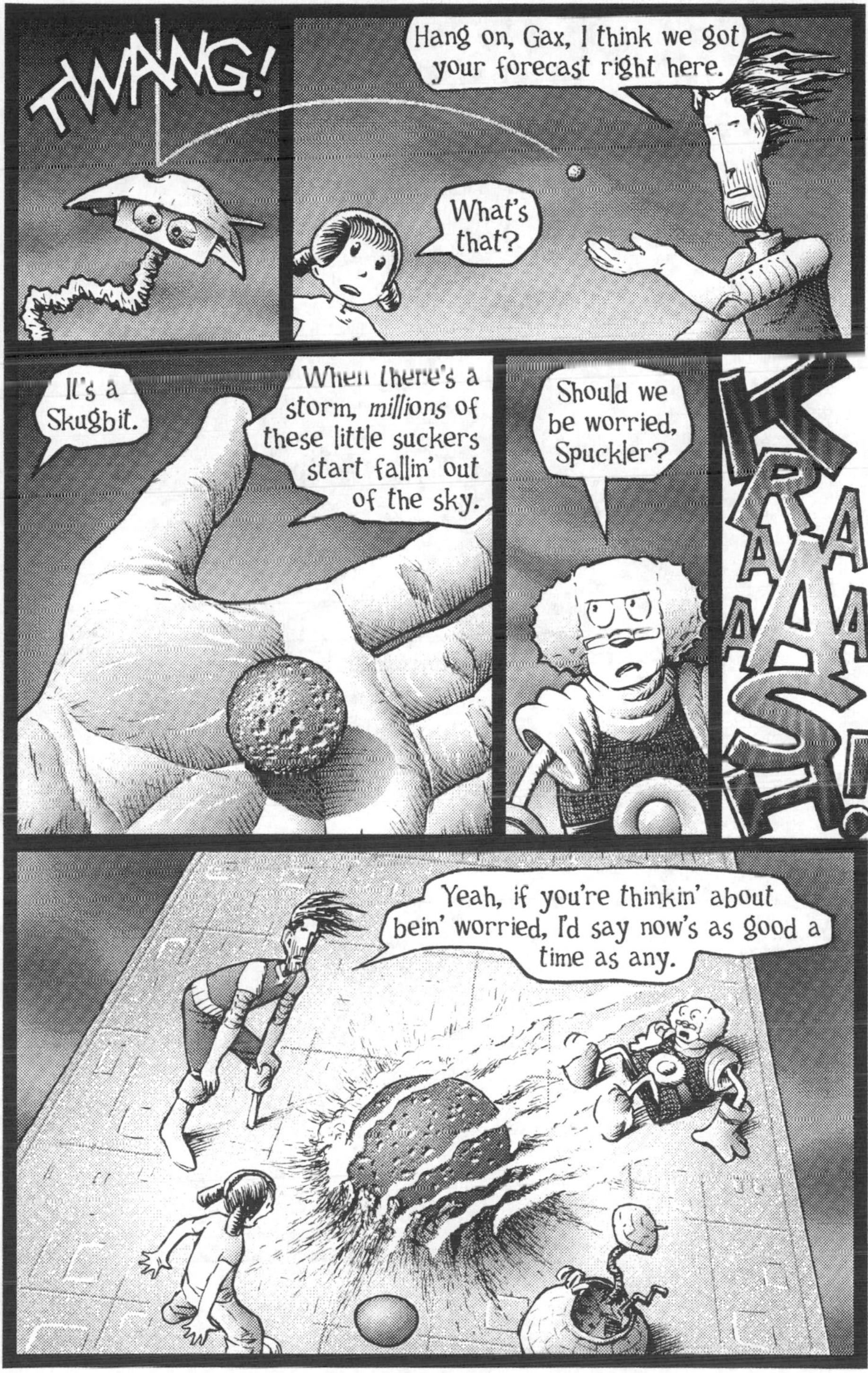
TWANG!
Hang on, Gax, I think we got your forecast right here.
What's that?
It's a Skugbit.
When there's a storm, *millions* of these little suckers start fallin' out of the sky.
Should we be worried, Spuckler?
KRAAAAASH!
Yeah, if you're thinkin' about bein' worried, I'd say now's as good a time as any.

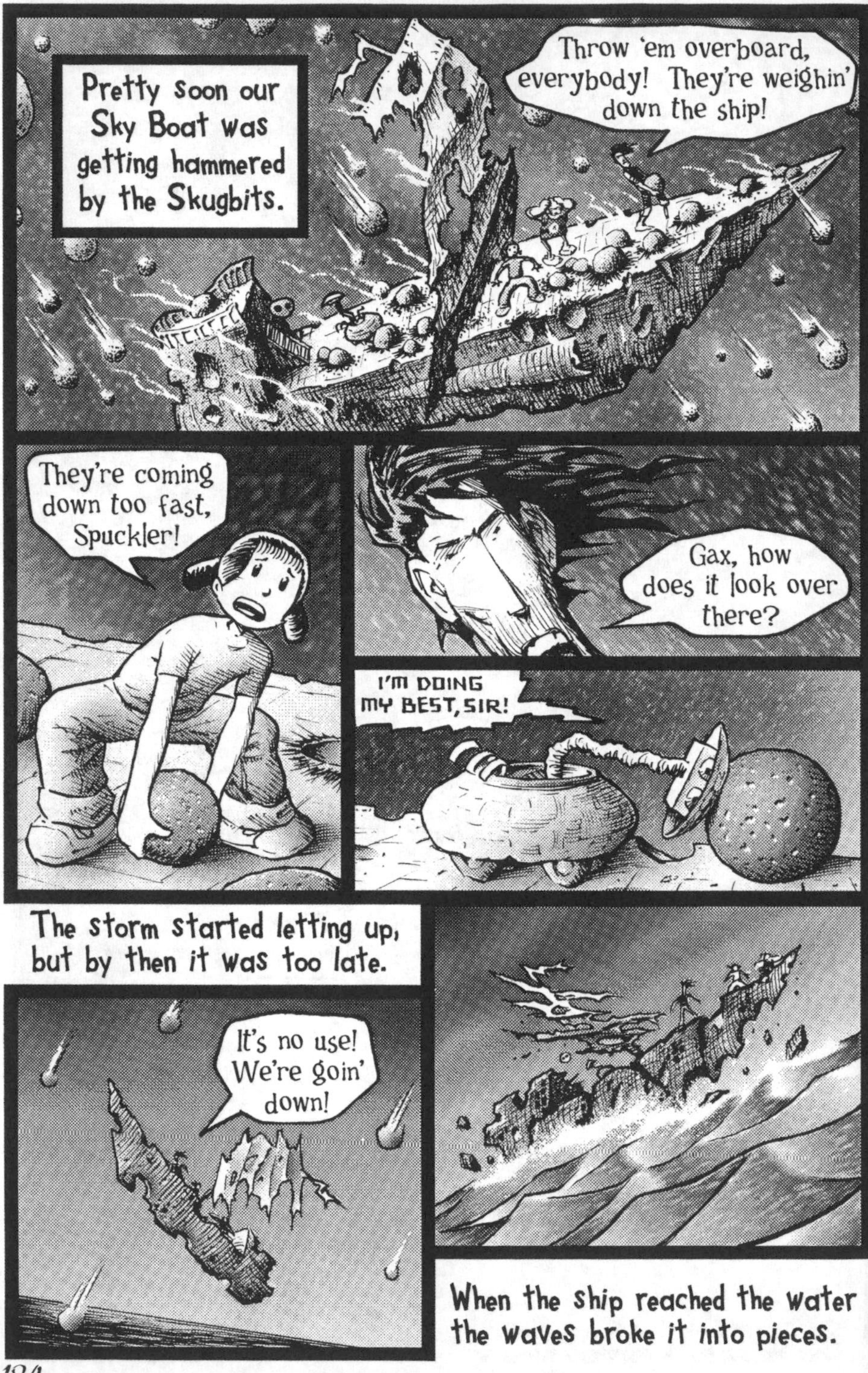
Pretty soon our Sky Boat was getting hammered by the Skugbits.
Throw 'em overboard, everybody! They're weighin' down the ship!
They're coming down too fast, Spuckler!
Gax, how does it look over there?
I'M DOING MY BEST, SIR!
The storm started letting up, but by then it was too late.
It's no use! We're goin' down!
When the ship reached the water the waves broke it into pieces.

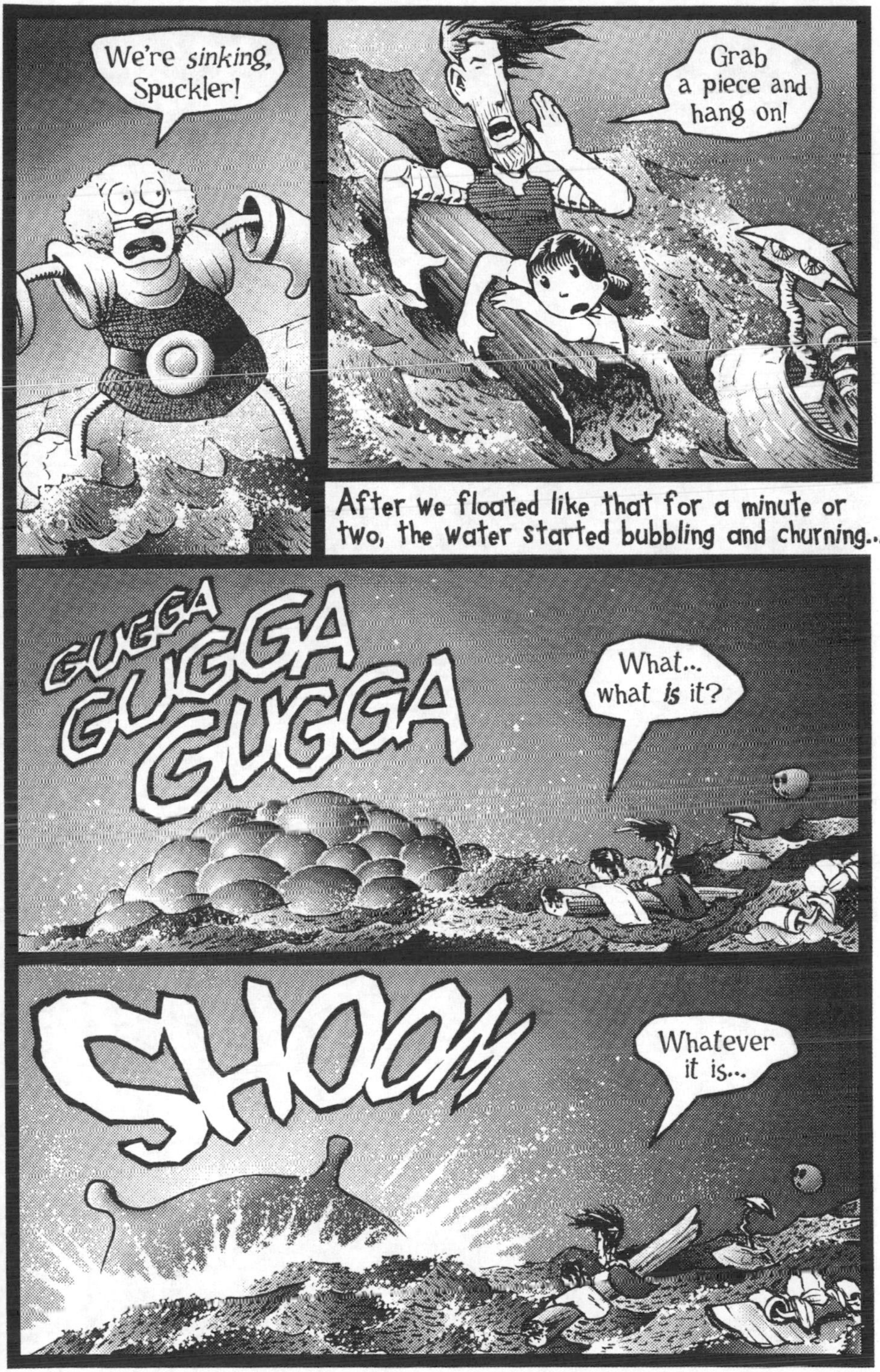
We're *sinking,* Spuckler!
Grab a piece and hang on!
After we floated like that for a minute or two, the water started bubbling and churning...
GUGGA GUGGA GUGGA
What... what *is* it?
SHOOM
Whatever it is...

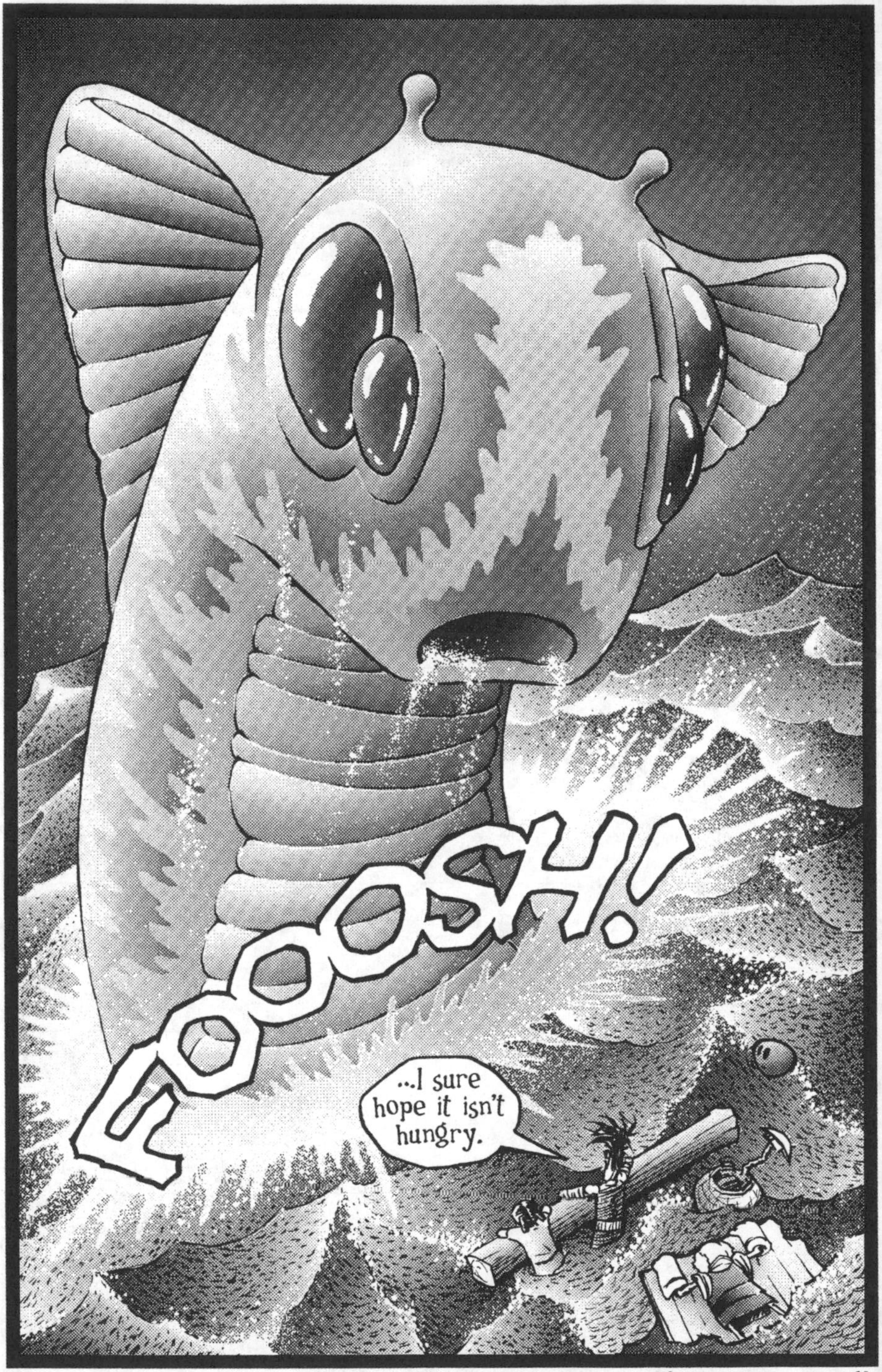
FOOOSH!
...I sure hope it isn't hungry.

Next Issue: "Inside Out"

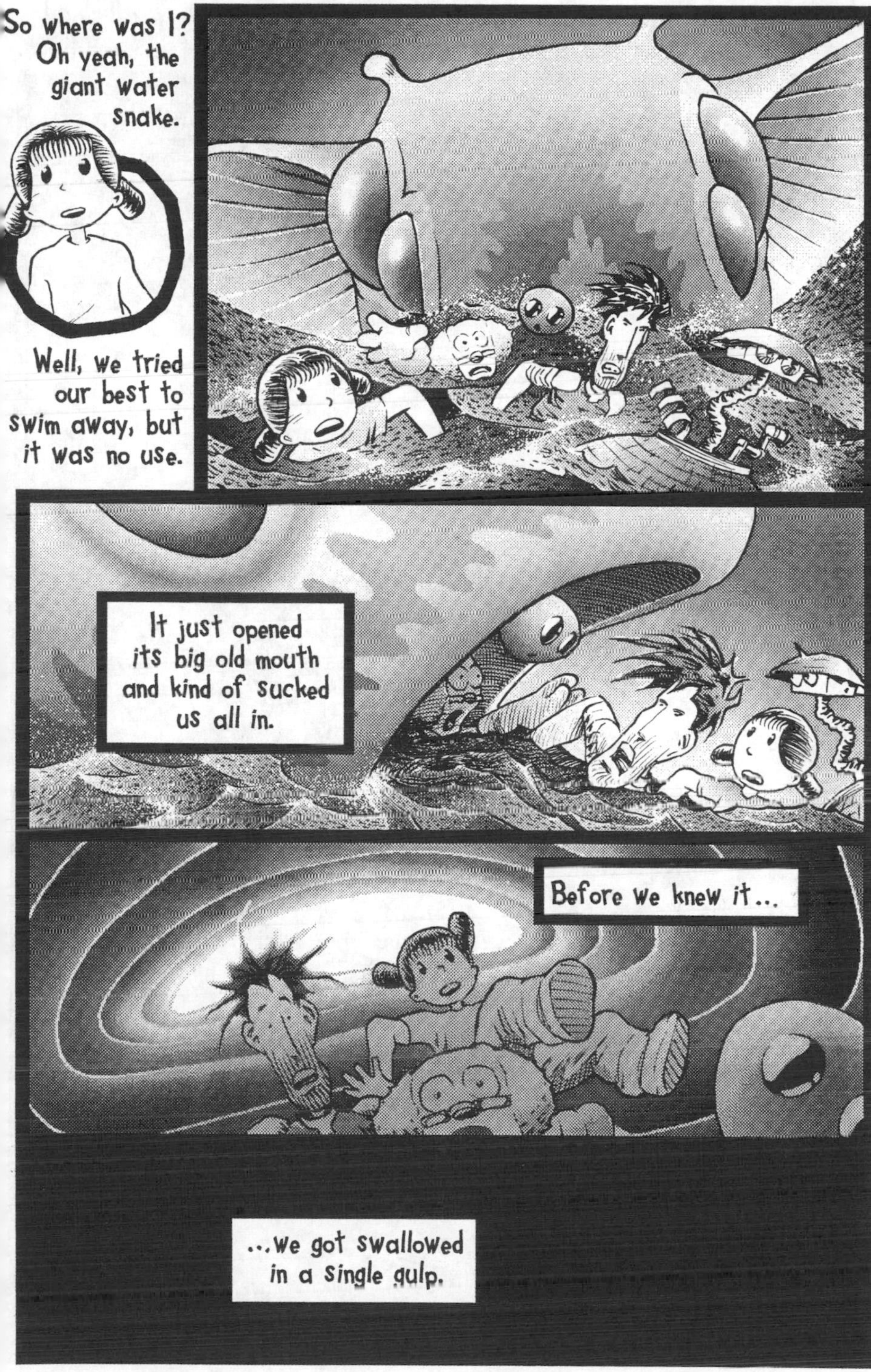
So where was I? Oh yeah, the giant water snake.
Well, we tried our best to swim away, but it was no use.
It just opened its big old mouth and kind of sucked us all in.
Before we knew it...
...we got swallowed in a single gulp.

A few minutes later, after I was almost certain we were all dead, there was a sudden flash of light just an inch or two from my face.

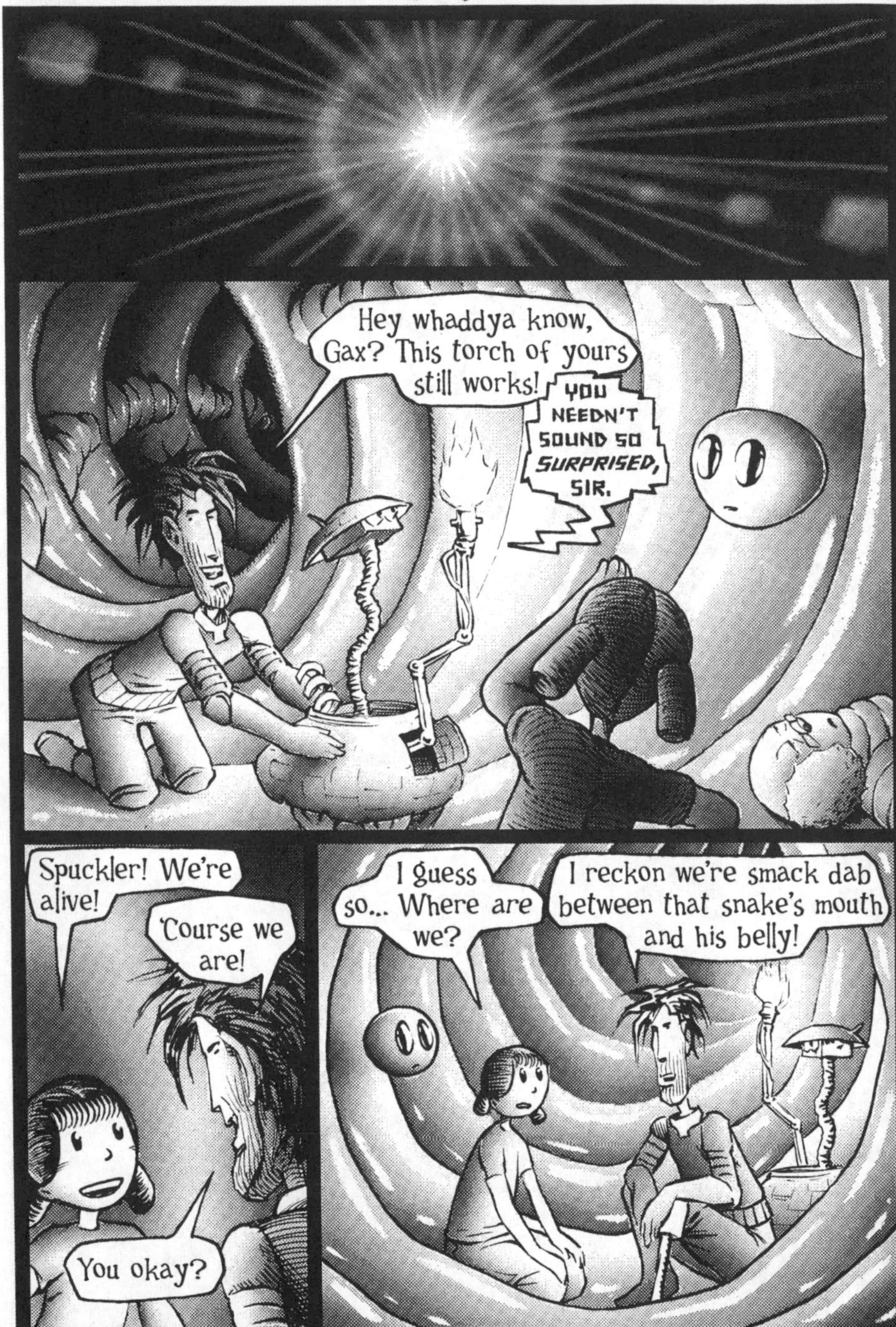
Hey whaddya know, Gax? This torch of yours still works!
YOU NEEDN'T SOUND SO SURPRISED, SIR.
Spuckler! We're alive!
'Course we are!
You okay?
I guess so... Where are we?
I reckon we're smack dab between that snake's mouth and his belly!

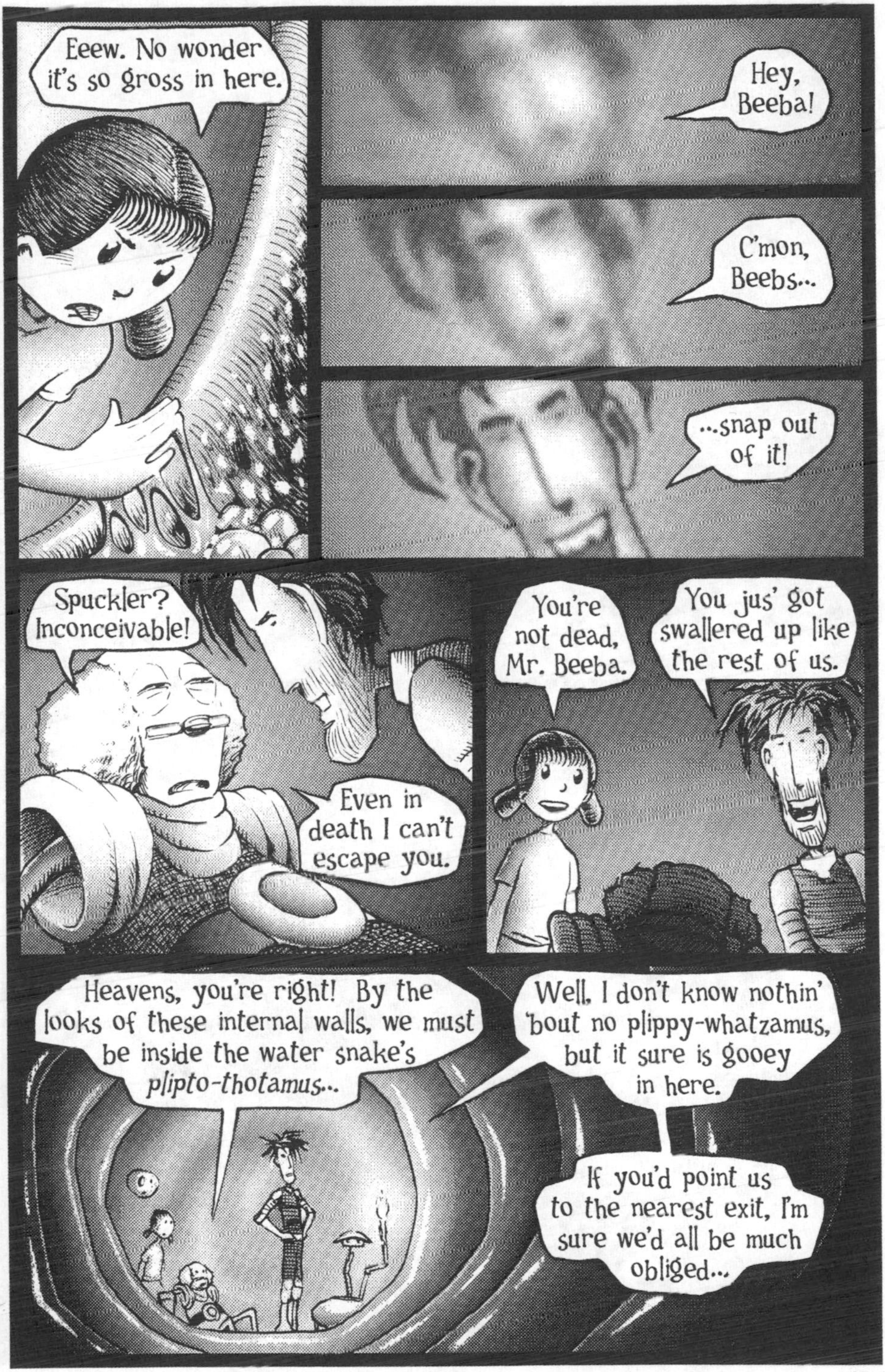
Eeew. No wonder it's so gross in here.
Hey, Beeba!
C'mon, Beebs...
...snap out of it!
Spuckler? Inconceivable!
Even in death I can't escape you.
You're not dead, Mr. Beeba.
You jus' got swallered up like the rest of us.
Heavens, you're right! By the looks of these internal walls, we must be inside the water snake's *plipto-thotamus*...
Well, I don't know nothin' 'bout no plippy-whatzamus, but it sure is gooey in here.
If you'd point us to the nearest exit, I'm sure we'd all be much obliged...

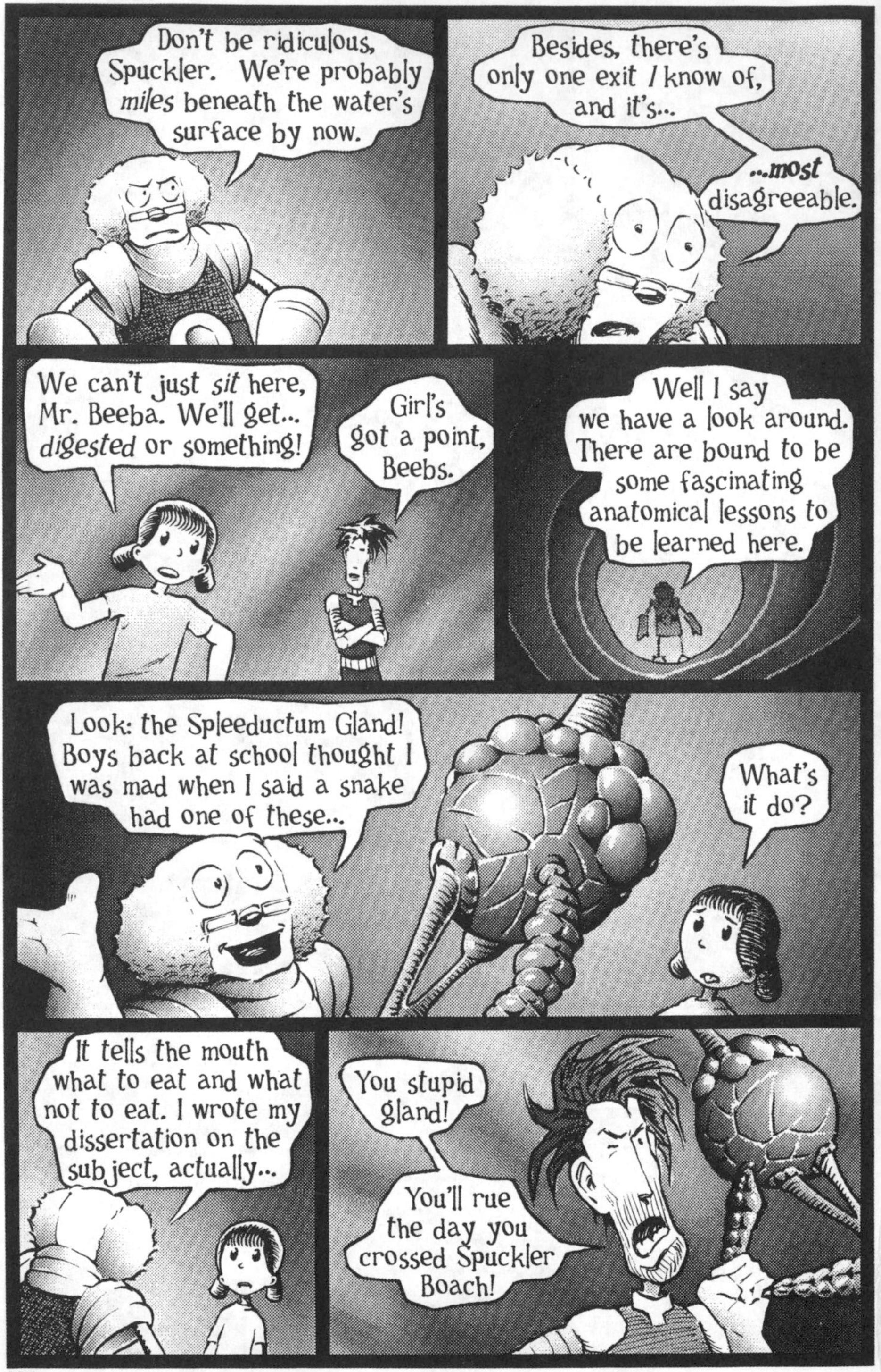
Don't be ridiculous, Spuckler. We're probably miles beneath the water's surface by now.
Besides, there's only one exit I know of, and it's...
...most disagreeable.
We can't just sit here, Mr. Beeba. We'll get... digested or something!
Girl's got a point, Beebs.
Well I say we have a look around. There are bound to be some fascinating anatomical lessons to be learned here.
Look: the Spleeductum Gland! Boys back at school thought I was mad when I said a snake had one of these...
What's it do?
It tells the mouth what to eat and what not to eat. I wrote my dissertation on the subject, actually...
You stupid gland!
You'll rue the day you crossed Spuckler Boach!

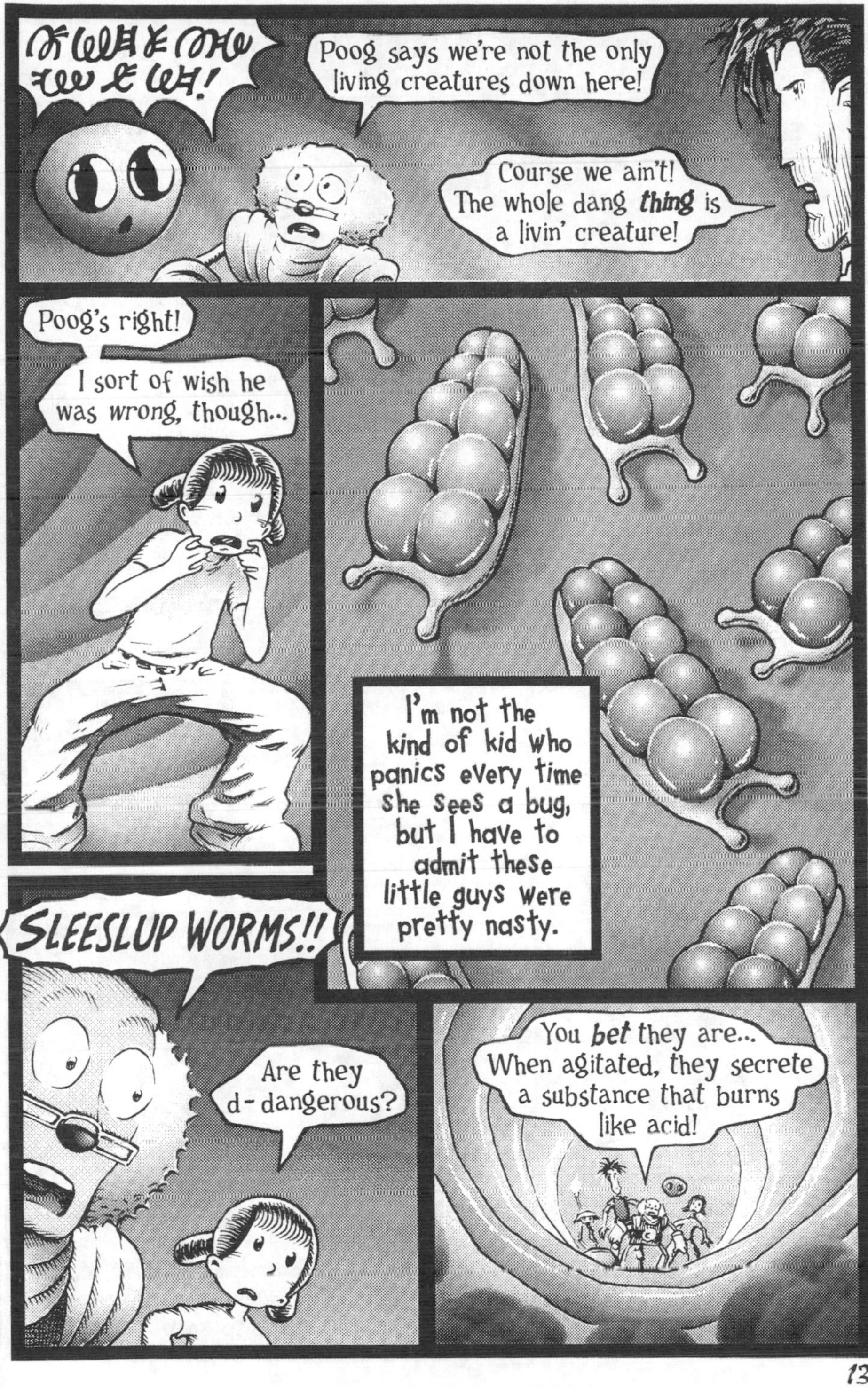
Poog says we're not the only living creatures down here!
Course we ain't! The whole dang *thing* is a livin' creature!
Poog's right!
I sort of wish he was *wrong*, though...
I'm not the kind of kid who panics every time she sees a bug, but I have to admit these little guys were pretty nasty.
SLEESLUP WORMS!!
Are they d-dangerous?
You *bet* they are... When agitated, they secrete a substance that burns like acid!

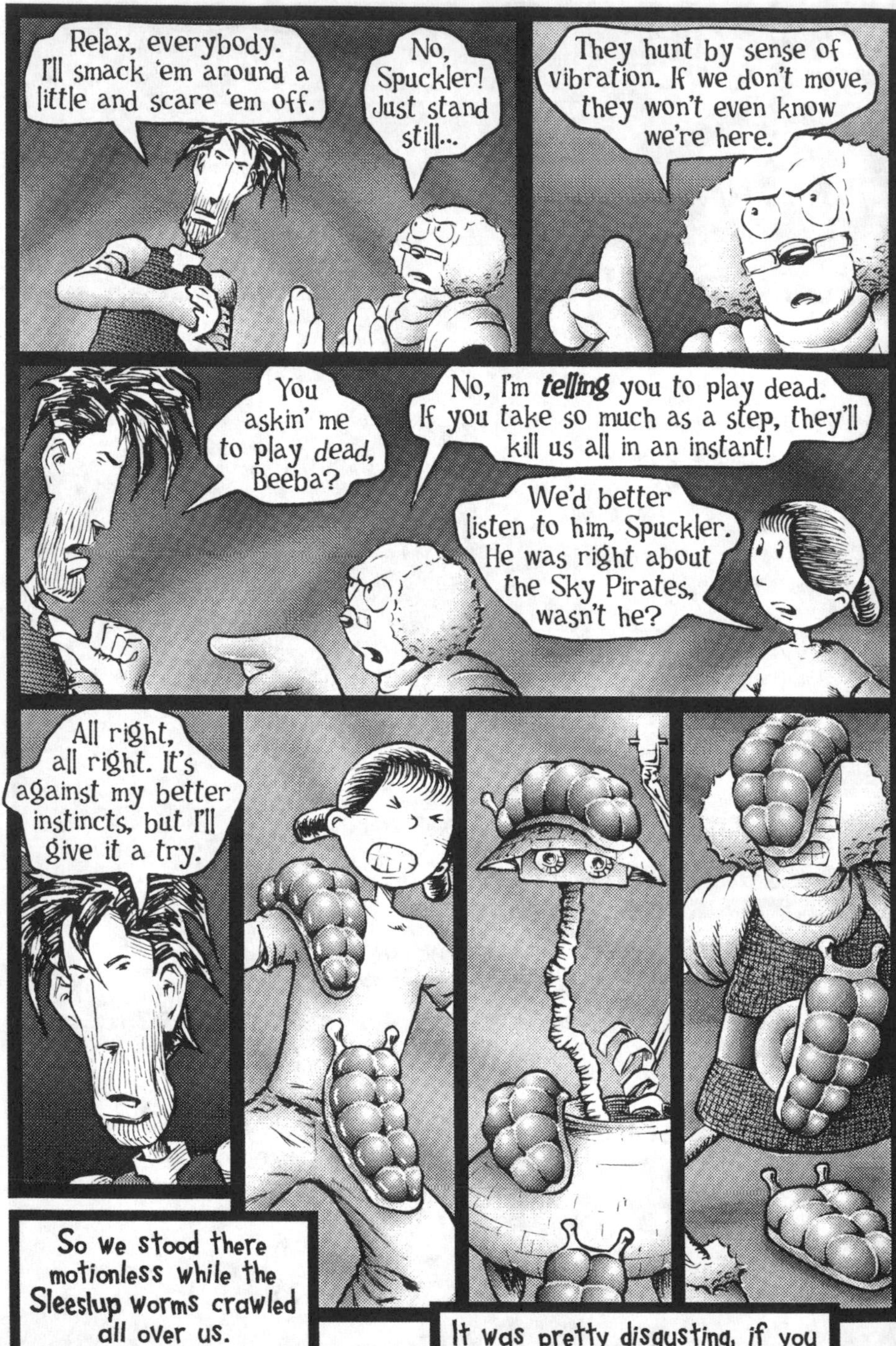
Relax, everybody. I'll smack 'em around a little and scare 'em off.
No, Spuckler! Just stand still...
They hunt by sense of vibration. If we don't move, they won't even know we're here.
You askin' me to play *dead,* Beeba?
No, I'm ***telling*** you to play dead. If you take so much as a step, they'll kill us all in an instant!
We'd better listen to him, Spuckler. He was right about the Sky Pirates, wasn't he?
All right, all right. It's against my better instincts, but I'll give it a try.
So we stood there motionless while the Sleeslup worms crawled all over us.
It was pretty disgusting, if you really want to know.

They never got anywhere *near* Poog. That's one of the advantages of being able to float.

Spuckler managed to control himself for once. Another minute or two and they'd have passed us by altogether.

AH AH AH

The only problem was Mr. Beeba was sort of allergic to worms.

Don't even *think* about sneezin', Beeba, now that you got us into this!

Please, Mr. Beeba!

I'll *kill* you, Beeba, I swear I will!

AH AH AH AH AH HA AH AH HA AH AH AH AH AH

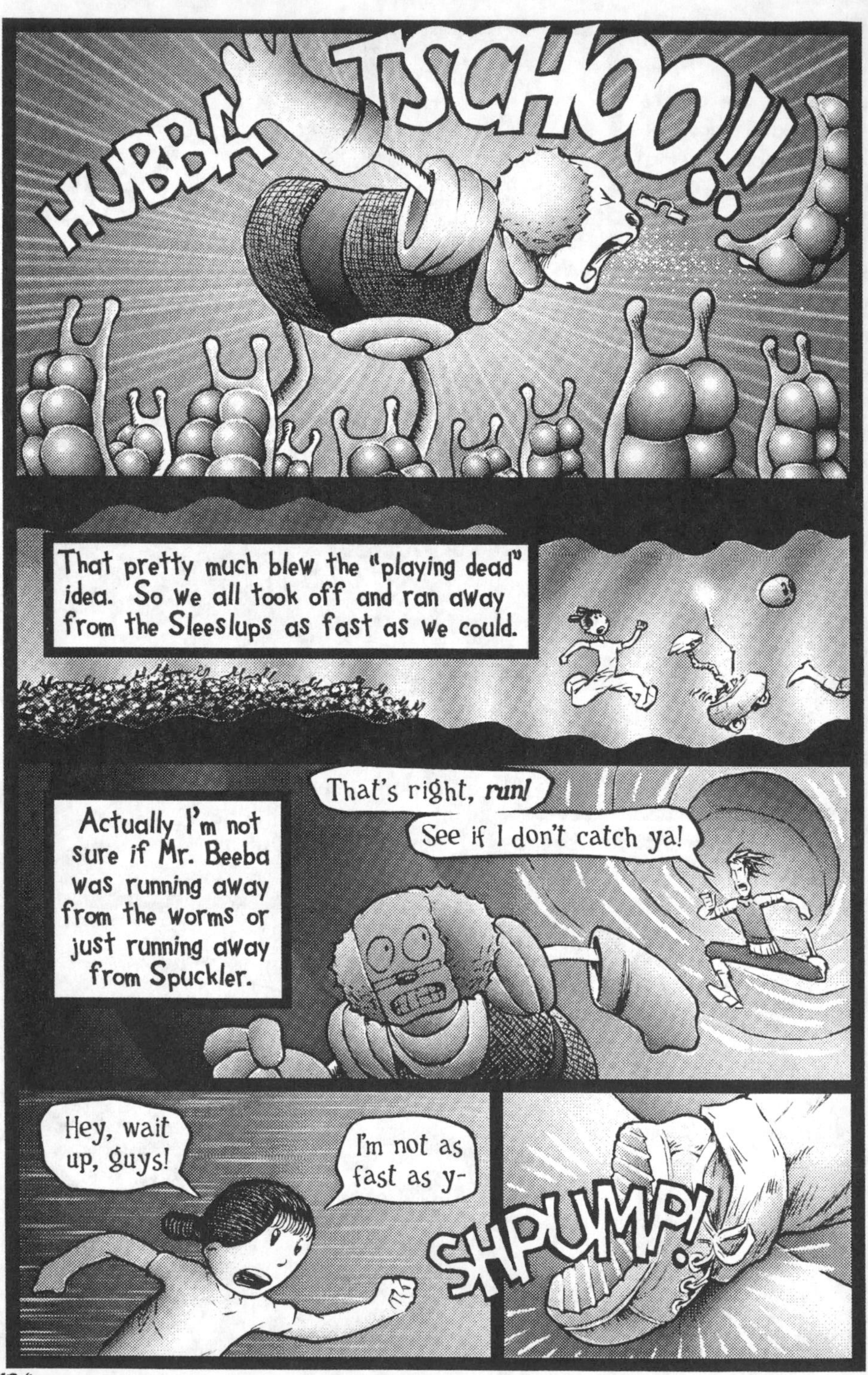
HUBBA TSCHOO!!
That pretty much blew the "playing dead" idea. So we all took off and ran away from the Sleeslups as fast as we could.
Actually I'm not sure if Mr. Beeba was running away from the worms or just running away from Spuckler.
That's right, run!
See if I don't catch ya!
Hey, wait up, guys!
I'm not as fast as y-
SHPUMP!

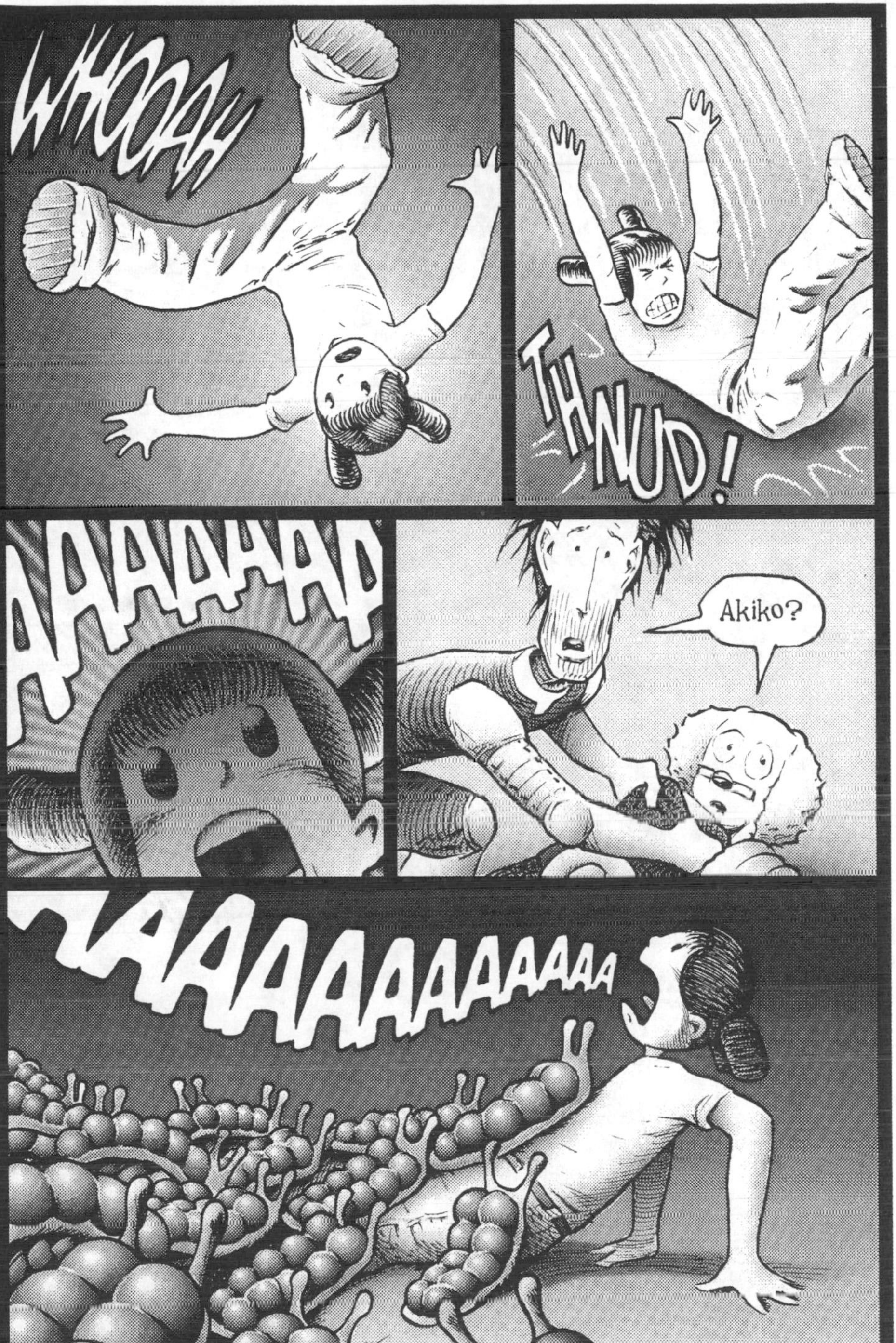
WHOOAH
THNUD!
AAAAAAAA
Akiko?
AAAAAAAAAAA

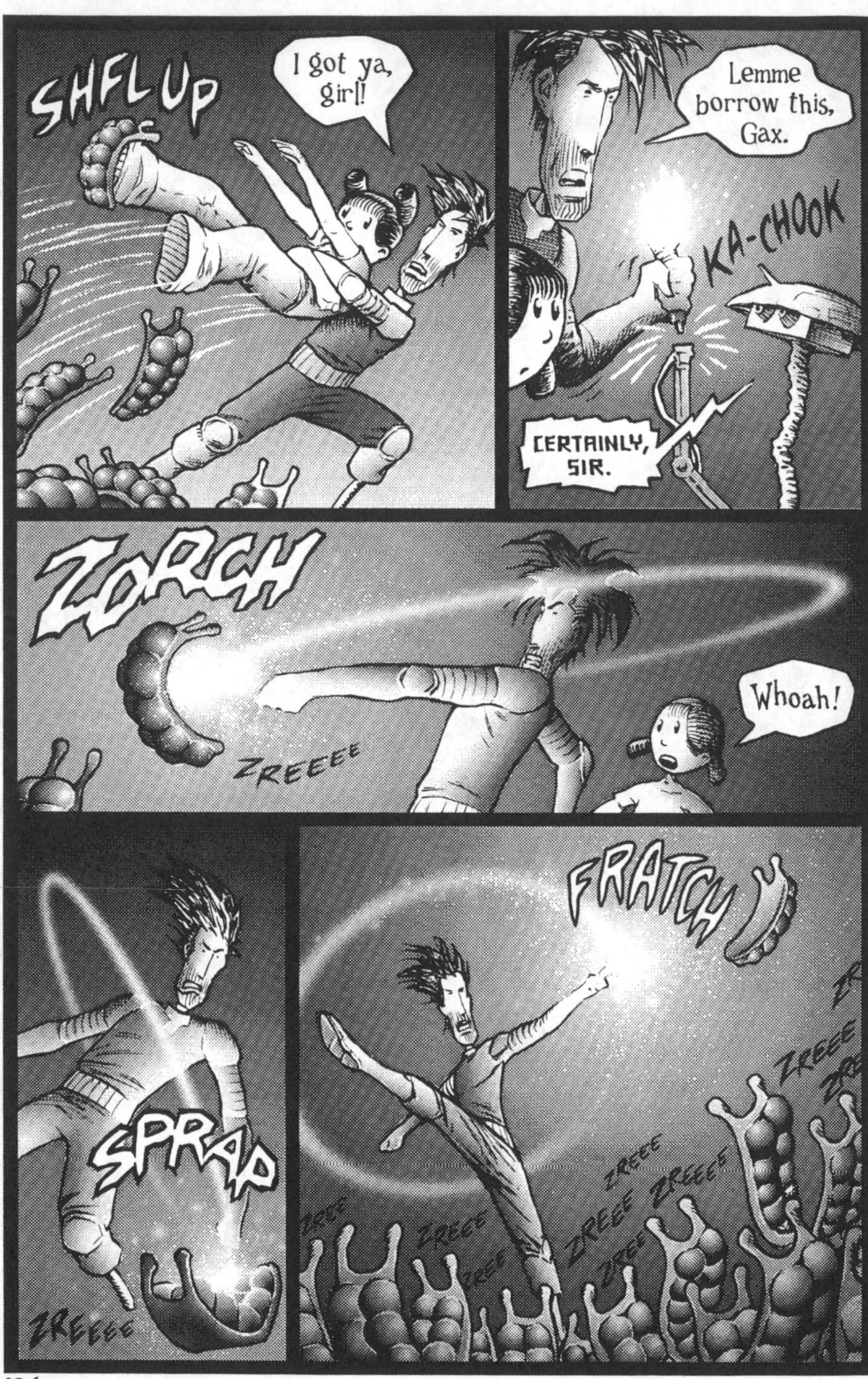
SHFLUP
I got ya, girl!
Lemme borrow this, Gax.
KA-CHOOK
CERTAINLY, SIR.
ZORCH
ZREEEE
Whoah!
SPRAP
ZREEEE
FRATCH
ZREEE
ZREEE
ZREEEE

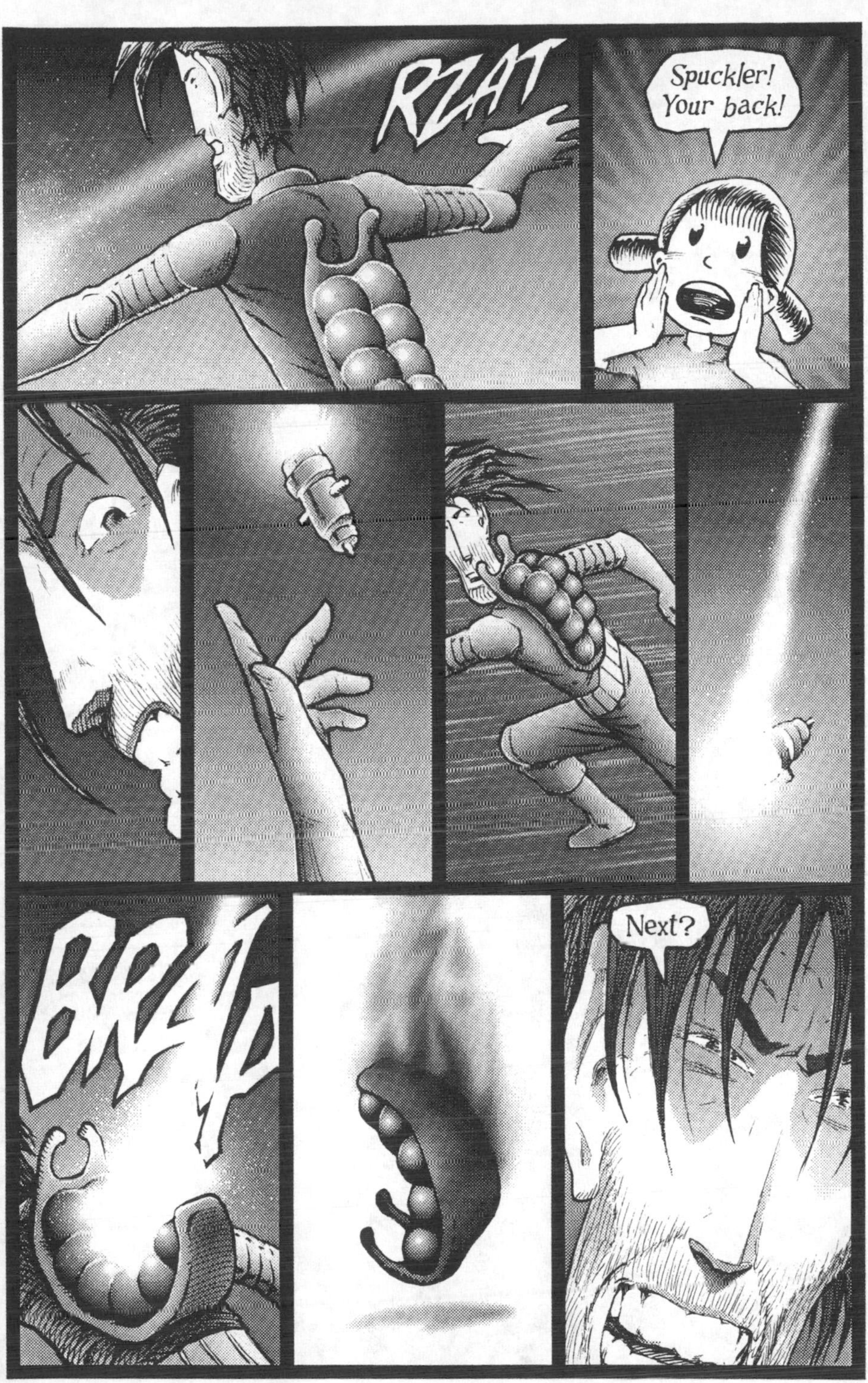
RZAT
Spuckler! Your back!
BRAP
Next?

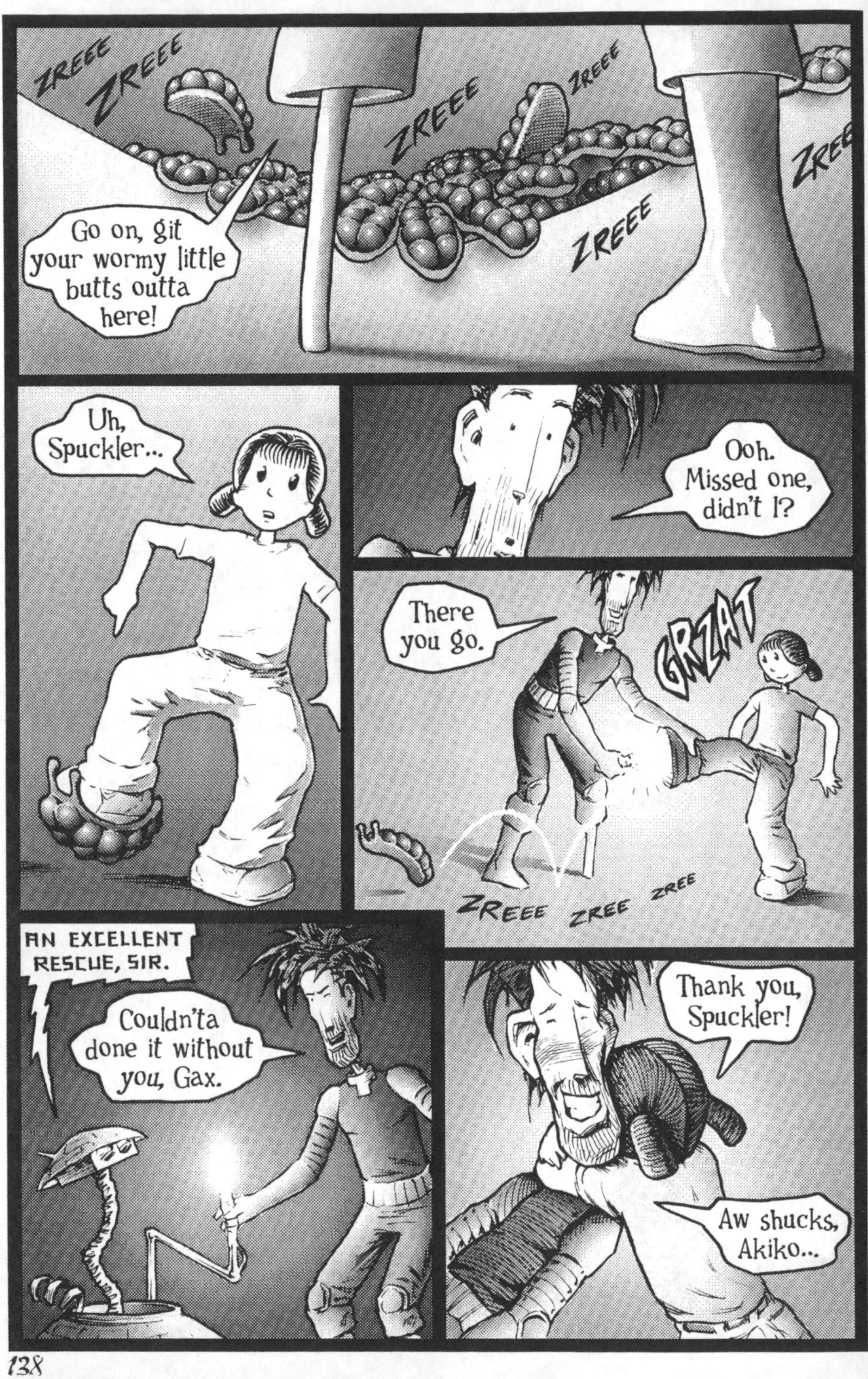
ZREEE
ZREEE
ZREEE
ZREEE
ZREEE
ZREE
Go on, git your wormy little butts outta here!
Uh, Spuckler...
Ooh. Missed one, didn't I?
There you go.
GRZAT
ZREEE
ZREE
ZREE
AN EXCELLENT RESCUE, SIR.
Couldn'ta done it without *you*, Gax.
Thank you, Spuckler!
Aw shucks, Akiko...

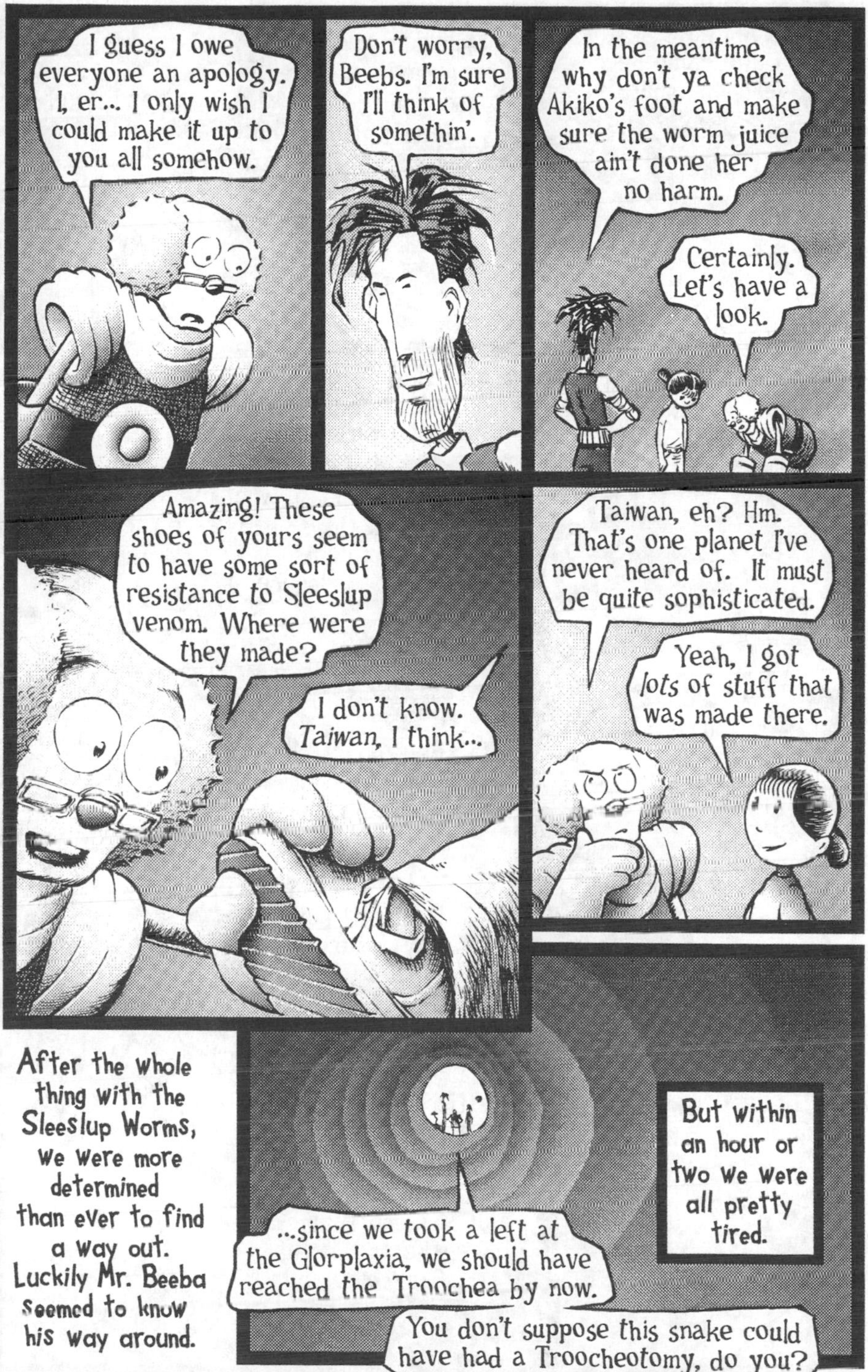
I guess I owe everyone an apology. I, er... I only wish I could make it up to you all somehow.
Don't worry, Beebs. I'm sure I'll think of somethin'.
In the meantime, why don't ya check Akiko's foot and make sure the worm juice ain't done her no harm.
Certainly. Let's have a look.
Amazing! These shoes of yours seem to have some sort of resistance to Sleeslup venom. Where were they made?
I don't know. *Taiwan*, I think...
Taiwan, eh? Hm. That's one planet I've never heard of. It must be quite sophisticated.
Yeah, I got *lots* of stuff that was made there.
After the whole thing with the Sleeslup Worms, we were more determined than ever to find a way out. Luckily Mr. Beeba seemed to know his way around.
But within an hour or two we were all pretty tired.
...since we took a left at the Glorplaxia, we should have reached the Troochea by now.
You don't suppose this snake could have had a Troocheotomy, do you?

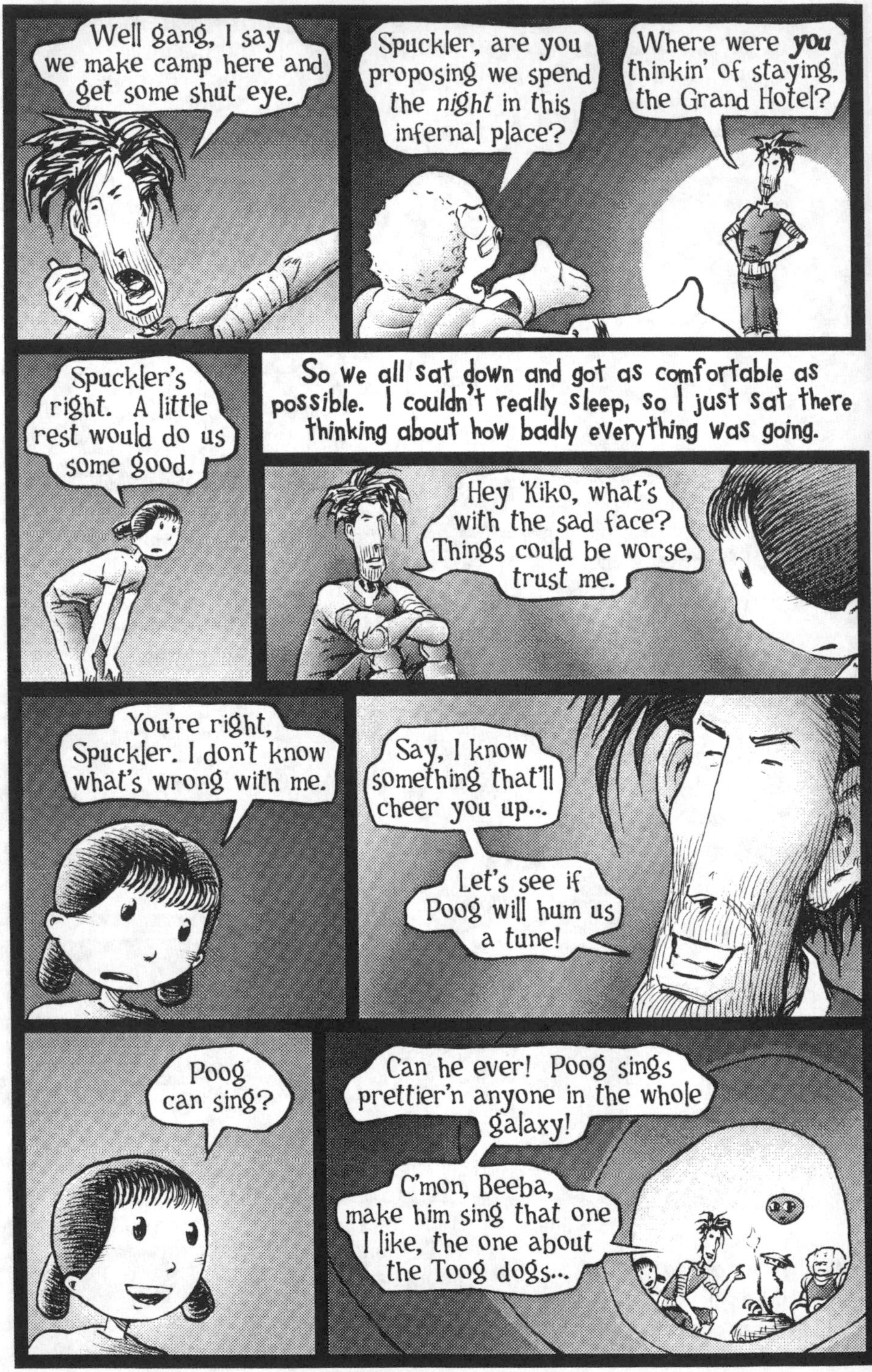

Well gang, I say we make camp here and get some shut eye.
Spuckler, are you proposing we spend the *night* in this infernal place?
Where were **you** thinkin' of staying, the Grand Hotel?
Spuckler's right. A little rest would do us some good.
So we all sat down and got as comfortable as possible. I couldn't really sleep, so I just sat there thinking about how badly everything was going.
Hey 'Kiko, what's with the sad face? Things could be worse, trust me.
You're right, Spuckler. I don't know what's wrong with me.
Say, I know something that'll cheer you up...
Let's see if Poog will hum us a tune!
Poog can sing?
Can he ever! Poog sings prettier'n anyone in the whole galaxy!
C'mon, Beeba, make him sing that one I like, the one about the Toog dogs...

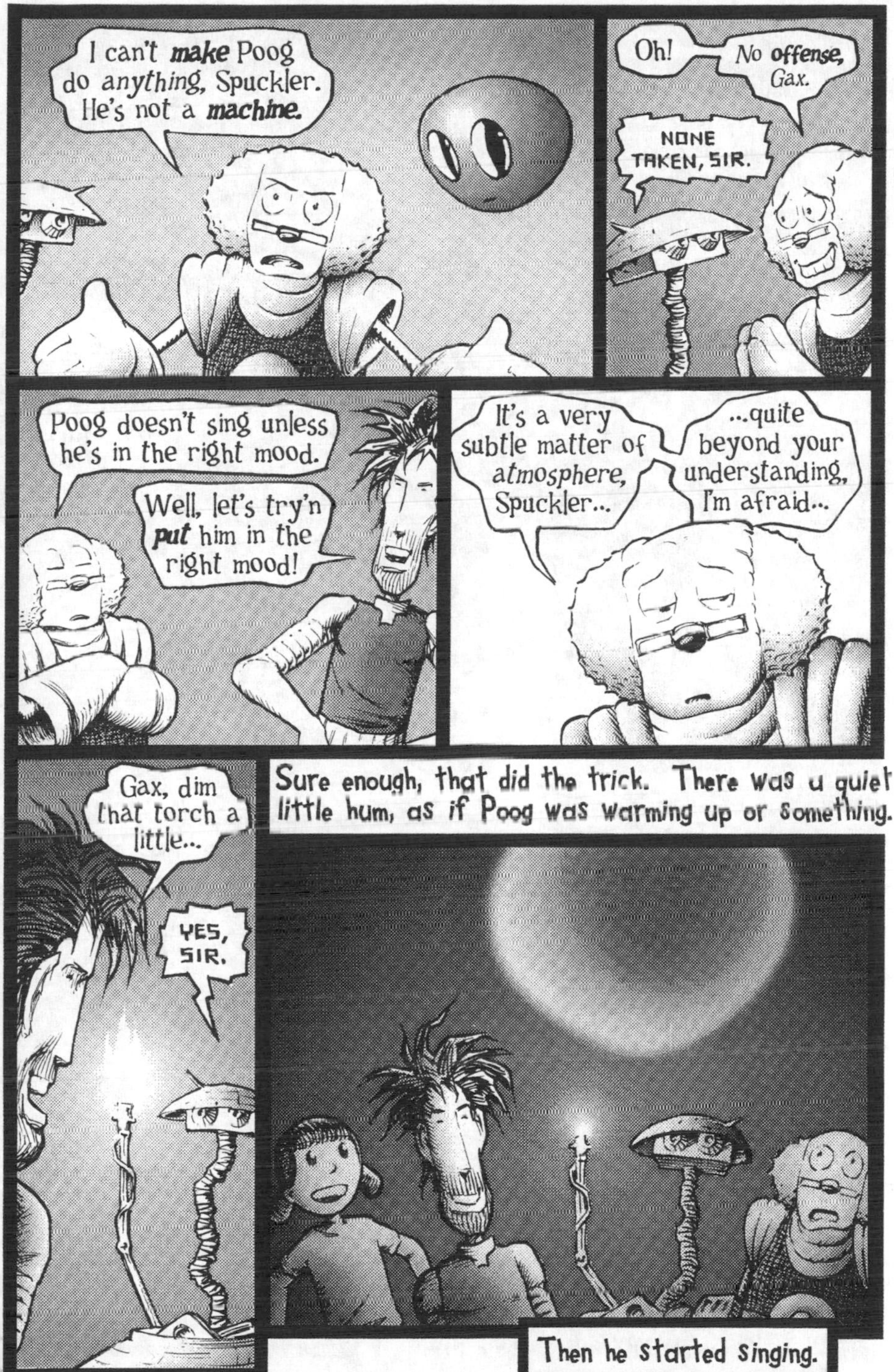
I can't **make** Poog do *anything*, Spuckler. He's not a **machine.**
Oh!
No **offense,** Gax.
NONE TAKEN, SIR.
Poog doesn't sing unless he's in the right mood.
Well, let's try'n ***put*** him in the right mood!
It's a very subtle matter of *atmosphere,* Spuckler...
...quite beyond your understanding, I'm afraid...
Gax, dim that torch a little...
YES, SIR.
Sure enough, that did the trick. There was a quiet little hum, as if Poog was warming up or something.
Then he started singing.

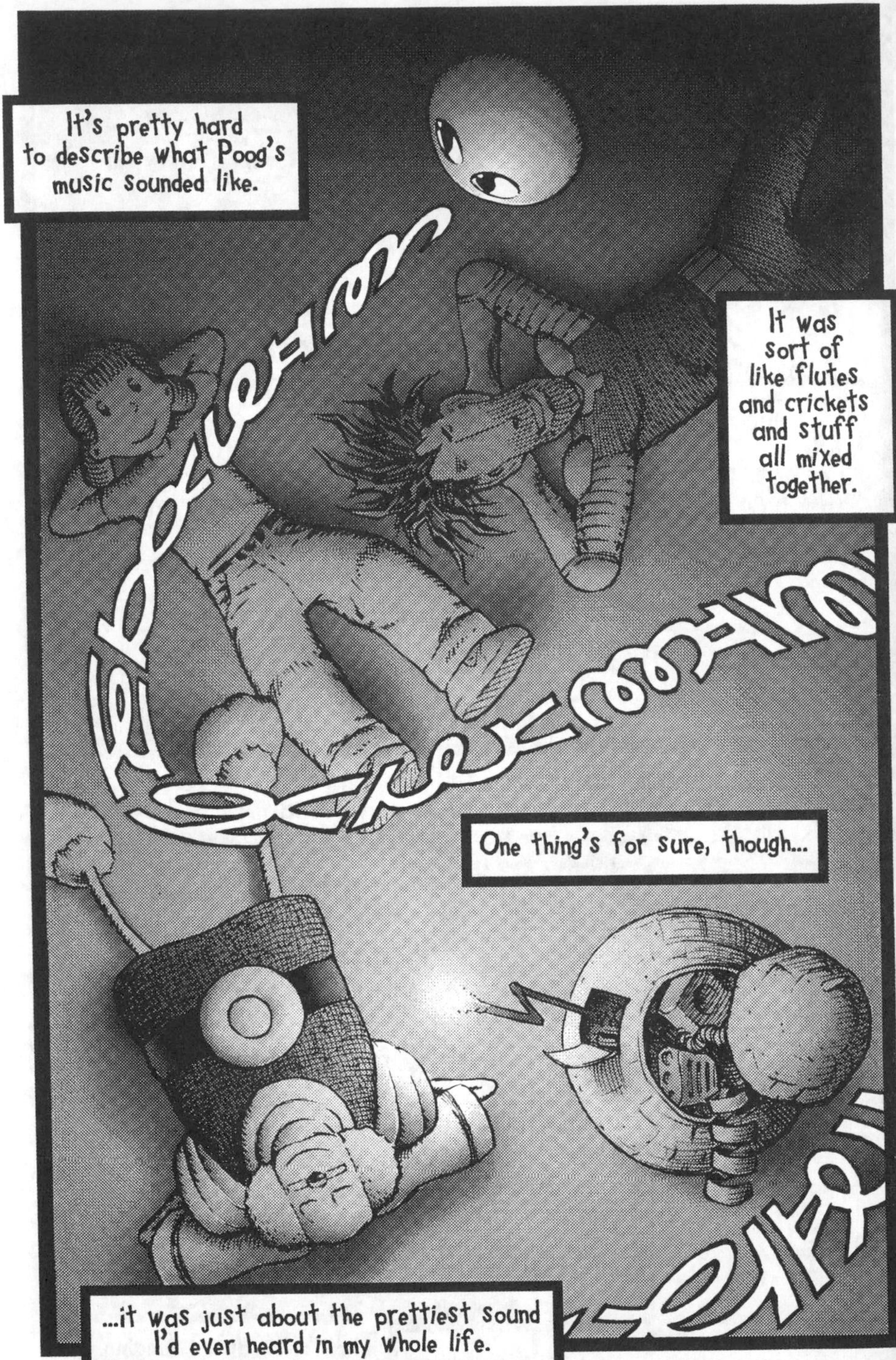
It's pretty hard to describe what Poog's music sounded like.
It was sort of like flutes and crickets and stuff all mixed together.
One thing's for sure, though...
...it was just about the prettiest sound I'd ever heard in my whole life.

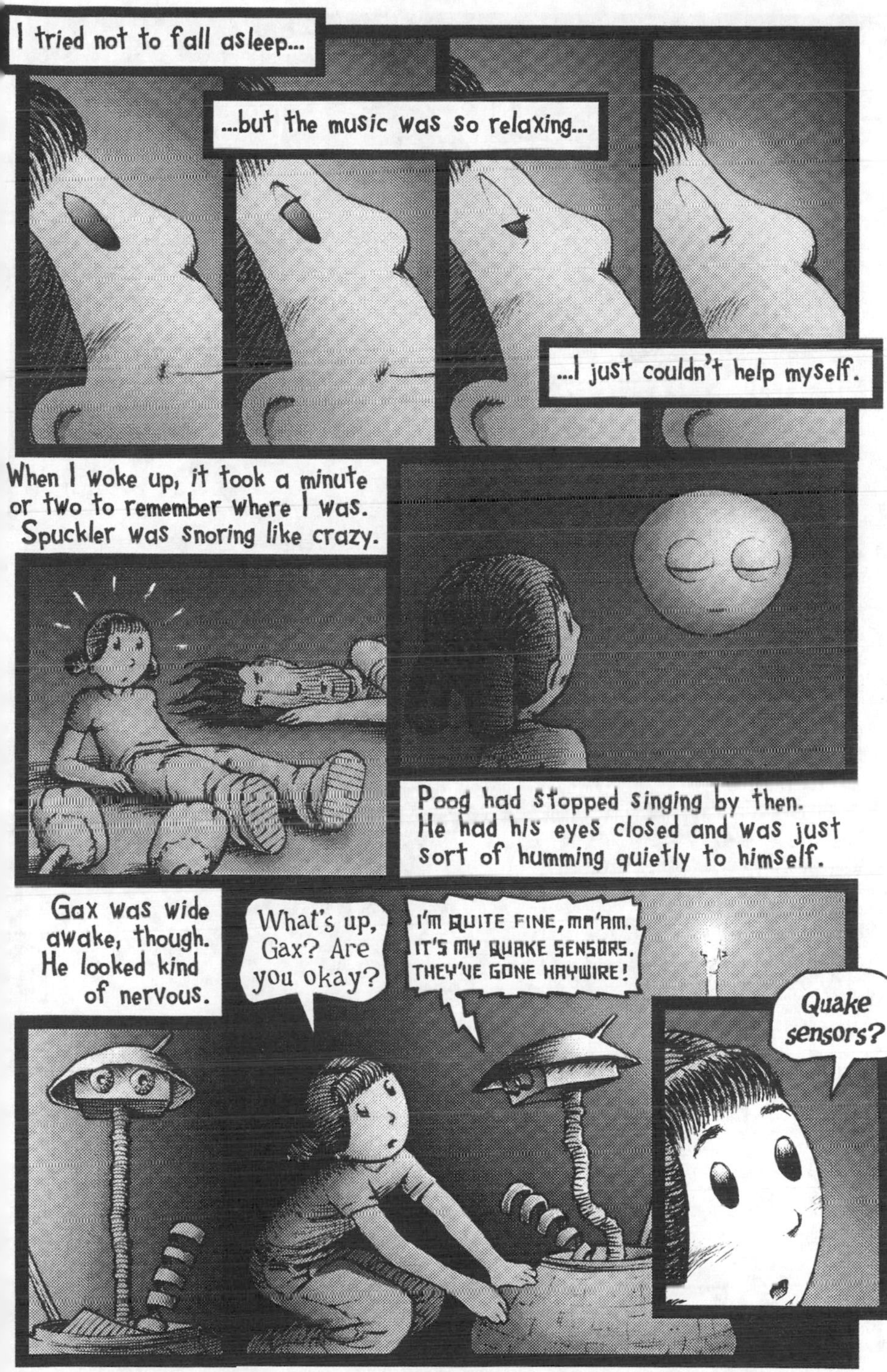
I tried not to fall asleep...
...but the music was so relaxing...
...I just couldn't help myself.
When I woke up, it took a minute or two to remember where I was. Spuckler was snoring like crazy.
Poog had stopped singing by then. He had his eyes closed and was just sort of humming quietly to himself.
Gax was wide awake, though. He looked kind of nervous.
What's up, Gax? Are you okay?
I'M QUITE FINE, MA'AM. IT'S MY QUAKE SENSORS. THEY'VE GONE HAYWIRE!
Quake sensors?

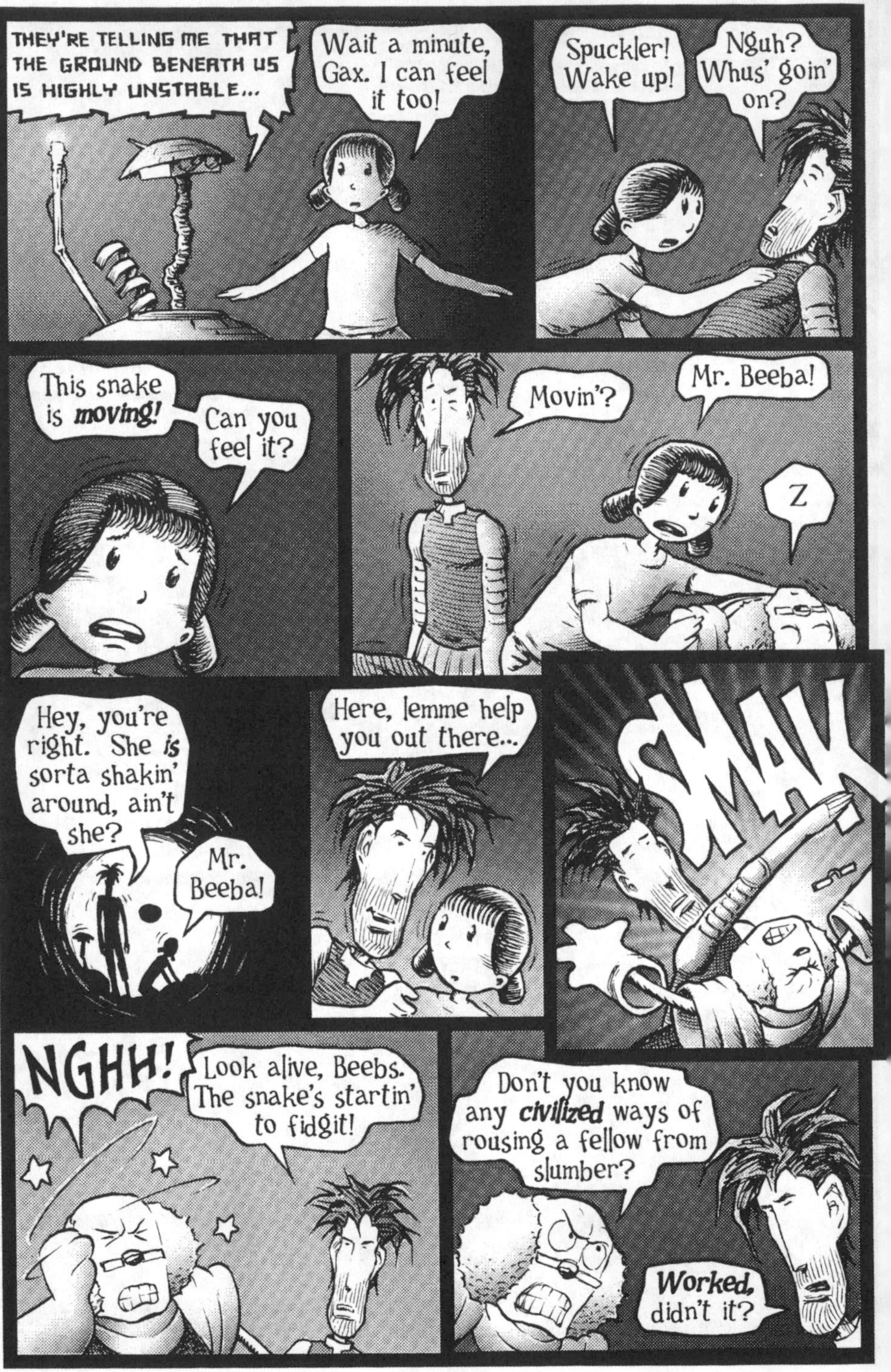

THEY'RE TELLING ME THAT THE GROUND BENEATH US IS HIGHLY UNSTABLE...
Wait a minute, Gax. I can feel it too!
Spuckler! Wake up!
Nguh? Whus' goin' on?
This snake is *moving!*
Can you feel it?
Movin'?
Mr. Beeba!
Z
Hey, you're right. She *is* sorta shakin' around, ain't she?
Mr. Beeba!
Here, lemme help you out there...
SMAK
NGHH!
Look alive, Beebs. The snake's startin' to fidgit!
Don't you know any *civilized* ways of rousing a fellow from slumber?
Worked, didn't it?

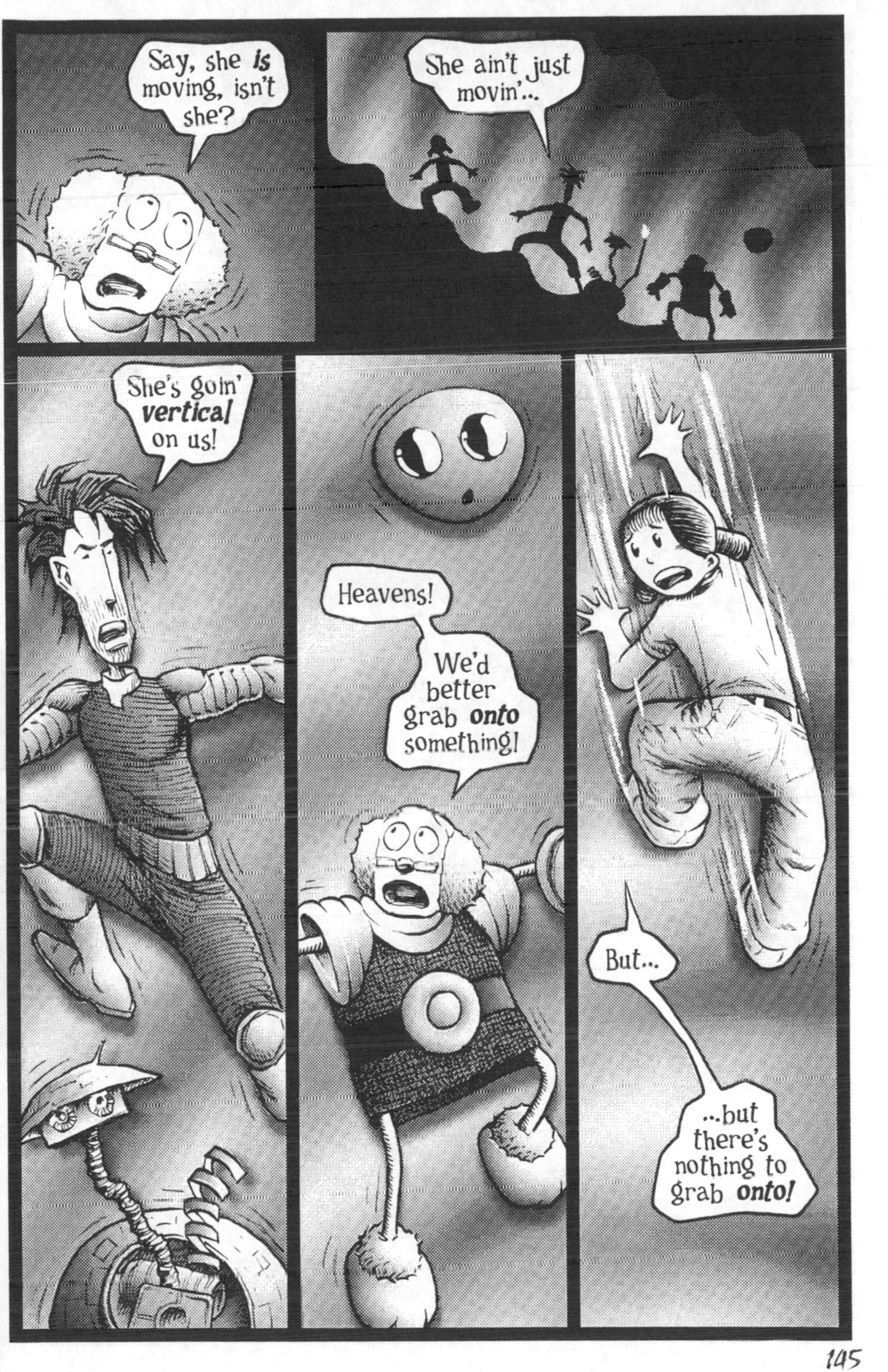
Say, she is moving, isn't she?
She ain't just movin'...
She's goin' vertical on us!
Heavens!
We'd better grab onto something!
But...
...but there's nothing to grab onto!

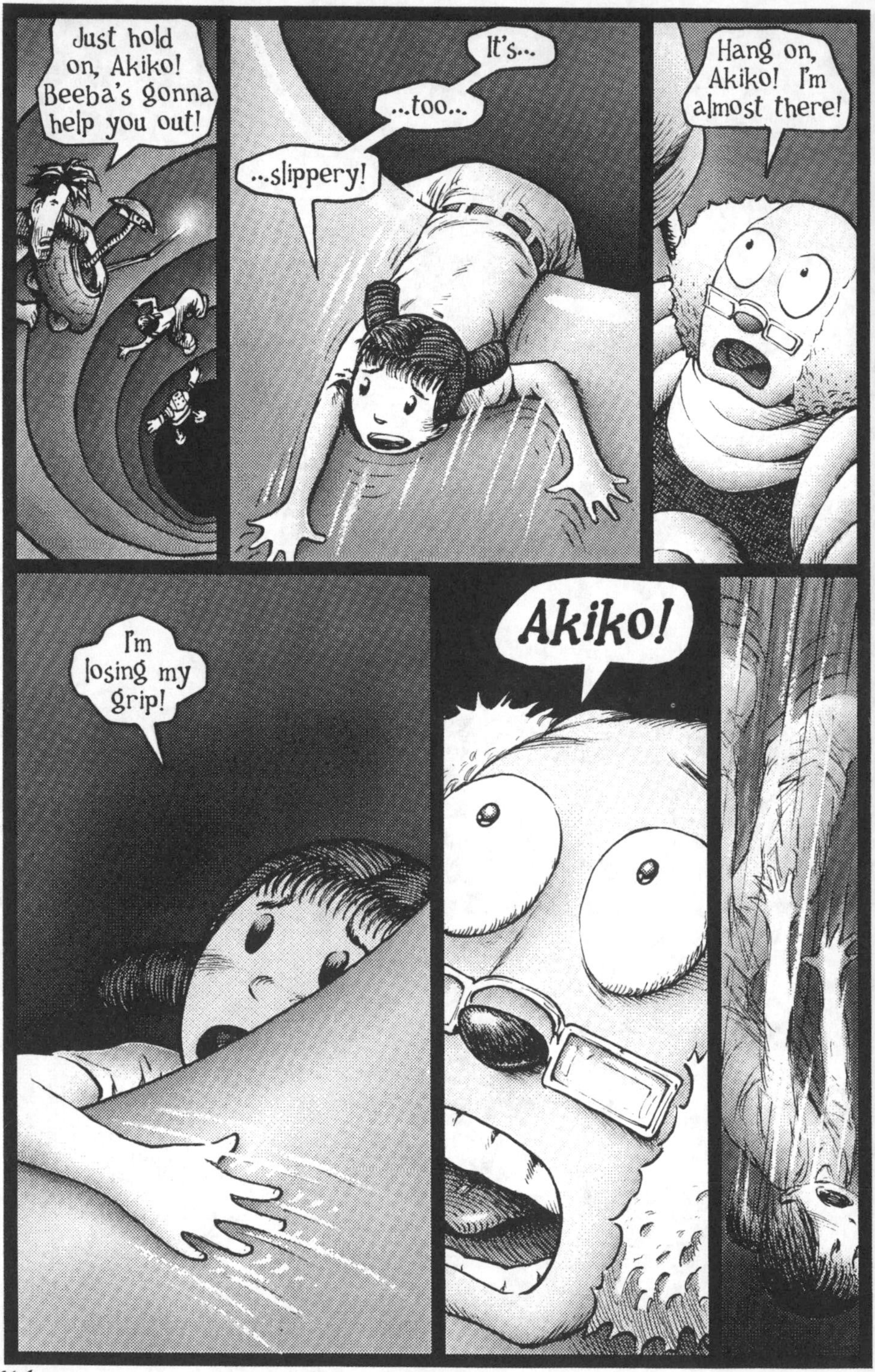

Just hold on, Akiko! Beeba's gonna help you out!
It's...
...too...
...slippery!
Hang on, Akiko! I'm almost there!
I'm losing my grip!
Akiko!

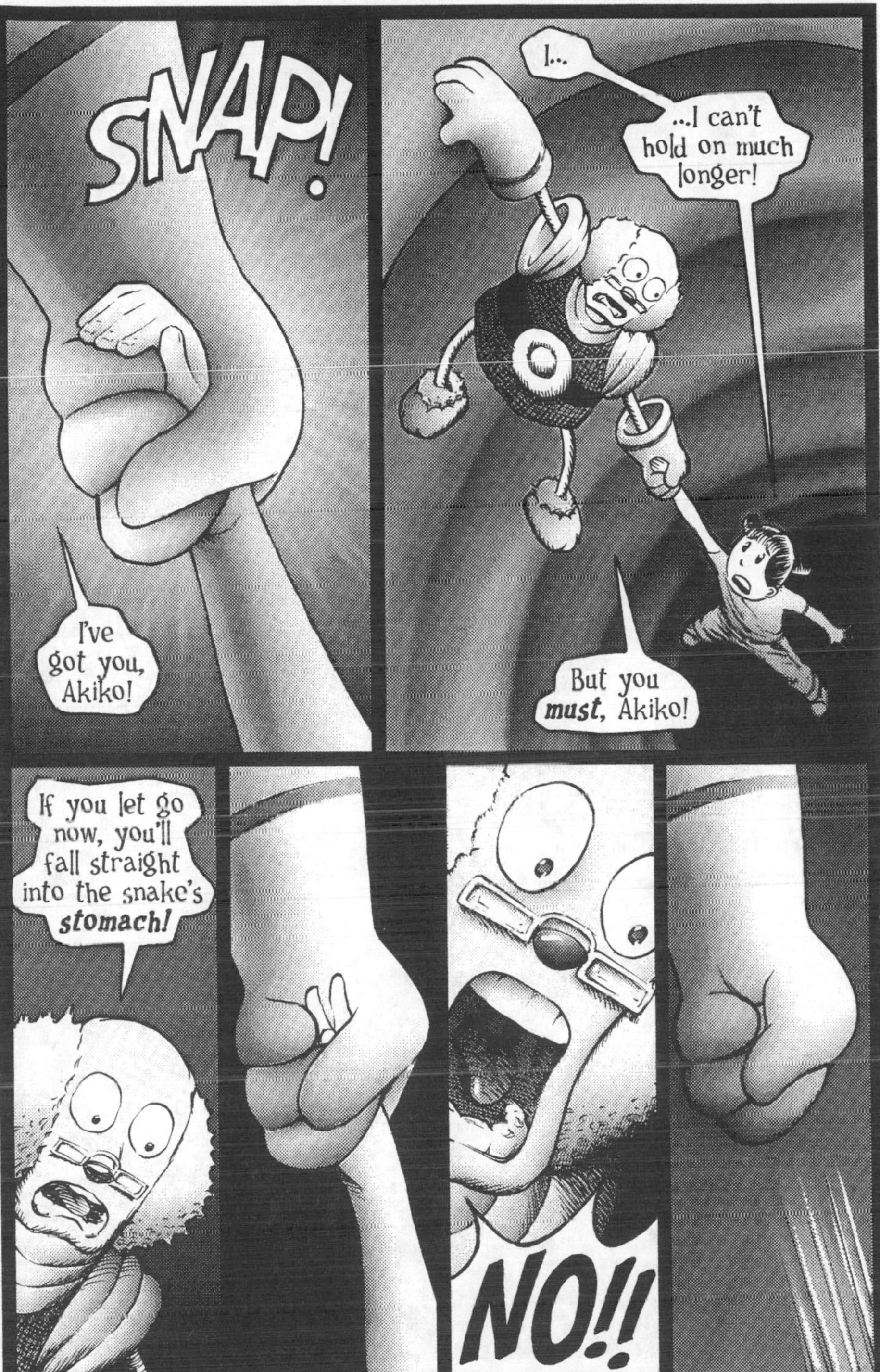
SNAP!
I've got you, Akiko!
I...
...I can't hold on much longer!
But you **must**, Akiko!
If you let go now, you'll fall straight into the snake's **stomach!**
NO!!

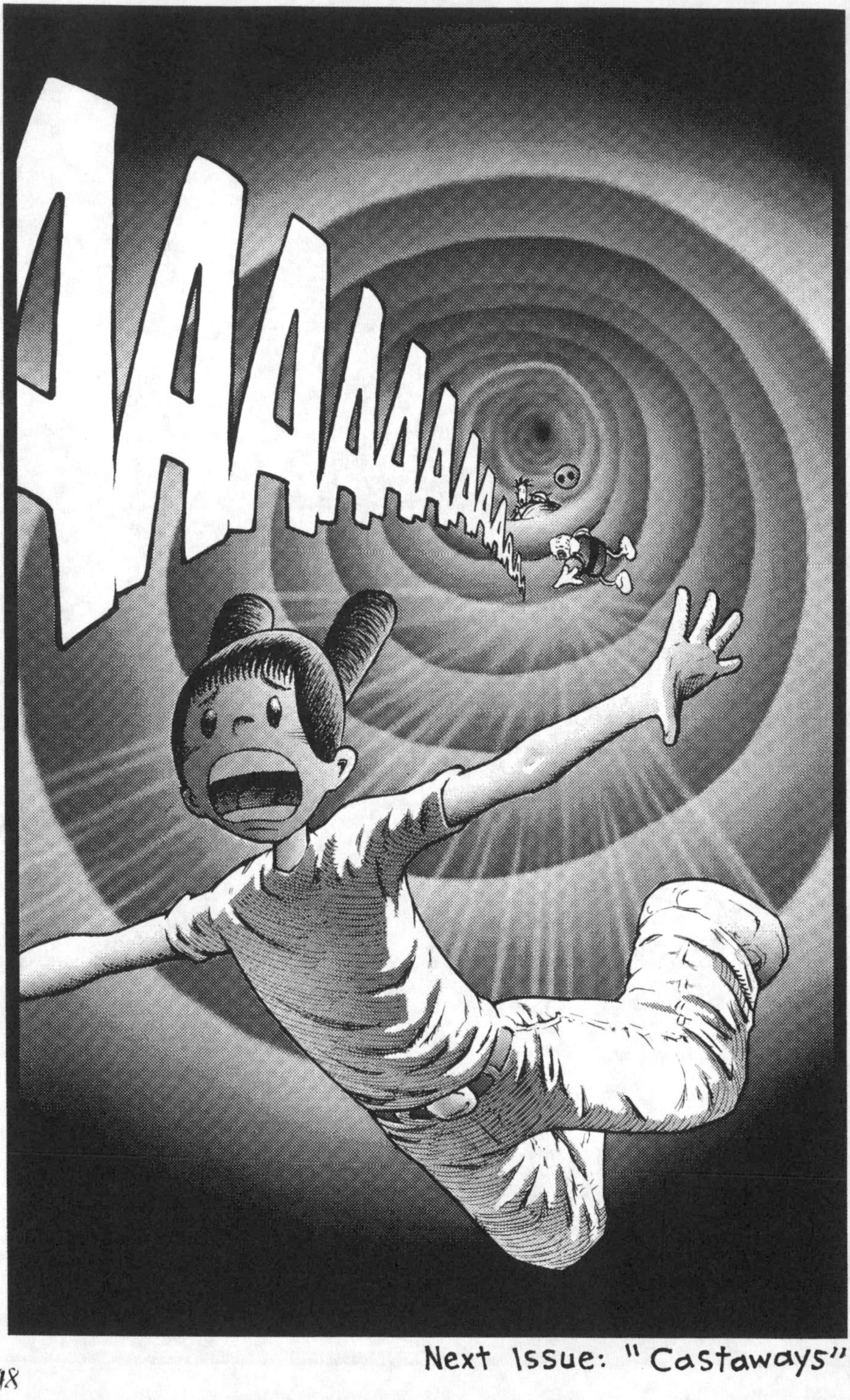
AAAAAAAAAAAAA

Next Issue: "Castaways"

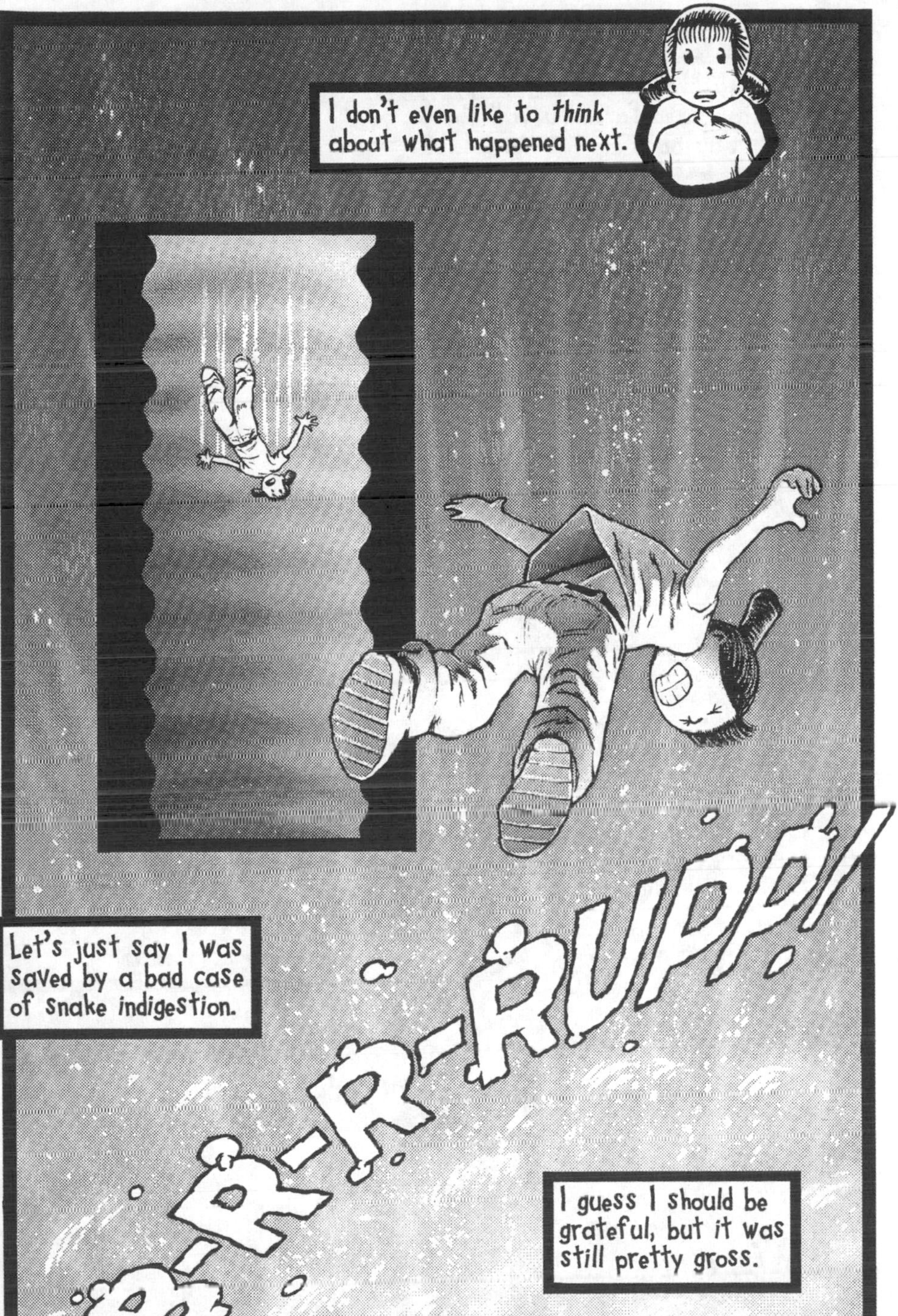
I don't even like to think about what happened next.
Let's just say I was saved by a bad case of snake indigestion.
B-R-R-R-RUPP!
I guess I should be grateful, but it was still pretty gross.

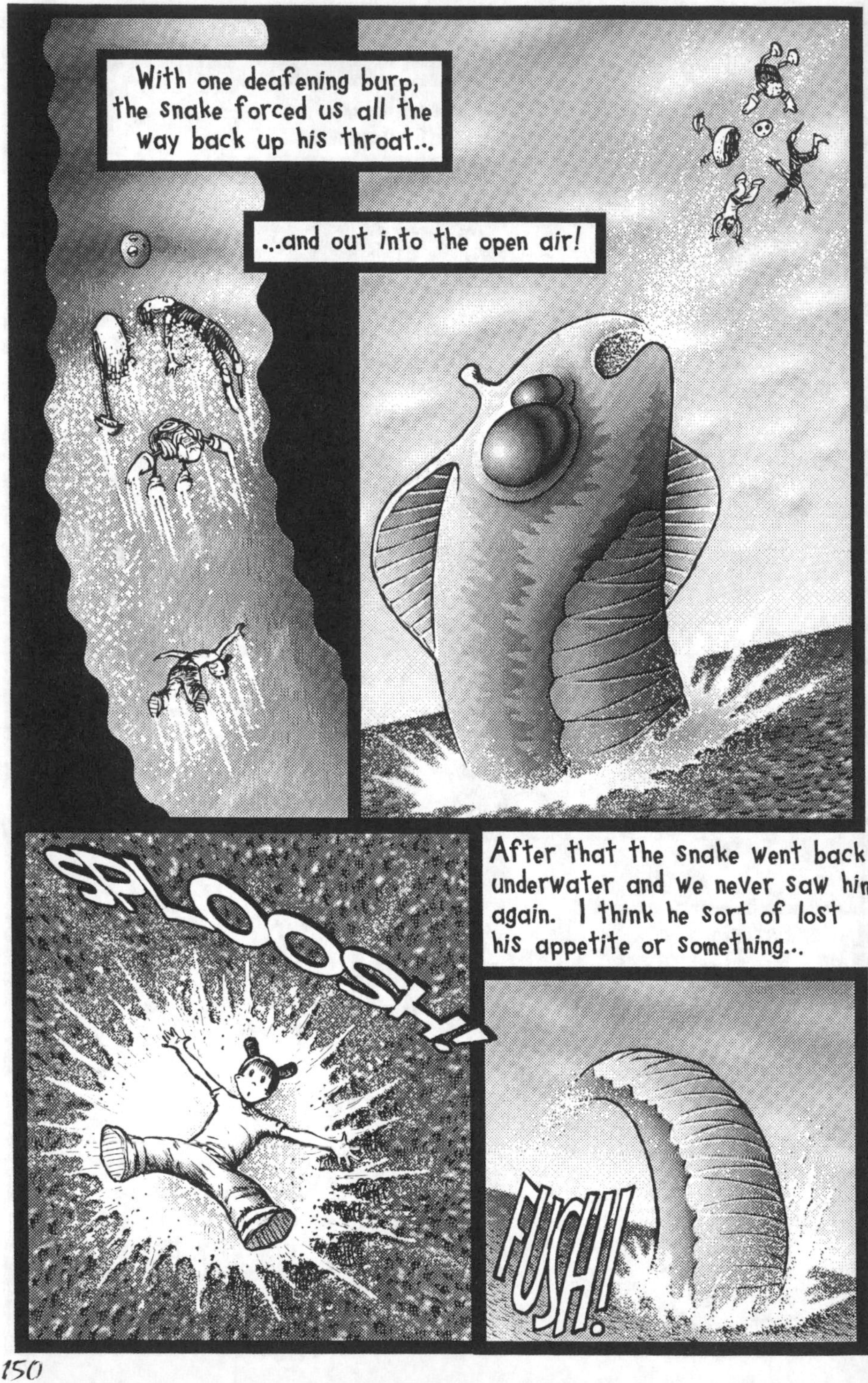
With one deafening burp, the snake forced us all the way back up his throat...
...and out into the open air!
SPLOOSH!
After that the snake went back underwater and we never saw him again. I think he sort of lost his appetite or something...
FUSH!

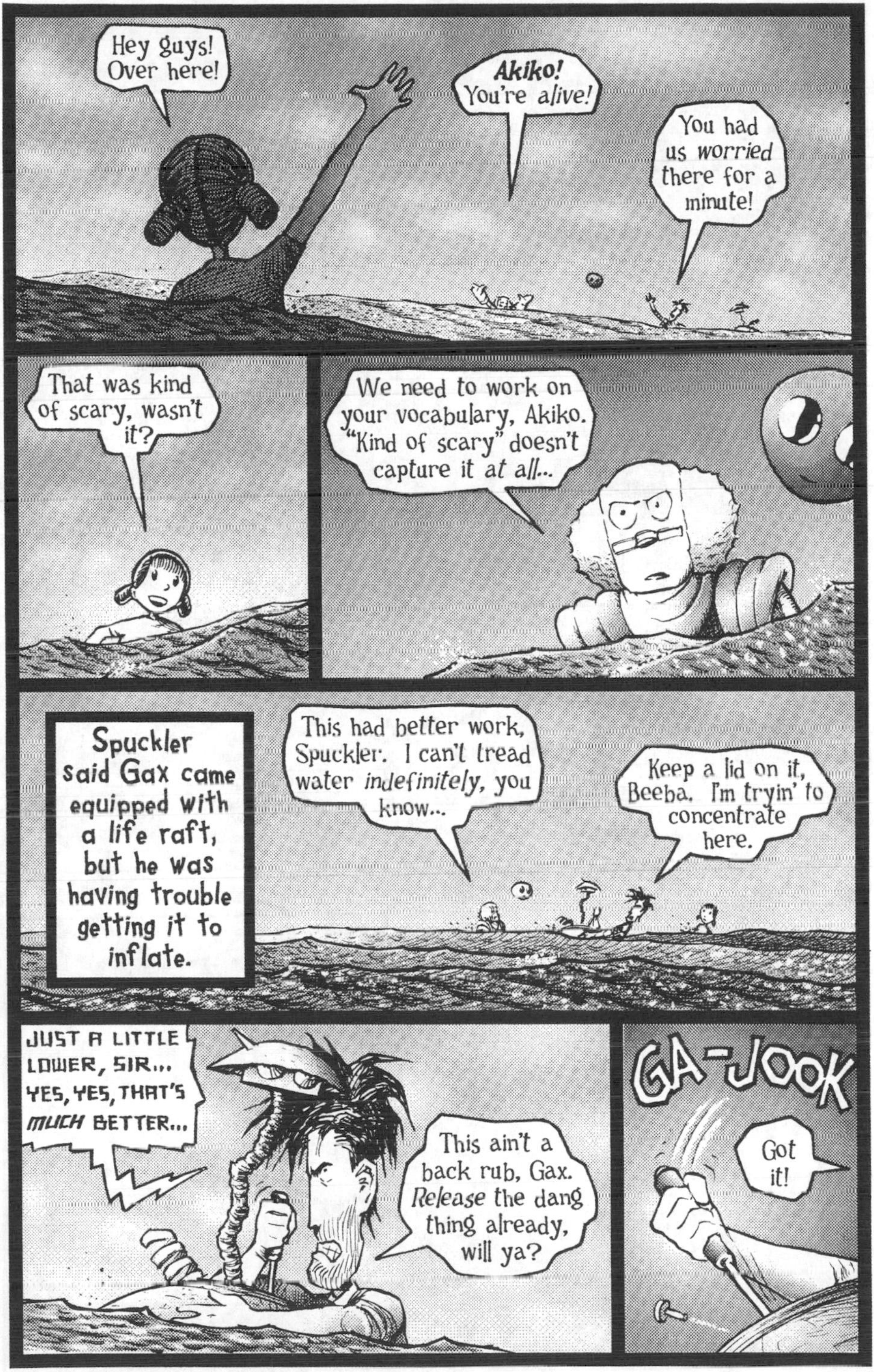
Hey guys! Over here!
Akiko! You're alive!
You had us worried there for a minute!
That was kind of scary, wasn't it?
We need to work on your vocabulary, Akiko. "Kind of scary" doesn't capture it at all...
Spuckler said Gax came equipped with a life raft, but he was having trouble getting it to inflate.
This had better work, Spuckler. I can't tread water indefinitely, you know...
Keep a lid on it, Beeba. I'm tryin' to concentrate here.
JUST A LITTLE LOWER, SIR... YES, YES, THAT'S MUCH BETTER...
This ain't a back rub, Gax. Release the dang thing already, will ya?
GA-JOOK
Got it!

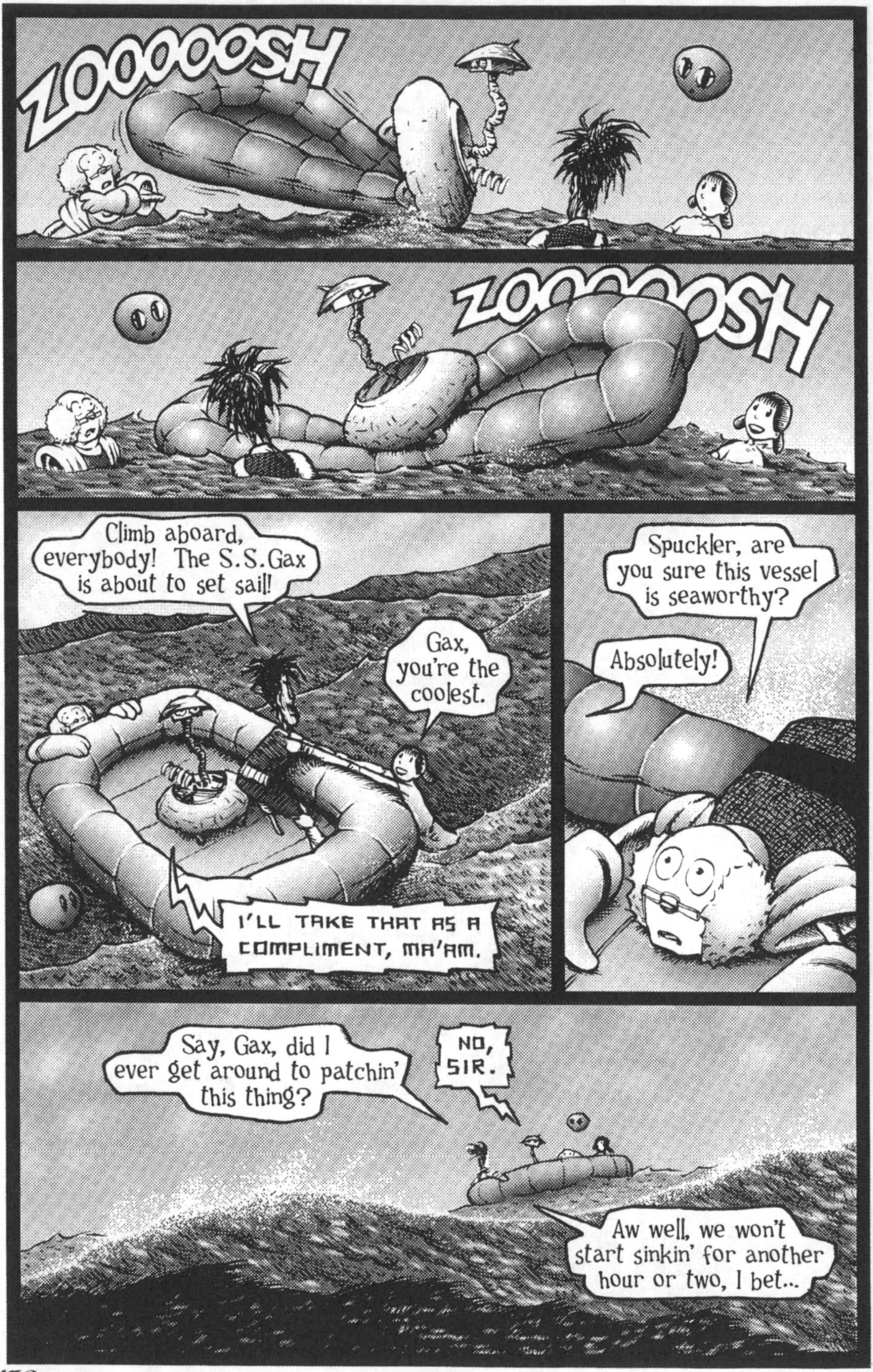
ZOOOOOSH
ZOOOOOSH
Climb aboard, everybody! The S.S.Gax is about to set sail!
Gax, you're the coolest.
I'LL TAKE THAT AS A COMPLIMENT, MA'AM.
Spuckler, are you sure this vessel is seaworthy?
Absolutely!
Say, Gax, did I ever get around to patchin' this thing?
NO, SIR.
Aw well, we won't start sinkin' for another hour or two, I bet...

After we floated along for a while, Mr. Beeba suggested we have a meeting to talk about how the mission was going.

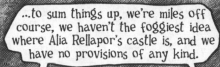

...to sum things up, we're miles off course, we haven't the foggiest idea where Alia Rellapor's castle is, and we have no provisions of any kind.

Questions?

I've got one...

Who *is* Alia Rellapor?

I...

...I don't understand the question.

What part don't you understand, "who," or "is?"

Yes, well, I'm afraid King Froptoppit has given us strict orders never to reveal her true identity to you.

What?! That's *ridiculous!*

Now, Akiko, we wouldn't hide nothin' from you if it wasn't for your own good.

You're still a child, after all...

I can't believe you guys. I'm soaked from head to toe in water snake spit, and you're telling me I'm not old enough to know what's going on!

You're absolutely right, Akiko. You're entitled to an explanation.

Spuckler?

153

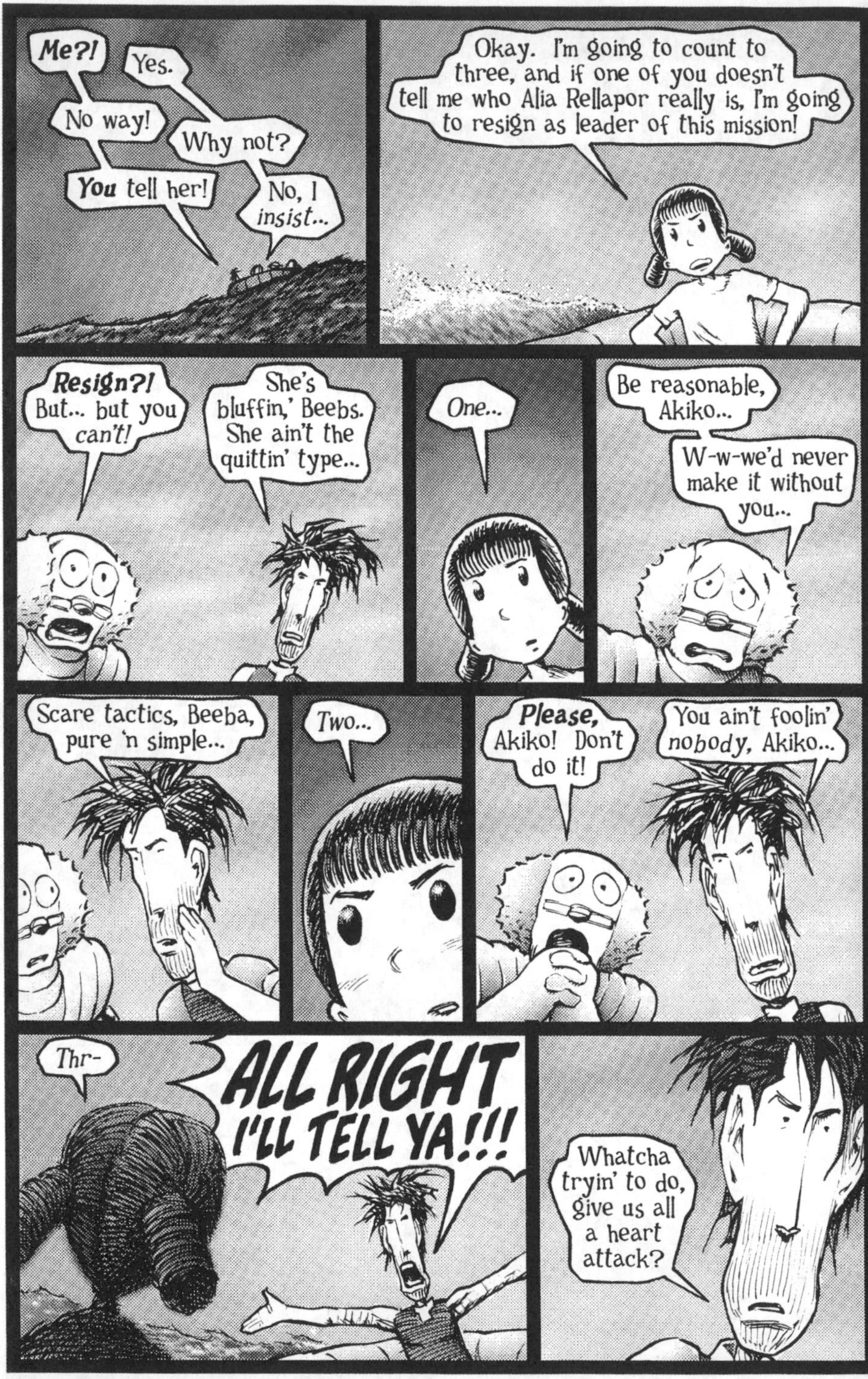
Me?!
Yes.
No way!
Why not?
You tell her!
No, I insist...
Okay. I'm going to count to three, and if one of you doesn't tell me who Alia Rellapor really is, I'm going to resign as leader of this mission!
Resign?! But... but you can't!
She's bluffin,' Beebs. She ain't the quittin' type...
One...
Be reasonable, Akiko...
W-w-we'd never make it without you...
Scare tactics, Beeba, pure 'n simple...
Two...
Please, Akiko! Don't do it!
You ain't foolin' nobody, Akiko...
Thr-
ALL RIGHT I'LL TELL YA!!!
Whatcha tryin' to do, give us all a heart attack?

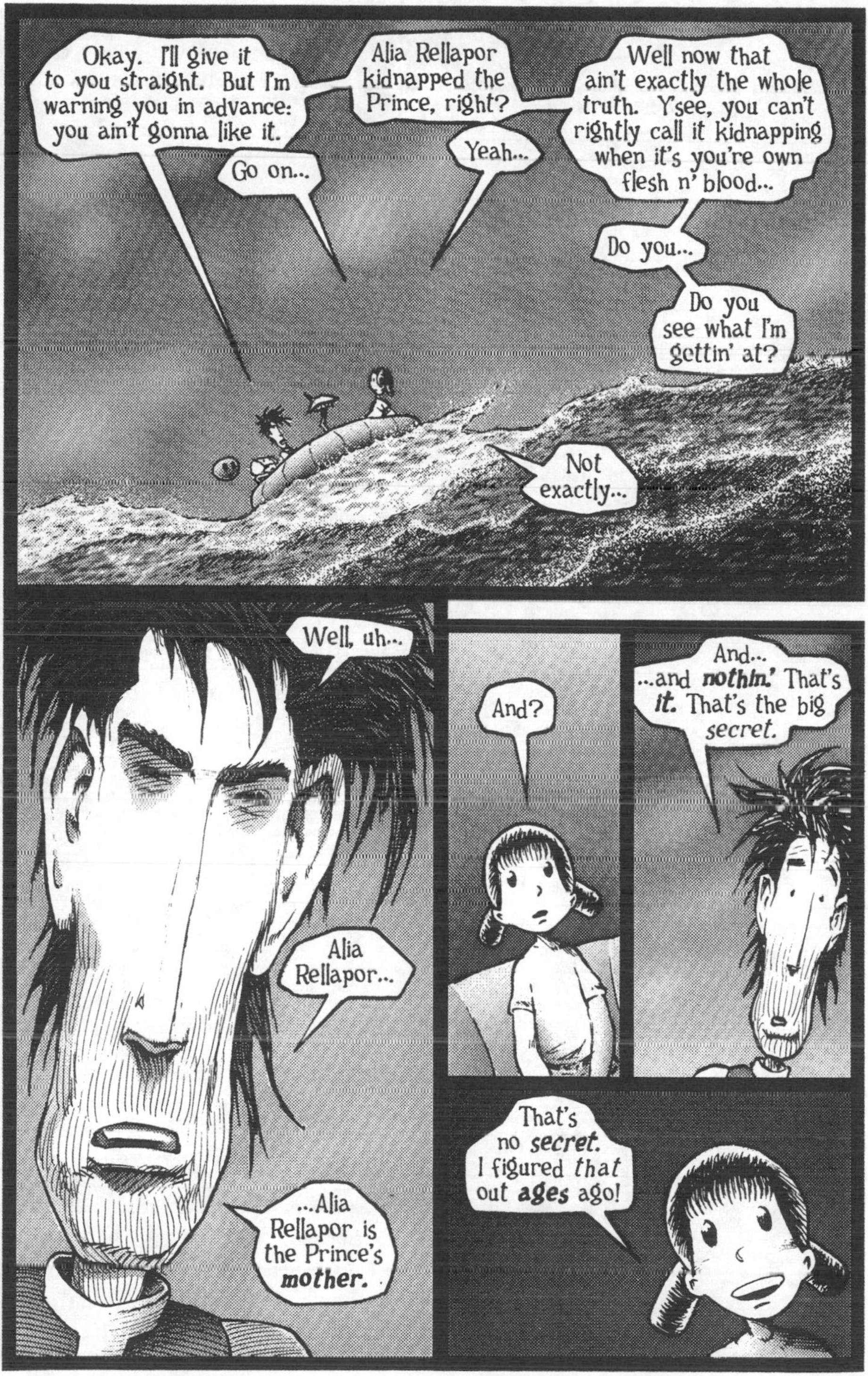
Okay. I'll give it to you straight. But I'm warning you in advance: you ain't gonna like it.
Go on...
Alia Rellapor kidnapped the Prince, right?
Yeah...
Well now that ain't exactly the whole truth. Y'see, you can't rightly call it kidnapping when it's you're own flesh n' blood...
Do you...
Do you see what I'm gettin' at?
Not exactly...
Well, uh...
Alia Rellapor...
...Alia Rellapor is the Prince's **mother.**
And?
And... ...and **nothin.'** That's ***it.*** That's the big *secret.*
That's no ***secret.*** I figured *that* out **ages** ago!

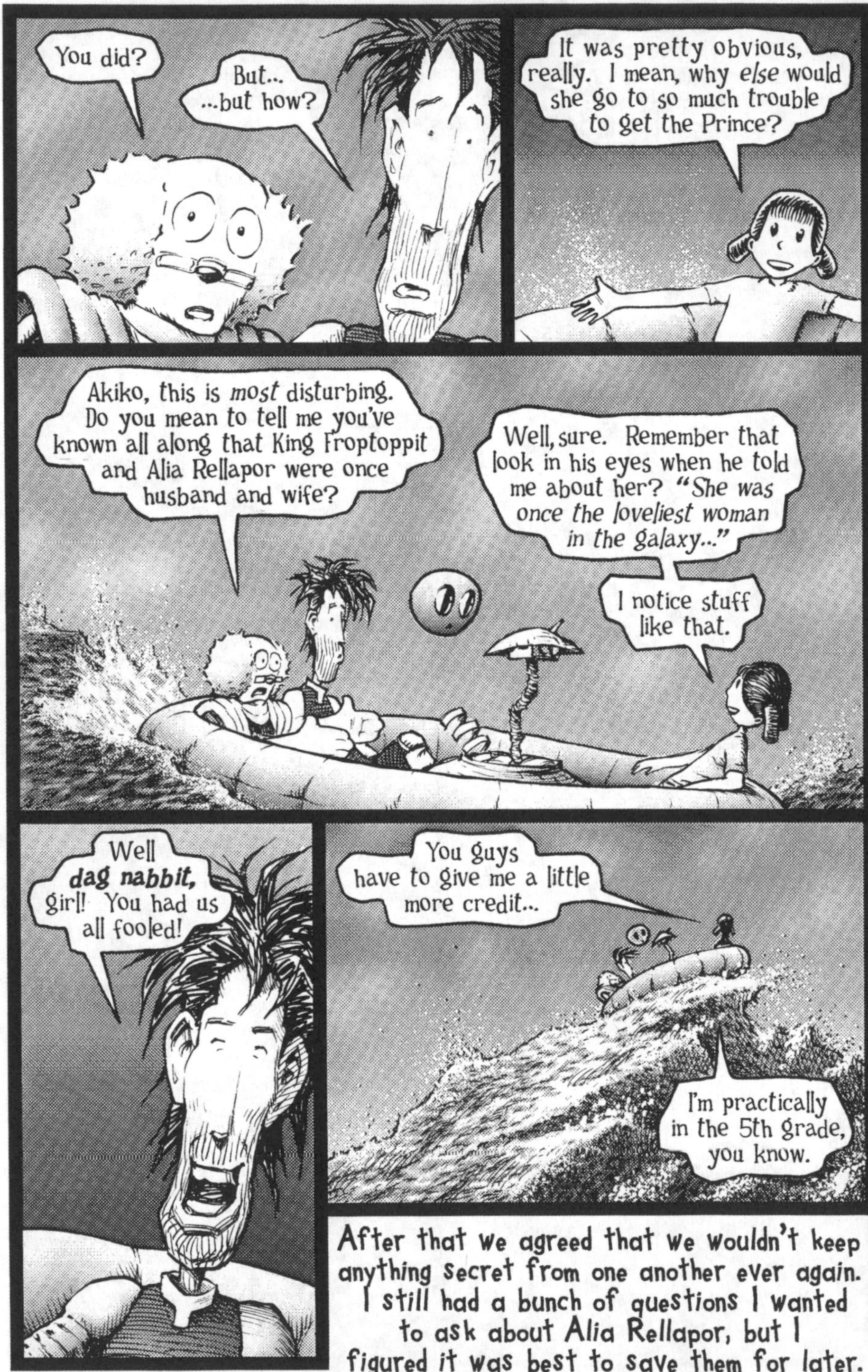
You did?
But... ...but how?
It was pretty obvious, really. I mean, why *else* would she go to so much trouble to get the Prince?
Akiko, this is *most* disturbing. Do you mean to tell me you've known all along that King Froptoppit and Alia Rellapor were once husband and wife?
Well, sure. Remember that look in his eyes when he told me about her? *"She was once the loveliest woman in the galaxy..."*
I notice stuff like that.
Well **dag nabbit,** girl! You had us all fooled!
You guys have to give me a little more credit...
I'm practically in the 5th grade, you know.

After that we agreed that we wouldn't keep anything secret from one another ever again. I still had a bunch of questions I wanted to ask about Alia Rellapor, but I figured it was best to save them for later.

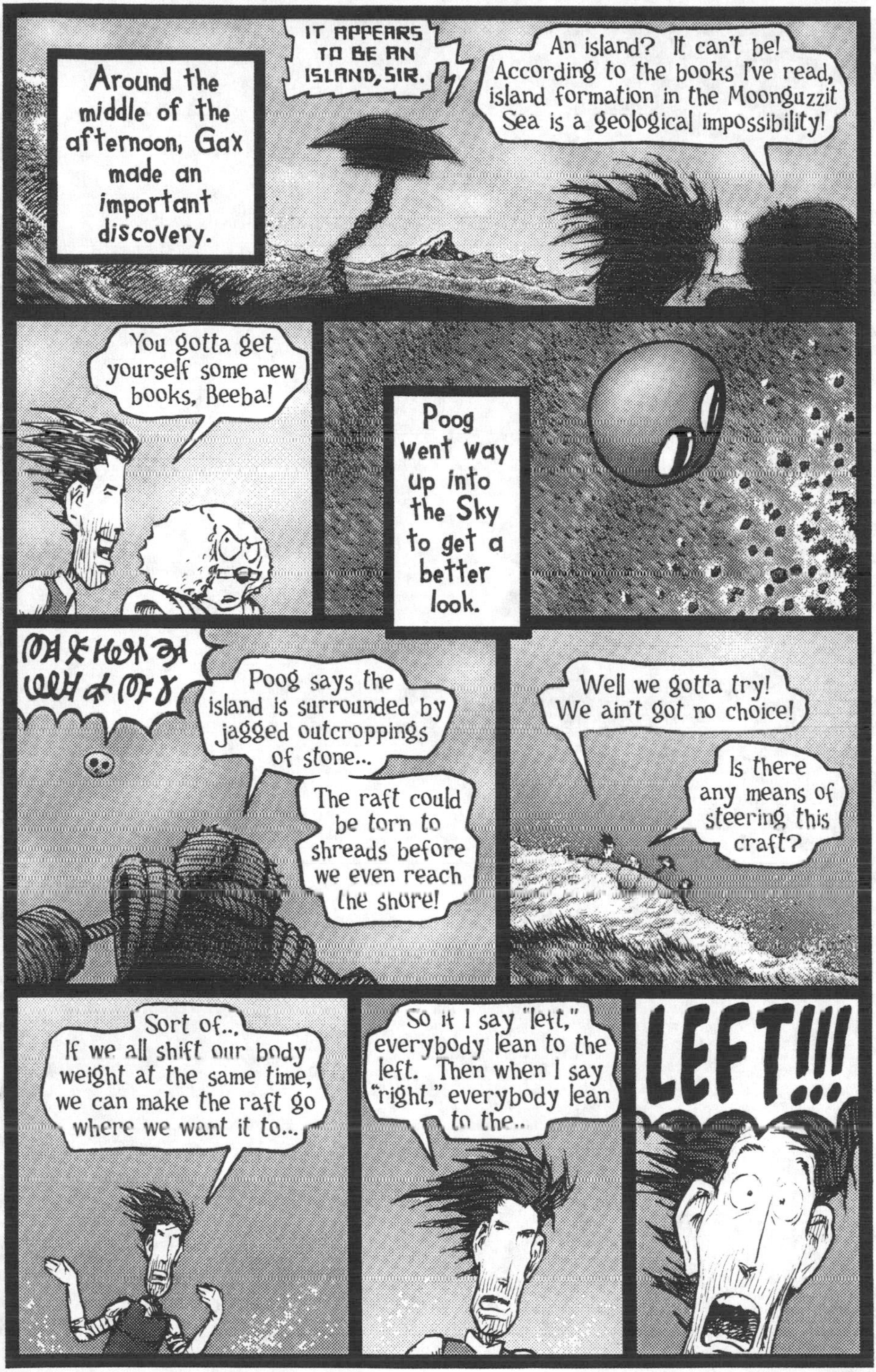
Around the middle of the afternoon, Gax made an important discovery.
IT APPEARS TO BE AN ISLAND, SIR.
An island? It can't be! According to the books I've read, island formation in the Moonguzzit Sea is a geological impossibility!
You gotta get yourself some new books, Beeba!
Poog went way up into the Sky to get a better look.
Poog says the island is surrounded by jagged outcroppings of stone...
The raft could be torn to shreads before we even reach the shore!
Well we gotta try! We ain't got no choice!
Is there any means of steering this craft?
Sort of... If we all shift our body weight at the same time, we can make the raft go where we want it to...
So if I say "left," everybody lean to the left. Then when I say "right," everybody lean to the..
LEFT!!!

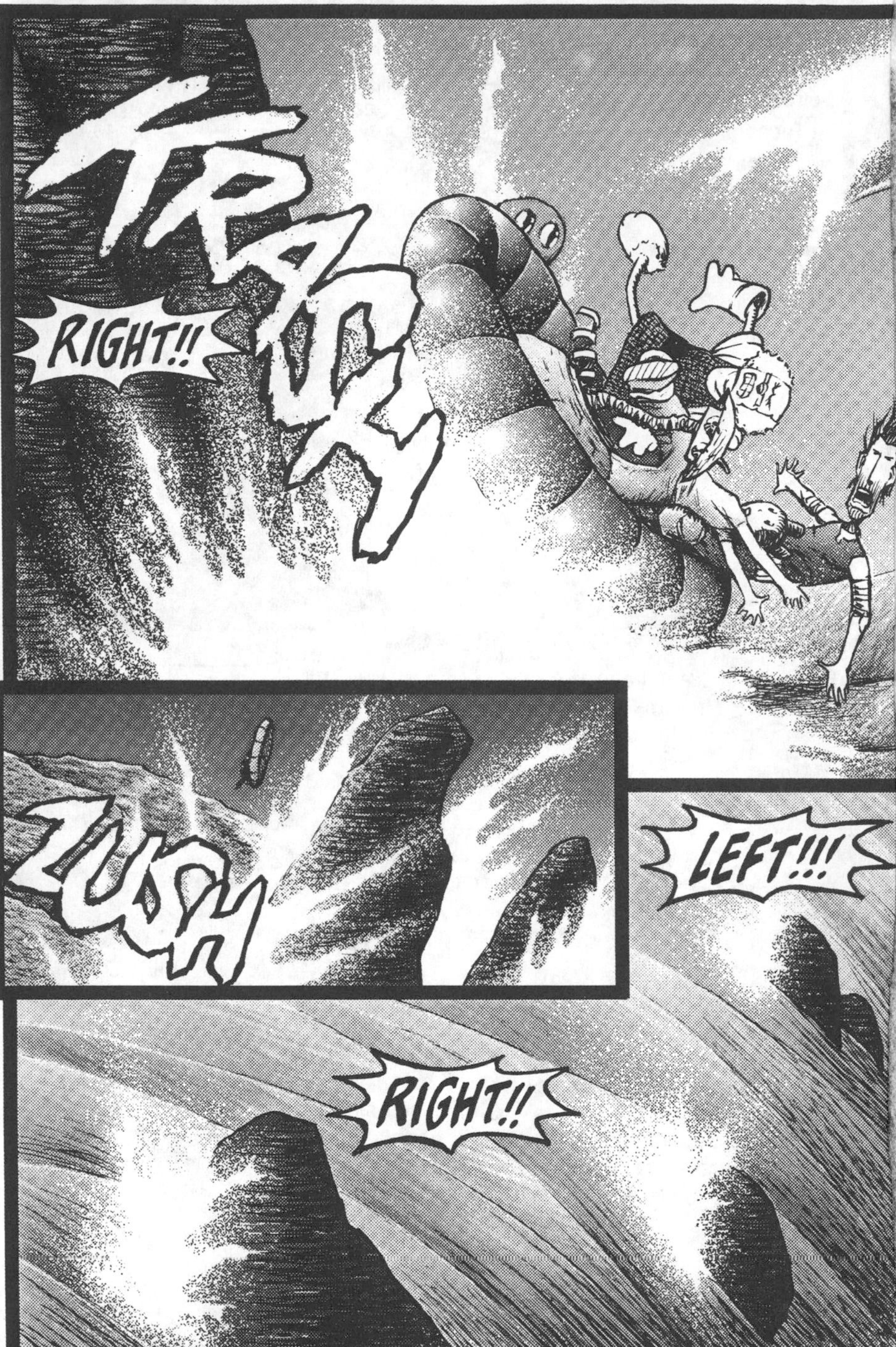
RIGHT!!
LEFT!!!
RIGHT!!

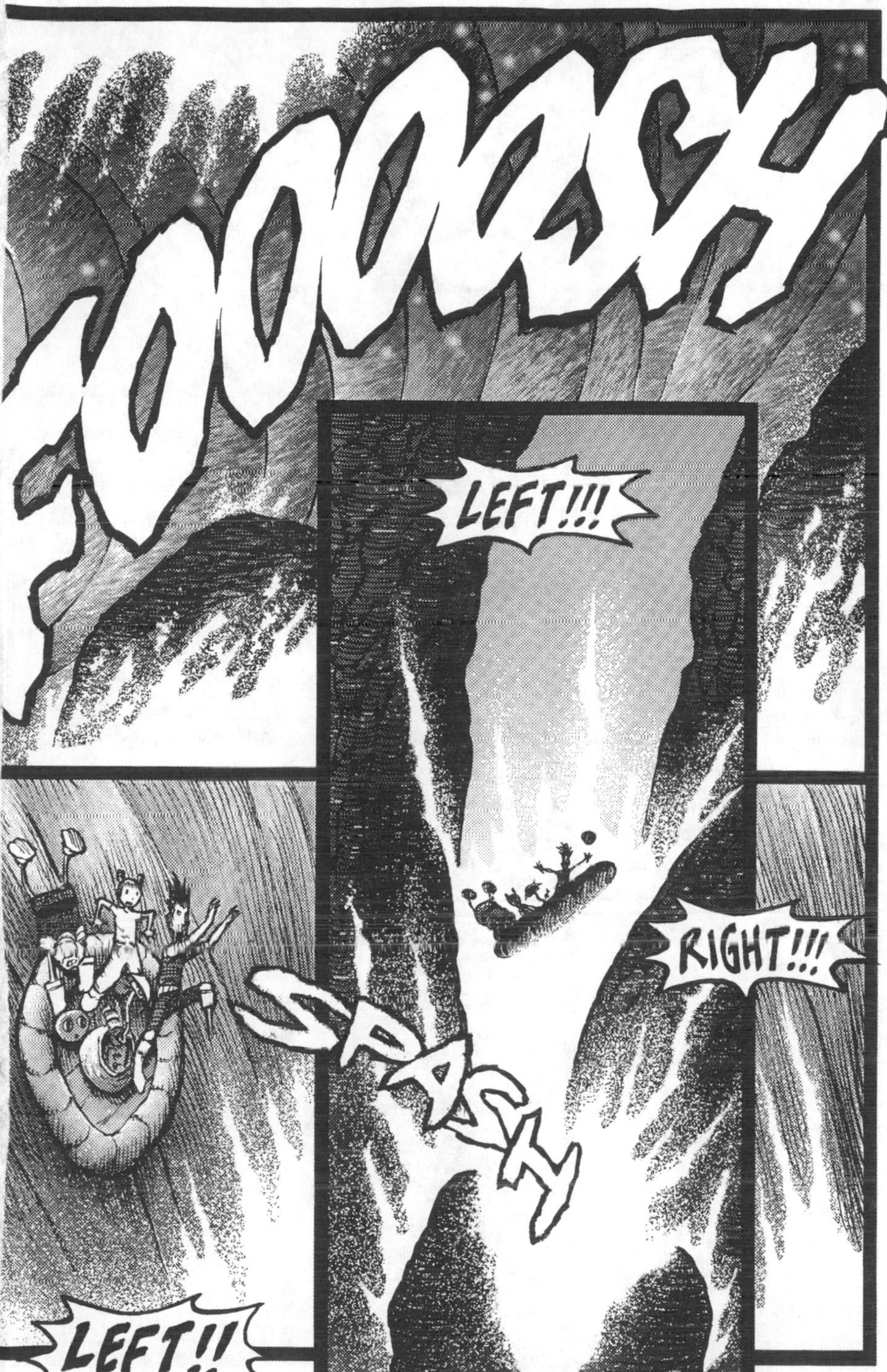

SQOOOCH
LEFT!!!
RIGHT!!!
SPASH
LEFT!!

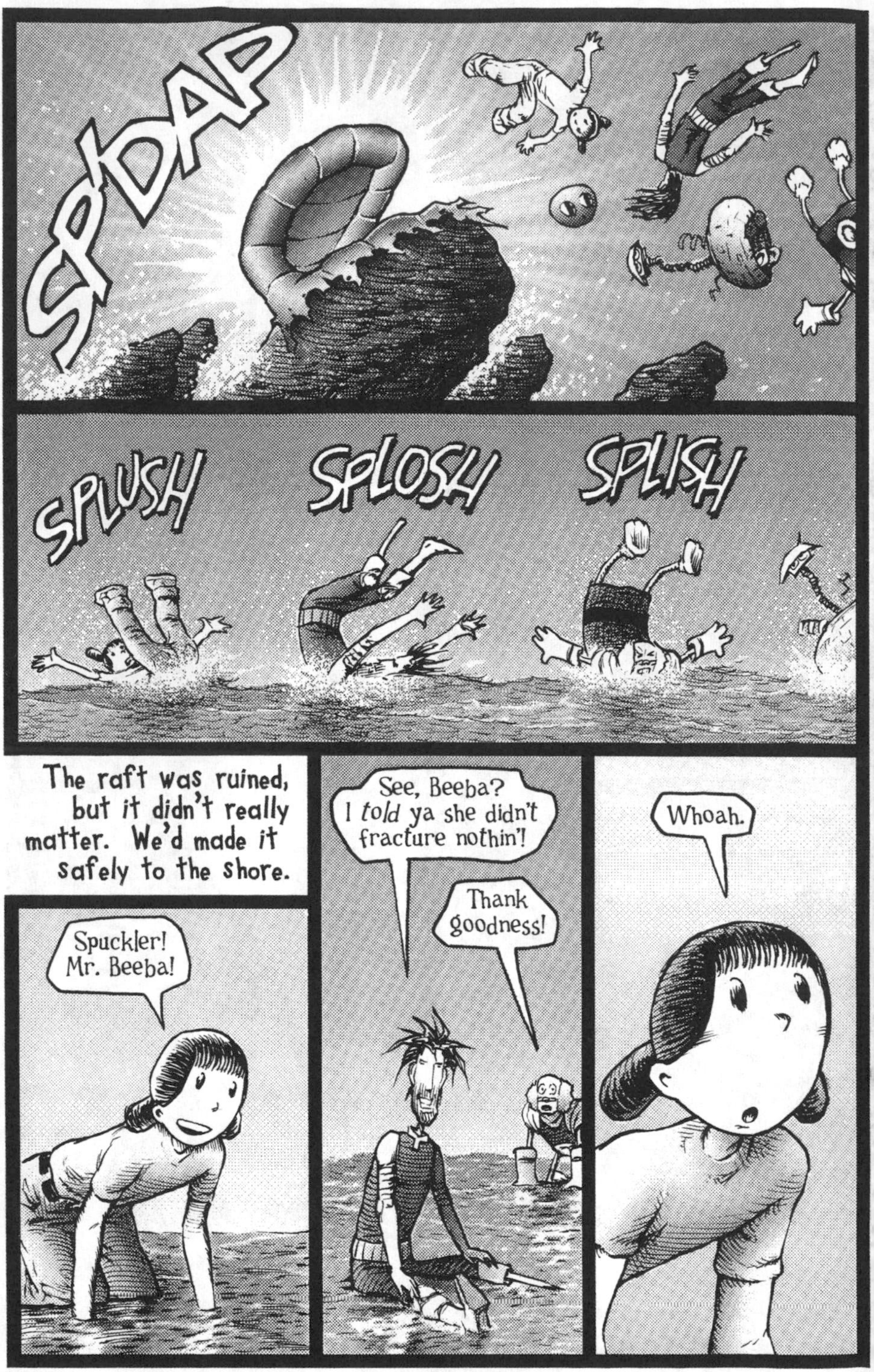
SPWAP
SPLUSH
SPLOSH
SPLISH
The raft was ruined, but it didn't really matter. We'd made it safely to the shore.
Spuckler! Mr. Beeba!
See, Beeba? I *told* ya she didn't fracture nothin'!
Thank goodness!
Whoah.

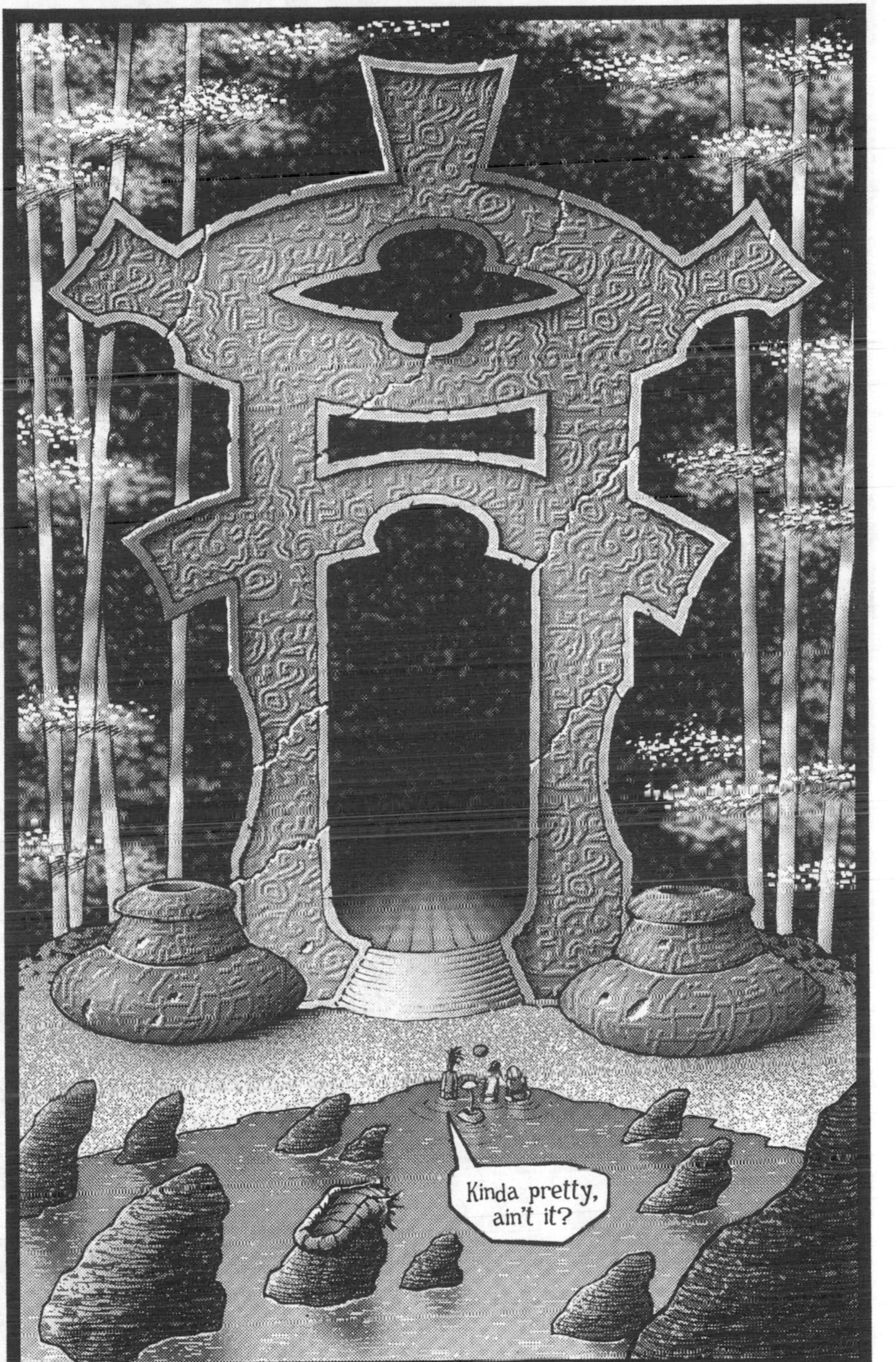
Kinda pretty,
ain't it?

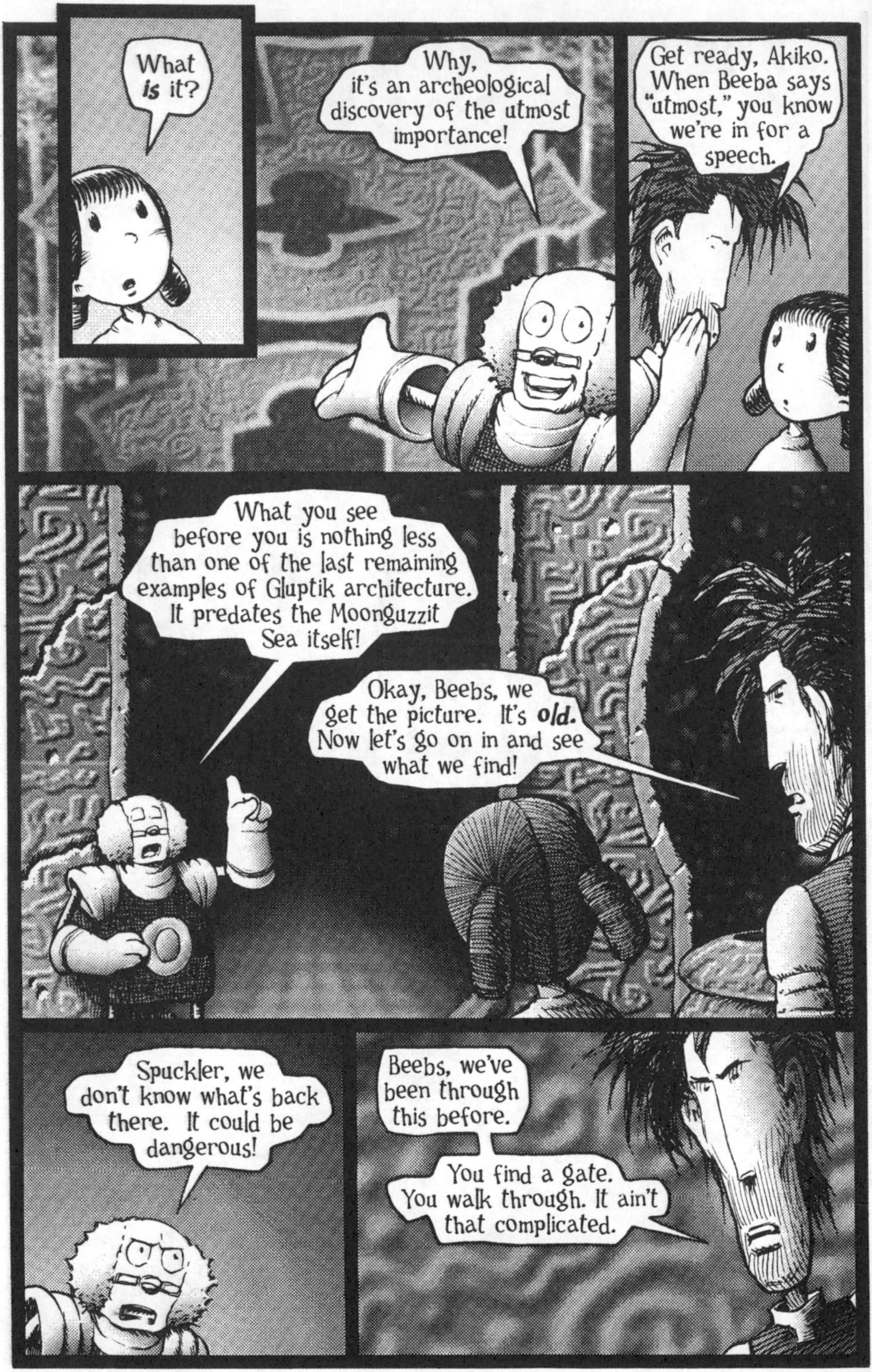
What is it?
Why, it's an archeological discovery of the utmost importance!
Get ready, Akiko. When Beeba says "utmost," you know we're in for a speech.
What you see before you is nothing less than one of the last remaining examples of Gluptik architecture. It predates the Moonguzzit Sea itself!
Okay, Beebs, we get the picture. It's *old.* Now let's go on in and see what we find!
Spuckler, we don't know what's back there. It could be dangerous!
Beebs, we've been through this before.
You find a gate. You walk through. It ain't that complicated.

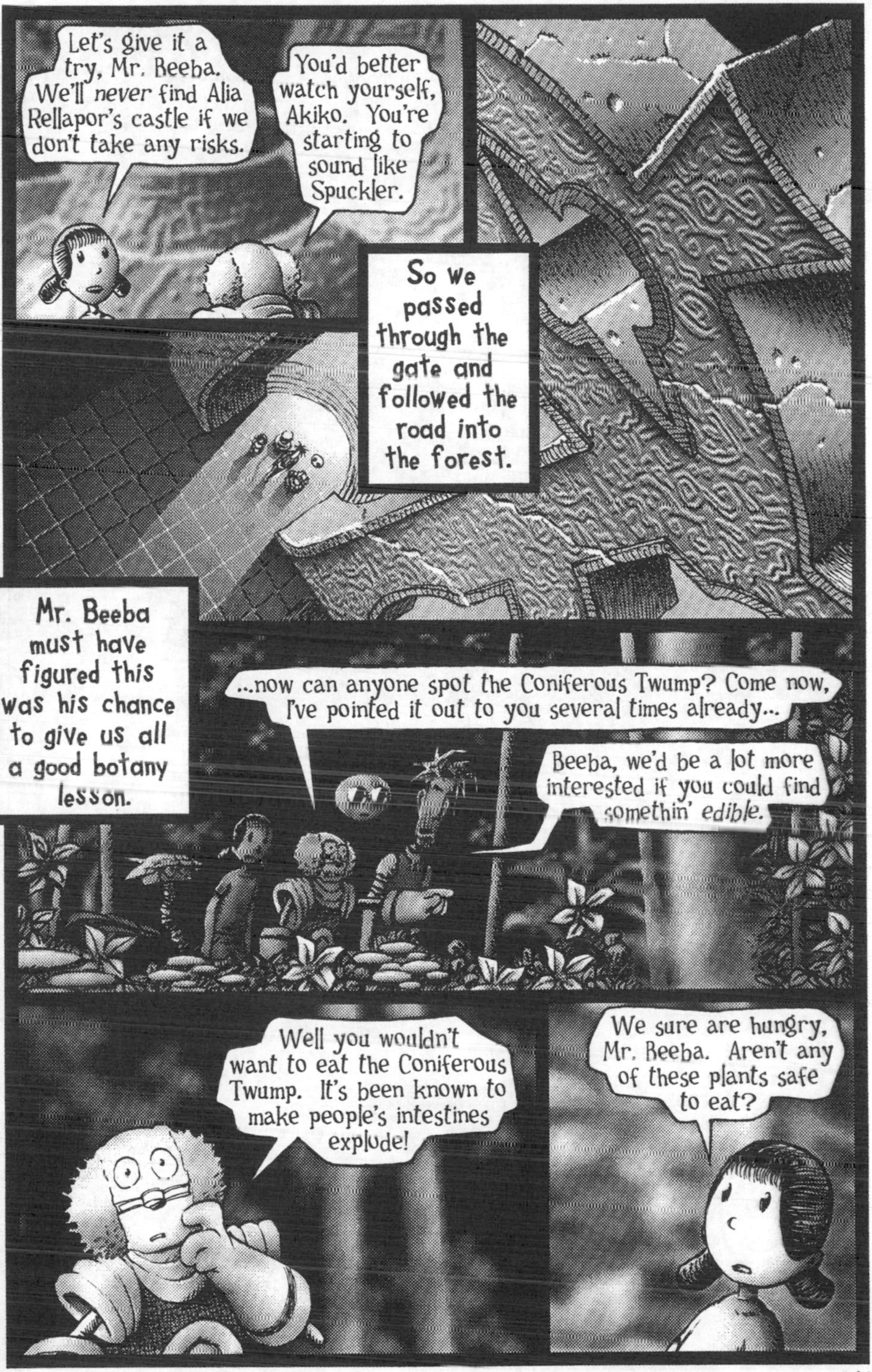
Let's give it a try, Mr. Beeba. We'll *never* find Alia Rellapor's castle if we don't take any risks.
You'd better watch yourself, Akiko. You're starting to sound like Spuckler.
So we passed through the gate and followed the road into the forest.
Mr. Beeba must have figured this was his chance to give us all a good botany lesson.
...now can anyone spot the Coniferous Twump? Come now, I've pointed it out to you several times already...
Beeba, we'd be a lot more interested if you could find somethin' *edible.*
Well you wouldn't want to eat the Coniferous Twump. It's been known to make people's intestines explode!
We sure are hungry, Mr. Beeba. Aren't any of these plants safe to eat?

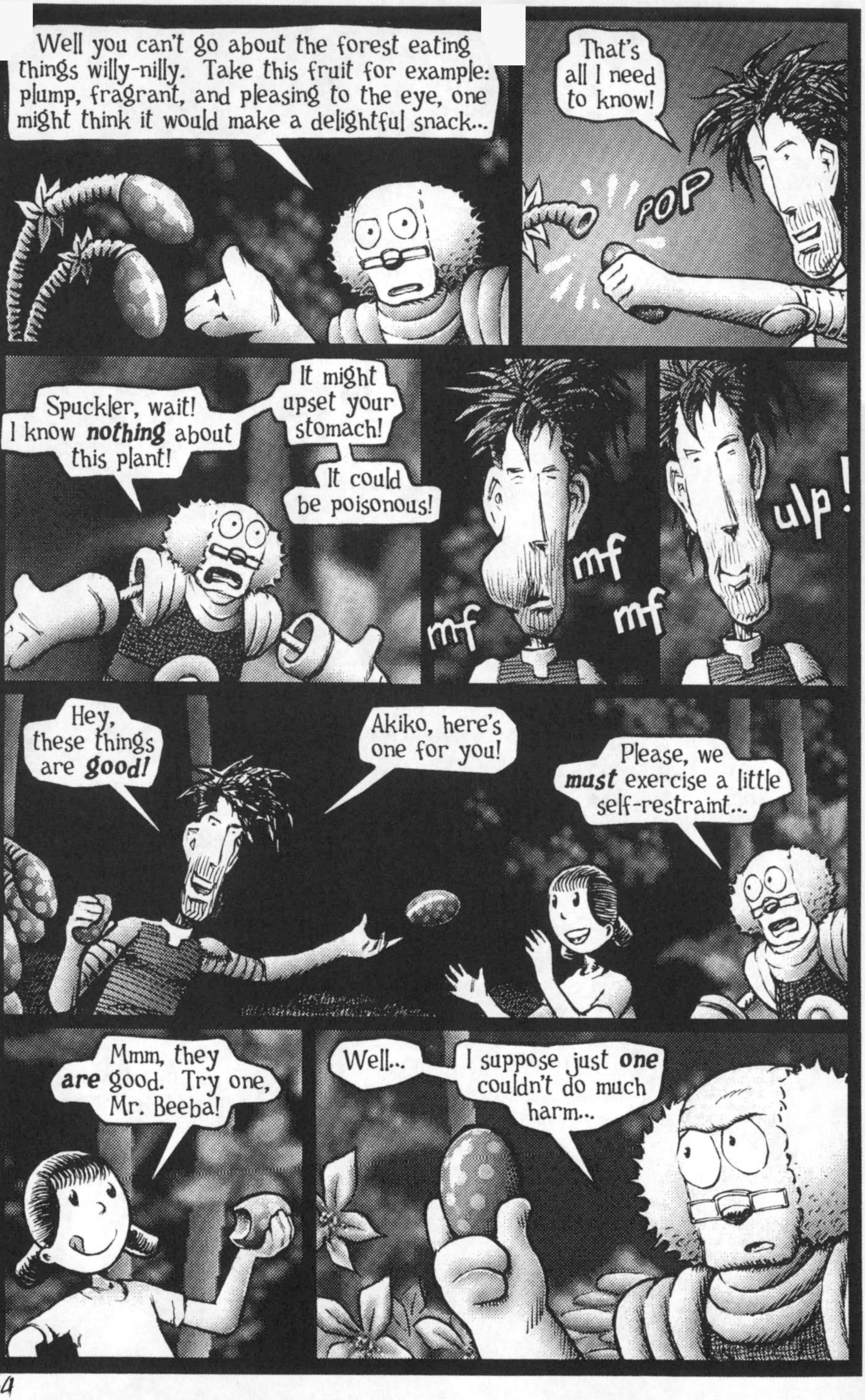

Well you can't go about the forest eating things willy-nilly. Take this fruit for example: plump, fragrant, and pleasing to the eye, one might think it would make a delightful snack...
That's all I need to know!
POP
Spuckler, wait! I know **nothing** about this plant!
It might upset your stomach!
It could be poisonous!
mf
mf
mf
ulp!
Hey, these things are **good**!
Akiko, here's one for you!
Please, we **must** exercise a little self-restraint...
Mmm, they **are** good. Try one, Mr. Beeba!
Well...
I suppose just **one** couldn't do much harm...

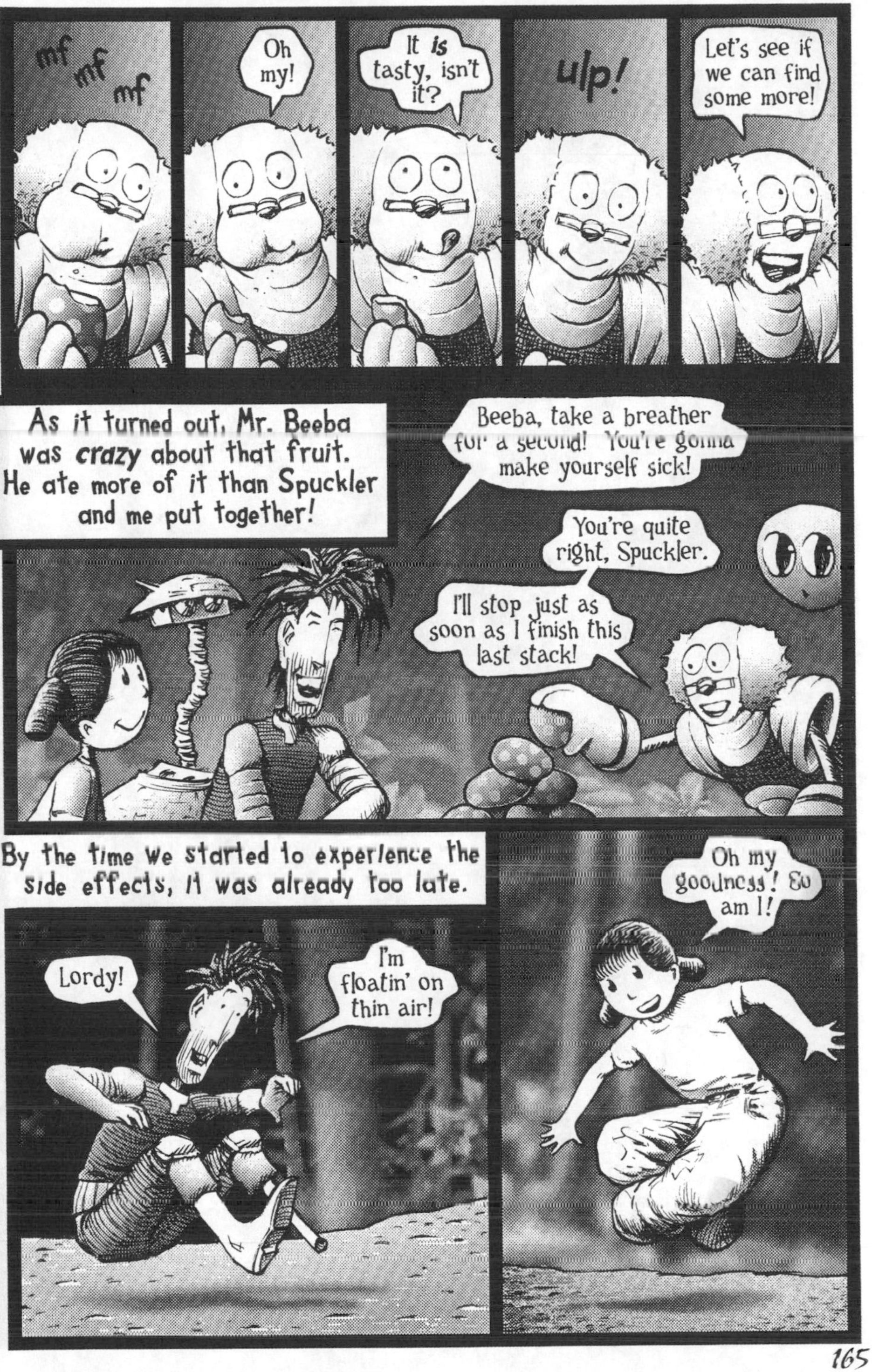
mf mf mf
Oh my!
It is tasty, isn't it?
ulp!
Let's see if we can find some more!
As it turned out, Mr. Beeba was crazy about that fruit. He ate more of it than Spuckler and me put together!
Beeba, take a breather for a second! You're gonna make yourself sick!
You're quite right, Spuckler.
I'll stop just as soon as I finish this last stack!
By the time we started to experience the side effects, it was already too late.
Lordy!
I'm floatin' on thin air!
Oh my goodness! So am I!

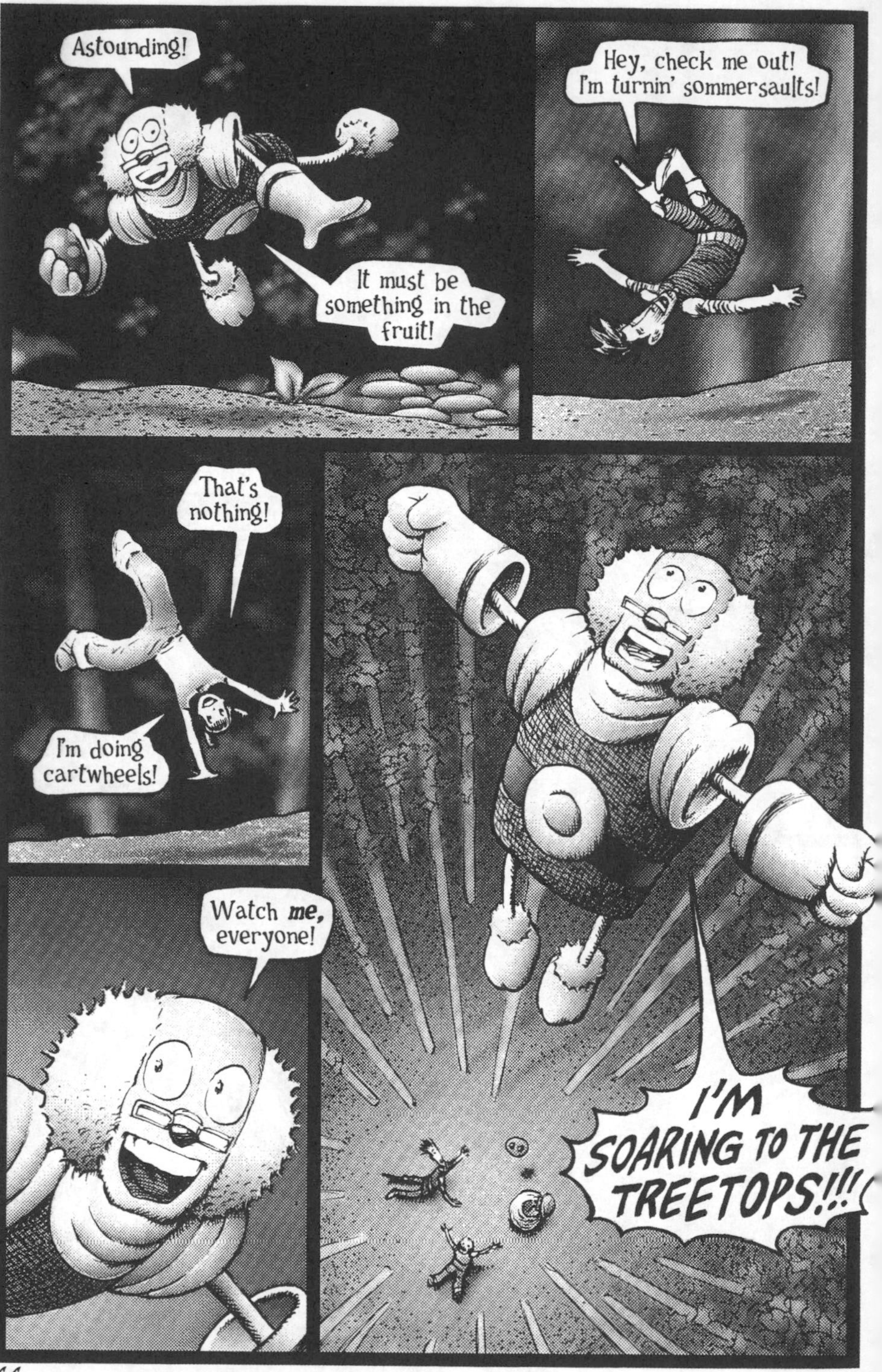
Astounding!
It must be something in the fruit!
Hey, check me out! I'm turnin' sommersaults!
That's nothing!
I'm doing cartwheels!
Watch *me,* everyone!
I'M SOARING TO THE TREETOPS!!!

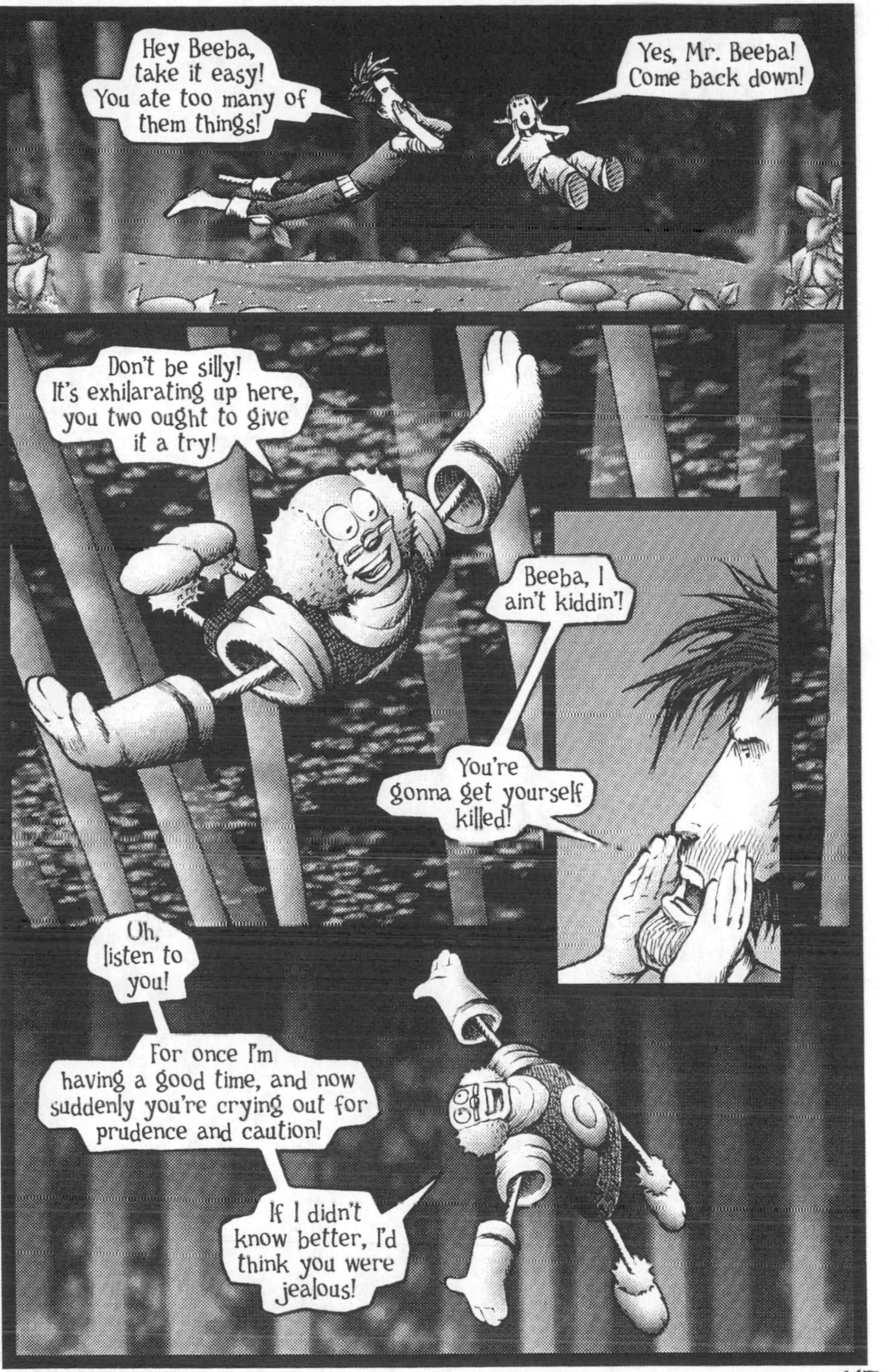
Hey Beeba, take it easy! You ate too many of them things!
Yes, Mr. Beeba! Come back down!
Don't be silly! It's exhilarating up here, you two ought to give it a try!
Beeba, I ain't kiddin'!
You're gonna get yourself killed!
Uh, listen to you!
For once I'm having a good time, and now suddenly you're crying out for prudence and caution!
If I didn't know better, I'd think you were jealous!

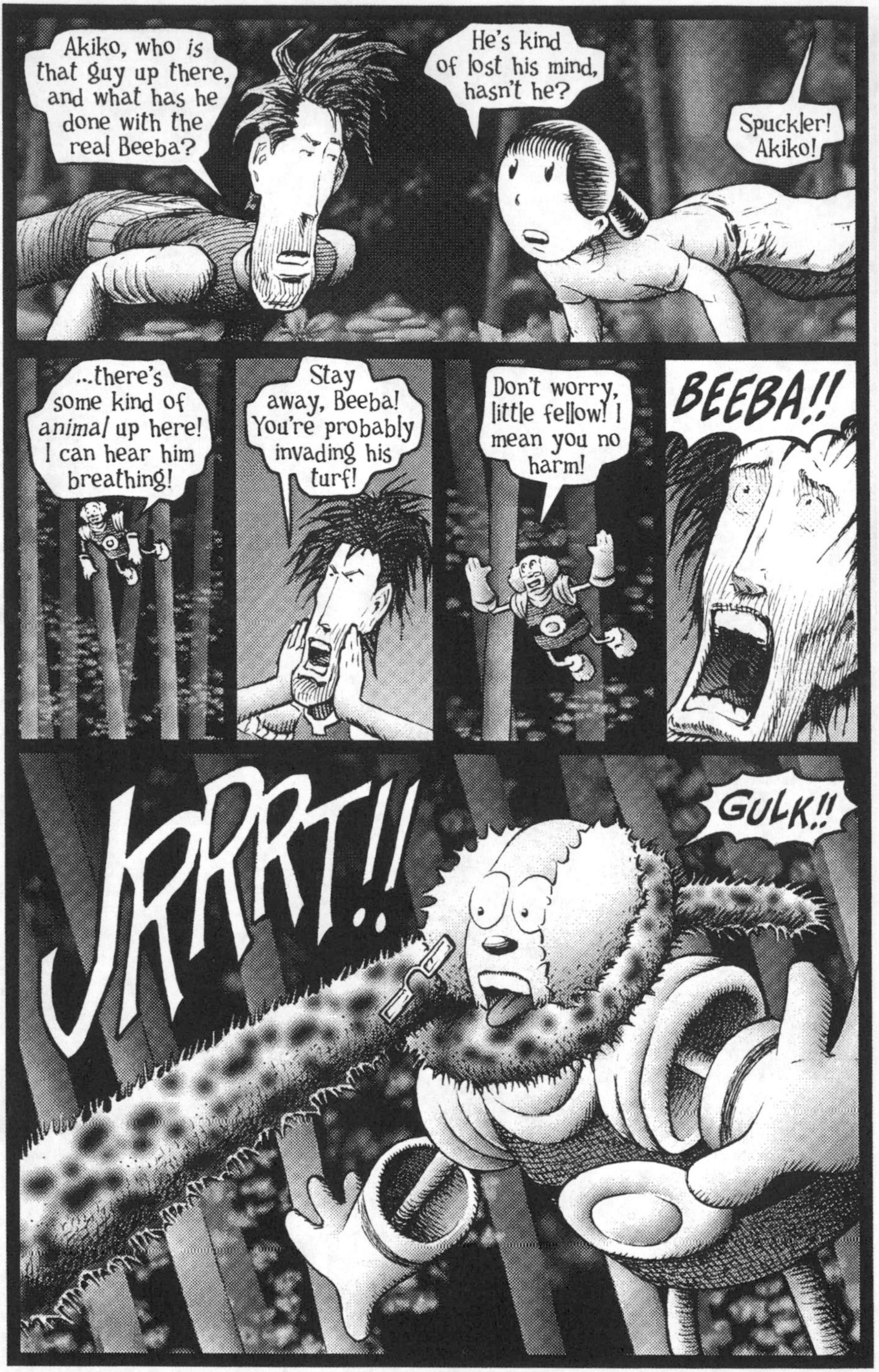
Akiko, who *is* that guy up there, and what has he done with the real Beeba?
He's kind of lost his mind, hasn't he?
Spuckler! Akiko!
...there's some kind of *animal* up here! I can hear him breathing!
Stay away, Beeba! You're probably invading his turf!
Don't worry, little fellow! I mean you no harm!
BEEBA!!
JRRRT!!
GULK!!

Next Issue: "Her Majesty"

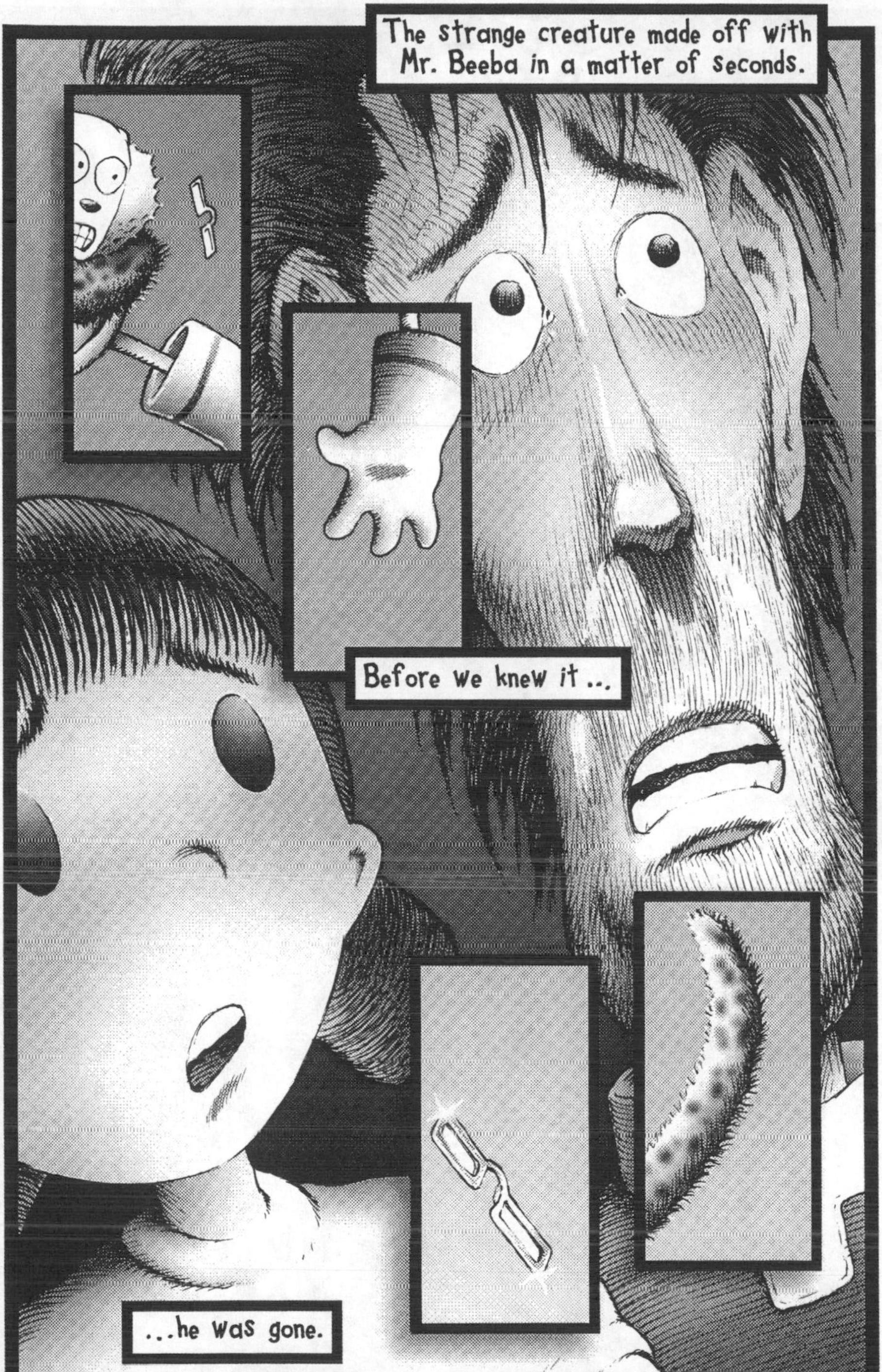
The strange creature made off with Mr. Beeba in a matter of seconds.
Before we knew it ...
...he was gone.

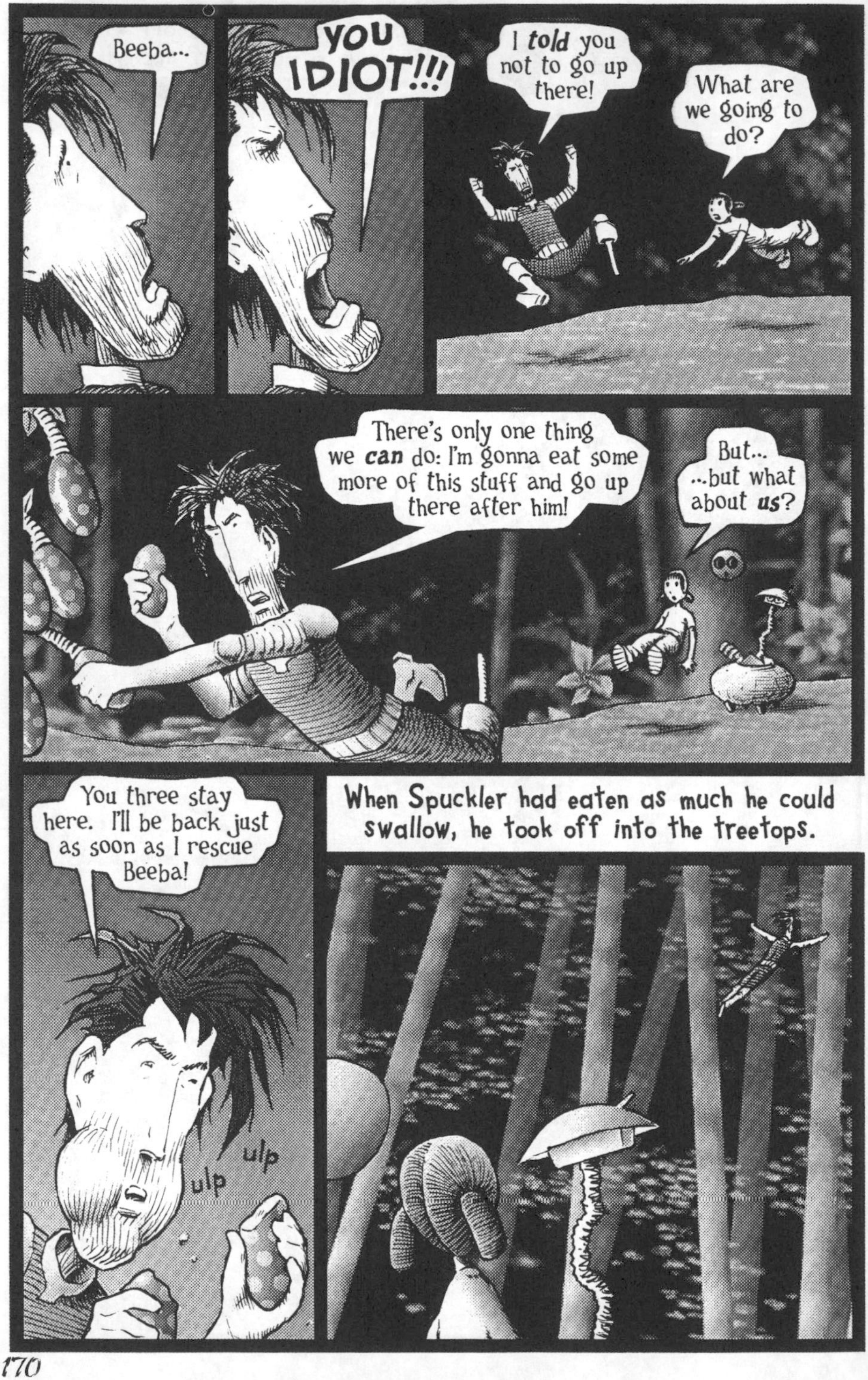
Beeba...
YOU IDIOT!!!
I told you not to go up there!
What are we going to do?
There's only one thing we can do: I'm gonna eat some more of this stuff and go up there after him!
But... ...but what about us?
You three stay here. I'll be back just as soon as I rescue Beeba!
ulp
ulp
When Spuckler had eaten as much he could swallow, he took off into the treetops.

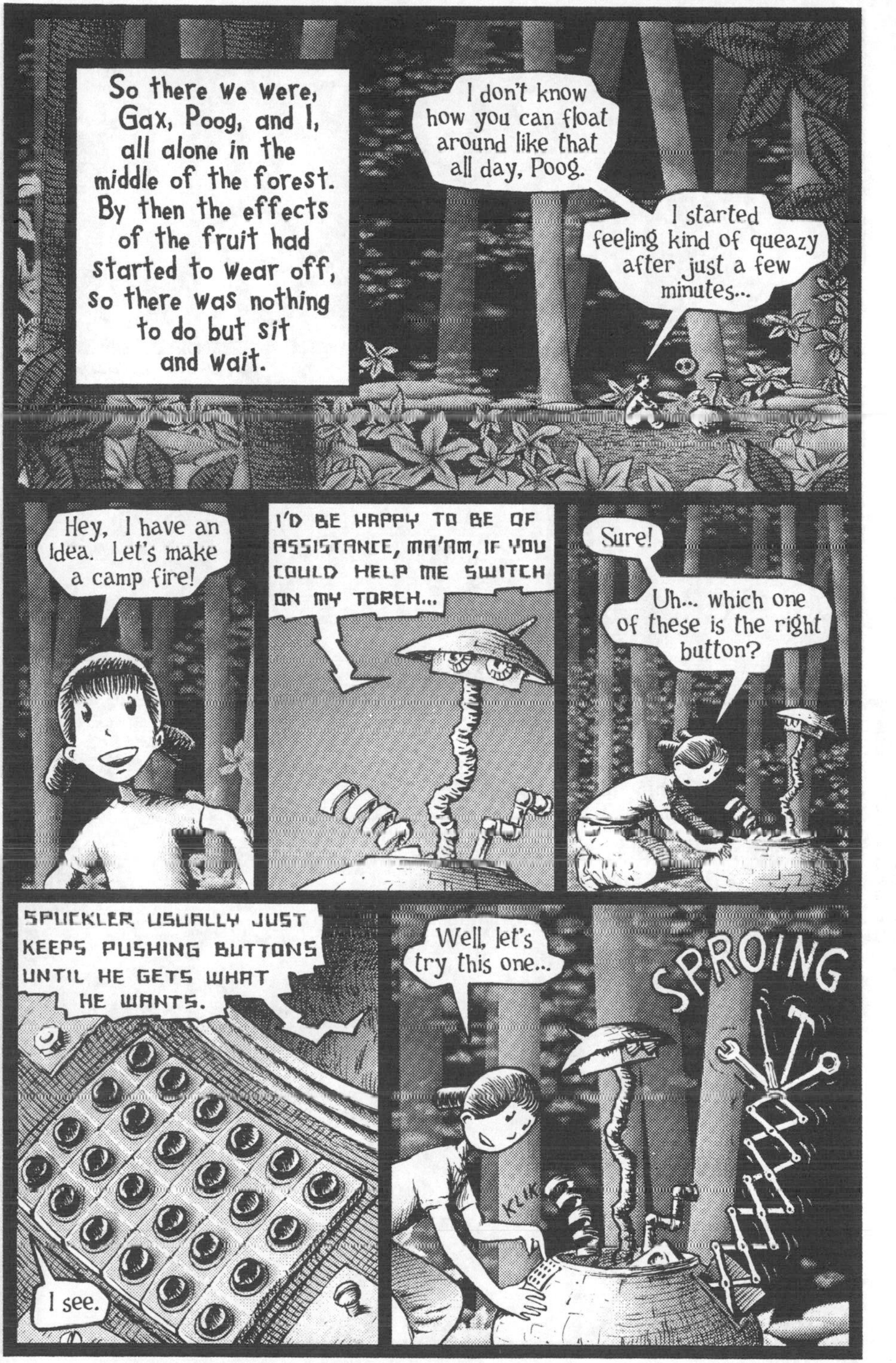
So there we were, Gax, Poog, and I, all alone in the middle of the forest. By then the effects of the fruit had started to wear off, so there was nothing to do but sit and wait.
I don't know how you can float around like that all day, Poog.
I started feeling kind of queazy after just a few minutes...
Hey, I have an Idea. Let's make a camp fire!
I'D BE HAPPY TO BE OF ASSISTANCE, MA'AM, IF YOU COULD HELP ME SWITCH ON MY TORCH...
Sure!
Uh... which one of these is the right button?
SPUCKLER USUALLY JUST KEEPS PUSHING BUTTONS UNTIL HE GETS WHAT HE WANTS.
I see.
Well, let's try this one...
KLIK
SPROING

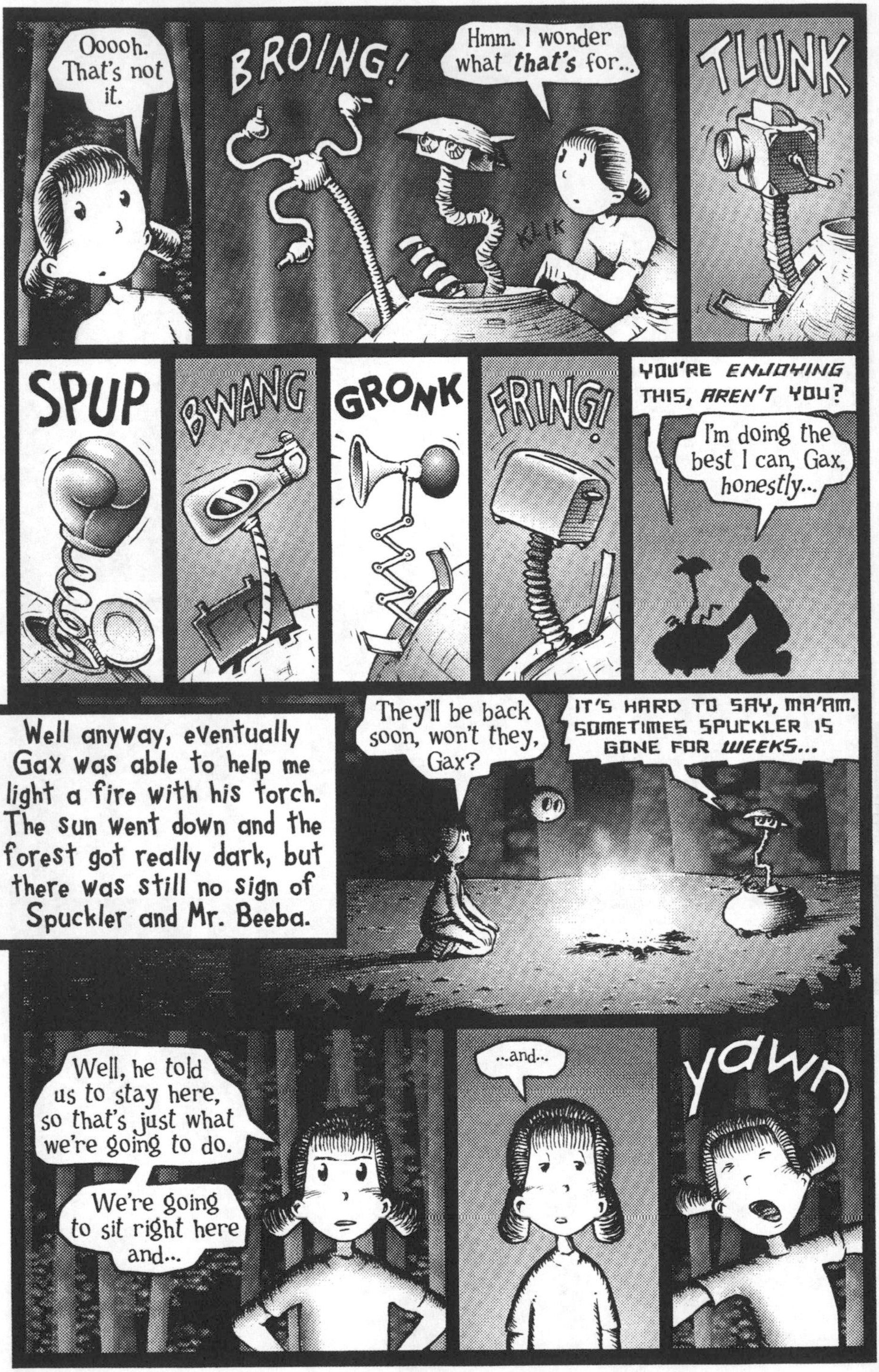

Ooooh. That's not it.
BROING!
Hmm. I wonder what *that's* for...
KLIK
TLUNK
SPUP
BWANG
GRONK
FRING!
YOU'RE *ENJOYING* THIS, *AREN'T* YOU?
I'm doing the best I can, Gax, *honestly*...
Well anyway, eventually Gax was able to help me light a fire with his torch. The sun went down and the forest got really dark, but there was still no sign of Spuckler and Mr. Beeba.
They'll be back soon, won't they, Gax?
IT'S HARD TO SAY, MA'AM. SOMETIMES SPUCKLER IS GONE FOR *WEEKS*...
Well, he told us to stay here, so that's just what we're going to do.
We're going to sit right here and...
...and...
yawn

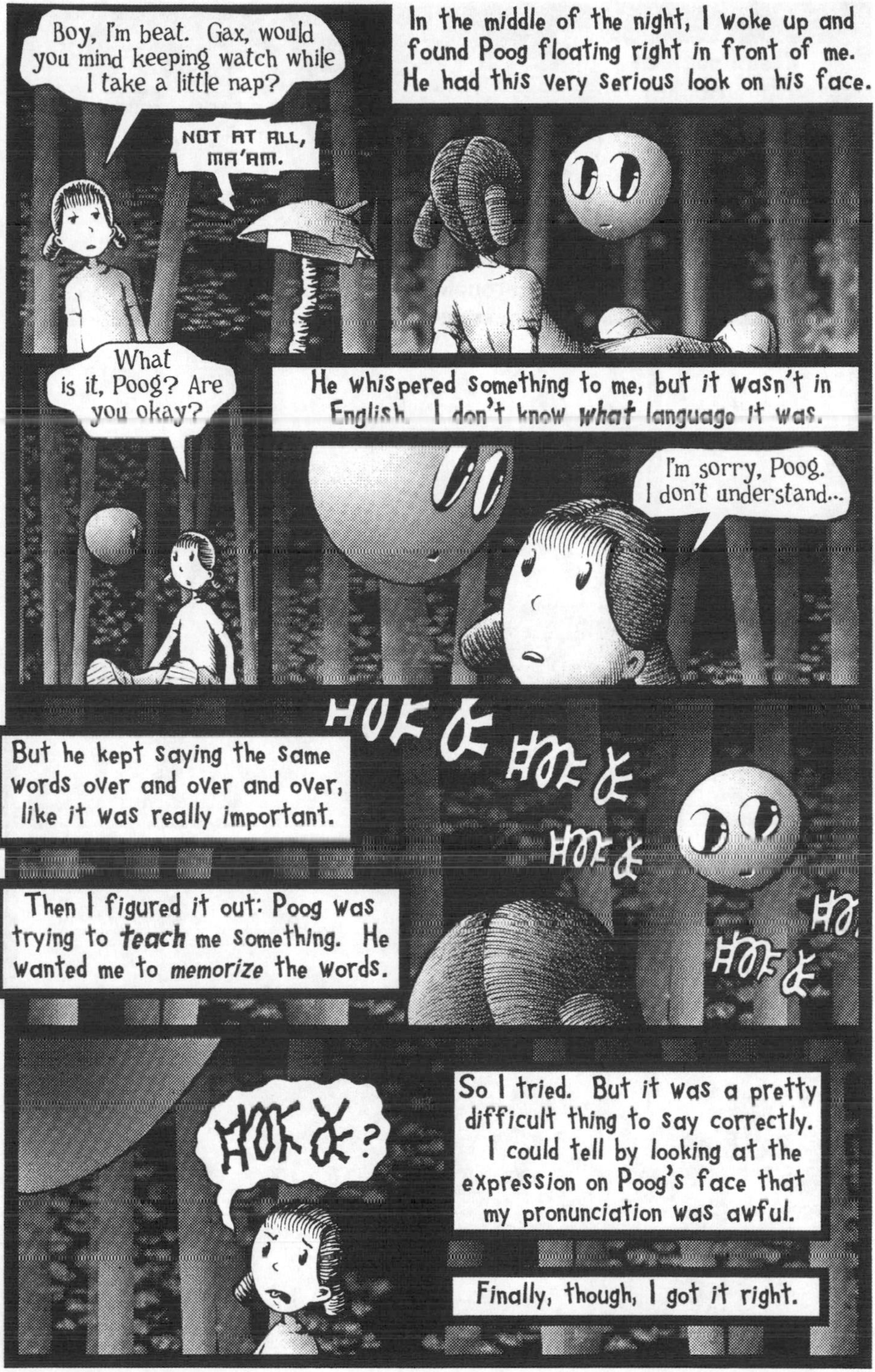
Boy, I'm beat. Gax, would you mind keeping watch while I take a little nap?
NOT AT ALL, MA'AM.
In the middle of the night, I woke up and found Poog floating right in front of me. He had this very serious look on his face.
What is it, Poog? Are you okay?
He whispered something to me, but it wasn't in English. I don't know *what* language it was.
I'm sorry, Poog. I don't understand...
But he kept saying the same words over and over and over, like it was really important.
Then I figured it out: Poog was trying to *teach* me something. He wanted me to *memorize* the words.
So I tried. But it was a pretty difficult thing to say correctly. I could tell by looking at the expression on Poog's face that my pronunciation was awful.
Finally, though, I got it right.

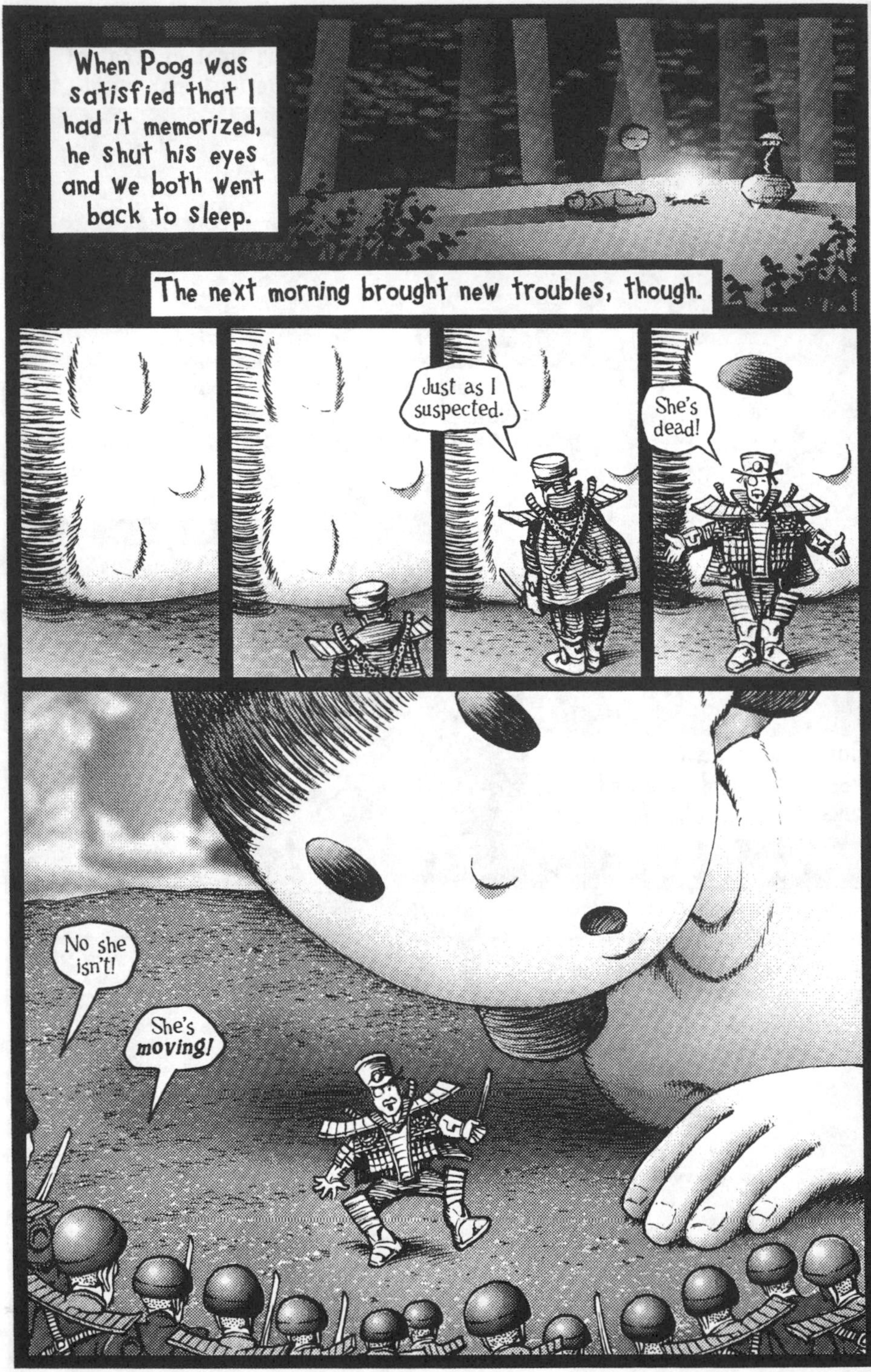

When Poog was satisfied that I had it memorized, he shut his eyes and we both went back to sleep.
The next morning brought new troubles, though.
Just as I suspected.
She's dead!
No she isn't!
She's *moving!*

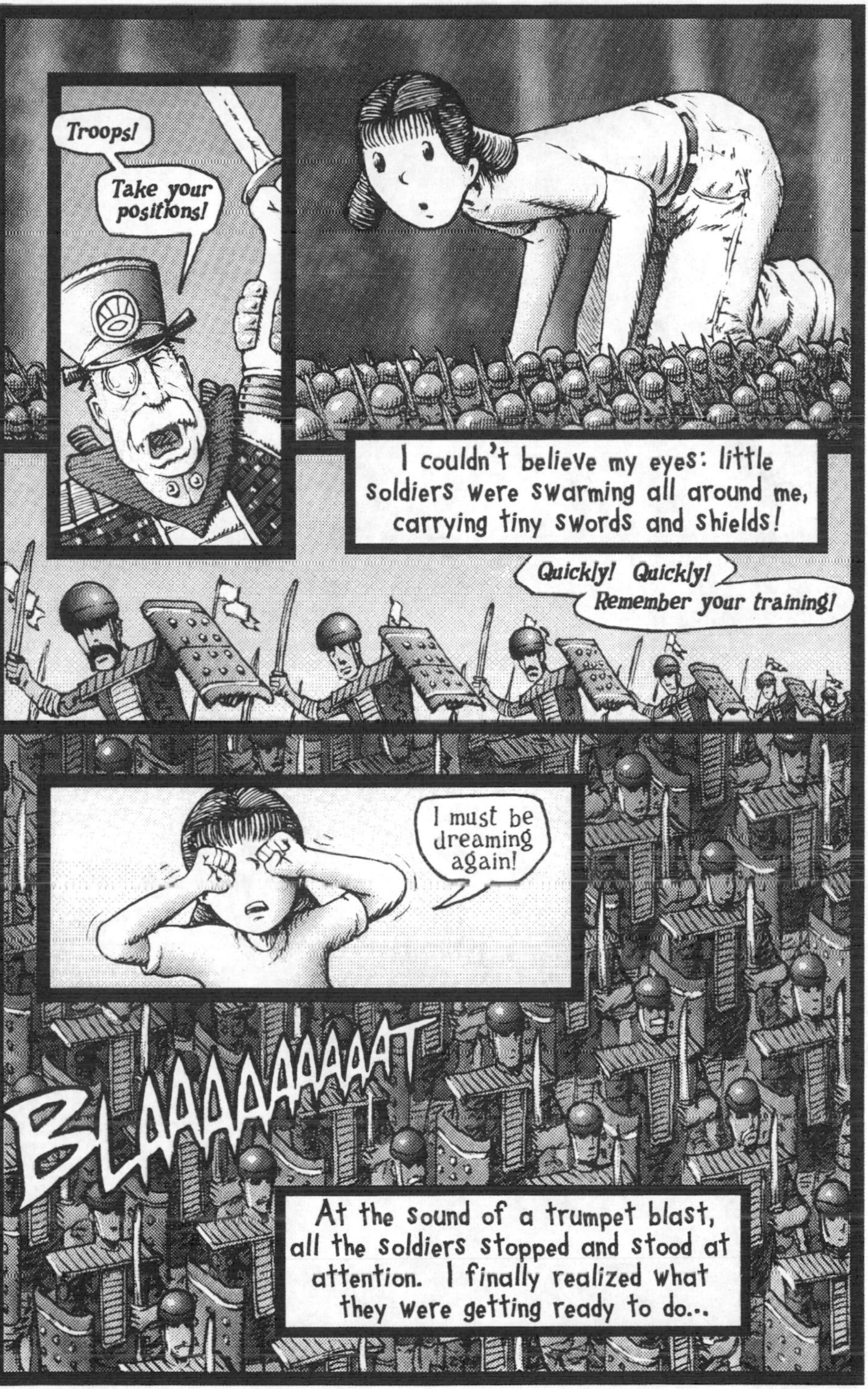
Troops!
Take your positions!
I couldn't believe my eyes: little soldiers were swarming all around me, carrying tiny swords and shields!
Quickly! Quickly!
Remember your training!
I must be dreaming again!
BLAAAAAAAAT
At the sound of a trumpet blast, all the soldiers stopped and stood at attention. I finally realized what they were getting ready to do...

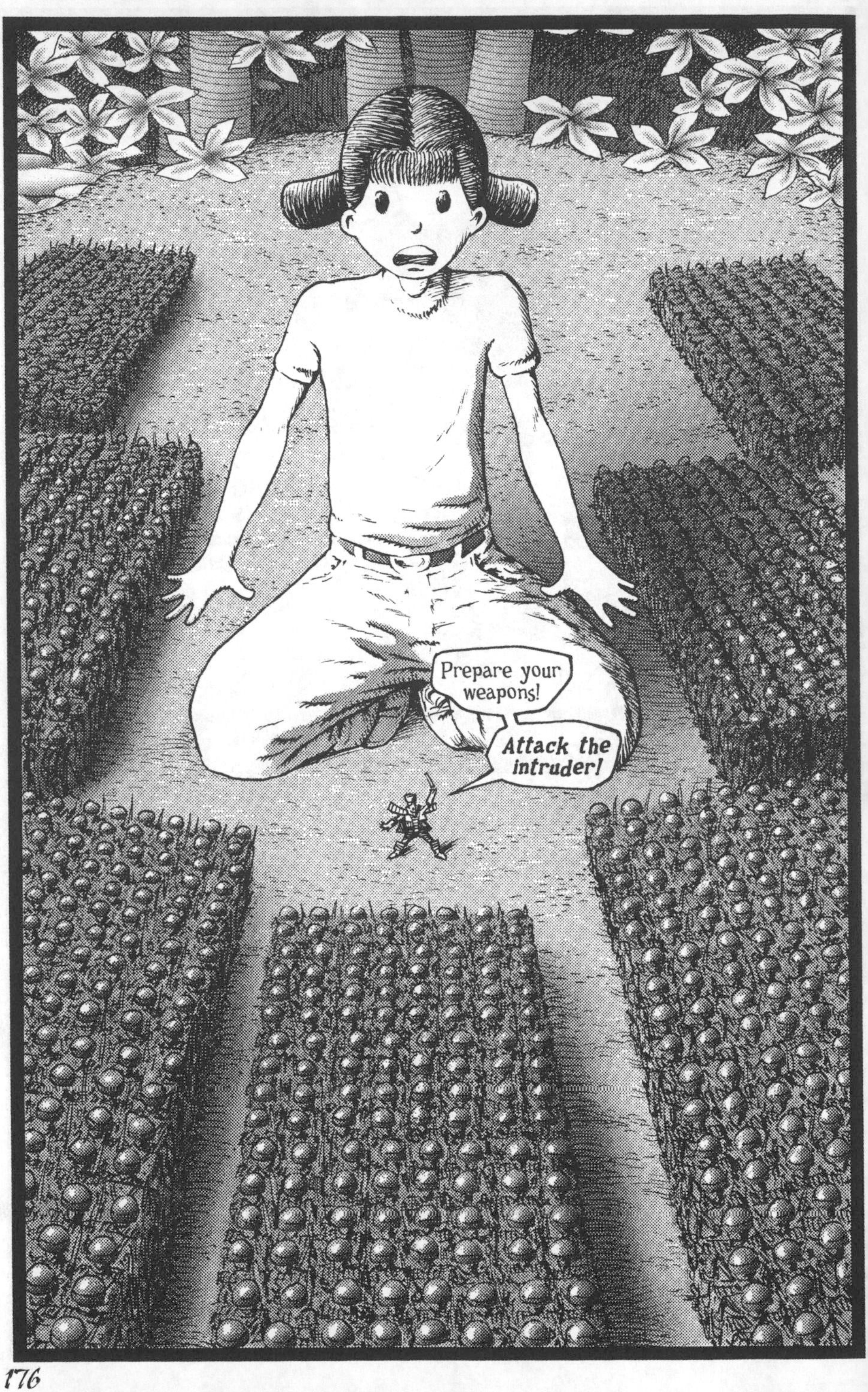
Prepare your weapons!
Attack the intruder!

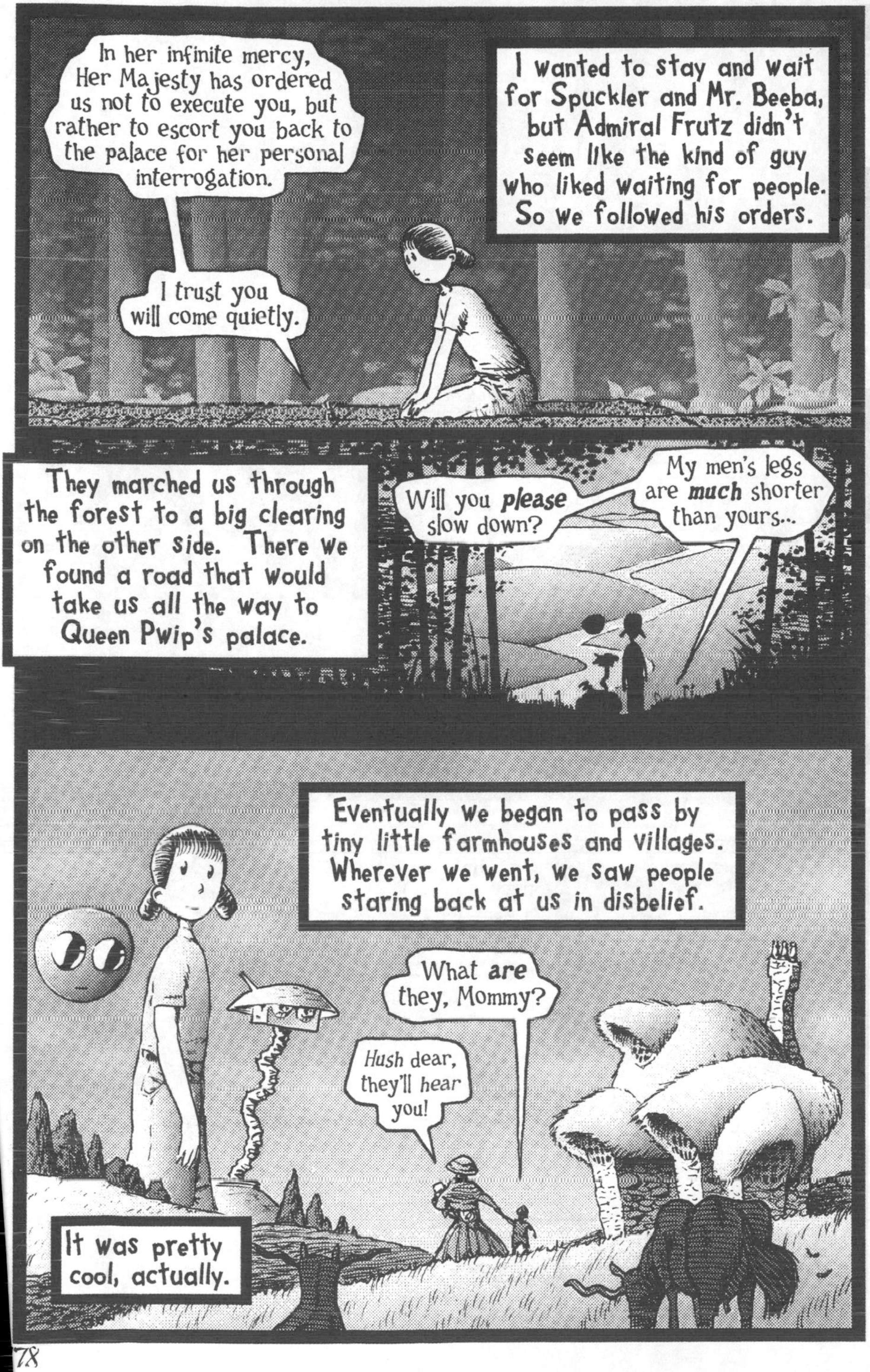
In her infinite mercy, Her Majesty has ordered us not to execute you, but rather to escort you back to the palace for her personal interrogation.
I wanted to stay and wait for Spuckler and Mr. Beeba, but Admiral Frutz didn't seem like the kind of guy who liked waiting for people. So we followed his orders.
I trust you will come quietly.
They marched us through the forest to a big clearing on the other side. There we found a road that would take us all the way to Queen Pwip's palace.
Will you *please* slow down?
My men's legs are *much* shorter than yours...
Eventually we began to pass by tiny little farmhouses and villages. Wherever we went, we saw people staring back at us in disbelief.
What **are** they, Mommy?
Hush dear, they'll *hear* you!
It was pretty cool, actually.

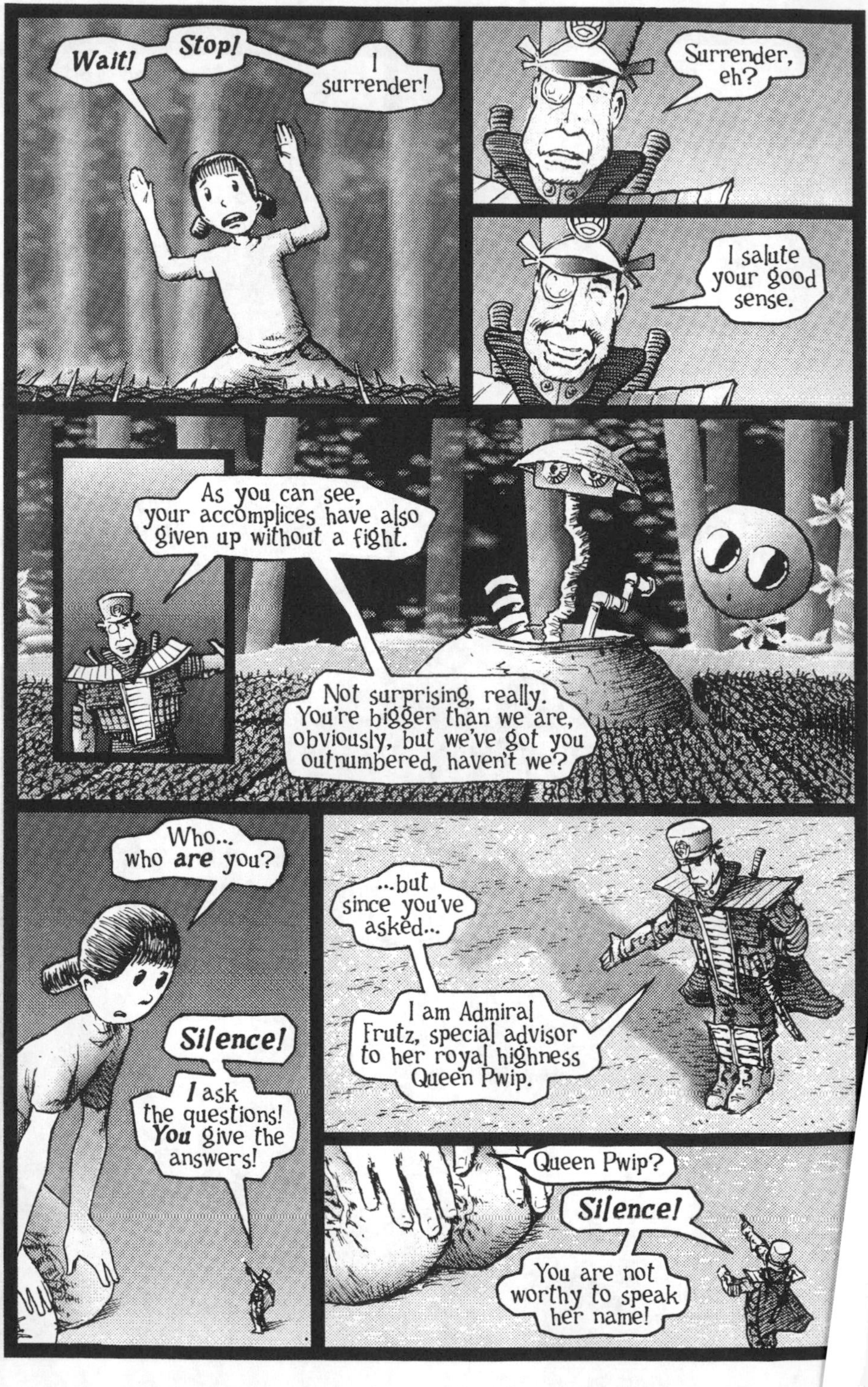
Wait!
Stop!
I surrender!
Surrender, eh?
I salute your good sense.
As you can see, your accomplices have also given up without a fight.
Not surprising, really. You're bigger than we are, obviously, but we've got you outnumbered, haven't we?
Who... who are you?
Silence!
I ask the questions! You give the answers!
...but since you've asked...
I am Admiral Frutz, special advisor to her royal highness Queen Pwip.
Queen Pwip?
Silence!
You are not worthy to speak her name!

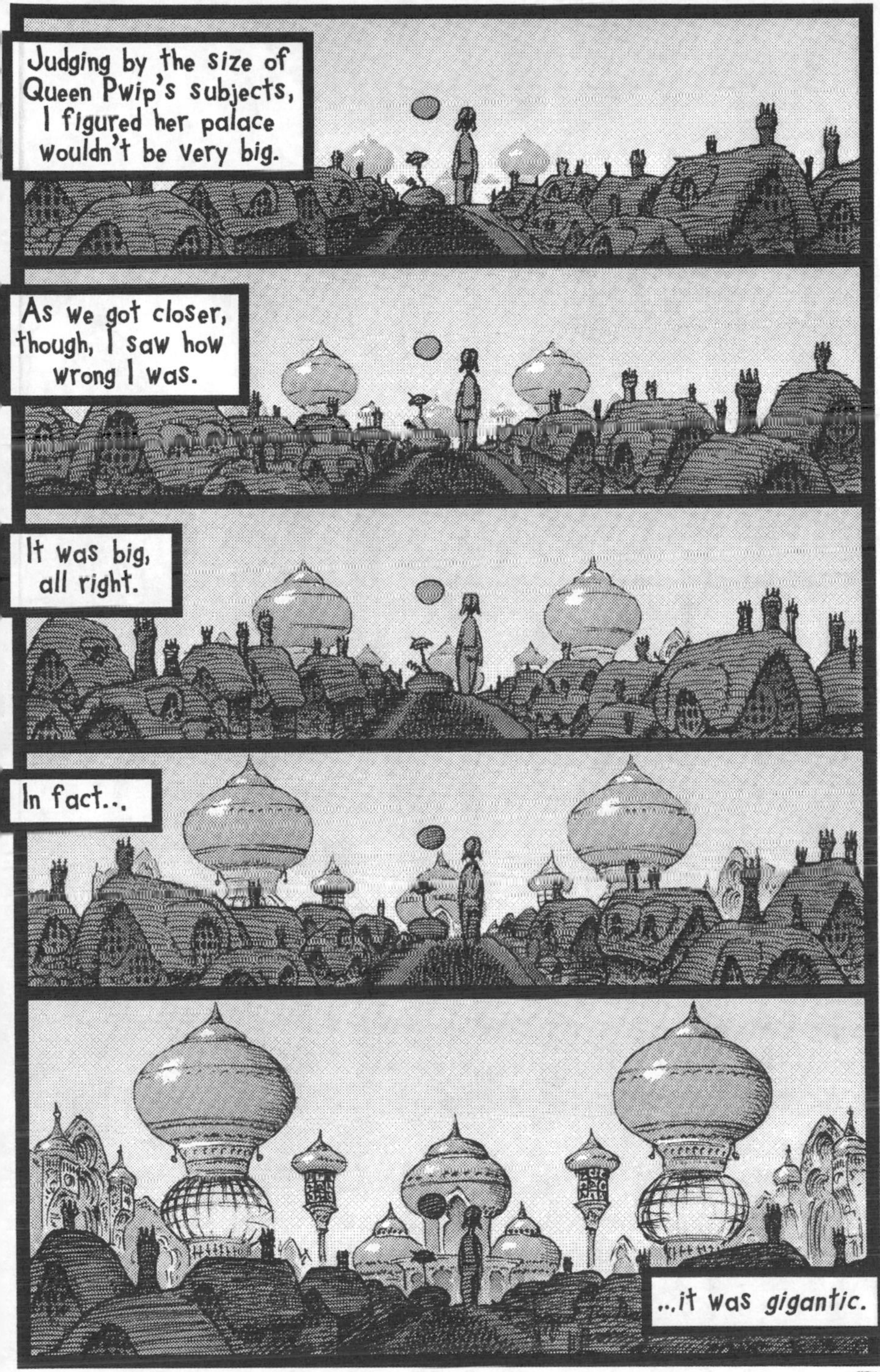
Judging by the size of Queen Pwip's subjects, I figured her palace wouldn't be very big.
As we got closer, though, I saw how wrong I was.
It was big, all right.
In fact...
...it was *gigantic*.

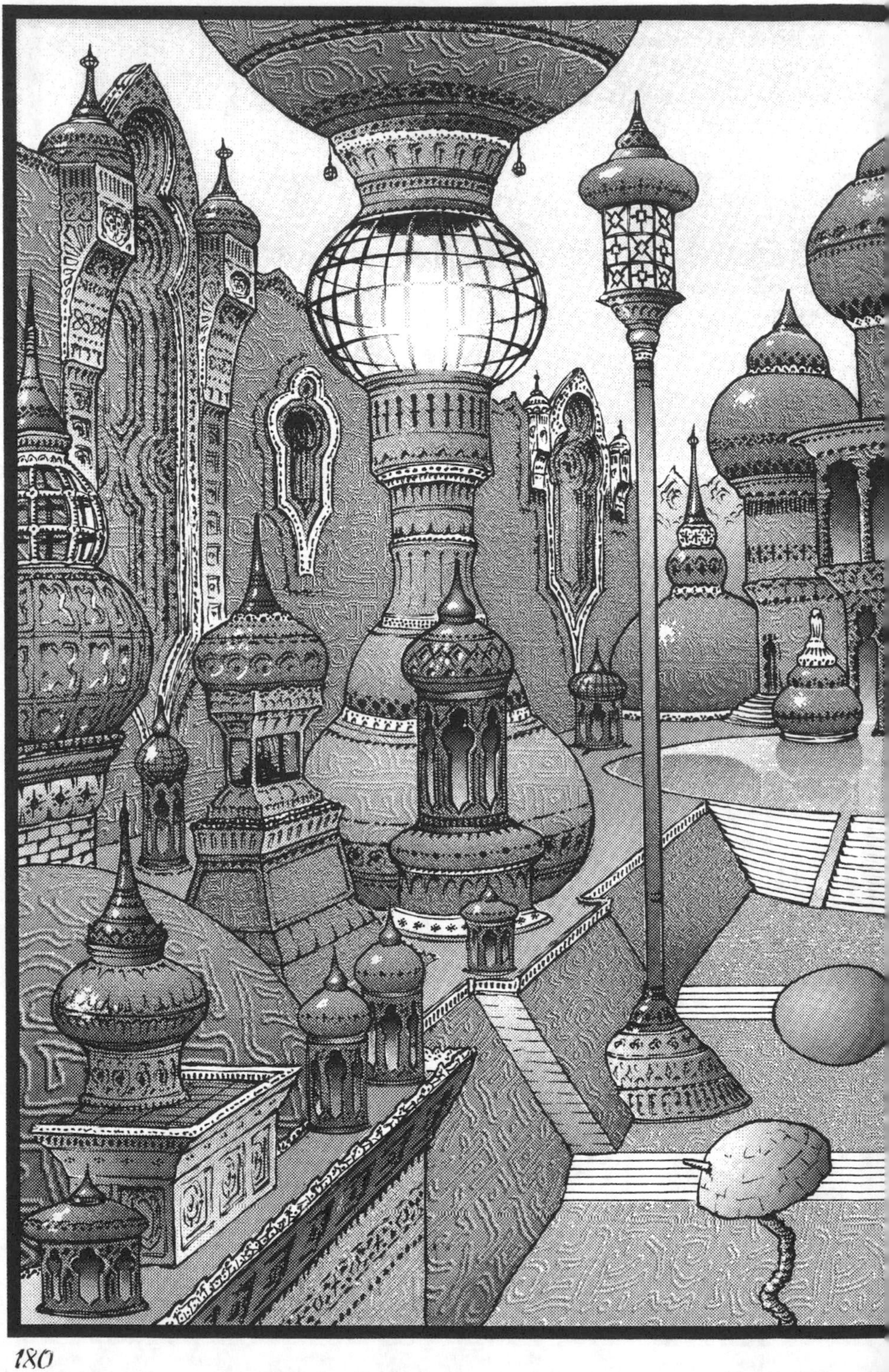

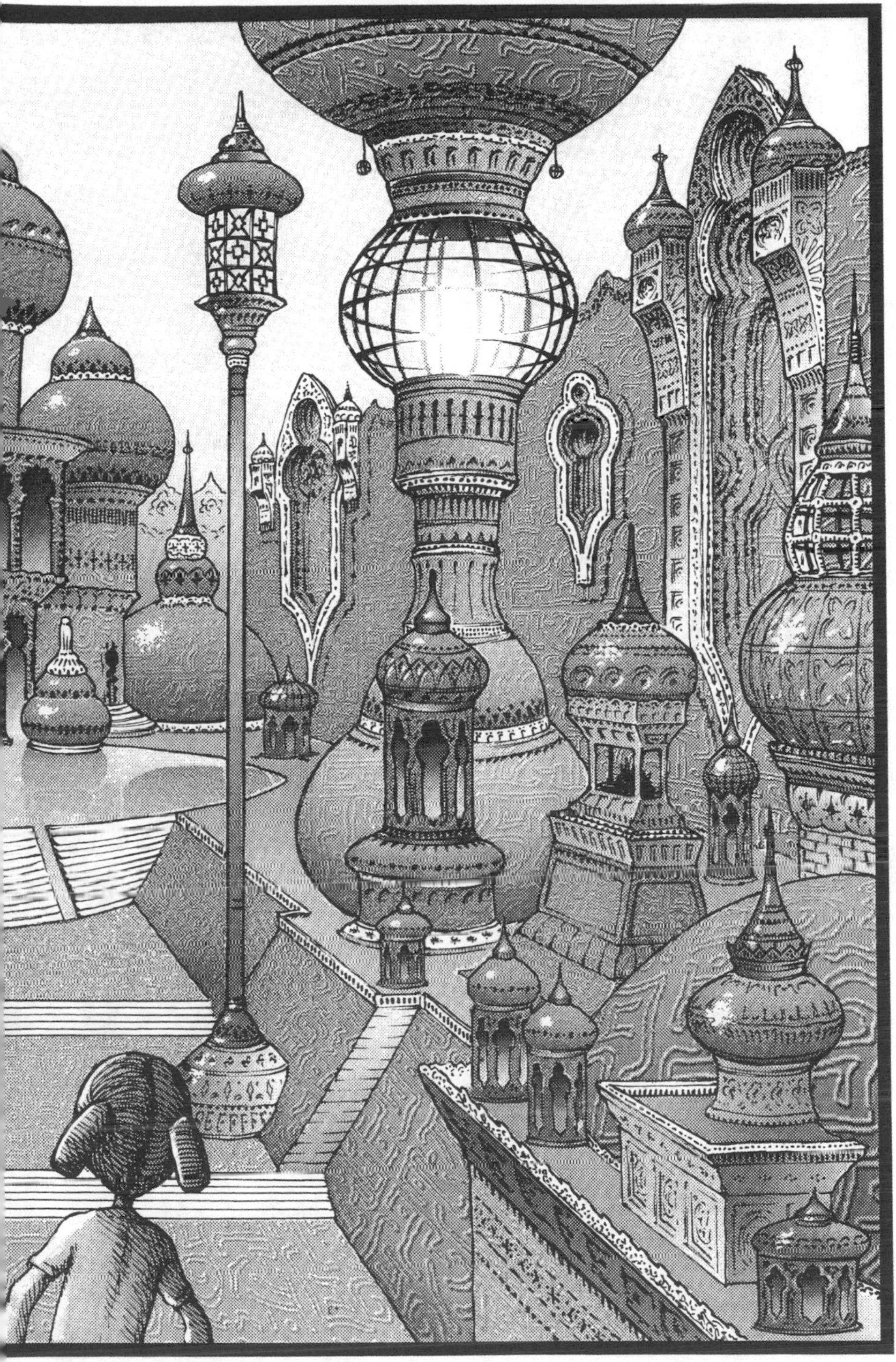

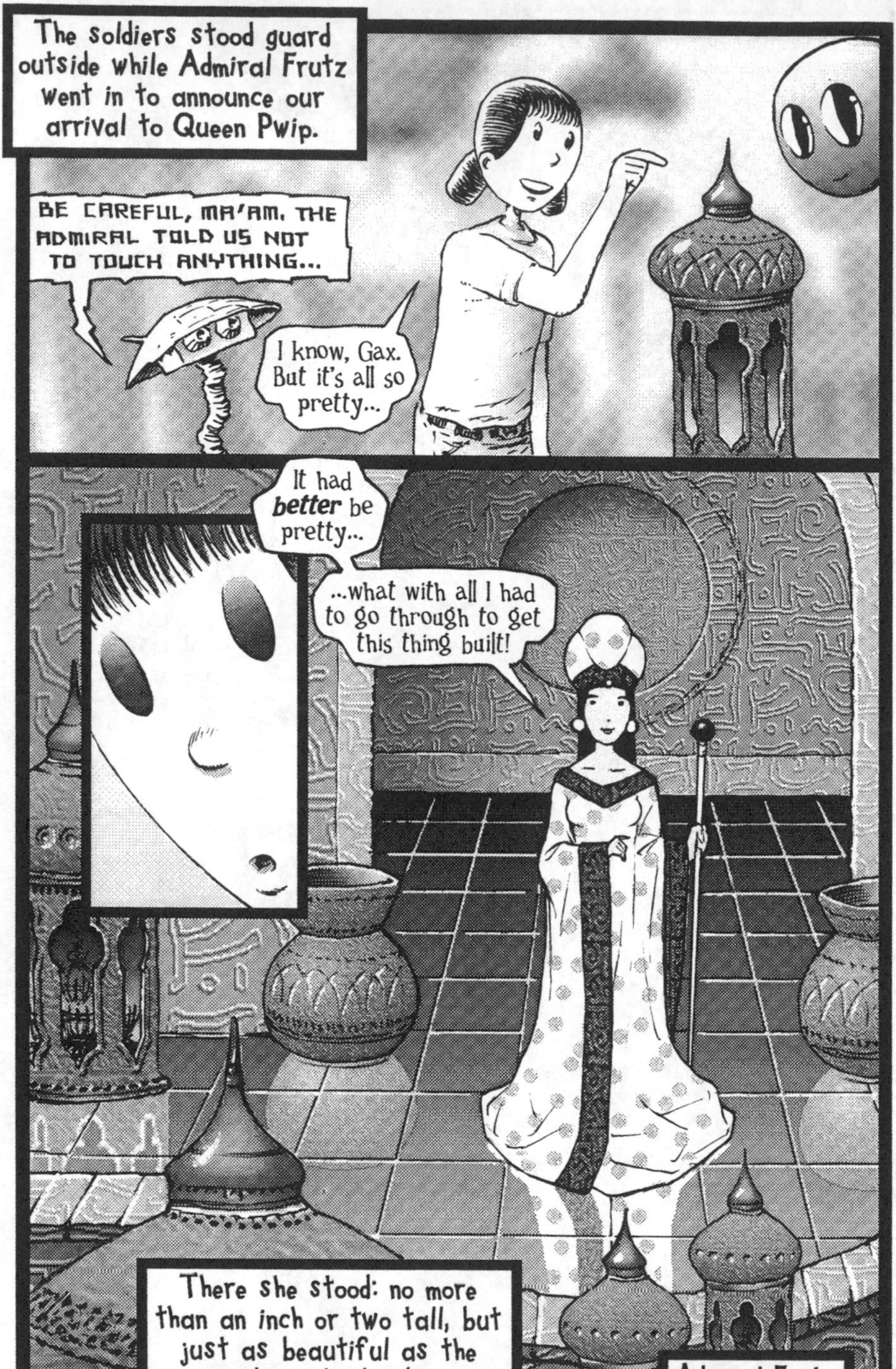
The soldiers stood guard outside while Admiral Frutz went in to announce our arrival to Queen Pwip.
BE CAREFUL, MA'AM. THE ADMIRAL TOLD US NOT TO TOUCH ANYTHING...
I know, Gax. But it's all so pretty...
It had **better** be pretty...
...what with all I had to go through to get this thing built!
There she stood: no more than an inch or two tall, but just as beautiful as the palace she lived in.
Admiral Frutz introduced her.

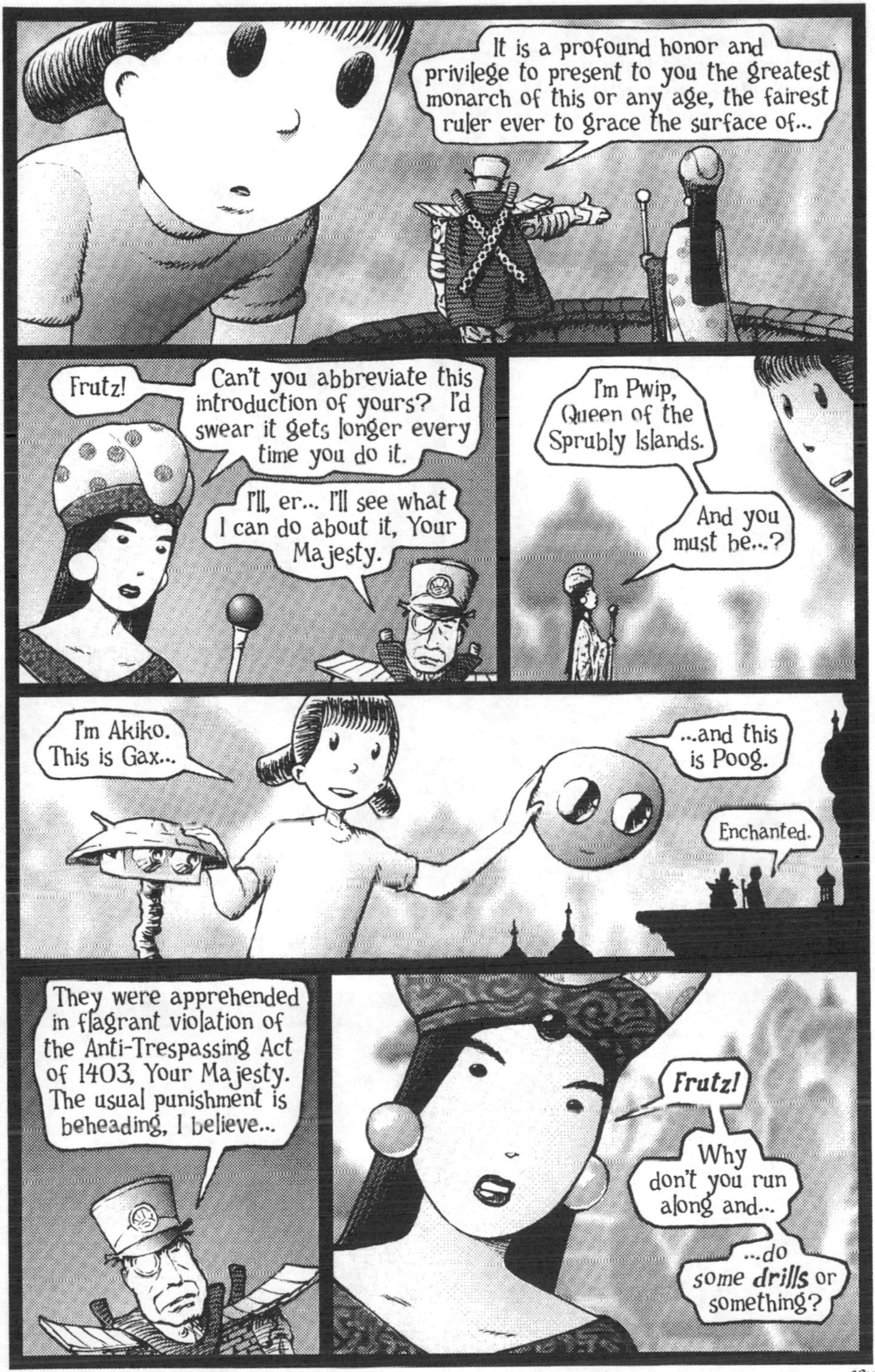

It is a profound honor and privilege to present to you the greatest monarch of this or any age, the fairest ruler ever to grace the surface of...
Frutz!
Can't you abbreviate this introduction of yours? I'd swear it gets longer every time you do it.
I'll, er... I'll see what I can do about it, Your Majesty.
I'm Pwip, Queen of the Sprubly Islands.
And you must be...?
I'm Akiko. This is Gax...
...and this is Poog.
Enchanted.
They were apprehended in flagrant violation of the Anti-Trespassing Act of 1403, Your Majesty. The usual punishment is beheading, I believe...
Frutz!
Why don't you run along and...
...do some drills or something?

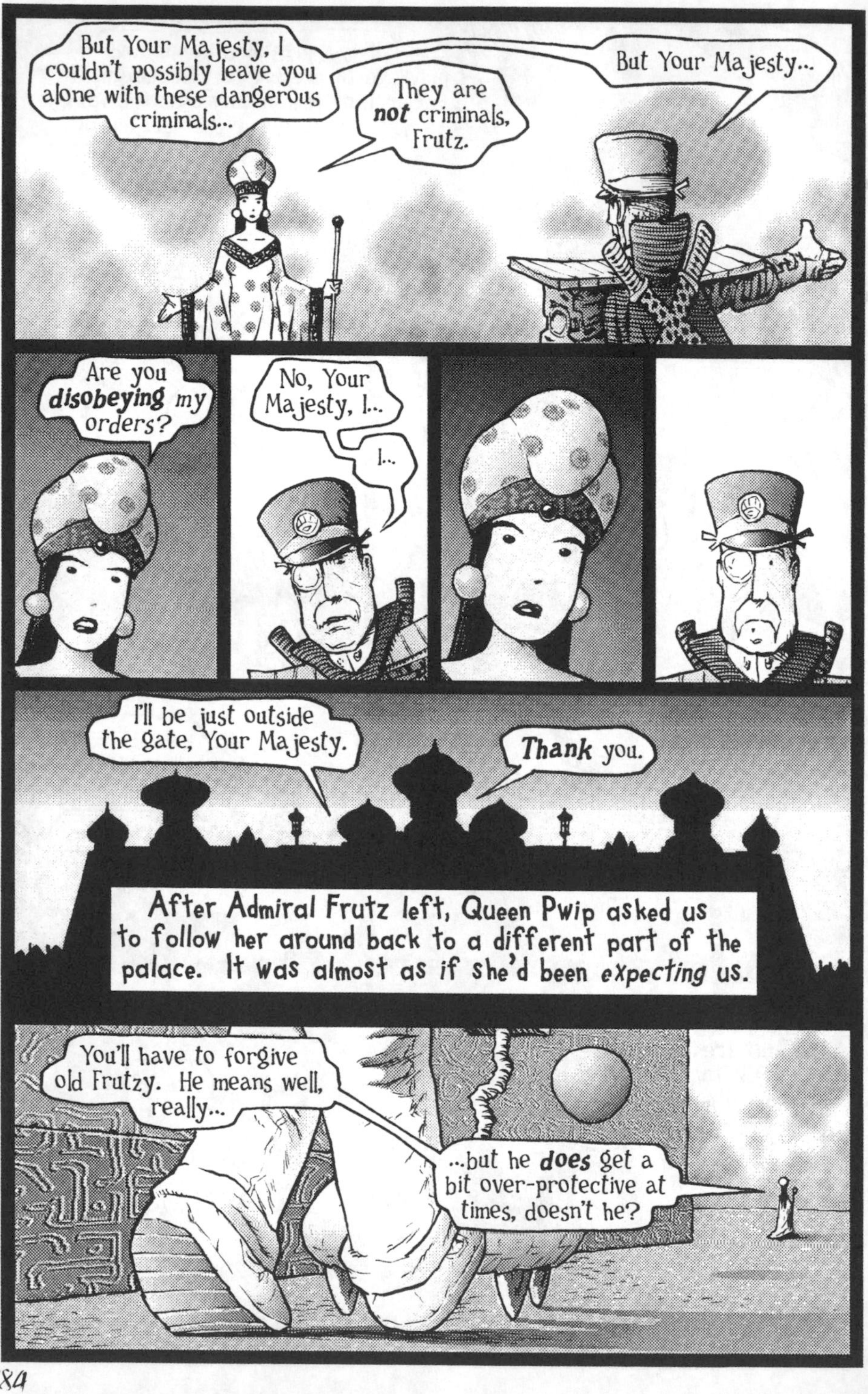
But Your Majesty, I couldn't possibly leave you alone with these dangerous criminals...
They are **not** criminals, Frutz.
But Your Majesty...
Are you **disobeying** my orders?
No, Your Majesty, I...
I...
I'll be just outside the gate, Your Majesty.
Thank you.
After Admiral Frutz left, Queen Pwip asked us to follow her around back to a different part of the palace. It was almost as if she'd been *expecting* us.
You'll have to forgive old Frutzy. He means well, really...
...but he **does** get a bit over-protective at times, doesn't he?

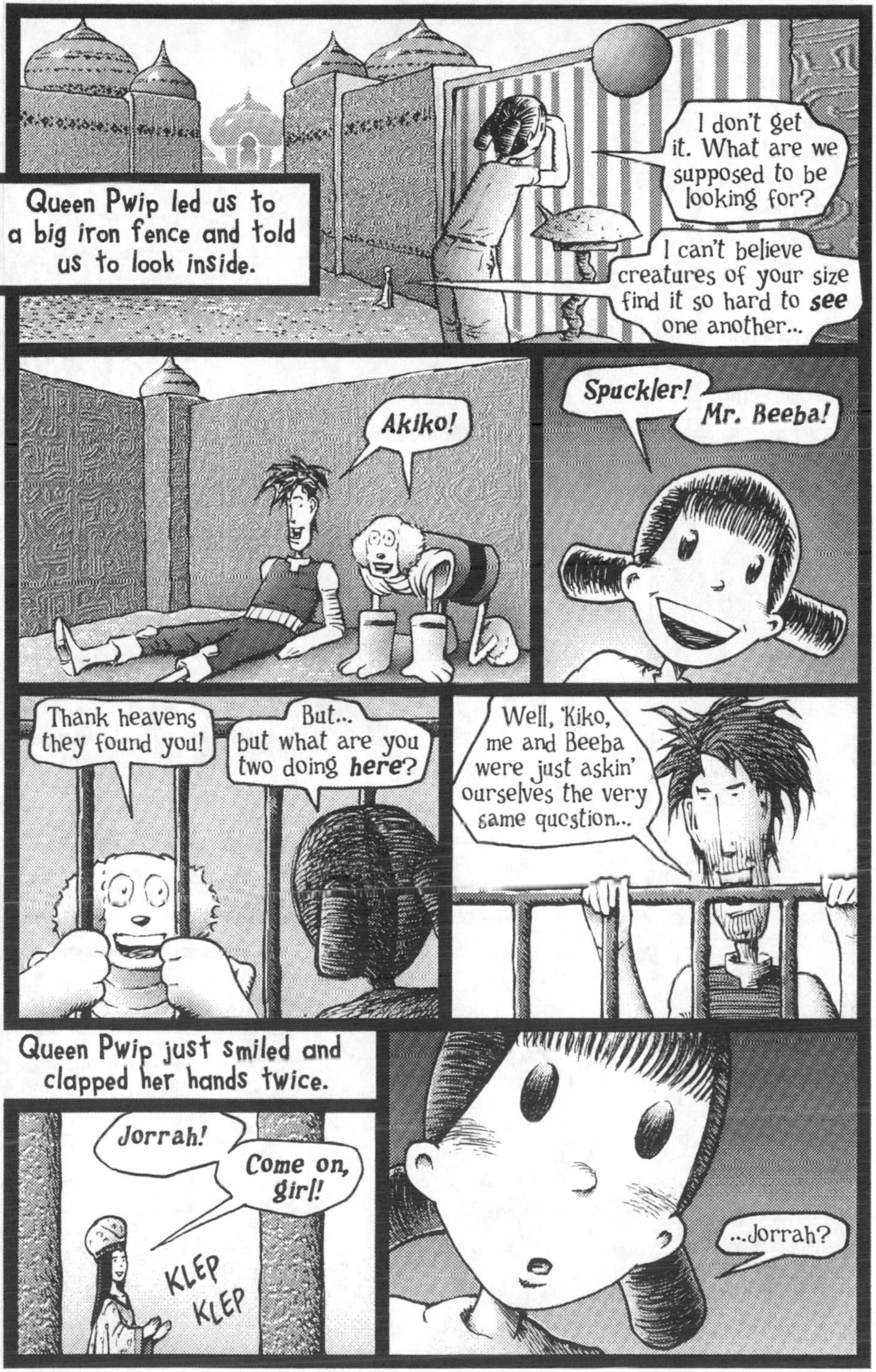

Queen Pwip led us to a big iron fence and told us to look inside.
I don't get it. What are we supposed to be looking for?
I can't believe creatures of your size find it so hard to see one another...
Akiko!
Spuckler!
Mr. Beeba!
Thank heavens they found you!
But... but what are you two doing here?
Well, 'Kiko, me and Beeba were just askin' ourselves the very same question...
Queen Pwip just smiled and clapped her hands twice.
Jorrah!
Come on, girl!
KLEP
KLEP
...Jorrah?

Jorrah, it turned out, was the name of the animal that had attacked Mr. Beeba out in the forest. She was sort of like Queen Pwip's pet or something.

RUHHH

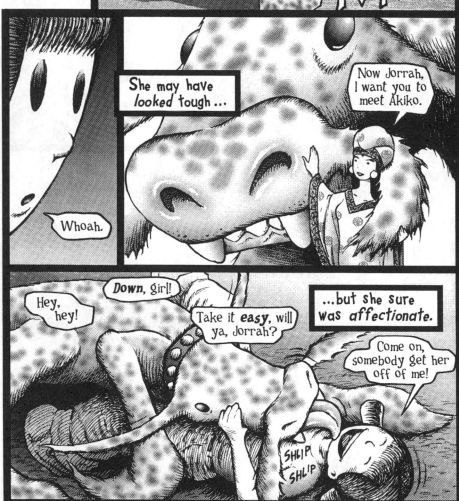

She may have *looked* tough...

Now Jorrah, I want you to meet Akiko.

Whoah.

Hey, hey!

Down, girl!

Take it **easy**, will ya, Jorrah?

...but she sure was affectionate.

Come on, somebody get her off of me!

SHLIP

SHLIP

186

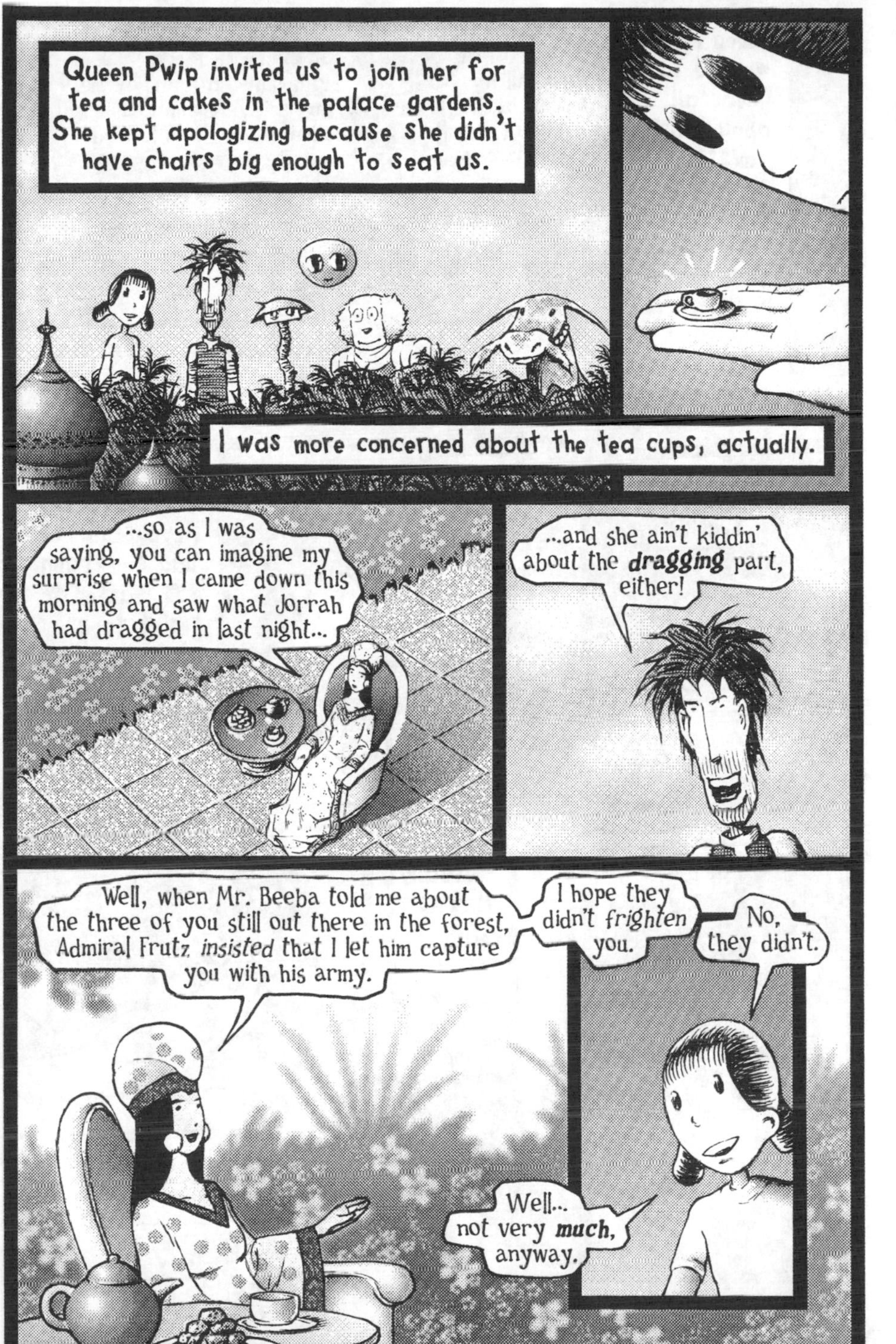
Queen Pwip invited us to join her for tea and cakes in the palace gardens. She kept apologizing because she didn't have chairs big enough to seat us.
I was more concerned about the tea cups, actually.
...so as I was saying, you can imagine my surprise when I came down this morning and saw what Jorrah had dragged in last night...
...and she ain't kiddin' about the *dragging* part, either!
Well, when Mr. Beeba told me about the three of you still out there in the forest, Admiral Frutz *insisted* that I let him capture you with his army.
I hope they didn't *frighten* you.
No, they didn't.
Well... not very *much*, anyway.

Queen Pwip wanted to hear all about our mission to rescue the Prince, so we each took turns telling her the whole story.

There I was, all by myself in the middle of the arena...

...with three Jaggasaurs in front of me, and a '57 Shnum Crusher comin' at me from behind...

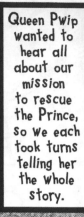

Stop *elaborating,* Spuckler!

Quiet, Beebs, you're breakin' my *rhythm* here...

When we were all done, Queen Pwip said she had something she wanted to give to us. She went back to the palace and returned carrying a big scroll.

This may be of use to you...

Actually it was a really *tiny* scroll, but you know what I *mean.*

What is it?

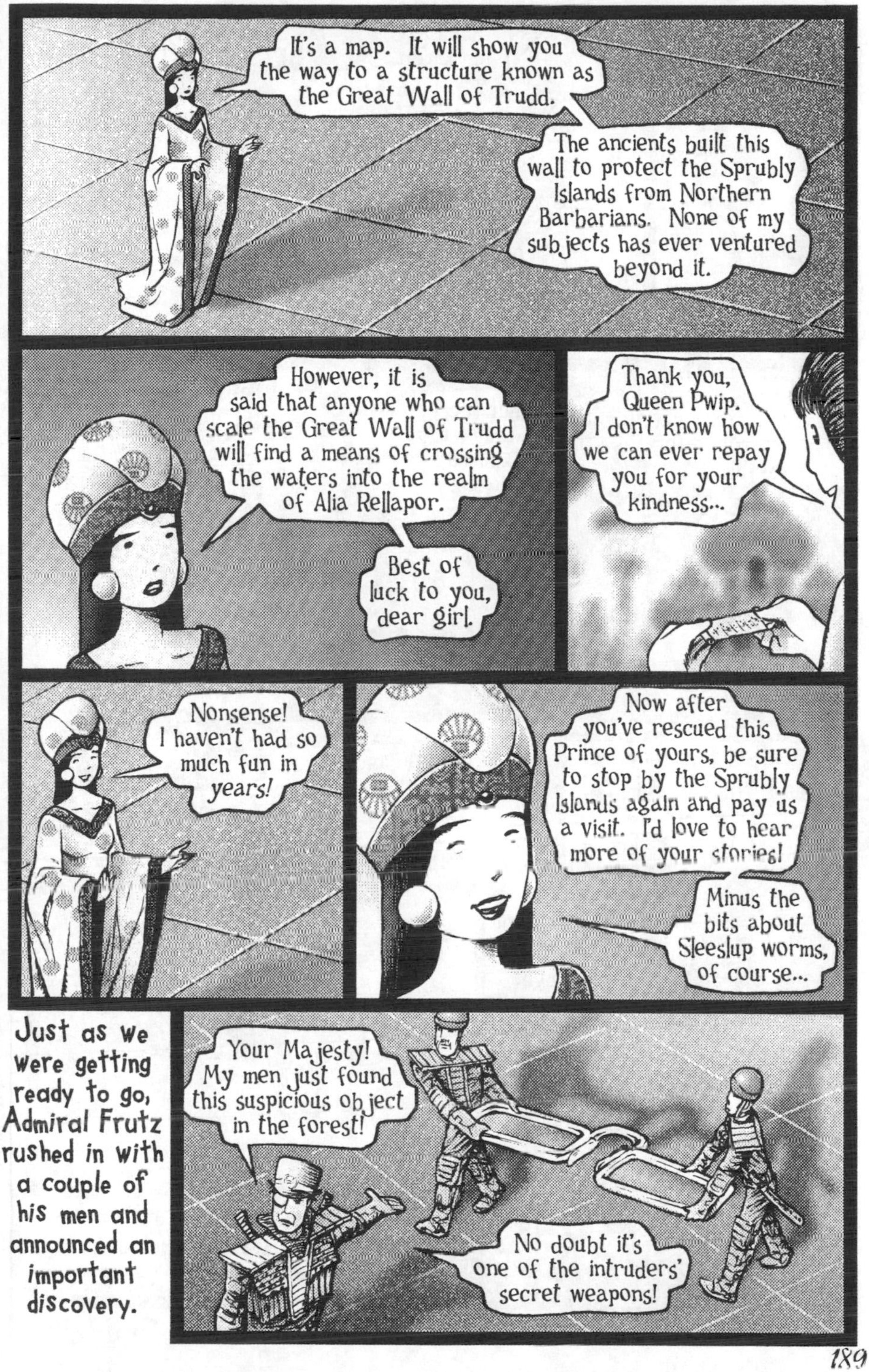
It's a map. It will show you the way to a structure known as the Great Wall of Trudd.
The ancients built this wall to protect the Sprubly Islands from Northern Barbarians. None of my subjects has ever ventured beyond it.
However, it is said that anyone who can scale the Great Wall of Trudd will find a means of crossing the waters into the realm of Alia Rellapor.
Best of luck to you, dear girl.
Thank you, Queen Pwip. I don't know how we can ever repay you for your kindness...
Nonsense! I haven't had so much fun in years!
Now after you've rescued this Prince of yours, be sure to stop by the Sprubly Islands again and pay us a visit. I'd love to hear more of your stories!
Minus the bits about Sleeslup worms, of course...
Just as we were getting ready to go, Admiral Frutz rushed in with a couple of his men and announced an important discovery.
Your Majesty! My men just found this suspicious object in the forest!
No doubt it's one of the intruders' secret weapons!

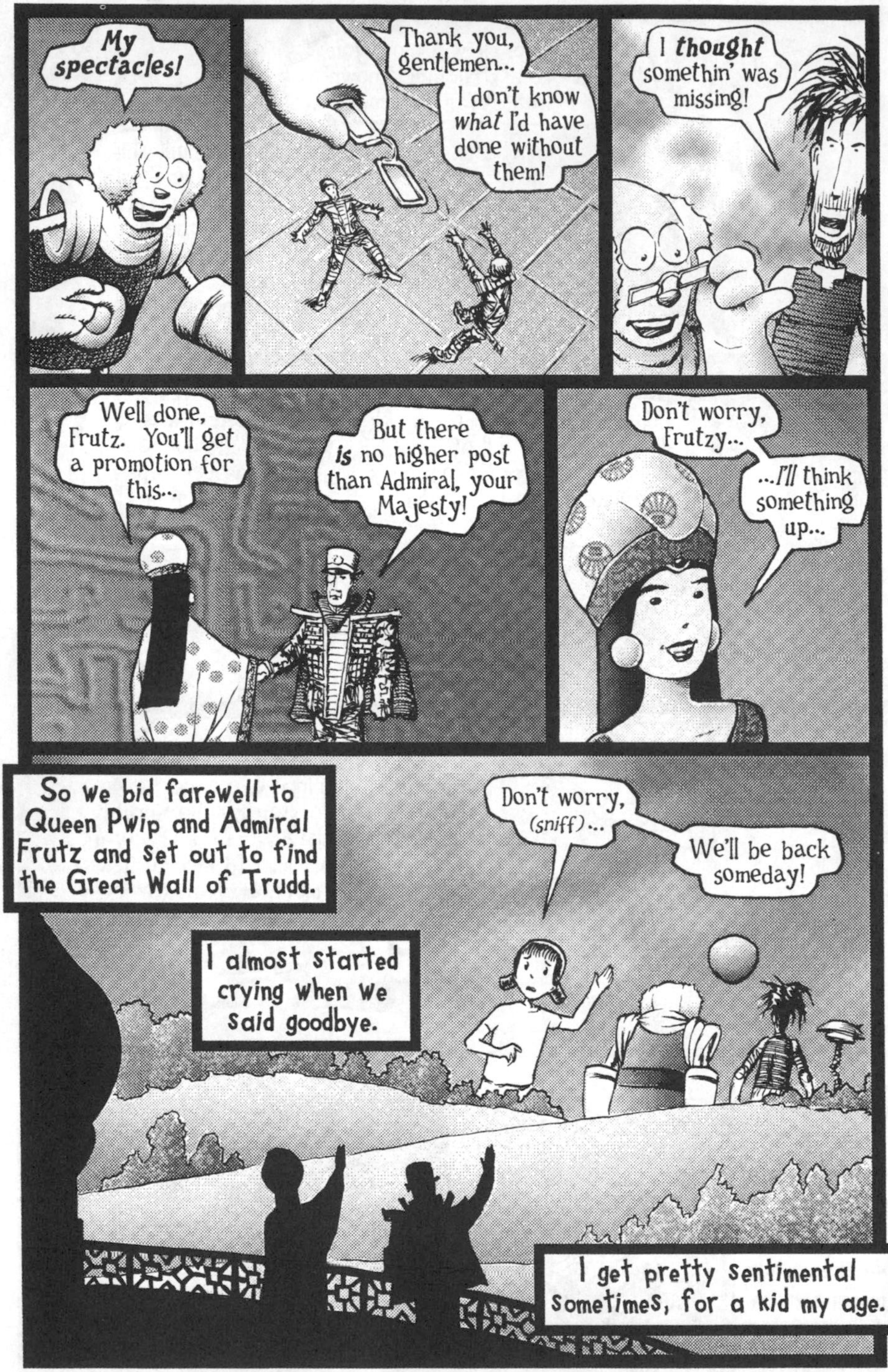
My spectacles!
Thank you, gentlemen...
I don't know what I'd have done without them!
I thought somethin' was missing!
Well done, Frutz. You'll get a promotion for this...
But there is no higher post than Admiral, your Majesty!
Don't worry, Frutzy...
...I'll think something up...
So we bid farewell to Queen Pwip and Admiral Frutz and set out to find the Great Wall of Trudd.
Don't worry, (sniff)...
We'll be back someday!
I almost started crying when we said goodbye.
I get pretty sentimental sometimes, for a kid my age.

Next Issue: "Trudd"